Golfing In
Idaho &
Montana

The *Complete* guide to Idaho & Montana's golf facilities

Montana

Idaho

Statewide Course Listings

Second Edition
by
Daniel MacMillan

Published by
MAC Productions

Waiver on Accuracy
We have gone to great lengths to provide the golfer with an up-to-date, accurate and comprehensive guide to golfing facilities in the states of Idaho and Montana; nevertheless, we all slice it out of bounds from time to time. Each course reserves the right to change their prices and policies at any time and we will not be held liable for any inaccuracies presented in this book.

Library of Congress Cataloging-in-Publication Data
MacMillan, Daniel E.
Golfing in Idaho & Montana; The complete guide to Idaho &
Montana's Golf facilities
(2nd edition)
1. Golf course guide-Idaho state
2. Travel-golf-related in Idaho state
3. Golf course guide-Montana state
4. Travel-golf-related in Montana state

Printed in Canada

Cover photos appear courtesy of:
Hidden Lakes Golf Resort
(Front cover), Sandpoint, Idaho
Sun Valley's Elkhorn Resort Golf Course
(Back cover), Sun Valley, Idaho

First Edition, April 1996
Second Edition, March 2000

ISBN 1-878591-24-X $10.95

Published by:
MAC Productions
P.O. Box 84
Duvall, Washington 98019 USA
Phone: (425) 884-8406
FAX: (425) 884-9245
Web address: www.macproductionsgolf.com
email address: mac.productions@gte.net

Preface

In this the second edition of **"Golfing in Idaho & Montana"** I hope it will be the most complete golf guide in these states published to date. The size is designed with the idea that the book will more easily fit in your glove box or golf bag. We have also provided small map inserts along with the driving directions to help you get to the golf facilities. As always you will find new golf courses, par 3's, and ranges just opened or due to open later in the season. Layouts, prices and yardage have been revised to reflect any changes that have occurred since the last edition. I hope you enjoy the book, see you on the links!

Acknowledgements

A special thanks to all the pros, owners and course managers who have been so helpful in providing us access to their courses and current information.

Thanks to Bob (the big picture) Valentine and his personal touch on these projects over the years, Thanks Robert!!

Thanks to the staff at Valco Graphics for the special touch they put on every cover of our golf guides. You guys are the best!

Thanks to Brian and Christie Kruhlak for the endless stream of phone calls that have to be made to keep the information current.

To my children Joshua Daniel, Sarah Gene and Christian Rogers for showing me what really is important in life.

Thanks to my loving wife Kristi Gene. Words cannot express the love and support she has given me on this project. I feel blessed to have a wife whom provided a loving, caring, Christ like atmosphere in which to produce this book in. Thanks Kristi Gene. Most importantly my Lord Jesus, for his gentle hand and firm grip with my life and this company.

Daniel

Title Page 1
ISBN page 2
Preface 3
Contents 4-6
About the Author 7
Abbreviations 8
How to use Golfing in
Idaho & Montana. 9
Idaho State grid maps 10-13

**IDAHO GOLF
COURSE LISTINGS**
93 Golf Ranch 14
American Falls Golf Course. ... 15
Aspen Acres............................. 16
Avondale Golf Course 17
BanBury Golf Club.................. 18
Bear Lake West Golf Course ... 19
Bigwood Golf Course 20
Blackfoot Golf Course 21
Blue Lakes Country Club 22
Boise Ranch Golf Course 23
Broadmore Country Club 24
Bryden Canyon Golf Course ... 25
Burley City Muni Golf Course 26
Candleridge Golf Course 27
Canyon Springs Golf Course ... 28
Cascade Golf Course 29
Centennial Golf Course 30
Central Links GC & RV Park .. 31
Challis Centennial 32
Cherry Lane Golf Club 33
Clear Lake Country Club......... 34
Coeur d'Alene Golf Club 35
Coeur d'Alene Resort G.C. 36
Council Mountain G.C. 37
Crane Creek Country Club 38
Desert Canyon Municipal GC . 39
Eagle Hills Golf Course. 40
Fairview Muni. Golf Course.... 41
Foxtail Golf Course 42
Fremont County Golf Course .. 43
Gem County Golf Course 44
Golf & Recreation Club, The .. 45

Gooding Country Club 46
Grangeville Country Club 47
Hayden Lake Country Club 48
Hazard Creek Golf Course 49
Heise Hills Golf Course........... 50
Hidden Lakes Golf Resort 51
Highland Golf Course............. 52
Highlands G. &C.C., The 53
Hillcrest Country Club 54
Idaho Falls Country Club 55
Indian Lake Golf Course 56
Island Park Village GC 57
Jefferson Hills Golf Course 58
Jerome Country Club 59
Juniper Hills Country Club 60
Krystal Lake Golf Course 61
Lewiston Golf & C.C. 62
Links Golf Club, The.............. 63
McCall Golf Course 64
Meadow Creek Golf & Field ... 65
Midas Golf Club 66
Mirror Lake Golf Course. 67
Montpelier Golf Course 68
Moscow Elks Golf Club. 69
Oregon Trail Country Club 70
Orofino Golf & C.C. 71
Pinecrest Muni. Golf Course ... 72
Pinehurst Golf Course 73
Pierce Park Greens 74
Plantation Golf Club, The 75
Pleasant Valley G.C. 76
Ponderosa Golf Course 77
Ponderosa Springs G.C. 78
Prairie Falls Golf Course 79
Preston Golf & Country Club .. 80
Priest Lake Golf Course 81
Purple Sage Golf Course 82
Quail Hollow Golf Club 83
Ranch Club Golf Course 84
Rexburg Muni Golf Course 85
Ridgecrest Golf Club 86
Rimrock Golf Course 87
River Bend Golf Course 88
River Park Golf Course 89

Riverside Golf Course 90
Rolling Hills Golf Course 91
Rupert Country Club 92
Sage Lakes Golf Course 93
Saint Maries Golf Course 94
Salmon Valley Golf Course 95
Sand Creek Golf Course 96
Sandpoint Elks Golf Course 97
Scotch Pines Golf Course 98
Shadow Valley Golf Course 99
Shamrock Golf Course 100
Shoshone Golf & Tennis Club. 101
Silver Sage Golf Course 102
Soldier Mtn. Ranch & Resort .. 103
Spurwing Country Club 104
Stoneridge Country Club 105
Sun Valley Resort G.C. 106
Sun Valley's Elkhorn
Resort Golf Course 107
Targhee Village Golf Course ... 108
Terrace Lakes Resort G.C. 109
Teton Lakes Golf Course 110
Thunder Canyon Golf Course . 111
Twin Falls Muni. Golf Course . 112
Twin Lakes Village 113
University Of Idaho G.C. 114
Valley Club, The 115
Vineyard Greens Golf Course . 116
Warm Springs Golf Club 117
Warm Springs Golf Course 118

**IDAHO DRIVING RANGES
& LEARNING CENTERS**

Desert Winds Golfing Range ... 119
Divotz Discount Golf & Range 119
Farm City Driving Range 119
Golf Shack, The 119
Green Links Driving Range 120
Outback Golf Park 120
Park Avenue Golf D.R. 120
Swing Scene 120

Golf Speciality Shops.......121-124

**Geographical Index by
City or Town**.....................125-126

Idaho Regional Map..............127

**Geographical Index
by Region**..........................128-130

Montana Title Page................131

**Montana State
grid maps**..........................132-135

**MONTANA GOLF
COURSE LISTINGS**

Airport Golf Club 136
Anaconda Country Club 137
Anaconda Hills Golf Course ... 138
Beartooth Golf & C.C. 139
Beaver Creek Golf Course 140
Beaverhead Golf Course 141
Big Sky Golf Club 142
Bill Roberts Muni G.C. 143
Briarwood, The 144
Bridger Creek 145
Buffalo Hill Golf Club............. 146
Butte Country Club.................. 147
Cabinet View Country Club 148
Cedar Creek Golf Course 149
Chinook G. & C.C. 150
Choteau Country Club 151
Circle Inn Golf Links............... 152
Cottonwood Country Club 153
Cottonwood Hills GC 154
Cut Bank Golf & C. C. 155
Deer Lodge Golf Club 156
Double Arrow Golf Resort 157
Eagle Bend G.C.................158-159
Emerald Greens 160
Exchange City Par 3 161
Fairmont Hot Springs Resort ... 162
Forsyth Country Club 163

Fort Custer Golf Club 164
Fox Ridge Golf Course 165
Glacier Park Golf Course 166
Glacier View Golf Club 167
Green Meadow Country Club . 168
Hamilton Golf Club 169
Harvest Hills Golf Course 170
Headwaters Public GC 171
Highland View Golf Club 172
Highlands Golf Club, The 173
Hilands Golf Club 174
Jawbone Creek Country Club .. 175
Judith Shadows Golf Course ... 176
King Ranch Golf Course 177
Lake Hills Golf Course 178
Lakeview Country Club 179
Larchmont Golf Course 180
Laurel Golf Club 181
Linda Vista Public G.C. 182
Livingston Golf &C.C. 183
Madison Meadows G.C. 184
Marian Hills Golf Course 185
Marias Valley Golf &C.C. 186
Meadow Creek Golf Course 187
Meadow Lake Resort 188
Meadow Lark Country Club 189
Miles City Town & C.C. 190
Mission Mountain C.C. 191
Missoula Country Club. 192
Mountain Crossroads G.C. 193
Northern Pines G.C. 194
Old Baldy Golf Course 195
Old Works Golf Club 196
Overland Golf Course 197
Par 3 on 93 G.C. & D.R. 198
Pete's Pitch & Putt 199
Peter Yegen, Jr. Golf Course ... 200
Pine Meadows Golf Club 201
Pine Ridge Country Club 202
Plains Golf Club 203
Plentywood Golf Club 204
Polson Country Club 205
Pondera Golf Club 206
Ponderosa Butte Public G.C. ... 207

Pryor Creek Golf Club 208
Red Lodge Mountain G.C. 209
River's Bend at
Thompson Falls Golf Course ... 210
Riverside Country Club 211
Robert O Speck Muni G.C. 212
Rolling Hills Golf Course 213
Scobey Golf Club 214
Sidney Country Club 215
Signal Point Golf Course 216
Sleeping Buffalo Resort 217
Stillwater Golf & Rec. 218
Sunnyside Golf &C.C. 219
Trestle Creek Golf Club 220
University Golf Course 221
Valley View Golf Club. 222
Village Greens 223
Whitefish Lake G.C...........224-225
Whitetail Golf Club 226
Yellowstone Country Club 227

**DRIVING RANGES &
LEARNING CENTERS**

National Driving Range 228
Skyline Driving Range 228

Golf Specialty Shops........229-230

**Geographical Index
by City or Town**...............231-232

Montana Regional Map..........233

**Geographical Index
by Region**...........................234-236

LinksTime.com.................237-238

Order Form 239

Upcoming Titles....................240

Daniel MacMillan has been an avid golfer for the past 16 years. He enjoys researching and playing the various golf courses of the Pacific Northwest (if it were only that easy!!). *Golfing in Washington* was the brainchild of Daniel and his previous partner Mark Fouty who, one day while playing a round at Snohomish Golf Course, discussed finding a guide to use themselves. When no such guide was available this one was written. The book has taken on many stages. It was originally called *Golfing in Western Washington*, which encompassed only the more populous half of the state. In 1988 it expanded to *Golfing in Washington* (now in it's 15th edition). Meanwhile Mark pursued a career in New York so Daniel bought out Mark's share of the company. The company has therefore become a real family operation. Daniel drags his wife Kristi and their three children throughout the west coast seeking information on new courses and facilities for upcoming publications. We hope all the thousands of miles and endless phone calls have paid off. This guide is designed to have all the information a golfer wants and needs to know about playing a course, and as a golfer Daniel has done just that.

Golfing in Oregon is the second book published by MAC Productions and written by Daniel. Now in its 10th edition it also is published on an annual basis. This book too has taken many forms it was originally called *Golfing in Oregon & Idaho*. In 1992 the book was changed to reflect the new format and now only includes the state of Oregon.

Golfing in Idaho & Montana is the third book published by MAC Productions and written by Daniel. The first edition of this book was called *Golfing In Idaho* and was published in 1994. Now in it's 2nd edition *Golfing In Idaho & Montana* is due out in spring of 2000. Look for it in a pro shop or book store near you.

The Birdie Book is another one of MAC Productions titles that was first published in November of 1998. It is a coupon book that offers the golfer nearly $2,500.00 worth of savings at many of Oregon and Washington's finest golf facilities and learning centers.

New territories are always being explored for writing golf course guides such as this. It takes many man hours and attention to detail to produce books of this nature. From start to finish a new book takes about two years to produce. Currently five more are in the works with many more in the initial planning stage. Look for the new publications at a pro shop or book store near you. Daniel's hope is that you will find this to be the best golf guide of its kind on the shelf. Visit us at our web site to look for new titles and the availablity of the region that you are interested in.

Our web site address is: **www.macproductionsgolf.com**

Abbreviations, Explanatory Notes and Disclaimers

Executive Course-An executive golf course is usually longer than a typical par 3 short course but shorter than a regulation course.

Private Course- A golf course that is not open to public play.

Semi-private- golf courses that are closed to the public at certain times during the week. Best to call ahead to reserve tee-times.

Tees: T-Tour; **C**-Championship; **M**-Men; **F**-Forward; **W**-Women.

W/D-Weekday; **W/E**-Weekend; **Hol.**-Holidays. **N/A**-Not available.

Course rating-This rates the degree of difficulty of course in the northwest and refers to the average number of shots per round a scratch golfer ought to shoot. It is figured by rating teams who factor in terrain, length and hazards of each course. The higher the rating the more difficult the course. Course ratings appear courtesy of the *Idaho Golf Association* , *Montana Golf Association* and the *Pacific Northwest Golf Association.*

Slope-This is similar to the course rating but it considers other factors as well. The slope rating takes into consideration the playing difficulty of a course for handicaps above scratch. The higher the number, the more difficult the golf course. Slope ratings appear courtesy of the *Idaho Golf Association* , *Montana Golf Association* and the *Pacific Northwest Golf Association.*

Green fees- prices are subject to change at any time. Because a number of Idaho and Montana courses close for the winter, the prices may reflect those of last year. When two prices are given, the first refers to the 18 hole fee, the second to the 9 hole fee. "Reciprocates" refers to the practice of private courses allowing members of other private courses to play their courses. However, because some courses only reciprocate with a limited number of other courses, it's best to call first.

Trail fee- the fee a course charges an individual to use their own power cart on the golf course.

Reservation policy- This refers to the maximum number of days the course allows reservations to made in advance under normal circumstances.

Winter condition- Dry, damp, wet refers to the club pro's opinion of the course's condition in rainy conditions. Also whether or not the course is closed during the winter months.

Terrain- flat, flat some hills, relatively hilly, very hilly.

Tees- Grass or mats are the alternatives.

Spikes- many of the area golf courses are going to a soft spike policy during the peak golfing season. Be sure to check each course prior to play as the policies vary a great deal from course to course.

Course layouts/yardage- My intent is to show tees in relation to greens, obvious hazards and other holes. Some hazards may not be adequately represented, nor are trees shown. Use these layouts as a reference at the kind of golf course you are planning to visit. The more the hazards the more difficult the golf course will play.

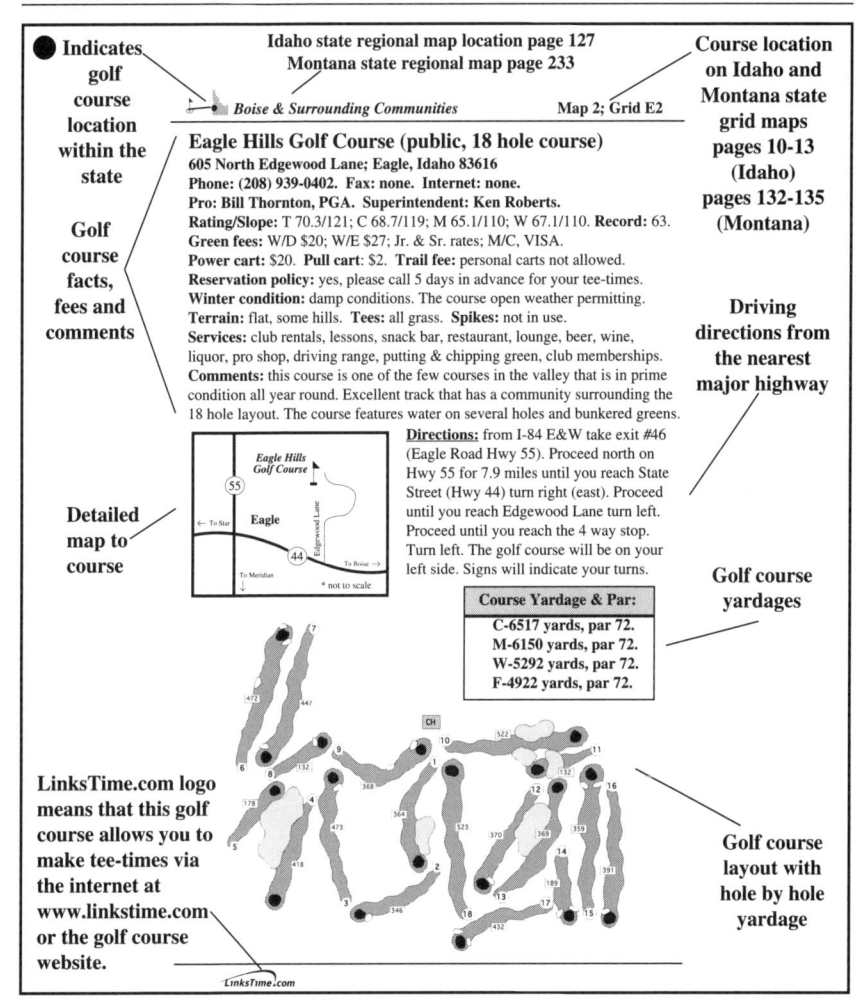

Indicates golf course location within the state

Golf course facts, fees and comments

Detailed map to course

LinksTime.com logo means that this golf course allows you to make tee-times via the internet at www.linkstime.com or the golf course website.

Idaho state regional map location page 127
Montana state regional map page 233

Boise & Surrounding Communities   Map 2; Grid E2

Eagle Hills Golf Course (public, 18 hole course)
605 North Edgewood Lane; Eagle, Idaho 83616
Phone: (208) 939-0402. Fax: none. Internet: none.
Pro: Bill Thornton, PGA. Superintendent: Ken Roberts.
Rating/Slope: T 70.3/121; C 68.7/119; M 65.1/110; W 67.1/110. Record: 63.
Green fees: W/D $20; W/E $27; Jr. & Sr. rates; M/C, VISA.
Power cart: $20. Pull cart: $2. Trail fee: personal carts not allowed.
Reservation policy: yes, please call 5 days in advance for your tee-times.
Winter condition: damp conditions. The course open weather permitting.
Terrain: flat, some hills. Tees: all grass. Spikes: not in use.
Services: club rentals, lessons, snack bar, restaurant, lounge, beer, wine, liquor, pro shop, driving range, putting & chipping green, club memberships.
Comments: this course is one of the few courses in the valley that is in prime condition all year round. Excellent track that has a community surrounding the 18 hole layout. The course features water on several holes and bunkered greens.

Directions: from I-84 E&W take exit #46 (Eagle Road Hwy 55). Proceed north on Hwy 55 for 7.9 miles until you reach State Street (Hwy 44) turn right (east). Proceed until you reach Edgewood Lane turn left. Proceed until you reach the 4 way stop. Turn left. The golf course will be on your left side. Signs will indicate your turns.

Course Yardage & Par:
C-6517 yards, par 72.
M-6150 yards, par 72.
W-5292 yards, par 72.
F-4922 yards, par 72.

Course location on Idaho and Montana state grid maps pages 10-13 (Idaho) pages 132-135 (Montana)

Driving directions from the nearest major highway

Golf course yardages

Golf course layout with hole by hole yardage

All **MAC Productions** golf guides are alphabetically arranged by golf course name for easy use. You can also find the golf course locations by using our geographical index located on pages 125-126 (ID), 231-232 (MT). Simply look up the nearest city or town to the location you will be visiting and the courses are listed accordingly. In addition to this feature we also include a geographical index that is arranged by regions within the states of Idaho and Montana. If you are visting Boise, for example, you would look in the geographical index by region on pages 128-130. Then find the Boise & surrounding cities region in this section and it will tell you the names of the golf courses located in that region.

The state maps on pages 10-13 (ID) 132-135 (MT) coincide with the map and grid numbers listed on the top right corner of each page. These maps are intended for approximate location within the state only. The detailed map grid and driving directions are provided on the listing page for accurate course locations.

Map 1

① Denotes approximate Golf Course Location.

Numbers on map correspond with golf course page numbers. R before a number represents range.

Grid → ↓	1	2	3	4

A

Idaho

* not to scale

N
W ← → E
S

② (Highway 2)

Bonners Ferry ⑥⑦

B

WA

⑧① Priest Lake

⑤⑦

⑨⑤

⑨⑦ ⑤①

⑧④ Priest River

Sandpoint

Chilco ⑧⑦

⑩⑤

Blanchard

⑥⑥ Garfield Bay

Montana

② (Highway 2)

Rathdrum ⑦⑨

⑪③

⑥③ ⑤③

⑰ ⑱

⑧⑤ ⑦⑧

Kellogg

Osborn

C

Coeur d' Alene ③⑥

⑨⓪ (I-90)

⑦③ ⑩①

⑨⓪ (I-90)

D

WA

⑨⑤

St. Maries ⑨④

③ (Highway 3)

Idaho

Montana

E

Moscow

⑪④ ⑥⑨

⑨⑤

F

③ (Highway 3)

⑦① Orofino

⑫ (Highway 12)

WA

②⑤ ⑥② Lewiston

Montana

G

⑫ (Highway 12)

⑨⑤

Idaho

Grangeville ④⑦

OR

Map 2

① Donotes approximate Golf Course Location.

Numbers on map correspond with golf course page numbers. R before a number represents range.

Grid → ↓	1	2	3	4

A

Montana

* not to scale

95

N
W ← → E
S

B

Idaho

C

65 New Meadows
64
McCall 55
Council 37
95
29 Cascade

D

OR
91 Weiser
75
1109 Garden Valley
Payette
98
21

E

R7 Emmett
44
44
88 Boise
Caldwell
84

Boise & Surrounding Cities

18 23 24 30 33 38 40
41 42 45 54 56 74 75
82 83 86 99 100 104 117
R2 R3 R4 R5

F

OR
84
20

G

Idaho
Mountain Home 39
R1 102
Glenns Ferry
116

11

Map 3

Map 3

① Donotes approximate Golf Course Location.

Numbers on map correspond with golf course page numbers. R before a number represents range.

| Grid→ | 1 | 2 | 3 | 4 |

A — 95 — * not to scale — N W←→E S

B — Salmon 95 — Montana

C — 32 Challis — Idaho

D — 28 — 93 Mackay 89 — 22

E — 75 — 20 Sun Valley — 106 107 — 118 Ketchum 115 — 20

F — 49 Aberdeen — Fairfield 103 — 46 — 15 American Falls — 24 — Twin Falls 15 27 28 112 — 84

G — Shoshone — Gooding — Rupert 92 — 14 Jerome 59 — 84 — 26 Burley 77 — 84 — 34 Buhl — Twin Falls — 76 Kimberly

Map 4

Grid→ ↓	1	2	3	4
A				
B				
C				
D				
E				
F				
G				

* not to scale

N
W ← → E
S

Montana

15
20
191

Ashton 16
St Anthony 43
Island Park 57
Rexbury 20
85 110
Rigby 58
50
Ririe
15
26
Driggs 108

Idaho Falls 55 93
72 96
Shelley 61
91
Idaho
26
21 Blackfoot

Pocatello 52
90 60 R6
86
15
34

Lava Hot Springs
30 111 31
70 Soda Springs

Montpelier 68
Preston 80
91
Fish Haven 19

93 Golf Ranch (public, 18 hole course)

406 East 200 South; P.O. Box 473; Jerome, ID 83338
Phone: (208) 324-9693. Fax: (208) 324-5619. Internet: none.
Manager: Ed Peterson. Superintendent: Ed Peterson.
Rating/Slope: the golf course will be rated in 2000. **Course record:** N/A.
Green fees: W/D $18/$10; W/E $18/$10; no special rates; no credit cards.
Power cart: $18/$10. **Pull cart:** $2. **Trail fee:** $10 for personal carts.
Reservation policy: please call ahead for your tee-times. No time limit.
Winter condition: the course is closed from December 15th to February 15th.
Terrain: relatively hilly. **Tees:** all grass. **Spikes:** soft spikes preferred.
Services: club rentals, beer, wine, restaurant, snack bar, pro shop, driving range. **Comments:** tight fairways puts an emphasis on your shot placement. The golf course offers a dual tee layout for 18 hole play. Creeks come into play on several holes. Course is much improved with a new pond on the 8th hole.

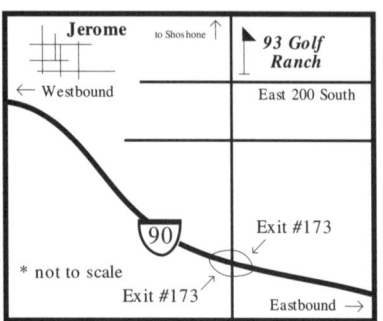

Directions: from I-84 E&W take exit #173 (Hwy 93). Travel northbound on Hwy 93 for 4.1 miles until you reach East 200 South. Turn right. The golf course is located immediately on your left.

Course Yardage & Par:
T-7218 yards, par 72.
C-6764 yards, par 72.
M-5990 yards, par 72.
W-5266 yards, par 72.

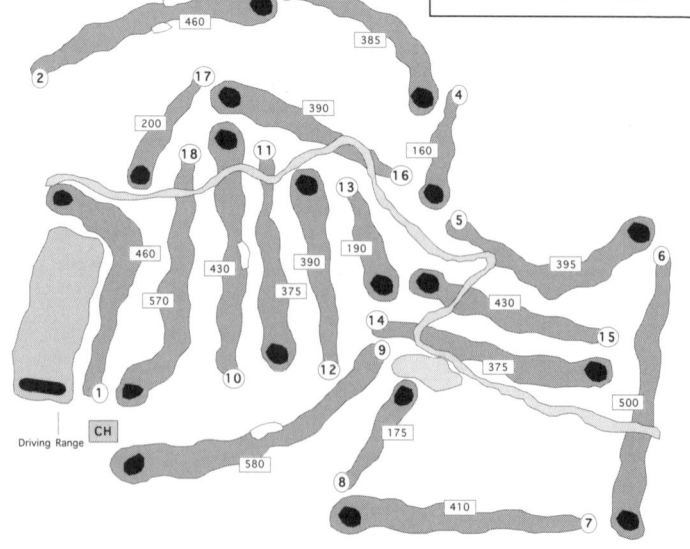

American Falls Golf Course (public, 9 hole course)

610 N Oregon Trail; American Falls, Idaho 83211
Phone: (208) 226-9631. Fax: none. Internet: none.
Pro: David Crozier, PGA. Superintendent: JohnStill.
Rating/Slope: M 62.3/96; W 65.0/109. **Course record:** 60.
Green fees: W/D $10/$8; W/E $12/$9; Jr. rates weekdays; VISA, M/C, AMEX.
Power cart: $15/$8. **Pull cart:** $2. **Trail fee:** personal carts not allowed.
Reservation policy: you may call up to 2 days in advance for tee times.
Winter condition: closed during the winter months. October through March.
Terrain: flat, some hills. **Tees:** all grass tees. **Spikes:** no spike policy.
Services: club rentals, lessons, snack bar, beer, pro shop, putting green.
Comments: lots of uphill and downhill lies on this short but challenging layout.
Greens are small in size and can be very difficult to hold. The golf course sports
2 sets of tees that gives this 9 hole course a different look the 2nd time around.

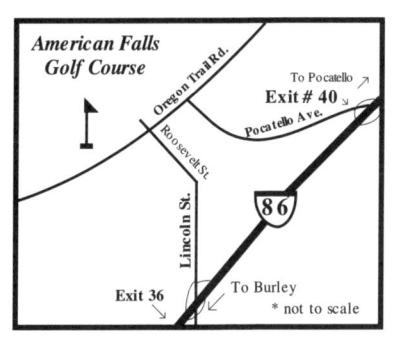

Directions: from I-86 heading eastbound
take exit #36. Proceed north on Lincoln
Street. Turn left on Roosevelt to the golf
course. From I-86 westbound take exit
#40. Proceed on Pocatello Avenue to
Oregon Trail Road. Turn left on Oregon
Trail Road to the golf course. Look for
signs marking your way to the course.

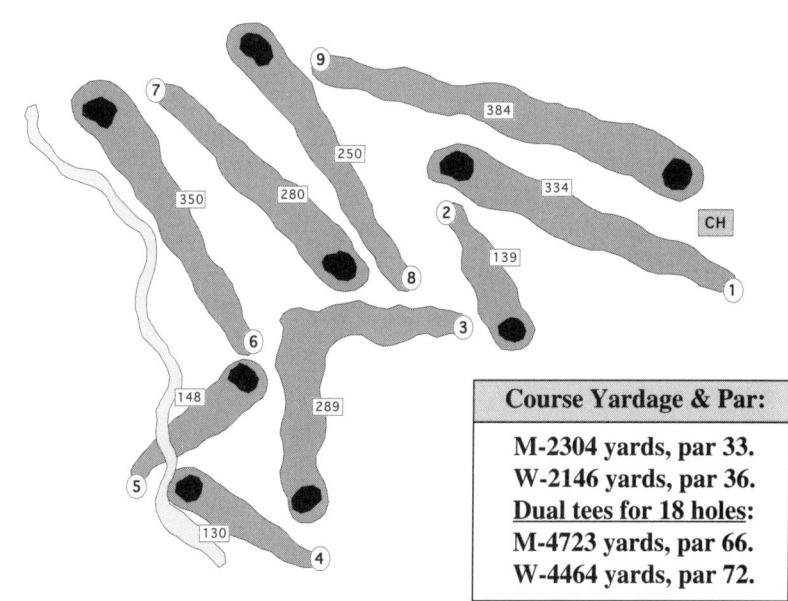

Course Yardage & Par:
M-2304 yards, par 33.
W-2146 yards, par 36.
Dual tees for 18 holes:
M-4723 yards, par 66.
W-4464 yards, par 72.

Aspen Acres Golf Club (public, 18 hole course)

4179 East 1100 North; Ashton, Idaho 83420
Phone: (208) 652-3524 or 1-800-845-2374. **Fax:** none. **Internet:** none.
Manager: A.P. Anderson. **Superintendent:** A.P. Anderson.
Rating/Slope: M 50.5/73; W 52.4/73. **Record:** 56.
Green fees: $10/$5.75; Jr. & Sr. rates; season tickets; VISA, M/C, AMEX.
Power cart: $12.50/$6.50. **Pull cart:** $1.80/$1.00. **Trail fee:** $3.50.
Reservation policy: yes, you can call ahead for reservations. No time limit.
Winter condition: the course is closed from mid October to the first of May.
Terrain: flat, some hills. **Tees:** all grass tees. **Spikes:** no policy.
Services: club rentals, snack bar, beverages, pro shop, RV park for overnighters.
Comments: challenging, fun golf course that is off the beaten path in very scenic eastern Idaho. Many RVers make this their vacation destination. Greens are on the small size with few hazards fronting them. Fairways are narrow in spots with trees coming into play off the tee and on your approach shots.

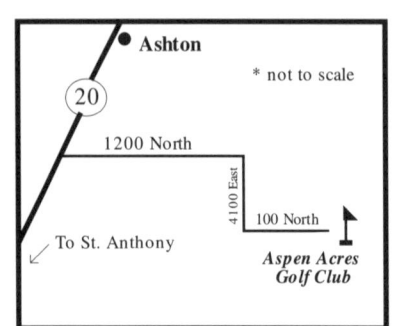

<u>Directions:</u> from Highway 20 at 1 mile south of Ashton, Idaho turn eastbound on 1200 North for 6.2 miles. Turn south on 4100 East for 1 mile. Turn eastbound on 1100 North for .75 miles. Follow signs to the golf course.

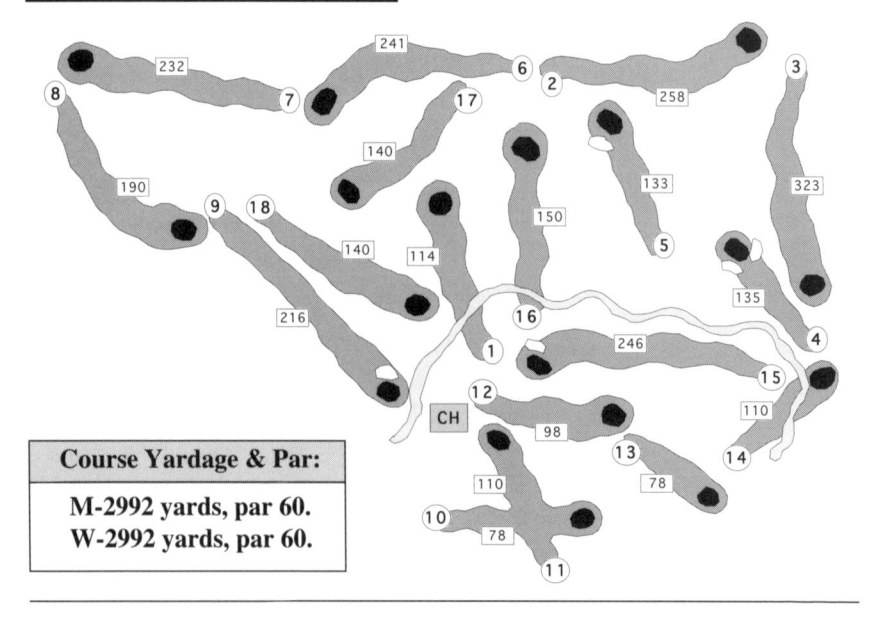

Course Yardage & Par:
M-2992 yards, par 60.
W-2992 yards, par 60.

Avondale Golf Course (semi-private, 18 hole course)

10745 Avondale Loop Road; Hayden Lake, Idaho 83835
Phone (208) 772-5963. Fax: (208) 762-8302. Intrernet: none.
Pro: Dan Porter, PGA. Superintendent: Tim Mack.
Rating/Slope: C 71.8/124; M 70.6/122; W 70.9/123. **Course record:** 64.
Green fees: W/D $38/$19; W/E $38/$19; $24 after 2:30pm; M/C, VISA.
Power cart: $22/$11. **Pull cart:** $3. **Trail fee:** $12 for personal carts.
Reservation policy: preferred tee times for stockholders. Others call ahead.
Winter condition: the golf course is open all year long, weather permitting.
Terrain: flat, some hills. **Tees:** all grass. **Spikes:** soft spikes only.
Services: club rentals, lessons, snack bar, restaurant, lounge, beer, wine, liquor, pop, pro shop, driving range, tennis courts, putting green, chipping green.
Comments: all the fairways are impeccably groomed and wander through spectacular scenery. Excellent course with large well bunkered greens. Public times are restricted at certain times so be sure to call ahead for your reservations.

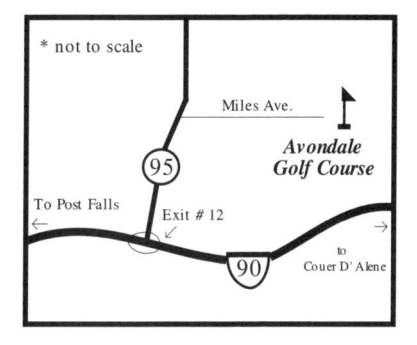

Directions: From I-90 East & West take the Highway 95 exit toward Hayden. You be going northbound on Highway 95. When you reach Miles Avenue go east (right). Proceed eastbound on Miles Avenue to the golf course. You will travel for about 4.3 miles on Highway 95 to Miles Ave. Look for signs marking to the course.

Course Yardage & Par:
T-6573 yards, par 72.
C-6335 yards, par 72.
M-6026 yards, par 72.
W-5357 yards, par 74.

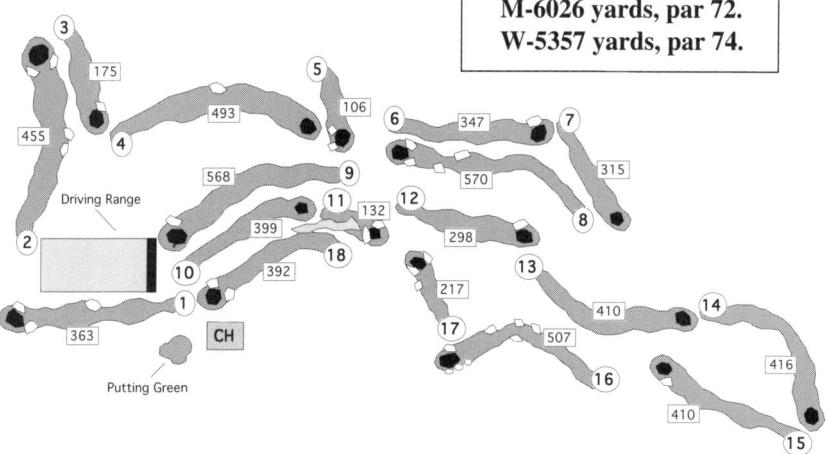

Banbury Golf Club (public, 18 hole course)

3023 South Eagle Road; Eagle, Idaho 83616
Phone: (208) 939-3600. Fax: (208) 939-6663. Internet: none.
Pro: Jerry Breaux, PGA. Superintendent: Clint Travis.
Rating/Slope: T 71.7/125; C 69.0/120; M 66.5/115; W 64.5/110. Record: 68.
Green fees: W/D $29/$17; W/E $39/$22; Jr./Sr. rates; VISA, M/C, AMEX.
Power cart: $11/$6.50. Pull cart: $4/$2. Trail fee: not allowed.
Reservation policy: you may call up to 7 days in advance for tee times.
Winter condition: the golf course is closed from December 1st to February 1st.
Terrain: flat, some hills. Tees: all grass. Spikes: soft spikes required.
Services: club rentals, beer, wine, liquor, lounge, restaurant, snack bar, lessons,
pro shop, driving range, putting & chipping greens, club memberships.
Comments: newer 18 hole, par 71 championship caliber golf course that is
crafted after the links of Scotland. This links style course is located along the
south channel of the Boise River. Great course that is a must play if in the area.

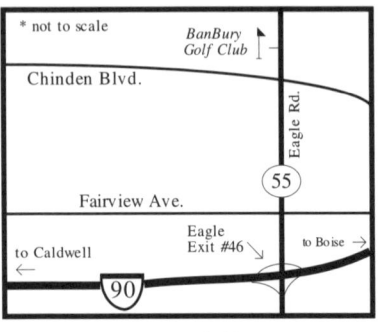

Directions: the course is located north of
Chinden on Eagle Road (Hwy 55), along
the Boise River. From I-84 take exit #46
(Eagle Road Hwy 55). Proceed northbound on Eagle Road to Oak Hampton (1st
left past Chinden Blvd. at the bottom of
the hill). Proceed to Mary Post Place and
turn right. The course is located ahead.

Course Yardage & Par:
T-6812 yards, par 71.
T-6761 yards, par 71.
C-6266 yards, par 71.
C-6216 yards, par 71.
M-5703 yards, par 71.
W-5257 yards, par 71.

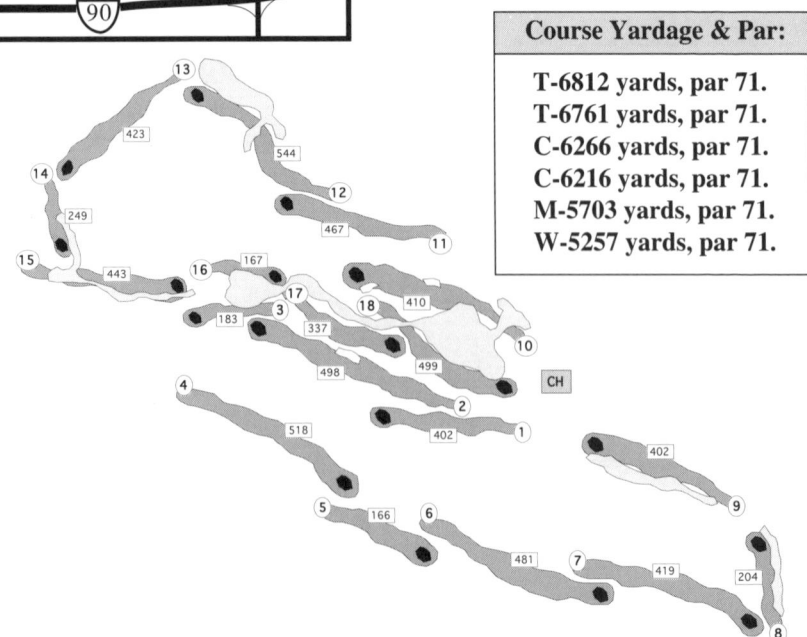

Bear Lake West Golf Course (public, 9 hole course)

Highway 89; P.O. Box 348; Fish Haven, Idaho 83287
Phone: (208) 945-2744. Fax: (208) 945-2215. Internet: none.
Rating/Slope: the golf course is not rated. **Course record:** 29.
Head Pro: Brodie Berg. Superintendent: none.
Green fees: Weekdays $12; Weekends $12; no special rates.
Power cart: $8 for 9 holes. **Pull cart:** $2. **Trail fee:** $4.
Reservation policy: you may call up to 1 week in advance for tee times.
Winter condition: the golf course is closed from November to May 1st.
Terrain: hill side course. **Tees:** grass. **Spikes:** soft spikes preferred.
Services: lessons, club rentals, beer, restaurant, beverages, pro shop.
Comments: good nine hole track located near the Utah-Idaho border. The course can play tough where water and sand come into play on several holes. Friendly atmosphere abounds at this track. Great course for a quick 9 holes.

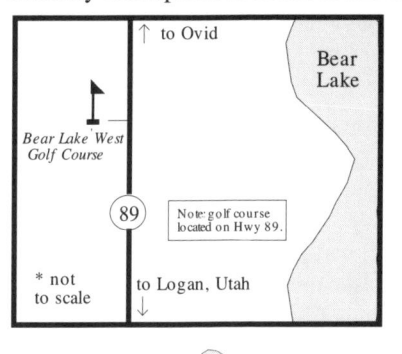

Directions: the golf course is located on Highway 89 just out of Fish Haven Idaho. If you are driving north on Highway 89 look for signs marking your way to the course. The golf course is located on the west side of the Highway.

Course Yardage & Par:
C- 2715 yards, par 33.
M-2524 yards, par 33.
W-2289 yards, par 33.

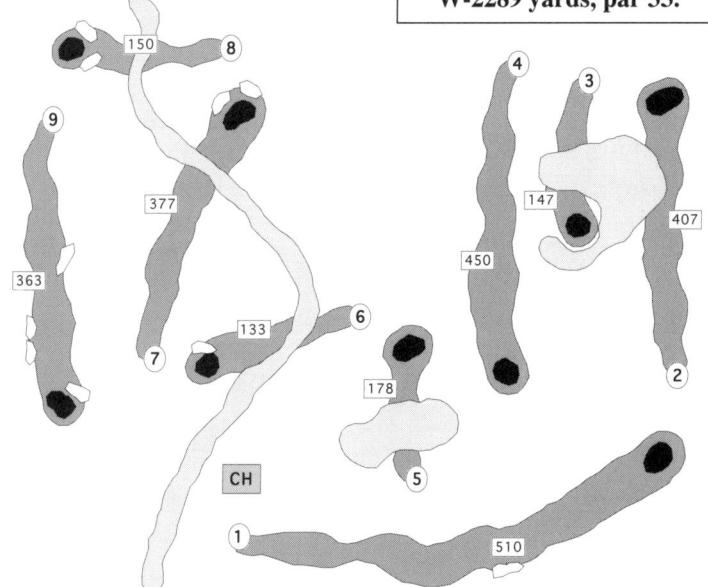

Bigwood Golf Course (semi-private, 9 hole course)

Mailing address: P.O. Box 2810; Sun Valley, Idaho 83353
Physical address: 125 Clubhonse Drive; Ketchum, Idaho 83340
Phone: (208) 726-4024. **Fax:** none. **Internet:** none.
Head Pro: Herbert Fash. **Superintendent:** Norm Shorts, Jr.
Rating/Slope: M 68.8/113; W 71.2/114. **Course record:** M 70 & W 73.
Green fees: W/D $34/$25; W/E $34/$25; M/C, VISA.
Power cart: $15/$11 (per person). **Pull cart:** $4. **Trail fee:** not allowed.
Reservation policy: please call the golf course ahead of time for the policy.
Winter condition: the golf course is closed from November 1st to April 15th.
Terrain: flat, some hills. **Tees:** all grass. **Spikes:** soft spikes preferred.
Services: club rentals, lessons, snack bar, restaurant, beer, wine, pop, pro shop, lockers, showers, driving range, putting & chipping greens, club memberships.
Comments: designed by Robert Muir Graves this beautiful 9 hole course is worth a special trip. Greens are large and have bunkers fronting them on nearly every hole. The track has two sets of tees for 18 hole play and can be found in excellent condition throughout the golfing season. Worth a special trip.

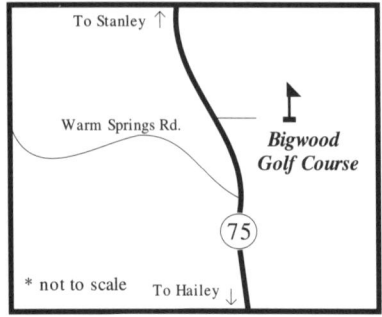

Directions: from I-84 E&W in Twin Falls take exit #173 (Hwy 93) north toward Shoshone. Proceed on Hwy 93 as it turns into Hwy 75 in Shoshone. Proceed on Hwy 75 north toward Ketchum. The golf course is located on Highway 75 at the north end of Ketchum Idaho. Look for Warm Springs Road and signs for your turn to the golf course.

Course Yardage & Par:
M-3200 yards, par 36.
W-2653 yards, par 36.
Dual tees for 18 holes:
M-6535 yards, par 72.
W-5620 yards, par 73.

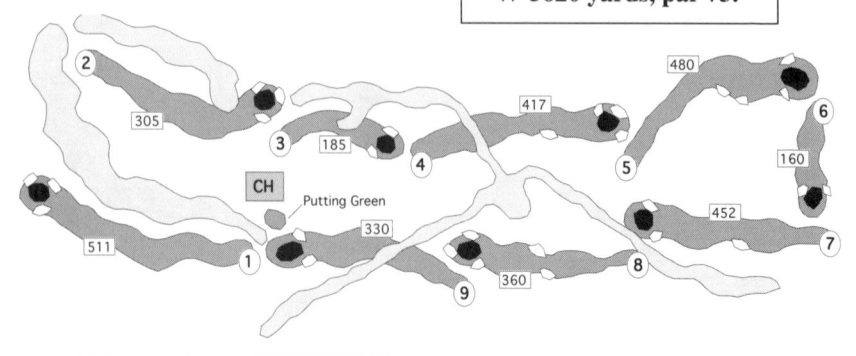

Blackfoot Golf Course (public, 18 hole course)

3115 Teeples Drive; Blackfoot, Idaho 83221
Phone: (208) 785-9960. **Fax:** (208) 785-8626. **Internet:** www.greens.com
Pro: Mike Dayley, PGA. **Superintendent:** Scott Hayes.
Rating/Slope: C 71.3/120; M 70.3/118; W 72.0/121. **Course record:** 64.
Green fees: W/D $16.75/$11.50; W/E $16.75/$11.50; M/C, VISA.
Power cart: $16/$11. **Pull cart:** $2. **Trail fee:** $10 for personal carts.
Reservation policy yes, please call ahead 7 days for all your tee times.
Winter condition: the golf course is closed from Thanksgiving to mid-March.
Terrain: flat (easy walking). **Tees:** all grass. **Spikes:** soft spikes preferred.
Services: club rentals, lessons, restaurant, lounge, beer, wine, beverages,
pro shop, lockers, showers, driving range, putting and chipping greens.
Comments: the tough front is very demanding from the tee as well as on your
approach shots. Greens are large with few bunkers fronting them. The course
plays very long from the back or middle tees leaving you with many long irons
to the greens from the fairway. Excellent public course that will not disappoint.

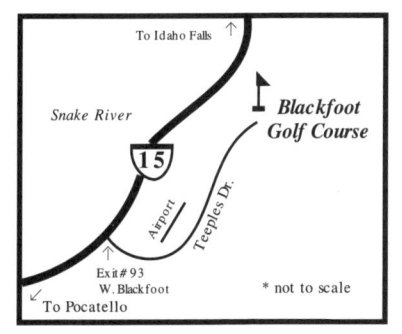

Directions: From I-15 North & South
take the West Blackfoot exit #93 in the
city of Blackfoot. Proceed left at first
stoplight (Bridge Street). Continue on
Bridge St. until you reach Parkway, turn
right. Proceed on until you reach the
golf course. The way is well marked.

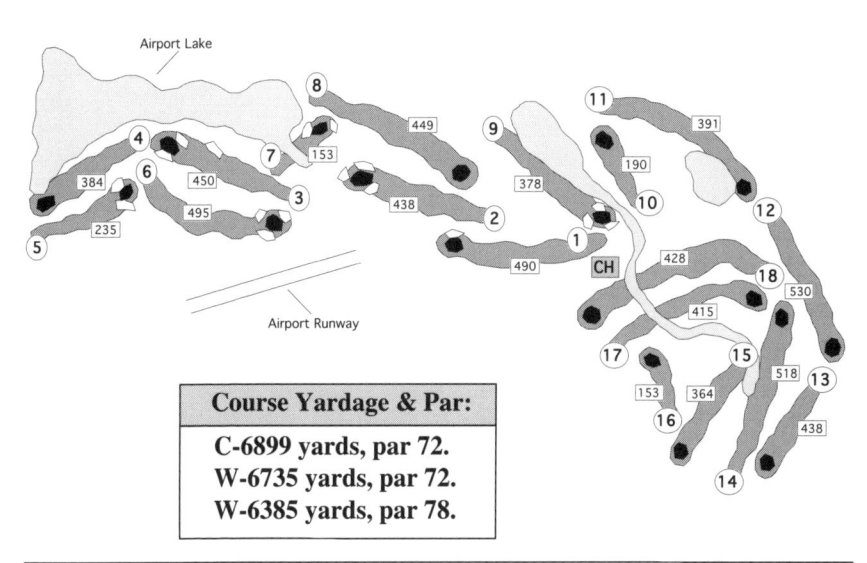

Course Yardage & Par:
C-6899 yards, par 72.
W-6735 yards, par 72.
W-6385 yards, par 78.

Blue Lakes Country Club (private, 18 hole course)

Blue Lakes Grade; P.O. Box 582; Twin Falls, Idaho 83303
Phone: (208) 733-2337. Fax: (208) 733-2583. Internet: none.
Pro: Rob Ellis, PGA. Superintendent: Jim Rasmussen
Rating/Slope: C 70.0/122; M 67.2/115; W 69.3/125. **Course record:** 66.
Green fees: private club, members only; reciprocates; no credit cards.
Power cart: private club. **Pull cart:** private club. **Trail fee:** not allowed.
Reservation policy: private golf club, members & guests of members only.
Winter condition: the golf course is open all year long. Damp conditions.
Terrain: relatively hilly. **Tees:** all grass. **Spikes:** soft spikes required.
Services: club rentals, lessons, snack bar, lounge, dining room, beer, wine,
liquor, pro shop, lockers, showers, driving range, club memberships.
Comments: well conditioned private facility that is spectacular. Unique setting
along the Snake River makes this course one of the best private courses in Idaho.

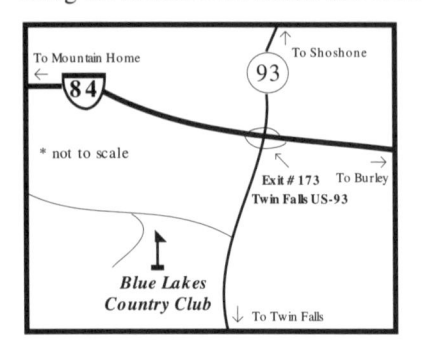

Directions: From 1-84 East & West
exit at south Hwy 93, #173. Proceed
southbound for 2 miles and turn right on
Golf Course Road. Proceed to the golf
course on your left.

Course Yardage & Par:
C-6474 yards, par 72.
M-5851 yards, par 72.
W-5236 yards, par 73.

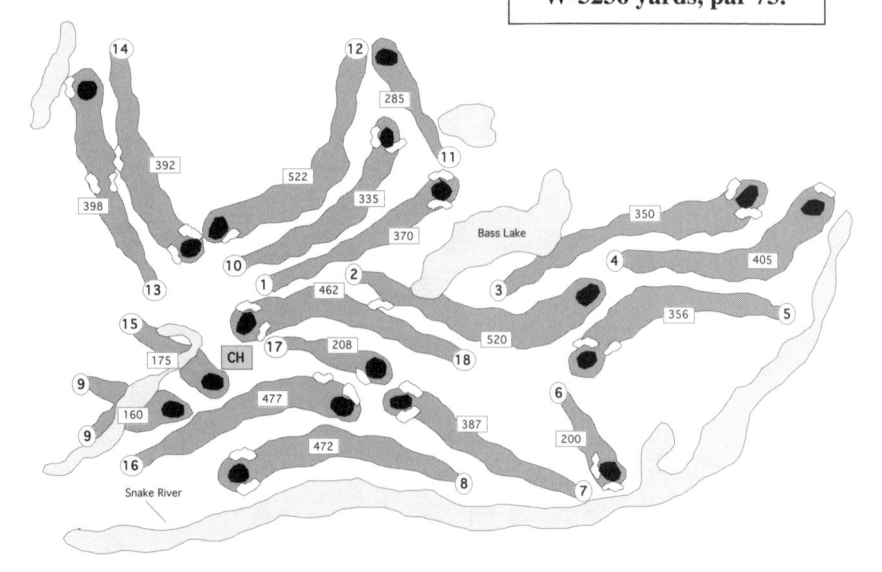

Boise Ranch Golf Course (public, 18 hole course)

6501 South Cloverdale Road; Boise, Idaho 83709
Phone: (208) 362-6501. Fax: (208) 362-6597. Internet: none.
Pro: Chad Watson, PGA. Manager: Russ Isbell.
Rating/Slope: T 70.3/112; C 68.1/108; M 66.3/104; W 67.4/109. **Record:** 63.
Green fees: Monday thru Thur. $18/$15; Friday thru Sunday & Hol. $24/$21.
Power cart: $20/$12. **Pull cart:** $4/$3. **Trail fee:** $8/$6 for personal carts.
Reservation policy: 1 week in advance in person; 5 days in advance by phone.
Winter condition: the golf course is open all year long, weather permitting.
Terrain: flat, some hills. **Tees:** all grass. **Spikes:** soft spikes required.
Services: club rentals, lessons, snack bar, beer, wine, pro shop, driving range.
Comments: A championship caliber design with 7 man-made lakes and wide
landing areas. The course can play tough so be sure to bring your "A" game.

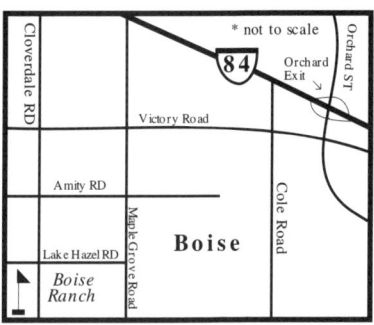

Directions: from I-84 E&W take the
Eagle Road exit #46. Travel south for 3
miles to Lake Hazel Road. Turn east on
Lake Hazel Road and travel 1 mile to
Cloverdale Road. The golf course is
located at the Southwest corner of Lake
Hazel Road and South Cloverdale.

Course Yardage & Par:
T-6574 yards, par 72.
C-6085 yards, par 72.
M-5830 yards, par 72.
W-5298 yards, par 72.

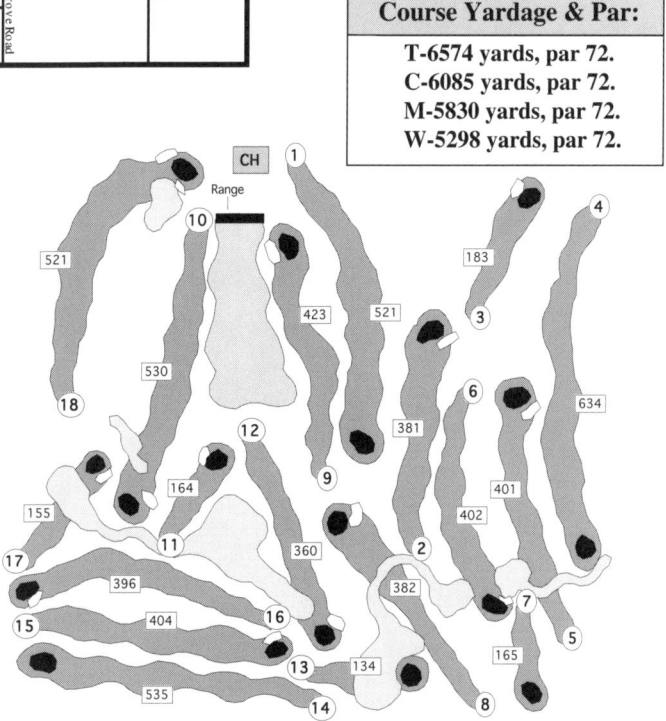

Broadmore Country Club (private, 9 hole course)

103 Shannon Drive; Nampa, Idaho 83687
Phone: (208) 466-0561. Fax: (208) 466-2872. Internet: none.
Pro: Roger Garner, PGA. Superintendent: Richard Rush.
Rating/Slope: M 68.1/111; W 70.2/123. **Course record:** 61.
Green fees: private club, members and guests of members only.
Power cart: members only. **Pull cart:** private club. **Trail fee:** private club.
Reservation policy: private club, members and guests of members only.
Winter condition: the golf course is open all year long weather permitting.
Terrain: flat, some hills. **Tees:** all grass. **Spikes:** soft spikes required.
Services: lessons, restaurant, beer, wine, beverages, pro shop, driving range.
Comments: private golf club located just west of Boise. This 9 hole course has two sets of tees for 18 hole play. Water comes into play on 7 holes which can make this golf course hard to score on. Greens are small in size and can be hard to hold. Fairways are tree-lined and narrow putting an emphasis on accuracy.

Directions: from I-84 East & Westbound take exit #35 (Nampa Boulevard). Proceed southbound, the golf course will be located on the right side of the road.

Course Yardage & Par:
M-3121 yards, par 36.
W-2842 yards, par 36.
Dual tees for 18 holes:
M-6211 yards, par 72.
W-5611 yards, par 72.

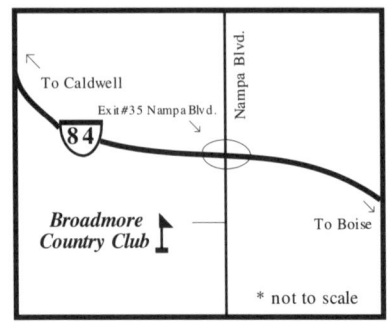

Bryden Canyon Golf Course (public, 18 hole course)

445 O'Conner Road; Lewiston, Idaho 83501

Phone: (208) 746-0863. **Fax:** (208) 746-4177. **Internet:** www.brydencanyon.com

Pro: Lee Roberts, PGA. **Superintendent:** Phil Brown.

Rating/Slope: M 68.3/111; W 70.2/111. **Course record:** 61.

Green fees: $17.85/$13.65 all week; season passes; Jr. Sr. rates; VISA, M/C.

Power cart: $21/$11. **Pull cart:** $2. **Trail fee:** $4 for personal carts.

Reservation policy: please call 7 days in advance for all your tee-times.

Winter condition: the golf course is open all year long, weather permitting.

Terrain: relatively hilly. **Tees:** all grass tees. **Spikes:** soft spikes preferred.

Services: club rentals, lessons, restaurant, beer, wine, beverages, snack bar, well stocked pro shop, driving range, putting & chipping greens, club memberships.

Comments: good public golf course that plays a lot tougher than the yardage will indicate. The course is built on a hilltop whichs gives the golfer a variety of lies from the fairway. Greens are medium in size with few hazards fronting them.

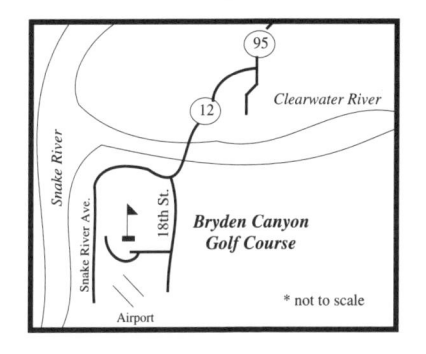

Directions: the golf course is located near the airport. While in Lewiston make sure you follow signs to the airport. This will get you to the golf course. The golf course is located in south Lewiston.

Course Yardage & Par:
M-6103 yards, par 71.
W-5294 yards, par 71.

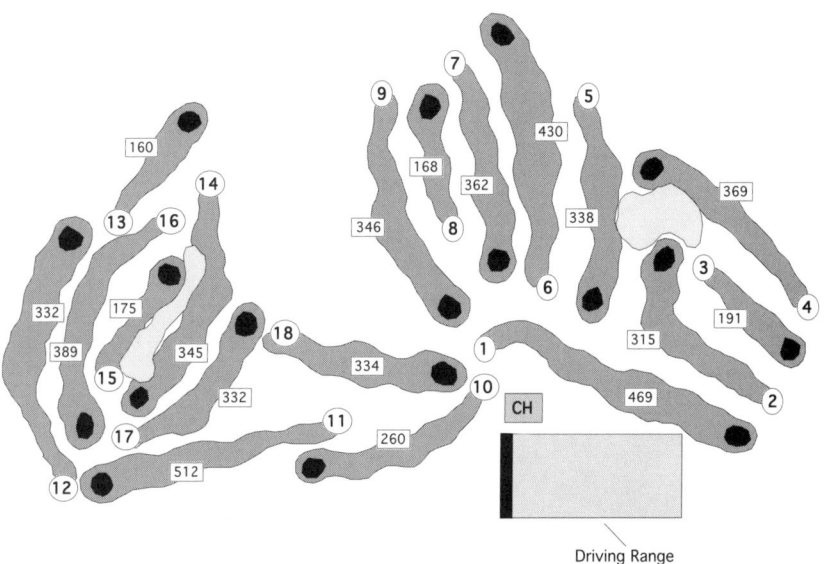

Driving Range

Burley City Municipal Golf Course (public, 18 hole course)
East 16th Street; P.O. Box 687; Burley, Idaho 83318
Phone: (208) 678-9807. Fax: none. Internet: none.
Pro: Mike Williams, PGA. Superintendent: Brent Winn.
Rating/Slope: C 70.5/116; M 68.5/112; W 70.8/119. **Course record:** 62.
Green fees: W/D $16/$10; W/E $16/$10; Sr. & Jr. rates (M-F); M/C, VISA.
Power cart: $18/$9. **Pull cart:** $2. **Trail fee:** $15 for personal carts.
Reservation policy: for weekday time call 1 day prior. For your weekend and holidays tee times make your call on the Wednesday prior to that weekend.
Winter condition: the course is closed from December to mid or late March.
Terrain: flat, some slight hills. **Tees:** all grass. **Spikes:** soft spikes required.
Services: club rentals, lessons, snack bar, beer, pro shop, driving range, putting green, club memberships. **Comments:** very scenic course that is bordered by the spectacular Snake River. The course has played host to many men's and ladies state amateur championships over the years. Great on course pro shop for those wanting to stock up on the essentials. Excellent public golf course.

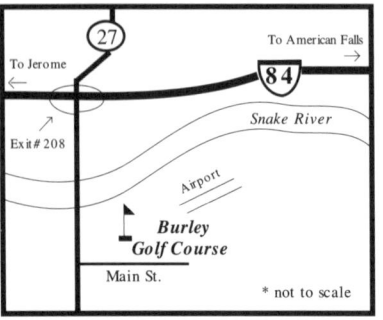

Directions: from I-84 take exit #208. Turn left across the Snake River to Main Street. Then turn left to the golf course which will be straight ahead. Look for a sign indicating your turn to the clubhouse.

Course Yardage & Par:
C-6283 yards, par 72.
M-6100 yards, par 72.
W-5597 yards, par 75.

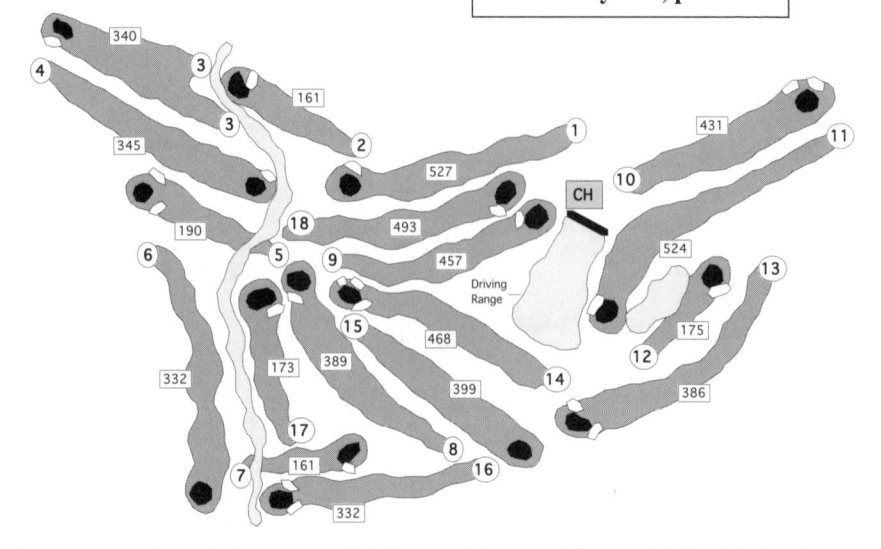

Candleridge Golf Course (public, 9 hole course)

2097 Candleridge Road; Twin Falls, Idaho 83301
Phone: (208) 733-6577, 800-733-6577. Fax: (208) 733-8893. Internet: none.
Pro: Brian Avran, PGA. Superintendent: Scott Swope.
Rating/Slope: C 59.0/86; M 58.6/86; W 57.8/80. **Course record:** 57.
Green fees: W/D $13.50/$9; W/E $16.50/$11; Jr./Sr. rates; VISA, M/C, DIS.
Power cart: $18/$9. **Pull cart:** $5. **Trail fee:** to be determined.
Reservation policy: you may call up to 1 day in advance for tee times.
Winter condition: the golf course is open all year long weather permitting.
Terrain: flat, some hills. **Tees:** all grass. **Spikes:** soft spikes preferred.
Services: club rentals, beer, restaurant, snack bar, pro shop, driving range.
Comments: built in 1997 this newer 9 hole course that sports a par of 62.
Not overly long this executive type course is fun to play for all levels and ages.
Greens are medium in size with few undulations running through them.

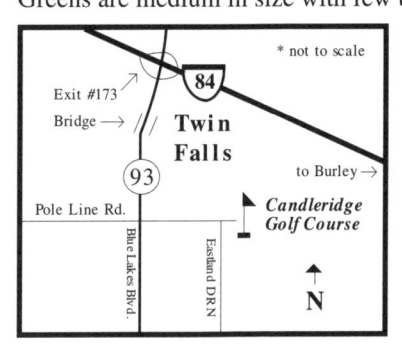

Directions: from I-84 E&W take exit #173 (Hwy 93). Travel southbound on Hwy 93 (Blue Lakes Road). Travel across the Perrin Bridge until you reach Pole Line Road, turn left. Proceed on Pole Line Road until you come to Candleridge Drive. The golf course is located on your right. The course is located near the intersections of Eastland Drive N and Pole Line Road.

Course Yardage & Par:
C-2005 yards, par 31.
M-1909 yards, par 31.
W-1798 yards, par 33.

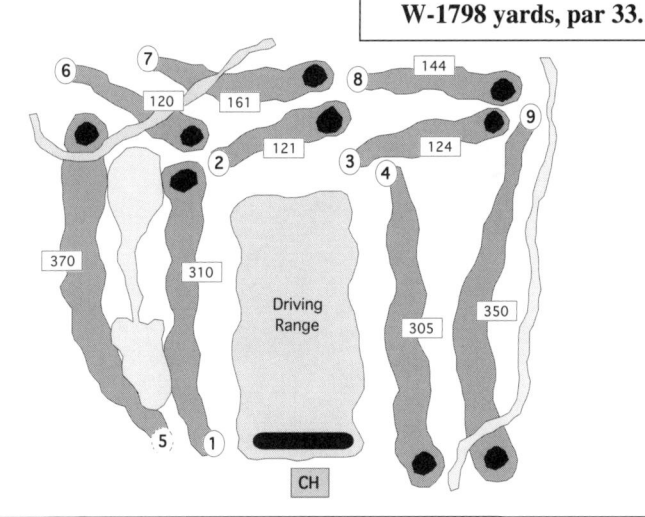

Canyon Springs Golf Course (public, 18 hole course)

199 Canyon Springs Road; P.O. Box 5912; Twin Falls, Idaho 83303
Phone: (208) 734-7609. **Fax:** (208) 735-9193. **Internet:** www.canyonsprings.com
Pro: Del Ericson, PGA. **Superintendent:** P.J. McGuire.
Rating/Slope: C 68.7/116; M 66.7/108; W 67.1/112. **Course record:** 64.
Green fees: W/D $19/$12; W/E $24; no credit cards.
Power cart: $22/$14. **Pull cart:** $4/$2.50. **Trail fee:** $10 for personal carts.
Reservation policy: please call 3 days in advance to make your tee-times.
Winter condition: the golf course is open all year long. Course drains well.
Terrain: relatively hilly. **Tees:** all grass. **Spikes:** soft spikes required.
Services: club rentals, lessons, snack bar, restaurant, lounge, beer, wine, liquor, pop, pro shop, lockers, showers, driving range, putting green, club memberships.
Comments: unique setting with lots of rock and water coming into play on several holes. The Snake River provides a perfect backdrop for this golf course.

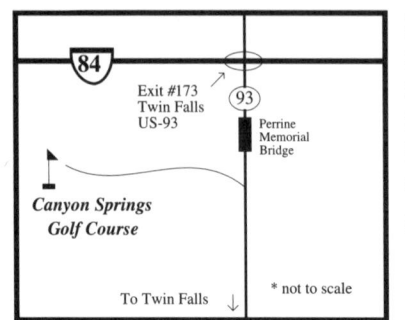

Directions: from I-84 take exit #173 (Hwy 93) in Twin Falls. Turn south and travel approximately 3 miles. Turn right at first turn beyond Perrine Bridge (Canyon Springs Road) this leads directly to the clubhouse. Signs indicate the turn to the golf course.

Course Yardage & Par:
C-6404 yards, par 72. **M-6027 yards, par 72.** **W-5043 yards, par 74.**

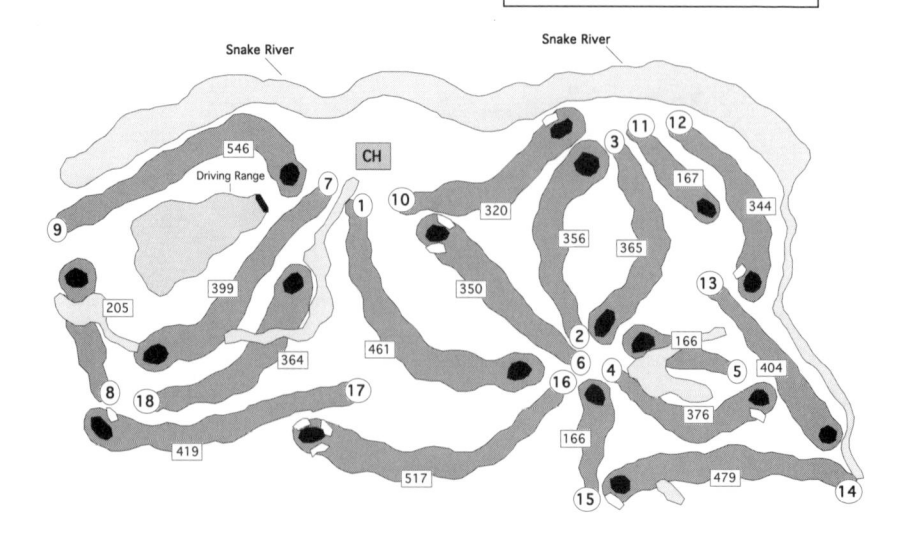

Cascade Golf Course (public, 9 hole course)

117 Lakeshore Drive; P.O. Box 238; Cascade, Idaho 83611
Phone: (208) 382-4835. Fax: none. Internet: none.
Managers: Jack & Donna Pingle. Superintendent: Jack Pingle.
Rating/Slope: M 63.2/96; W 64.6/99. **Course record:** 30.
Green fees: weekdays $12; weekends $15; no credit cards.
Power cart: $18. **Pull cart:** $2.50. **Trail fee:** not allowed.
Reservation policy: yes, call ahead up to 1 week in advance for tee-times.
Winter condition: closed during the winter months (November thru March).
Terrain: flat with rolling hills. **Tees:** all grass. **Spikes:** no policy.
Services: club rentals, snack bar, restaurant, lounge, beer, wine, putting green.
Comments: the course has many hills and water to contend with. Shot placement is a must on many of the holes as fairways are narrow in spots. The course runs along the Cascade Reservoir and offers fantastic views from every tee.

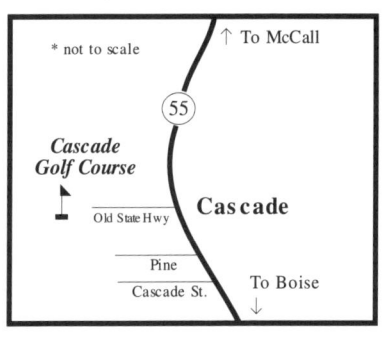

Directions: from Highway 55 turn west on "Old State Highway." Travel .5 miles to Lakeshore Drive and the golf course clubhouse which will be located on your left. Look for signs. The course is located approximatley 73 miles north of Boise, Idaho.

Course Yardage & Par:
M-2566 yards, par 33.
W-2315 yards, par 38.
Dual tees for 18 holes:
M-5141 yards, par 66.
W-4609 yards, par 76.

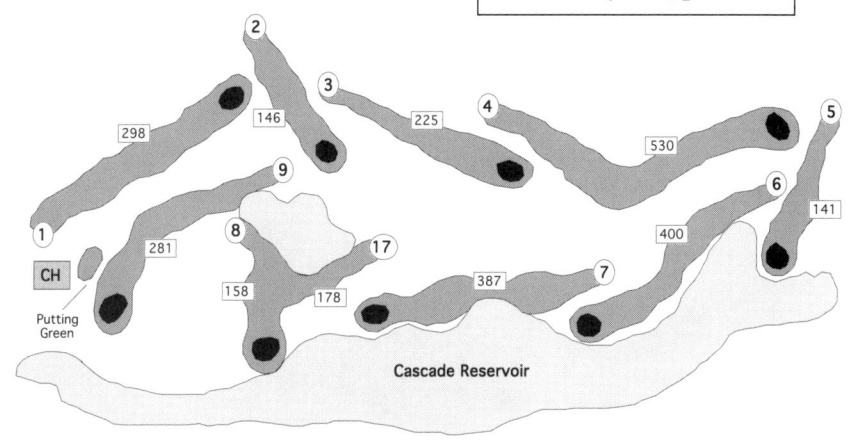

Cascade Reservoir

Centennial Golf Course (public, 18 hole course)
2600 Centennial Drive; P.O. Box 52; Nampa, Idaho 83653
Phone: (208) 467-3011, 888-7559. Fax: (208) 465-4476.
Pro: John Lewis, PGA. Supt.: Eric Robinson. Internet: golfcentennial.com
Rating/Slope: C 69.6/113; M 68.2/109; W 69.6/112. **Course record**: 62.
Green fees: Mon.-Thur. $15; Fri.-Sunday $18; Jr., twilight rates; M/C, VISA.
Power cart: $17/$11. **Pull cart:** $3. **Trail fee:** $11 for personal carts.
Reservation policy: yes, please call ahead 2 days in advance for your tee times.
Winter condition: damp, the course is open all year round weather permitting.
Terrain: relatively hilly. **Tees:** all grass tees. **Spikes:** soft spikes preferred.
Services: club rentals, lessons, snack bar, beer, wine, pro shop, driving range,
putting & chipping greens. **Comments:** nice public facility that gets a lot of
play during the summer months. The course sports wide open fairways with
medium to large greens. Water comes into play and can be a factor off the tee.

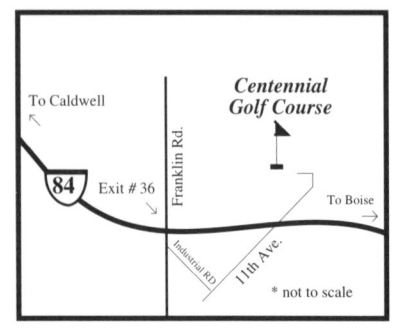

Directions: From I-84 take exit #36
(Franklin). Go southbound 1 block, then
turn left on Industrial Rd. Proceed to 11th
Avenue and turn left. Go to Centennial
Drive and turn left to the golf course.

Course Yardage & Par:
C-6655 yards, par 72.
M-6213 yards, par 72.
W-5483 yards par 72.

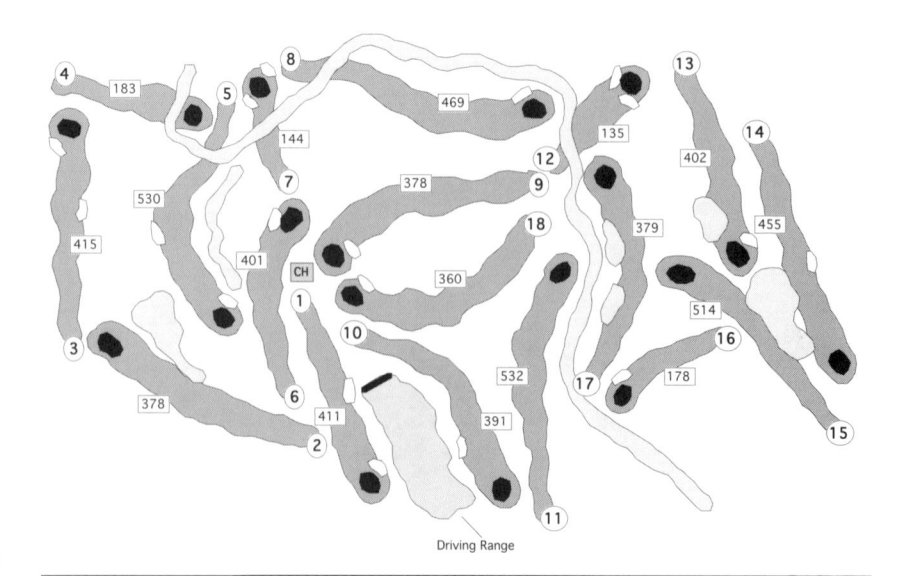

Central Links Golf Course & RV Park (public, 9 hole course)

1750 Gibson Lane; Grace, Idaho 83241
Phone: (208) 425-3233. Fax: (208) 425-3585. Internet: none.
Manager's: Bart & Cherie Christensen.
Rating/Slope: M 59.7/89; W 62.0/103. **Course record:** 32.
Green fees: $13/$7 all week long; Jr. rates; season passes available.
Power cart: $14/$7. **Pull cart:** $2. **Trail fee:** $3 for personal carts.
Reservation policy: advance tee-times are not needed or required.
Winter condition: the golf course is open April 1st to October 15th.
Terrain: flat, some hills. **Tees:** all grass tees. **Spikes:** soft spikes preferred.
Services: club rentals, pro shop, driving range, beverages, candy, snacks.
Comments: challenging and fun golf course that is isolated from the traffic and noise. It is built among lava outcroppings and nearby farm land. This newer course is planning an RV park that is due to open in 2000. Very friendly course.

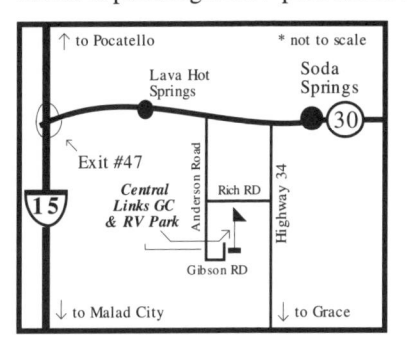

Directions: follow golf signs 2 miles north of Grace Idaho on Highway 34 or at milepost 383 on Highway US 30. Signs will take you to the course which is ahead 4.5 miles from the main road. The course is located 11 miles west of Soda Springs and 9 miles east of Lava Hot Springs off of Highway US 30. Look for signs.

Course Yardage & Par:
M-2192 yards, par 33. **W-1995 yards, par 33.**

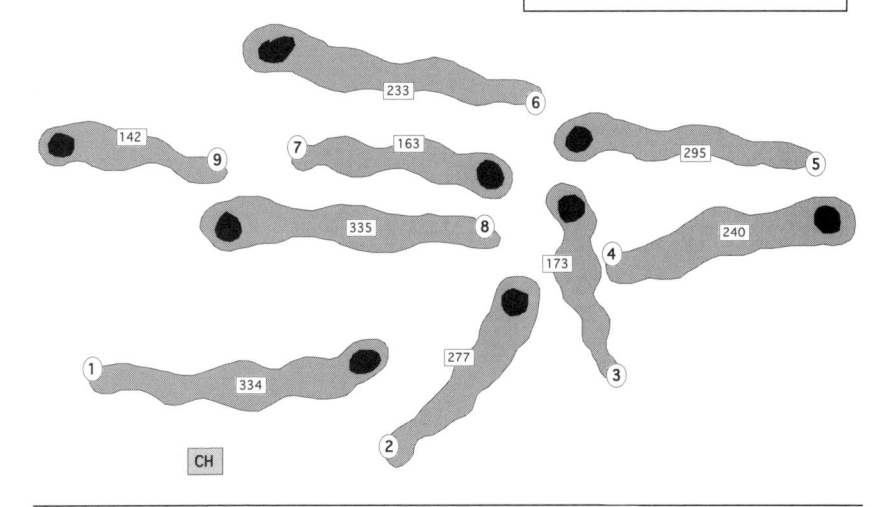

Challis Centennial Golf Course (public, 9 hole course)
Off Main Street; Challis, Idaho 83226
Phone: (208) 879-5440. Fax: none. Internet: none.
Pro: Larry Weiner. Manager: none. Superintendent: none.
Rating/Slope: M 69.2/117; W 69.3/116. **Course record:** 65.
Green fees: $10 all week long; no credit cards are accepted.
Power cart: none available. **Pull cart:** none. **Trail fee:** not allowed.
Reservation policy: none needed, course often played on the honor system.
Winter condition: course closed during the winter months, Nov. to March.
Terrain: flat with rolling hills. **Tees:** all grass. **Spikes:** no policy.
Services: Very limited services. The golfers clubhouse is very primitive.
Comments: a rural course which caters to the local community. Greens and fairways are rough, leaving the golfer battling the local terrain. The golf course is situated against the foothills in the heart of the town of Challis Idaho.

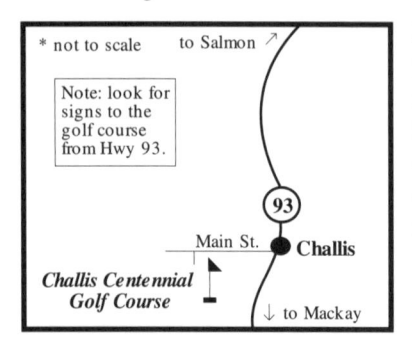

Directions: from Highway 93 southbound turn right on Main Street. Follow Main St. for 1.25 miles to the course on your left. From Highway 93 northbound turn left on Main Street. Proceed 1.2 miles to course on your left. There are many signs indicating your turn from Highway 93.

Course Yardage & Par:
M-3273 yards, par 36.
W-2729 yards, par 36.

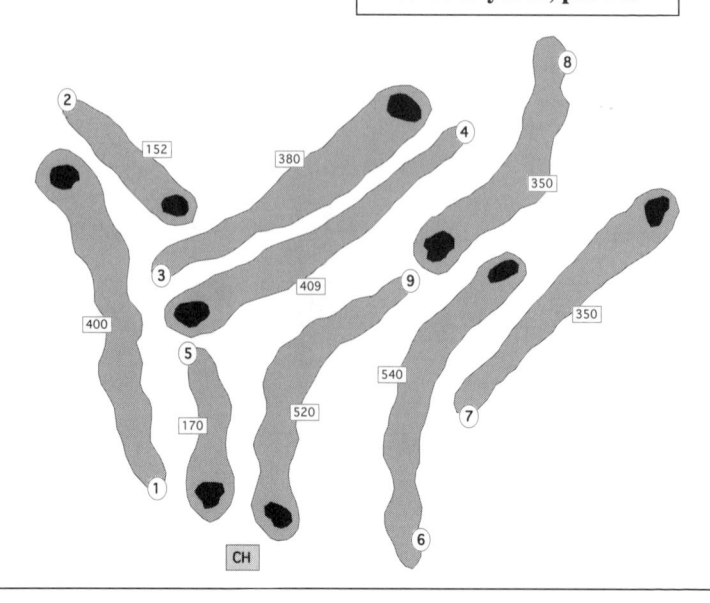

Cherry Lane Golf Club (public, 18 hole course)
4200 West Talamore; Meridian, Idaho 83642
Phone: (208) 888-4080. Fax: (208) 888-4022. Inernet: none.
Pro: Tad Holloway, PGA. Superintendent: Tom Link.
Rating/Slope: C 68.5/114; M 67.1/111; W 68.3/112. **Course record:** 63.
Green fees: W/D $17/$13; W/E $19/$13; winter rates; M/C, VISA.
Power cart: $18/$10. **Pull cart:** $2. **Trail fee:** $8.50/$7 for personal carts.
Reservation policy: yes, call 3 days in advance weekend play only.
Winter condition: the golf course is open weather permitting. Damp.
Terrain: flat, very easy to walk. **Tees:** all grass. **Spikes:** soft spikes required.
Services: club rentals, lessons, snack bar, beer, wine, pro shop, driving range,
putting green. **Comments:** the golf course is flat, easy to walk. Great course for
the senior. The golf course plays much tougher than the yardage would indicate.

Directions: from I-84 E&W take exit
#44 (Meridian/McCall). Travel north for
1 mile to Fairview/Cherry Lane. Turn
left on Cherry Lane and proceed for 2.6
miles to West Talamore, turn right to
the golf course. Look for signs.

Course Yardage & Par:
C-6521 yards, par 72.
M-6223 yards, par 72.
W-5257 yards, par 72.

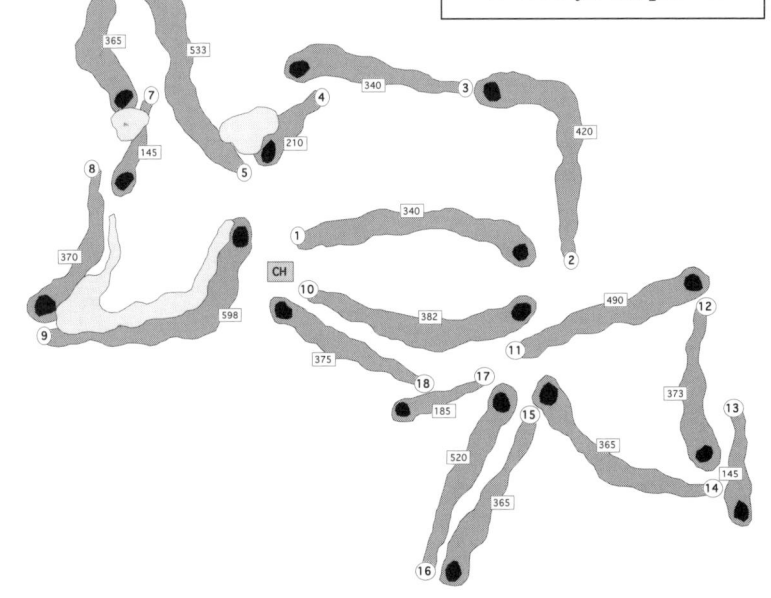

Clear Lake Country Club (semi-private, 18 hole course)

Route 4; Box 225; 403 Clear Lake Lane; Buhl, Idaho 83316
Phone: (208) 543-4849. Fax: none. Internet: none.
Pro: Matt Echeverria, PGA. Superintendent: Denny Kuntz.
Rating/Slope: C 67.6/108; M 67.0/106; W 70.2/116. **Course record:** 68.
Greens fee: W/D $19/$13; W/E $21/$13; VISA, M/C.
Power cart: $16/$8. **Pull cart**: $4/$2. **Trail fee:** $6 for personal carts.
Reservation policy: yes, please call Thursday for your weekend tee-times.
Winter condition: the golf course is open all year long weather permitting. Dry.
Terrain: relatively hilly. **Tees:** all grass. **Spikes:** soft spikes preferred.
Services: club rentals, lessons, snack bar, restaurant, lounge, beer, wine,
liquor, pro shop, lockers, showers, driving range, RV park, fly fishing.
Comments: course is very scenic with tree-lined fairways. The layout is set in
the Snake River Canyon. Nice facility that is worth a special trip if in the area.

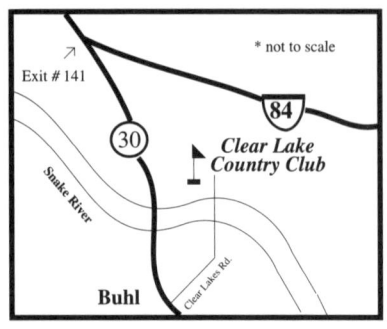

Directions: from Highway 30 in Buhl
turn northbound on Clear Lakes Road.
Follow this for 7.8 miles to the golf
course. Look for signs on the highway
indicating the turn to the golf course.

Course Yardage & Par:
C-6015 yards, par 72.
M-5905 yards, par 72.
W-5378 yards, par 73.

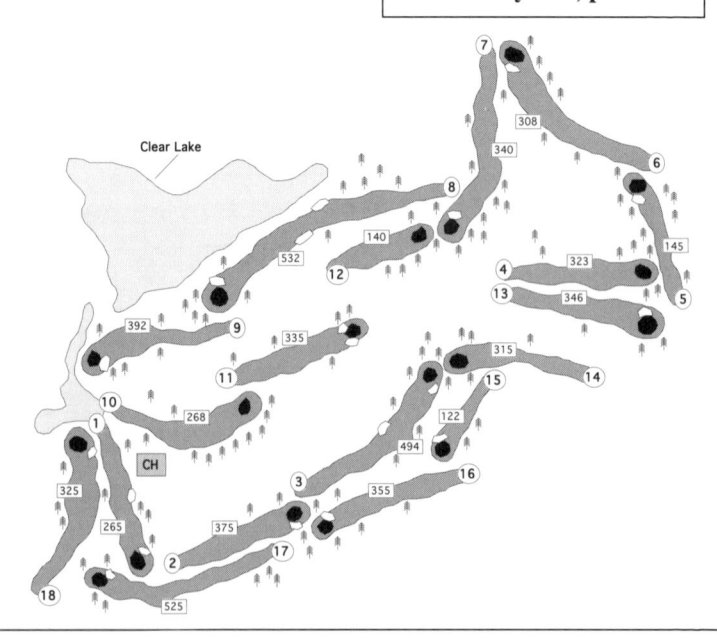

Coeur d'Alene Golf Club (public, 18 hole course)

2201 Fairway Drive; Coeur d'Alene, Idaho 83814
Phone: (208) 765-0218. Fax: (208) 667-5286. Internet: none.
Pro: Dave Lowe, PGA. Superintendent: unavailable.
Rating/Slope: C 69.5/116; M 68.3/113; W 71.4/119. **Course record: 61.**
Green fees: $18/$12.50; $24/$18 out of state residents; Jr/Sr rates; M/C, VISA.
Power cart: $22/$12. **Pull cart:** $3. **Trail fee:** $5 for personal carts.
Reservation policy: yes, 2 days in advance. Call on Thursday for the weekend.
Winter condition: the course is closed from November 15th to March 15th.
Terrain: flat, some hills. **Tees:** all grass. **Spikes:** soft spikes preferred.
Services: club rentals, lessons, snack bar, restaurant, beer, wine, pro shop,
driving range, putting green, club memberships. **Comments:** the golf course is
kept in excellent condition. Fairways are narrow in size putting a premium on
accuracy off the tee. Greens are large in size leaving the golfer with ample room.

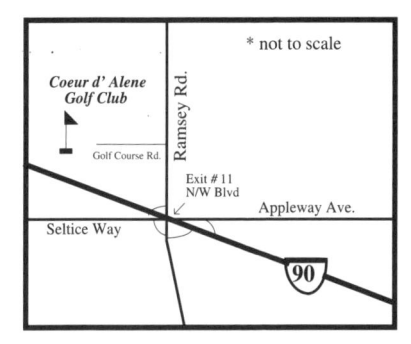

Directions: from I-90 E&W take the NW
Boulevard exit. Proceed northbound to
Appleway Ave. Turn left on Appleway to
Fairway Drive. Proceed to the golf course.

Course Yardage & Par:
C-6295 yards, par 72.
M-6037 yards, par 72.
W-5560 yards, par 74.

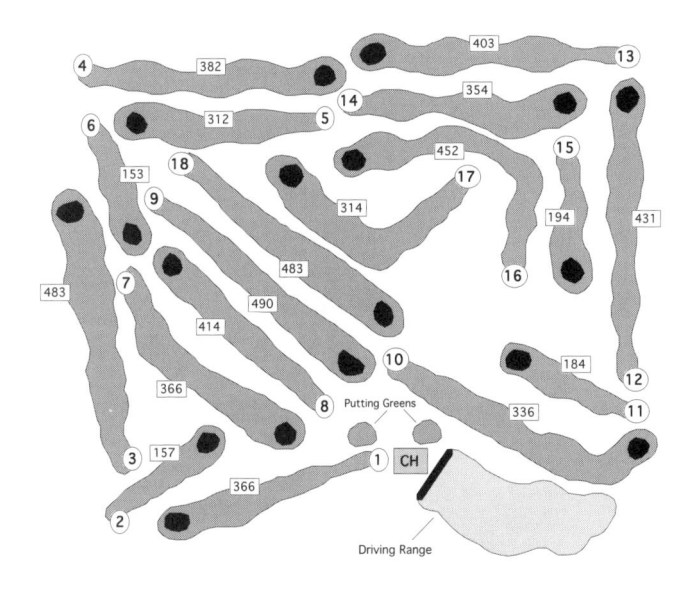

Coeur d'Alene Resort Golf Course, The (resort, 18 hole course)

2255 Mullan Avenue; Coeur d'Alene, Idaho 83814
Phone: (208) 667- 4653, reservations 800-688-5253; **Fax:** (208) 667-5683
Pro: Mike DeLong, PGA. **Supt.:** John Anderson. **Internet:** www.cdaresort.com
Rating/Slope: C 69.9/121; M 68.2/117; M 66.0/113; W 64.5/105. **Record:** 61.
Green fees: $200 non guests; $155 resort guests; M/C, VISA, AMEX, DIS, DN.
Power cart: included in the greens fee. **Pull cart:** none. **Trail fee:** not allowed.
Reservation policy: tee times are made at the time of room reservations.
Winter condition: the golf course is closed during the winter months.
Terrain: flat, some hills. **Tees:** all grass. **Spikes:** soft spikes are required.
Services: club rentals, lessons, snack bar, restaurant, beer, wine, liquor,
pro shop, driving range, putting & chipping greens, full service four star resort.
Comments: this is one of the most beautiful golf courses in the state of Idaho.
This facility has received numerous awards for outstanding service and golf
course design. The now famous floating green on the #14 hole is spectacular.

Directions: from I-90 East & West take exit #15. Proceed southbound to Mullan Ave. The resort is located on Mullan Ave. **Note:** the golf resort can be seen from I-90.

Course Yardage & Par:
C-6309 yards, par 71.
M-5899 yards, par 71.
M-5490 yards, par 71.
W-4446 yards, par 71.

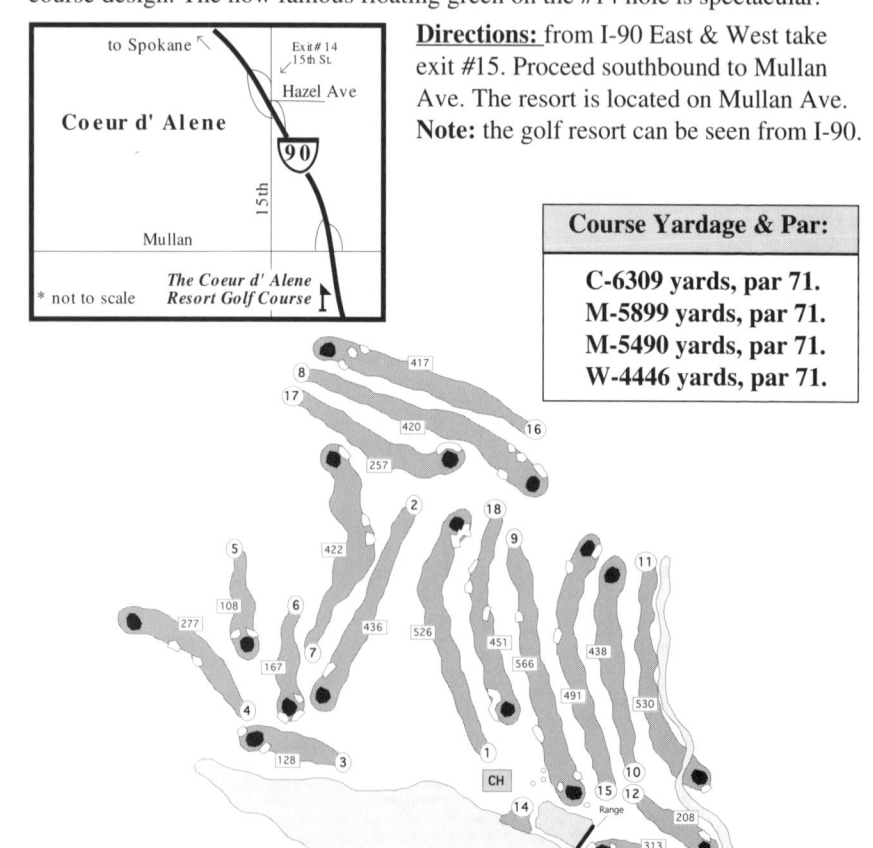

Council Mountain Golf Course (public, 9 hole course)

1918 Highway 95 South; P.O. Box 7; Council, Idaho 83612
Phone: (208) 253-4357. Fax: none. Internet: none.
Manager: Jeff Muller. Superintendent: Jeff Muller.
Rating/Slope: M 67.0/102; W 69.4/104. **Course record:** 32.
Green fees: W/D $11/$9; W/E $12/$10; VISA, M/C, AMEX.
Power carts: $15/$11. **Pull cart:** $2. **Trail fee:** personal carts not available.
Reservation policy: tee times are accepted up to 2 days in advance.
Winter condition: closed during the winter months, November thru mid-March.
Terrain: flat, some hills. **Tees:** all grass. **Spikes:** no spike policy.
Services: club rentals, restaurant, snack bar, beer, wine, liquor, small pro shop.
Comments: a nice country course to visit while traveling through Idaho.
The golf course is nestled up in the foothills in the heart of Council, Idaho.
Greens are small to medium in size and have few hazards fronting them.

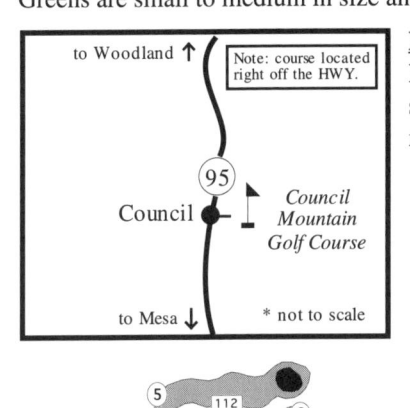

Directions: the golf course is located on Highway 95 in Council, Idaho on the west side of the highway. Look for a white sign marking the golf course.

Course Yardage & Par:
M-3003 yards, par 36.
W-2696 yards, par 36.
Dual tees for 18 holes:
M-6113 yards, par 72.
W-5480 yards, par 72.

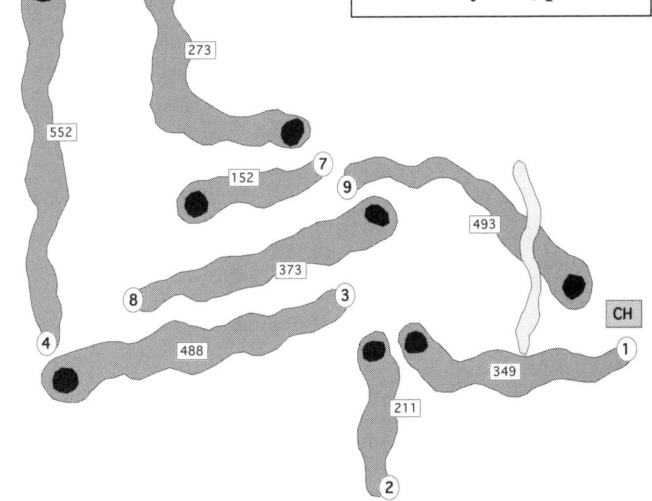

Crane Creek Country Club (private, 18 hole course)

500 West Curling Drive; Boise, Idaho 83702
Phone: (208) 344-9313. Fax: none. Internet: none.
Pro: Stoney Brown, PGA. Superintendent: Jerry Flaher.
Rating/Slope: C 71.0/124; M 69.8/120; W 71.4/127. **Course record:** 62.
Green fees: private club members & guests only; reciprocates; M/C, VISA.
Power cart: private club. **Pull cart:** none. **Trail fee:** not allowed.
Reservation policy: private club, members and guests of members only.
Winter condition: the golf course is open all year long, weather permitting.
Terrain: very hilly. **Tees:** all grass. **Spikes:** soft spikes only.
Services: club rentals, lessons, snack bar, restaurant, lounge, beer, wine, liquor, pro shop, showers, driving range, putting green, chipping green.
Comments: scenic course with a large canyon bordering the front side. Greens are large and can be hard to hold in summer. Well maintained private facility.

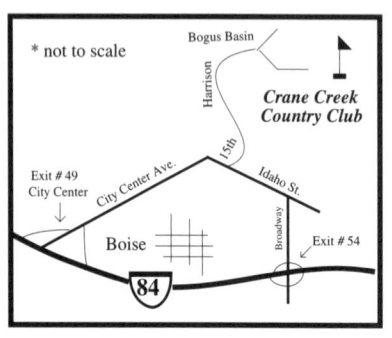

Directions: I-84W take City Center exit to 15th St. Left on 15th to Hayes St. Left on Hayes which becomes Harrison Blvd. Go north on Harrison Boulevard which becomes Bogus Basin Road. North on Bogus Basin to Curling Road. Right on Curling to Braenere, left to course. I-84E take Broadway exit. North on Broadway beyond University, road veers left into Idaho Street. Proceed to 15th and follow directions above to the golf course.

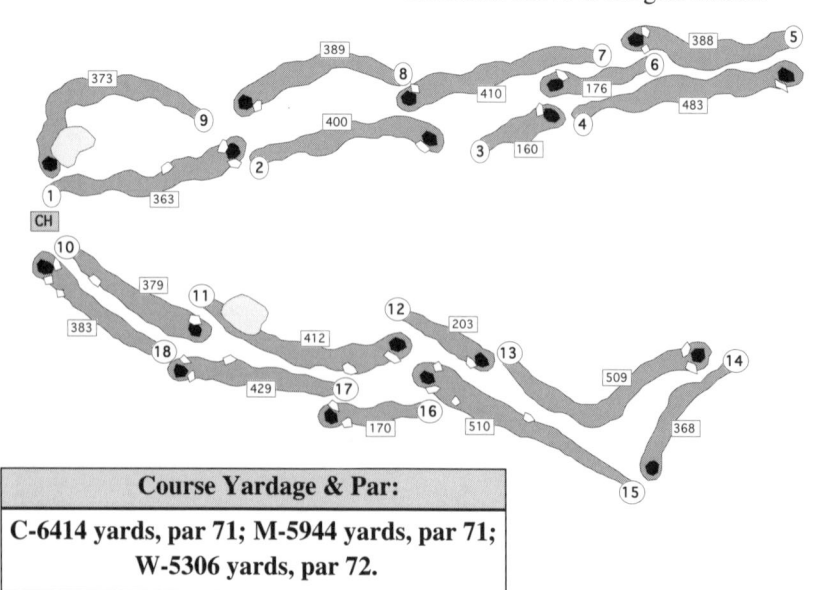

Course Yardage & Par:
C-6414 yards, par 71; M-5944 yards, par 71; W-5306 yards, par 72.

Desert Canyon Golf Course (public, 9 hole course)
1880 East 8th North; Mountain Home, Idaho 83647
Phone: (208) 587-3293. Fax: (208) 587-1352. Internet: none.
Pro: Lance Price, PGA. Superintendent: Brian Rodgers.
Rating/Slope: C 69.8/117; M 68.0/110; W 67.9/105. **Course record:** 63.
Green fees: $18/$14 all week lomg; Jr. rates (M-F); M/C, VISA.
Power cart: $20/$12. **Pull cart:** $3/$2. **Trail fee:** $10 for personal carts.
Reservation policy: yes, please call 2 days in advance for tee times.
Winter condition: the golf course is open all year long, weather permitting.
Terrain: flat (easy walking). **Tees:** grass. **Spikes:** soft spikes only.
Services: club rentals, lessons, snack bar, restaurant, beer, wine, beverages, pop, pro shop, driving range, putting & chipping greens, club memberships.
Comments: built in 1969 this course features small, elevated greens that make for tricky approach shots. Fairways are wide in the landing area's and water comes into play on 4 holes. Course plays tougher than the yardage indicates.

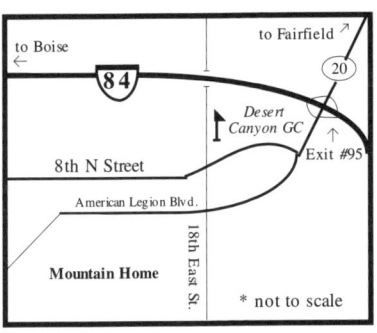

Directions: From I-84 E&W take exit #95. Proceed southbound to an immediate right on 8th Street. After you turn right on 8th Street proceed for .5 miles to the golf course. Look for signs.

Course Yardage & Par:
M-3198 yards, par 36.
W-2786 yards, par 37.
Dual tees for 18 holes:
M-6270 yards, par 72.
W-5624 yards, par 74.

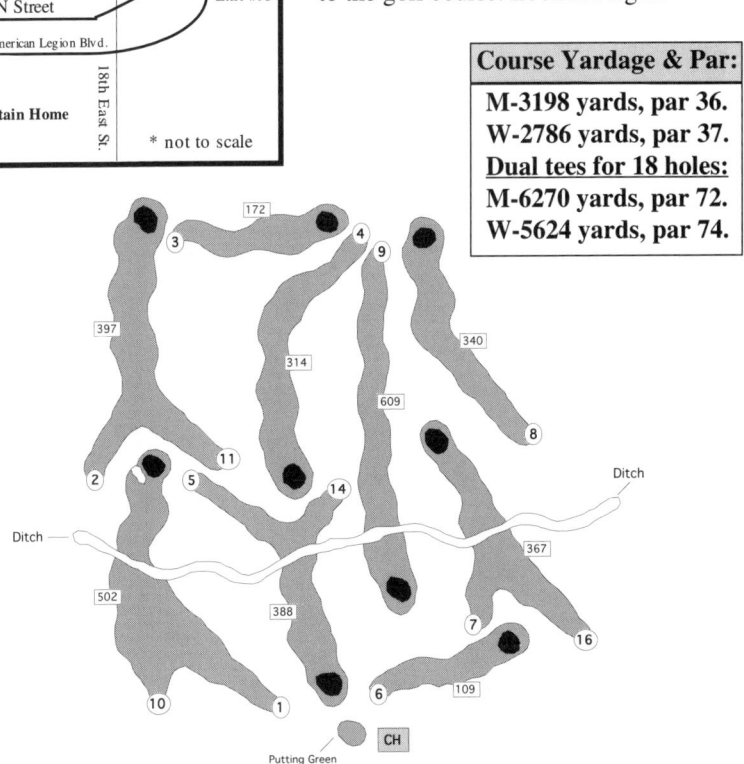

Eagle Hills Golf Course (public, 18 hole course)

605 North Edgewood Lane; Eagle, Idaho 83616
Phone: (208) 939-0402. Fax: (208) 939-8309. Internet: none.
Pro: Bill Thornton, PGA. Superintendent: Ken Roberts.
Rating/Slope: T 70.3/121; C 68.7/119; M 65.1/114; W 67.1/118. **Record:** 63.
Green fees: W/D $19; W/E $27; Jr. & Sr. rates; M/C, VISA.
Power cart: $20. **Pull cart**: $2. **Trail fee:** personal carts not allowed.
Reservation policy: yes, please call 5 days in advance for your tee-times.
Winter condition: damp conditions. The course open weather permitting.
Terrain: flat, some hills. **Tees:** all grass. **Spikes:** soft spikes preferred.
Services: club rentals, lessons, snack bar, restaurant, lounge, beer, wine,
liquor, pro shop, driving range, putting & chipping green, club memberships.
Comments: this course is one of the few courses in the valley that is in prime
condition all year round. Excellent track that has a community surrounding the
18 hole layout. The course features water on several holes and bunkered greens.

Directions: from I-84 E&W take exit #46
(Eagle Road Hwy 55). Proceed north on
Hwy 55 for 7.9 miles until you reach State
Street (Hwy 44) turn right (east). Proceed
until you reach Edgewood Lane turn left.
Proceed until you reach the 4 way stop.
Turn left. The golf course will be on your
left side. Signs will indicate your turns.

Course Yardage & Par:
C-6517 yards, par 72.
M-6150 yards, par 72.
W-5292 yards, par 72.
F-4922 yards, par 72.

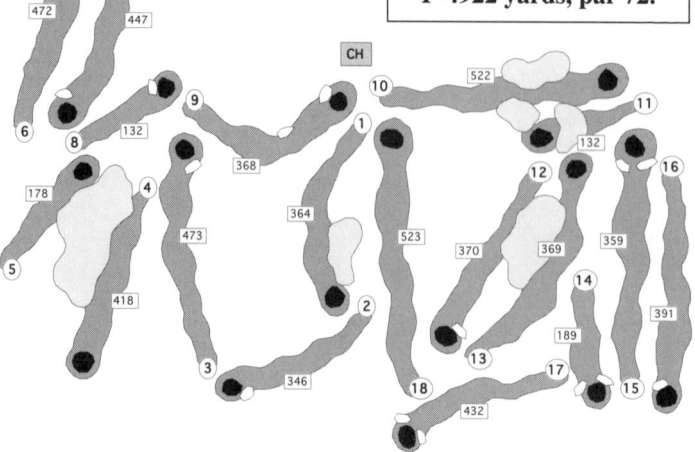

Fairview Municipal Golf Course (public, 9 hole course)

816 Grant Street; Caldwell, Idaho 83605
Phone (208) 455-3090. Fax: (208) 375-3256. Internet: none.
Pro: Lenny Stroup, PGA. Superintendent: Gordie Crockett.
Rating/Slope: M 63.2/99; W 68.5/112. **Course record:** 59.
Green fees: W/D $10; W/E & Holidays $13; no special rates; M/C, VISA.
Power cart: $7.75. **Pull cart:** $3/$1.50. **Trail fee:** $8.25 for personal carts.
Reservation policy: none, tee-times are on first come first served basis.
Winter condition: the course open weather permitting. Damp conditions.
Terrain: flat, some hills. **Tees:** all grass tees. **Spikes:** soft spikes only.
Services: club rentals, lessons, snack bar, beer, pro shop, putting green.
Comments: built in the early 1900's this course is one of the oldest in the state of Idaho. Small greens and many trees will challenge the skill of any golfer. There are no sand traps on this course so greens are fairly wide open in the front.

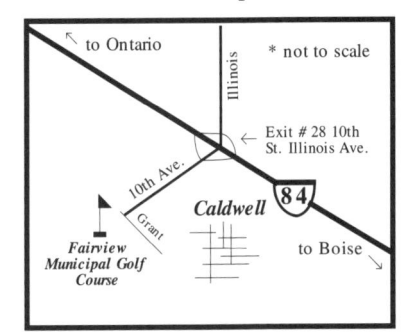

Directions: from I-84 take exit #28 to 10th Avenue. Left on 10th to Grant Street. Right on Grant Street to the golf course. Look for signs marking the way.

Course Yardage & Par:
M-2500 yards, par 35.
W-2500 yards, par 35.

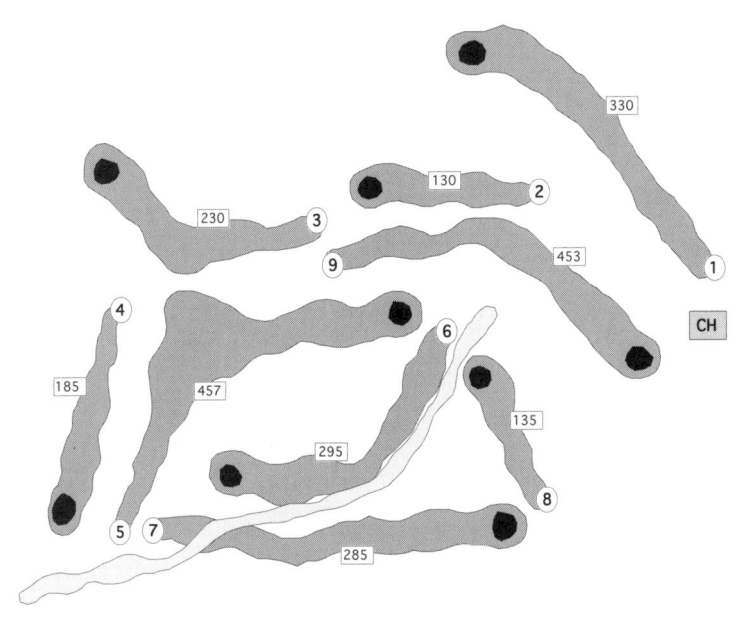

Foxtail Golf Course (public, 18 hole executive course)

990 West Chinden Boulevard; Meridian, Idaho 83642
Phone: (208) 887-4653. Fax:(208) 887-3970. Internet: none.
Pro/Manager: Tad Holloway, PGA. Superintendent: Todd Crockett.
Rating/Slope: M 59.3/91; W 59.3/91. **Course record:** 54.
Green fees: $15/$10 all week long; no special rates; VISA, M/C, AMEX.
Power cart: $14/$7. **Pull cart:** $2. **Trail fee:** $7 per nine holes.
Reservation policy: yes, please call up to 7 days in advance for your tee-fimes.
Winter condition: the golf course is open all year long, weather permitting.
Terrain: flat, some hills. **Tees:** all grass. **Spikes:** soft spikes required.
Services: club rentals, lessons, snacks & beverages, driving range, putting green.
Comments: the course's main hazard is water which comes into play on 5 of the 18 holes. Great iron golf course that will test you at every turn. If you are looking for a change of pace give Foxtail Golf Course a try it will not disappoint.

Directions: from I-84 E&W take exit #44 (Meridian Road). Proceed northbound on Merdian Road to Chinden Blvd. Turn left on Chinden Blvd. to the golf course which will be located on your right hand side. Look for a sign at your turn.

Course Yardage & Par:
C-3994 yards, par 61.
M-3784 yards, par 61.
W-3536 yards, par 61.

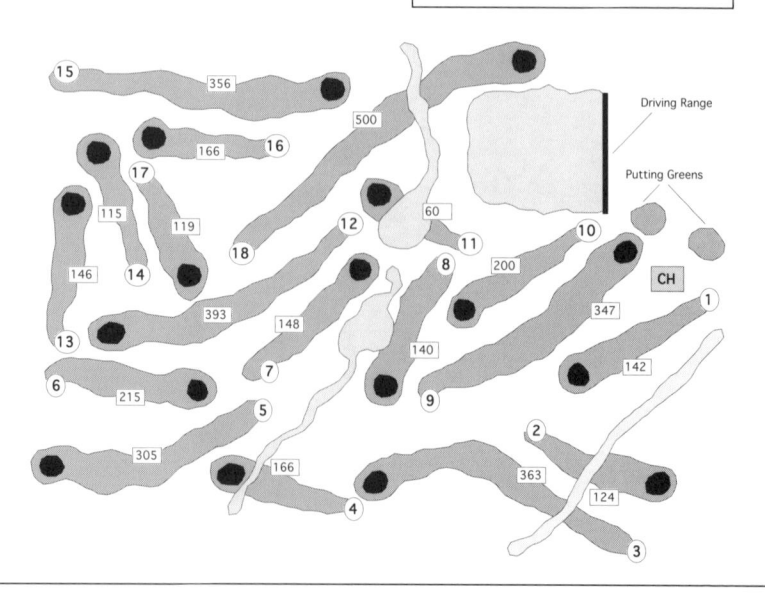

Fremont County Golf Course (public, 9 hole course)

674 Golf Course Road; P.O. Box 23; Saint Anthony, Idaho 83445
Phone: (208) 624-7074. Fax: none. Internet: none.
Pro: Chris Enstinan, PGA. Superintendent: Mike Rice.
Rating/Slope: M 67.6/115; W 70.0/122. **Course record:** 29.
Green fees: weekdays $15/$9; weekends $18/$10; VISA, M/C.
Power cart: $20/$10. **Pull cart:** $2/.$1. **Trail fee:** $15 for personal carts.
Reservation policy: yes, taken for weekends only. Call 7 days in advance.
Winter condition: the golf course is closed from November 1st to April 1st.
Terrain: flat, some hills. **Tees:** all grass. **Spikes:** soft spikes preferred.
Services: club rentals, lessons, snack bar, beer, wine coolers, pro shop,
lockers, showers, driving range, club memberships, putting & chipping greens.
Comments: the course has lots of variety. You will use every club in your bag.
OB comes into play on the right of every hole putting an emphasis on accuracy.

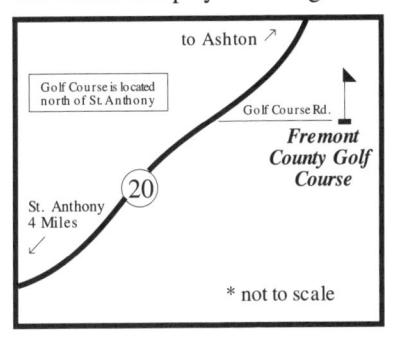

Directions: from Highway 20 proceed for 4.25 miles north of Saint Anthony to Golf Course Road. The course will be located on your right hand side. Look for signs that are posted along the way.

Course Yardage & Par:
M-3151 yards, par 36.
W-2748 yards, par 37.
Dual tees for 18 holes:
M-6244 yards, par 72.
W-5556 yards, par 74.

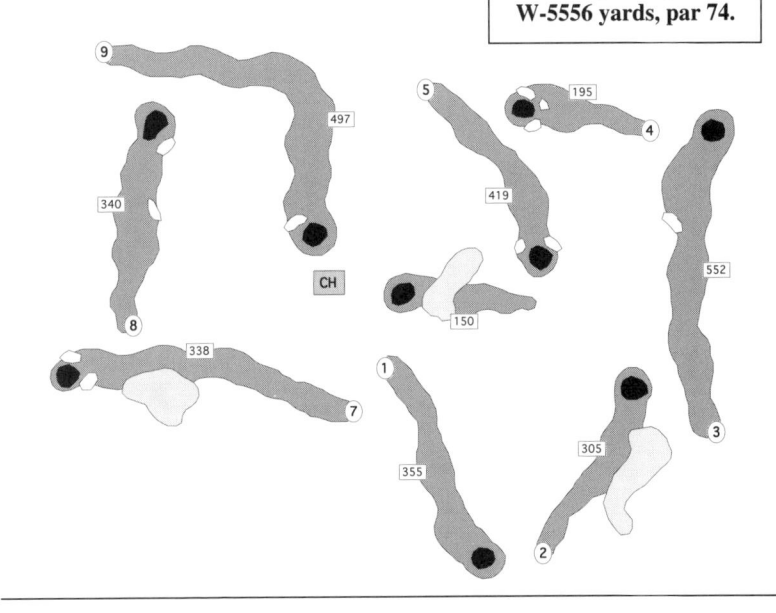

Gem County Golf Course (public, 9 hole course)

2102 West Salesyard Road; Emmett, Idaho 83617
Phone: (208) 365-2675. **Fax:** none. **Internet:** none.
Manager: Emmett City Golf Association. **Superintendent:** Dell Kroush.
Rating/Slope: M 67.6/109; W 72.4/115. **Course record:** 68.
Green fees: Weekdays $10.50; Weekends $12.60; M/C, VISA, AMEX.
Power cart: $15/$10. **Pull cart:** $2. **Trail fee:** to be determined.
Reservation policy: no restrictions. Please call in advance for your tee times.
Winter condition: the course is closed from December 15th to February 1st.
Terrain: flat (easy walking). **Tees:** all grass. **Spikes:** soft spikes only.
Services: club rentals, lessons, restaurant, lounge, beer, wine, liquor, pro shop.
Comments: the golf course is very narrow with challenging greens. Water comes into play on many of the holes and is a major factor. Good 9 hole course.

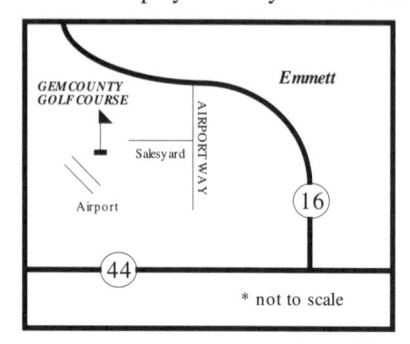

Directions: from Highway 44 E&W proceed to Hwy 16. Turn north on Hwy 16. Proceed northbound on Hwy 16 for 16 miles to Emmett Idaho. Turn left on Airport Way for .7 miles to Salesyard Road. Turn right on Salesyard Road to the golf course. Look for signs.

Course Yardage & Par:
M-3099 yards, par 36.
W-2822 yards, par 36.
Dual tees for 18 holes:
M-5991 yards, par 72.
W-5606 yards, par 72.

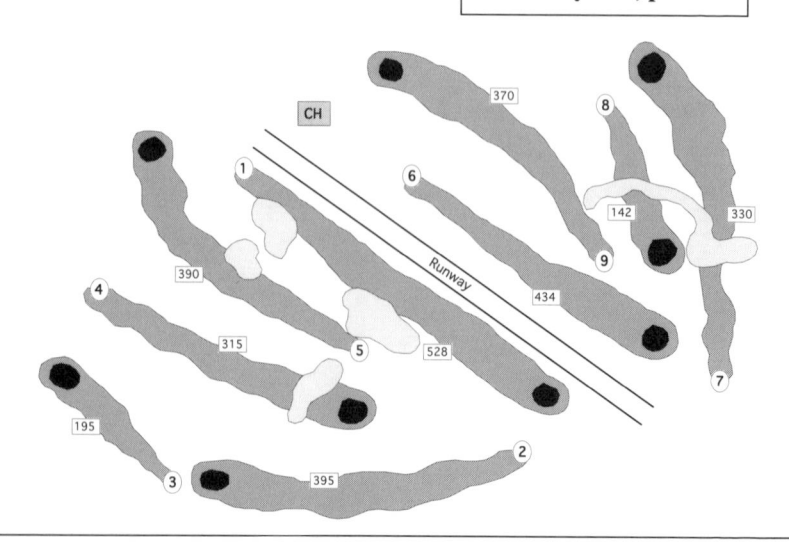

Golf & Recreation Club (public, 9 hole executive course)
3883 South Orchard Street; Boise, Idaho 83705
Phone: (208) 344-2008. Fax: (208) 344-2332. Internet: none.
Owner: Ray Sorensen. Superintendent: Terry Anderson.
Rating/Slope: the golf course is not rated. **Course record:** 23.
Green fees: $12/$9 all week long; Senior rates $8; M/C, VISA, DIS, AMEX.
Power cart: $7. **Pull cart:** $1. **Trail fee:** personal carts are not allowed.
Reservation policy: no restrictions on tee times. First come, first served.
Winter condition: the golf course is closed from November to February.
Terrain: flat, some hills. **Tees:** all grass. **Spikes:** soft spikes preferred.
Services: club rentals, lessons, snack bar, beer, wine, beverages, golf supplies, lighted driving range, lighted batting cages, lighted go-kart track, pro shop.
Comments: great course to take the whole family to. The facility has many family recreation activities. It calls itself "the nicest little course in Boise".

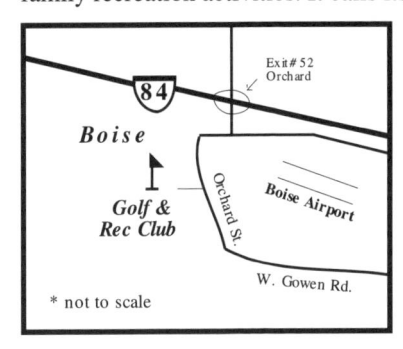

Directions: from I-84 E&W take exit #52 (Orchard). Proceed southbound for approximately 1 mile to the golf course Look for a sign at the turn.

Course Yardage & Par:
M-1295 yards, par 28.
W-1295 yards, par 32.

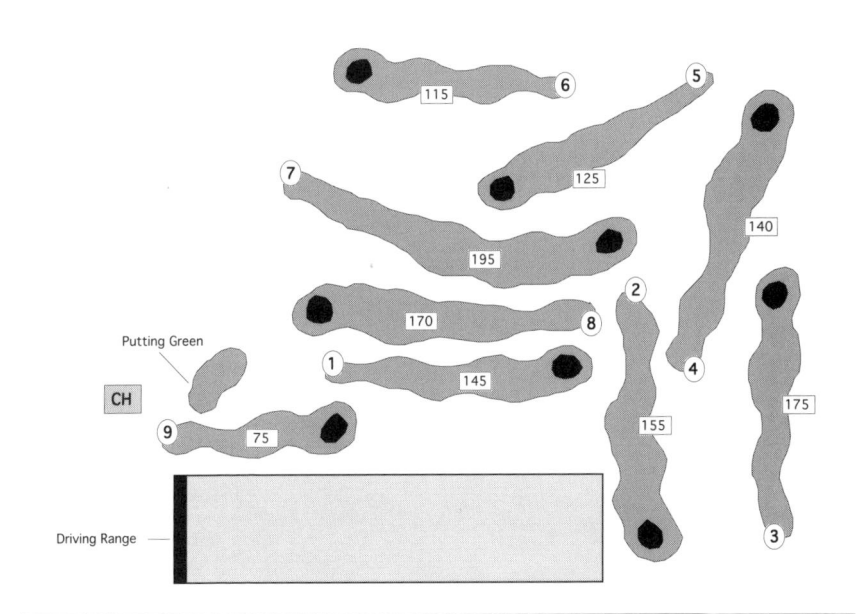

Gooding Country Club (public, 9 hole course)

1951 US Hwy 26; Route 2 Box 194; Gooding, Idaho 83330
Phone: (208) 934-9977. **Fax:** (208) 934-5783. **Internet:** none.
Pro: Troy Vitek, PGA. **Superintendent:** Kelly McIntyre.
Rating/Slope: M 67.1/108; W 67.9/115. **Course record:** Men 60, Women 66.
Green fees: W/D $14; W/E $17.50; no special rates; VISA, M/C.
Power cart: $17/$11. **Pull cart:** $3/$2.50. **Trail fee:** $4 for personal carts.
Reservation policy: please make tee times 3 days in advance for the weekend.
Winter condition: the golf course is closed from November 15th to March 1st.
Terrain: flat, some hills. **Tees:** all grass. **Spikes:** soft spikes preferred.
Services: club rentals, lessons, restaurant, snack bar, beer, beverages,
pro shop, driving range, putting & chipping greens, club memberships.
Comments: the course is very playable for golfers of all levels. Good course
that has medium sized greens with few hazards fronting them. The course plays
longer than the scorecard yardage would indicate.

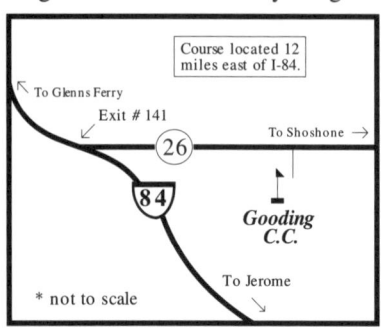

Directions: from I-84 E&W exit at the Wendall exit #157. Proceed north on Hwy 26 for 9.5 miles toward Gooding. When in Gooding the course is located right off Hwy 26. Look for signs.

Course Yardage & Par:
M-2943 yards, par 35.
W-2572 yards, par 37.
Dual tees for 18 holes:
M-6084 yards, par 71.
W-5213 yards, par 74.

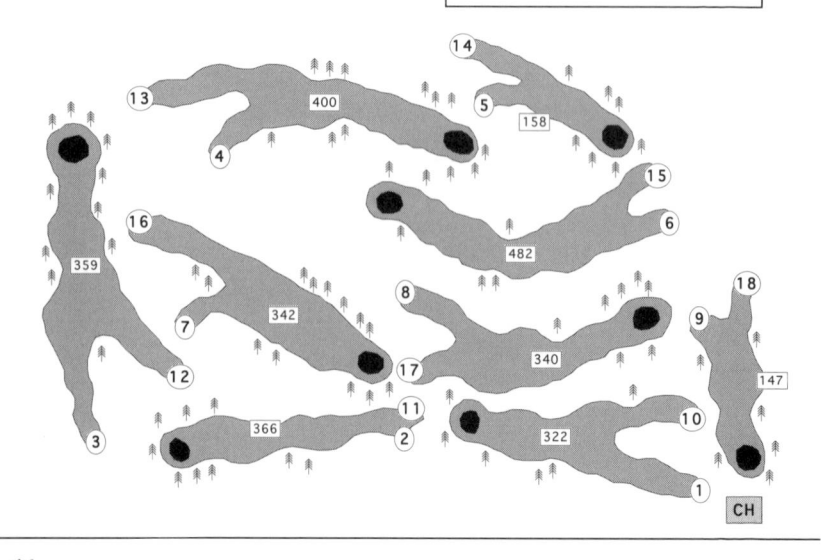

Grangeville Country Club (semi-private, 9 hole course)

Route 2 Box 845; Highway 95; Grangeville, Idaho 83530
Phone: (208) 983-1299. Fax: none. Internet: none.
Pro: unavailable. Superintendent: Larry Pulley.
Rating/Slope: M 66.5/113; W 72.0/117. **Course record:** 60.
Green fees: W/D $15/$10; W/E $18/$10; VISA, M/C.
Power cart: $18/$10. **Pull cart:** $2/$1. **Trail fee:** $5 for personal carts.
Reservation policy: none, tee-times are on a first come first served basis.
Winter condition: the golf course is closed from November 1st to April 1st.
Terrain: flat, some hills. **Tees:** all grass. **Spikes:** soft spikes preferred.
Services: club rentals, lessons, lounge, restaurant, snack bar, beer, wine, liquor, beverages, driving range, pro shop, putting/chipping greens, club memberships.
Comments: the course is fairly short but the small undulating greens will challenge your skill for getting up and down. Fairways are fairly wide open with few hazards coming into play. Dual tees are available for those playing 18 holes.

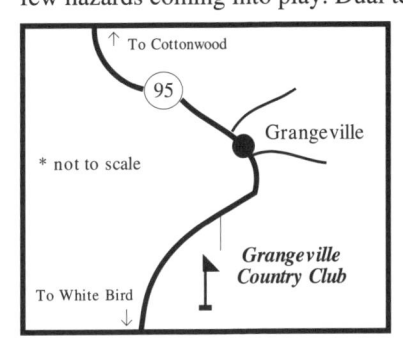

Directions: the course is located south of Grangeville on Hwy 95, 1.6 miles out of town. Proceed south on Hwy 95. The golf course is located right off the highway. Look for signs at your turn.

Course Yardage & Par:
M-2936 yards, par 35.
W-2742 yards. par 35.
Dual tees for: 18 holes:
M-5867 yards, par 70.
W-5341 yards, par 70.

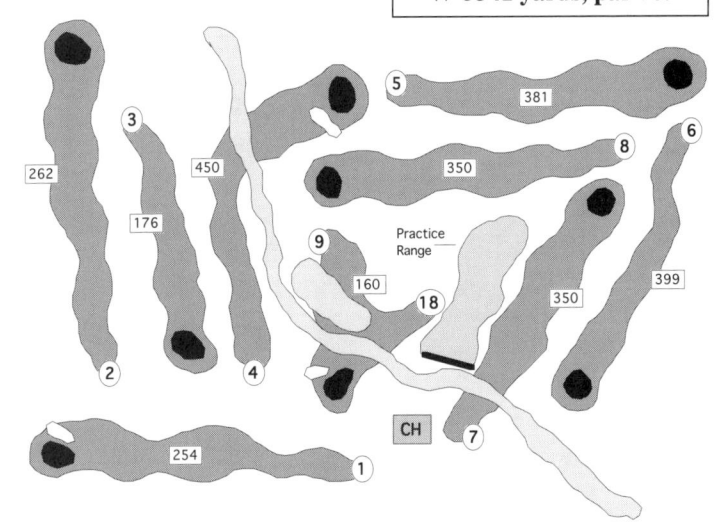

Hayden Lake Country Club (private, 18 hole course)

1800 E. Bozanta Drive; Hayden Lake, Idaho 83835
Phone: (208) 772-0555. **Fax:** (208) 772-5856. **Internet:** haydengolf@compaq.net
Pro: Chad Stoddard, PGA. **Superintendent:** Scott Schillington.
Rating/Slope: C 68.3/117; M 67.0/114; W 72.0/122. **Course record:** 62.
Green fees: private club, members & guests only; reciprocates; VISA, MC.
Power cart: private club. **Pull cart:** private club. **Trail fee:** private club.
Reservation policy: private club, members & guests of members only.
Winter condition: the golf course is closed during winter. November to March.
Terrain: flat, some hills. **Tees:** all grass. **Spikes:** soft spikes only.
Services: club rentals, lessons, lounge, restaurant, snack bar, beer, wine, liquor,
beverages, limited flight driving range, pro shop, putting & chipping greens.
Comments: a beautiful course situated on the shores of Hayden Lake. Fairways
are lined with evergreens and most greens are guarded by bunkers. Hayden Lake
Country Club is regarded as the oldest course in Idaho being established in 1907.

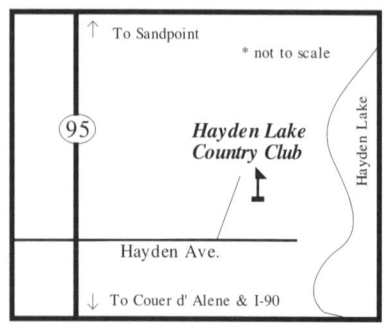

Directions: from I-90 E&W take exit
#12 (Hwy 95). Proceed northbound after
you exit. Proceed north on Hwy 95 to
Hayden Avenue. Turn right on Hayden
Avenue. Proceed for 1.5 miles to the
golf course entrance.

Course Yardage & Par:
C-6073 yards, par 70.
M-5814 yards. par 70.
W-5657yards, par 72.

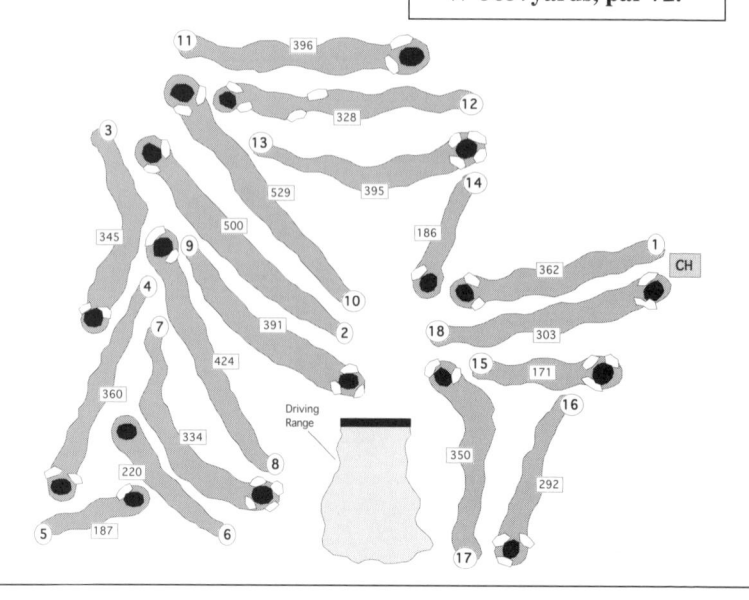

Hazard Creek Golf Course (public, 9 hole course)

419 East Bingham Street; Aberdeen, Idaho 83210
Phone: (208) 397-5308. Fax: none. Internet: none.
Manager: Danny Behrend. Superintendent: Danny Behrend.
RatinWSlope: M 66.1/108; W 69.7/123. Course record: 66.
Green fees: W/D $14/$9; W/E $15/$11; no credit cards accepted.
Power cart: $18/$10. **Pull cart:** $2. **Trail fee:** $10 for personal carts.
Reservation policy: call ahead for tee times. Drop-ins welcome.
Winter condition: the golf course is closed from mid-November to mid-March.
Terrain: flat, some slight hills. **Tees:** all grass. **Spikes:** soft spikes only.
Services: club rentals, snack bar, pro shop, putting green, club memberships.
Comments: Hazard Creek winds its way through the course and will affect your
play on holes 4, 5, 6, 7, & 8. Dual tees are available for a full 18 hole variety.

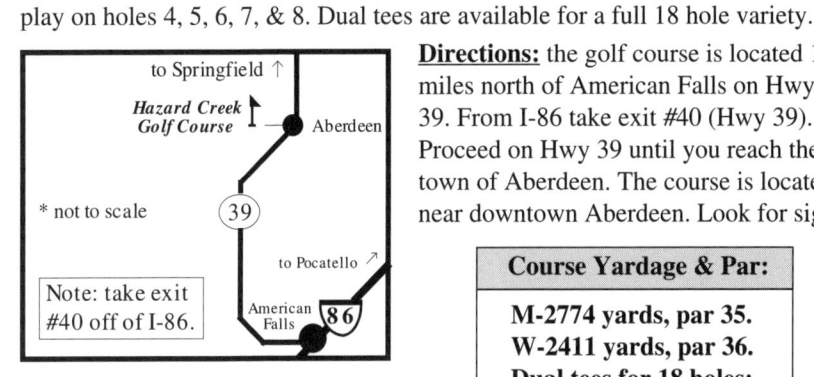

Directions: the golf course is located 16
miles north of American Falls on Hwy
39. From I-86 take exit #40 (Hwy 39).
Proceed on Hwy 39 until you reach the
town of Aberdeen. The course is located
near downtown Aberdeen. Look for signs.

Course Yardage & Par:
M-2774 yards, par 35.
W-2411 yards, par 36.
Dual tees for 18 holes:
M-5681 yards, par 70.
W-5155 yards, par 72.

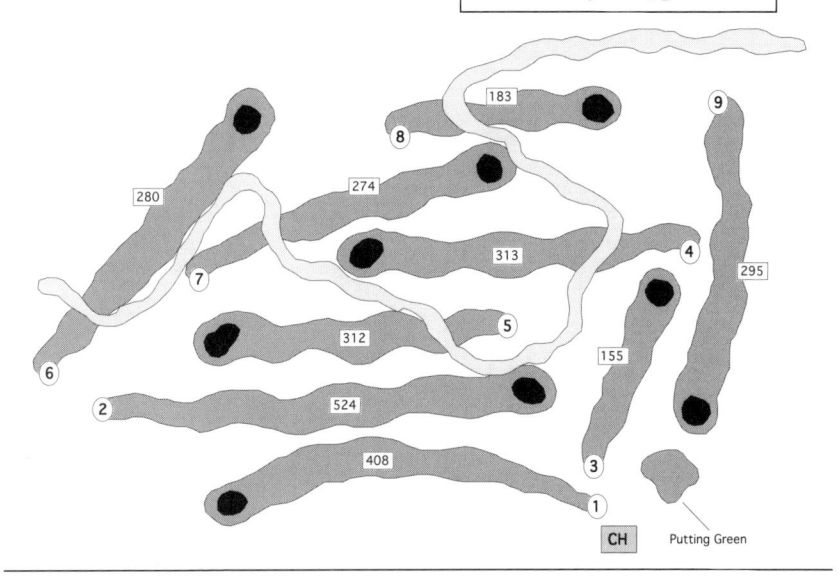

Heise Hills Golf Course (public, 9 hole executive course)

5136 East Heise; Ririe, Idaho 83443
Phone: (208) 538-7327. Fax: none. Internet: none.
Owner: Mike Quinn. Superintendent: Mike Quinn.
Rating/Slope: the golf course is not rated. **Course record:** 25.
Green fees: $6 for 9 holes all week long; no credit cards.
Power cart: not available. **Pull cart:** $2. **Trail fee:** personal carts not allowed.
Reservation policy: yes, please call up to 1 week in advance for tee times.
Winter condition: the golf course is closed from November to March.
Terrain: flat (easy walking). **Tees:** all grass. **Spikes:** no policy.
Services: club rentals, snack bar, beer, wine, restaurant, putting green, pro shop.
Comments: this is a good short course for beginners or a place to bring the laid back golfer. There is a restaurant serving pizza on site for those wanting to dine.

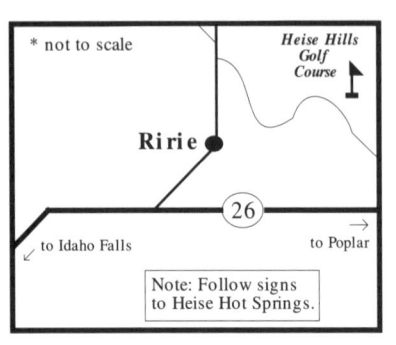

Directions: the golf course is located 5 miles northeast of Ririe Idaho off of Hwy 26. Exit at Heise Road and travel for approximately 3 miles to the golf course.

Course Yardage & Par:
M-1270 yards, par 29.
W-1270 yards. par 29.

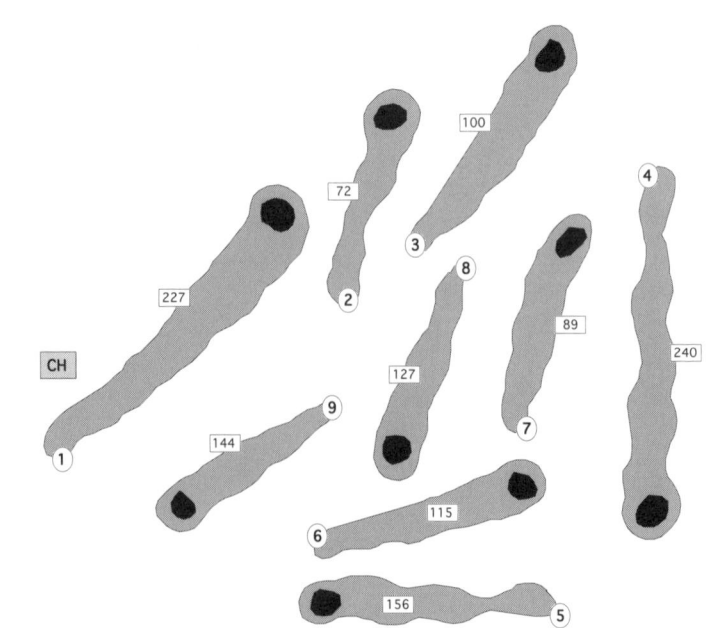

Hidden Lakes Golf Resort (public, 18 hole course)

89 Lower Pack River Road; Sandpoint, Idaho 83864
Phone: (208) 263-1642. Fax: (208) 263-1925. Internet: www.hiddenlakes.com
GM: Ken Parker. Pro: Mike Deprez, PGA. Superintendent: Tim Heeney.
Rating/Slope: T 71.7/132; C 69.4/124; M 66.5/118; W 69.1/119. **Record:** 69.
Green fees: $34/$22 (+tax) all week long; member fees lower; VISA, M/C.
Power cart: $25/$18. **Pull cart:** $5/$3. **Trail fee:** $5 for personal carts.
Reservation policy: yes, please call 1 week in advance for your tee times.
If you pay by credit card your time is unlimited within the calender year.
Winter condition: the golf course is closed from November to March.
Terrain: flat, some hills. **Tees:** all grass. **Spikes:** soft spikes preferred.
Services: club rentals, lessons, snack bar, lounge, beer, wine, pro shop, range.
Comments: water and sand bunkers come into play on nearly every hole. The
course has beautiful scenery and great golf. This course is worth a special trip.
The course is re-designing four holes that will enhance an already great layout.

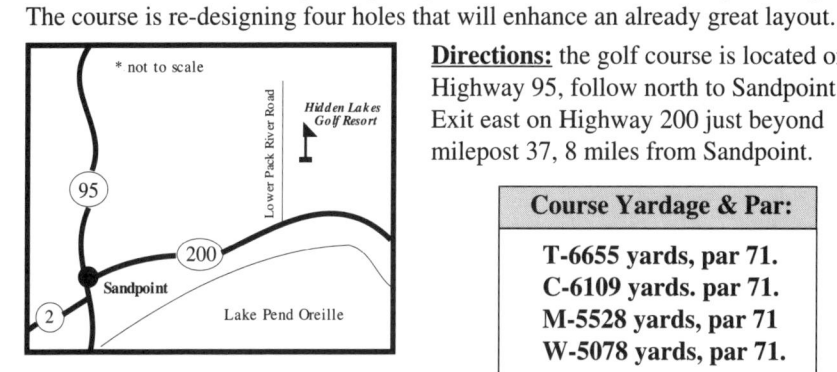

Directions: the golf course is located on
Highway 95, follow north to Sandpoint.
Exit east on Highway 200 just beyond
milepost 37, 8 miles from Sandpoint.

Course Yardage & Par:
T-6655 yards, par 71.
C-6109 yards. par 71.
M-5528 yards, par 71
W-5078 yards, par 71.

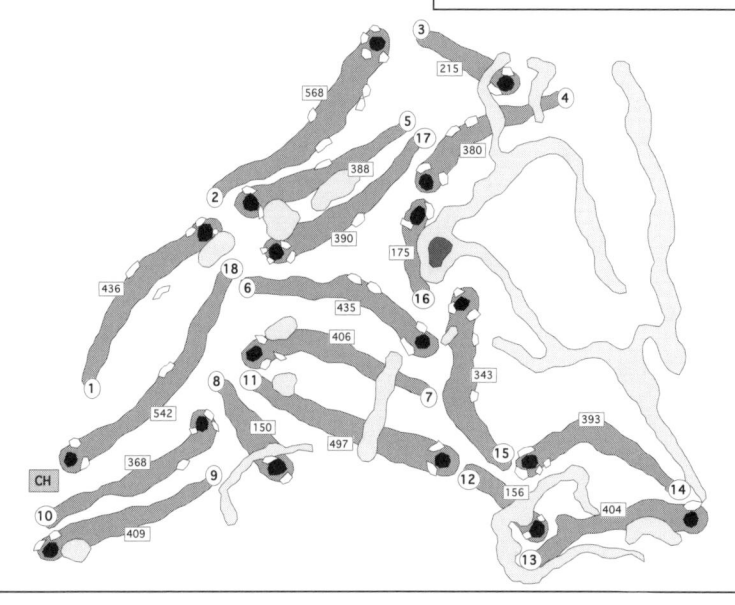

Highland Golf Course (public, 18 hole course)

201 Von Elm Lane; P.O. Box 2164; Pocatello, Idaho 83201
Phone: (208) 237-9922. Fax: none. Internet: none.
Pro: Gary Tawzer, PGA. Superintendent: Gary Otte.
Rating/Slope: C 70.0/118; M 69.8/117; W 73.2/124. **Course record:** 62.
Green fees: W/D $15/$12; W/E $17/$13; Jr. & Sr. rates; VISA, M/C.
Power cart: $18.90/$10.50. **Pull cart:** $2/$1. **Trail fee:** $8.
Reservation policy: yes, call Thursday morning for your weekend tee-times.
Winter condition: the golf course is closed from November to February.
Terrain: very hilly. **Tees:** all grass. **Spikes:** soft spikes only.
Services: club rentals, lessons, restaurant, beer, coolers, pro shop, driving range.
Comments: this course is wide open with large very tricky greens. The course can get very busy during the summer so be sure to call ahead for your tee-time.

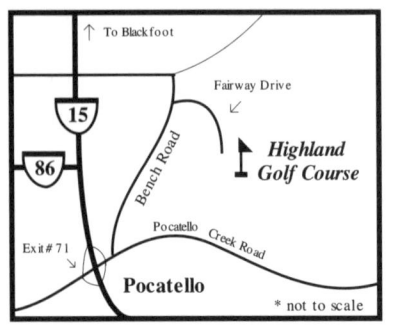

Directions: from I-15N exit at Pocatello Creek Road (#71). Turn left on Bench Road for 1 mile. Proceed past the High School. Take the first right, then the next available right to the course. From I-15S take a right on Bench Road and follow the above directions. Look for signs.

Course Yardage & Par:
C-6481 yards. par 71.
M-6222 yards, par 71
W-6100 yards, par 71.

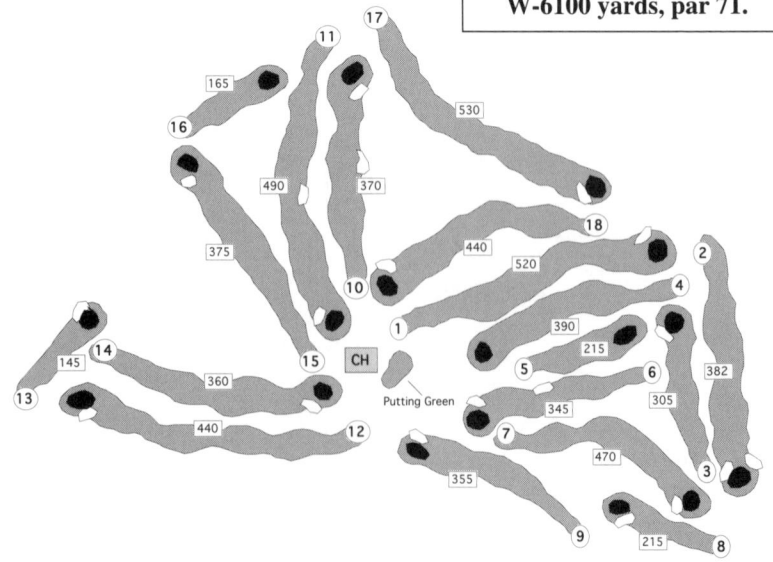

Highlands Golf & Country Club, The (public, 18 hole course)

North 701 Inverness Drive; Post Falls, Idaho 83854
Phone: (208) 773-3673 or 800-797-7339. Fax: none. Internet: none.
Pro: Sean Stiller, PGA. Superintendent: unavailable.
Rating/Slope: C 70.7/125; M 68.7/121; W 69.5/121. **Course record:** 65.
Green fees: W/D $23/$17; W/E $25/$19; Jr. & Sr. rates, MC, VISA, AMEX.
Power cart: $22.50/$12. **Pull cart:** $3. **Trail fee:** $5 for personal carts.
Reservation policy: yes, you may call 1 week in advance for your tee-times.
Winter condition: the golf course is closed from December 1st to March 1st.
Terrain: flat, some hills. **Tees:** all grass. **Spikes:** soft spikes only.
Services: club rentals, lessons, restaurant, lounge, beer, wine, liquor, lockers,
showers, pro shop, driving range, putting & chipping greens, club memberships.
Comments: this course is very challenging and offers beautiful views of the
entire valley and surrounding mountains. This course is worth a trip anytime.

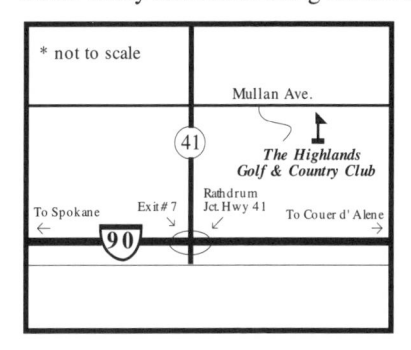

Directions: from 1-90 E&W take exit #7.
Take Hwy 41. Proceed north for 5 miles
to Mullan Street and turn right. Proceed
up the hill .25 miles and turn right to the
golf course at the of the hill. Look for
signs marking your way to the course.

Course Yardage & Par:
C-6369 yards, par 72.
M-6041 yards, par 72.
W-5115 yards, par 73.

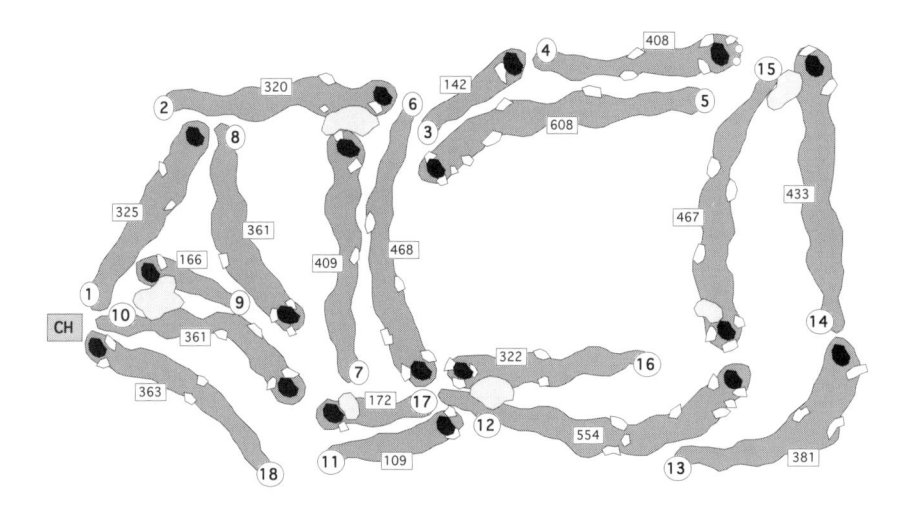

Hillcrest Country Club (private, 18 hole course)

4610 Hillcrest Drive; Boise, Idaho 83705
Phone: (208) 343-1769. Fax: none. Internet: none.
Pro: unavailable. Superintendent: Kevin Hicks.
Rating/Slope: C 70.9/125; M 69.1/122; W 71.4/121. **Course record:** 61.
Green fees: private club members only; reciprocates; M/C, VISA, AMEX.
Power cart: private club. **Pull cart:** private club. **Trail fee:** not allowed.
Reservation policy: private club members & guests of members only.
Winter condition: the golf course is open all year long. Dry conditions.
Terrain: flat, some hills. **Tees:** all grass. **Spikes:** soft spikes only.
Services: rentals, lessons, restaurant, lounge, beer, wine, coolers, liquor,
pro shop, lockers, driving range, putting/chipping greens, club memberships.
Comments: one of the top 3 golf courses in Idaho that is impeccably manicured
and maintained. The course sports somewhat narrow tree-lined fairways and
large undulating greens. This golf course is a bear to score on anytime of year.

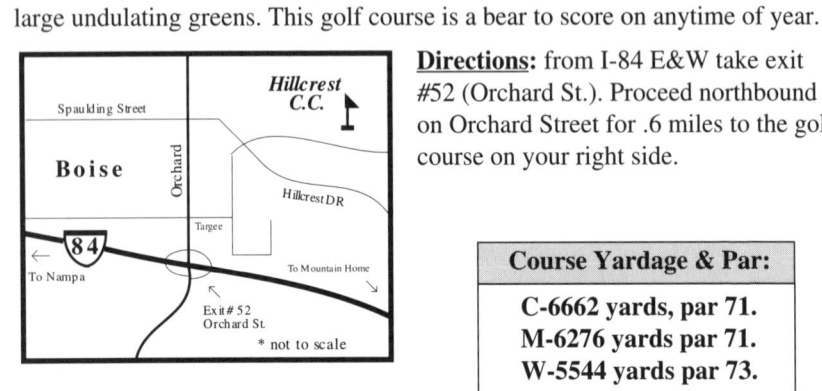

Directions: from I-84 E&W take exit
#52 (Orchard St.). Proceed northbound
on Orchard Street for .6 miles to the golf
course on your right side.

Course Yardage & Par:
C-6662 yards, par 71.
M-6276 yards par 71.
W-5544 yards par 73.

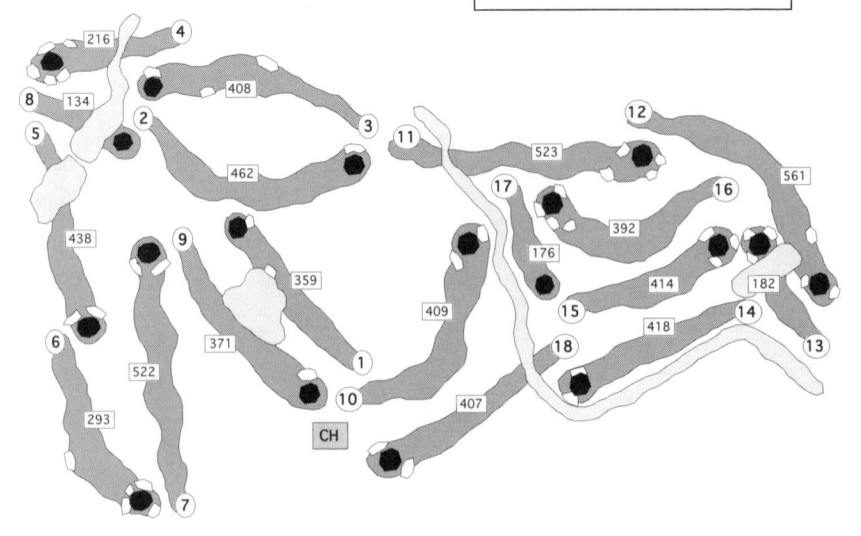

Idaho Falls Country Club (private, 18 hole course)

Physical address: 11611 S Country Club Drive; Idaho Falls, Idaho 83405
Mailing address: P.O. Box 51076; Idaho Falls, Idaho 83405
Phone: (208) 523-5762. **Fax:** none. **Internet:** none.
Pro: Jon Potter, PGA. **Superintendent:** Randy Ernst.
Rating/Slope: C 71.6/125; M 70.0/120; W 71.5/127. **Course record:** 63.
Green fees: private club members and guests only; reciprocates; VISA, M/C.
Power cart: private club. **Pull cart:** private club. **Trail fee:** not allowed.
Reservation policy: private club, members & guests of members only.
Winter condition: the golf course is open all year long, weather permitting.
Terrain: flat, some slight hills. **Tees:** all grass. **Spikes:** soft spikes preferred.
Services: club rentals, lessons, snack bar, restaurant, lounge, beer, wine liquor, beverages, pro shop, driving range, putting/chipping greens, club memberships.
Comments: good, older private course with tough greens and narrow fairways. The terrain varies giving the golfer a wide variety of lies from the fairway.

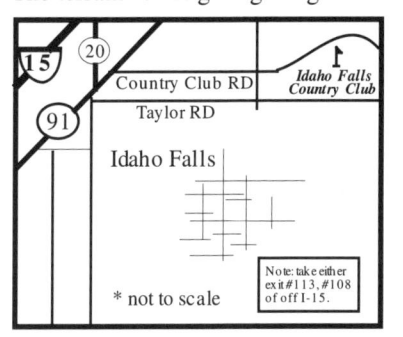

Directions: from I-15 N&S exit at the first Idaho Falls exit. Turn east off the exit. Proceed to York Rd. Turn east on York Rd. Proceed to St. Claire Road and turn left. Proceed to Country Club Dr. and turn left. Proceed to the golf course.

Course Yardage & Par:
C-6755 yards, par 72.
M-6392 yards, par 72.
W-5988 yards, par 75.

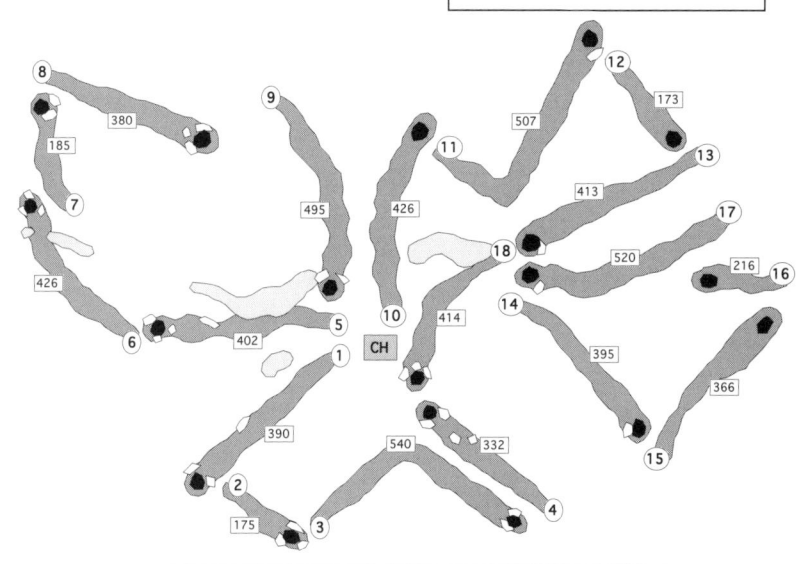

Indian Lake Golf Course (public, 9 hole course)

4700 South Umatilla Avenue; Boise, Idaho 83709
Phone: (208) 362-5771. Fax: (208) 362-5772. Internet: www.indianlakesgolf.com
Pro: Jeff Thomsen, PGA. Superintendent: Mel Ricketts.
Rating/Slope: M 66.7/112; W 68.6/117. **Course record:** 60.
Green fees: M-Th $17.50/$13.50; Fri-Sun $22/$15.50; Jr./Sr. rates; M/C, VISA.
Power cart: $20/$13. **Pull cart:** $3/$1.50. **Trail fee:** $12 for personal carts.
Reservation policy: yes, please call 7 days in advance for all your tee-times.
Winter condition: the golf course is open all year long. Dry conditions.
Terrain: flat (easy walking). **Tees:** all grass. **Spikes:** soft spikes only.
Services: club rentals, lessons, snack bar, restaurant, lounge, beer, wine, liquor, pop, pro shop, driving range, putting & chipping greens, club memberships.
Comments: the golf course sport's two very tough par 3's that have extremely quick greens. Tree lined fairways and tough lies result in creative shot making. This course has a fantastic on course driving range for those wanting to practice.

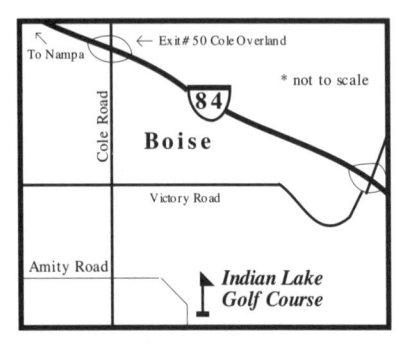

Directions: I-84 exit #50 (South Cole). Get on South Cole, follow for 3 miles. Turn left on Amity and follow to the golf course. Look for signs marking your turn.

Course Yardage & Par:
M-3019 yards, par 35.
W-2705 yards, par 35.
<u>Dual tees for 18 holes:</u>
M-6046 yards, par 70.
W-5360 yards, par 70.

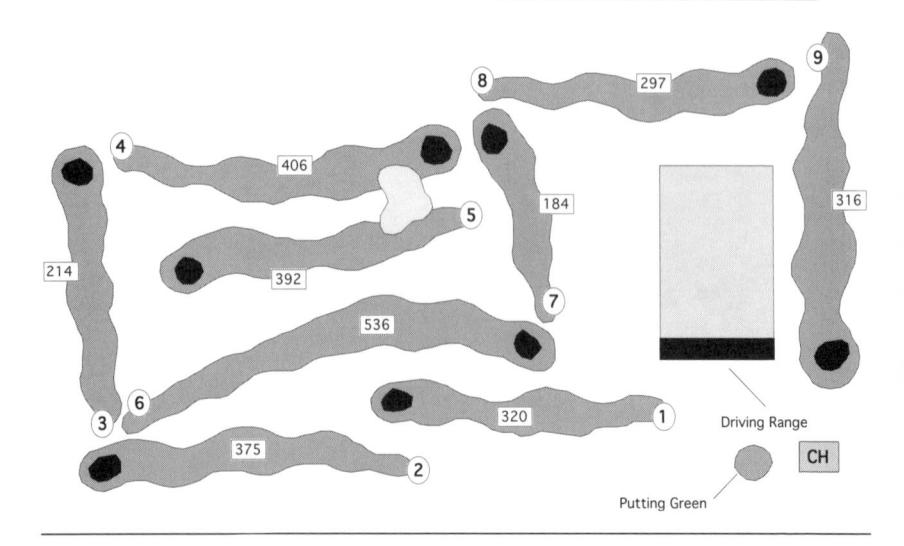

Island Park Village Golf Course (semi-private, 9 hole course)

Hist County Road 66; P.O. Box 12; Island Park, Idaho 83429
Phone: (208) 558-7550. Fax: none. Internet: none.
Manager: Richard Zimmerman. Superintendent: Trenna Biron.
Rating/Slope: the golf course is not rated. **Course record:** 31.
Green fees: W/D $14/$9; W/E $17/$13; M/C, VISA, AMEX.
Power cart: $12/$8. **Pull cart:** $3/$2. **Trail fee:** $4 for personal carts.
Reservation policy: yes, call up to 3 days in advance for your tee-time.
Winter condition: the course is closed from approximately October thru May.
Terrain: flat (easy to walk). **Tees:** all grass. **Spikes:** soft spikes preferred.
Services: club rentals, snack bar, beer, showers, lockers, tennis courts, pool,
putting green, racquetball, saunas. **Comments:** course is located at the gateway
to Yellowstone Park, it provides a peaceful round of golf while on a vacation in
the park. If you get a chance be sure to stop in at this very friendly facility.

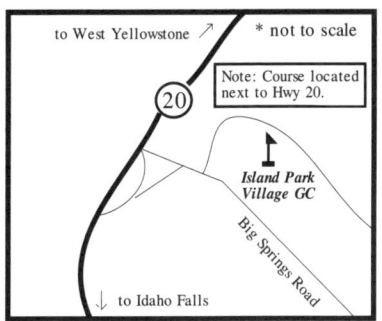

Directions: from Idaho Falls take Hwy
20 toward Yellowstone National Park
(northeast). While on Hwy 20 exit at the
Island Park Village exit (east). When
you come to the resort you will turn left.
Follow the signs to the golf course.

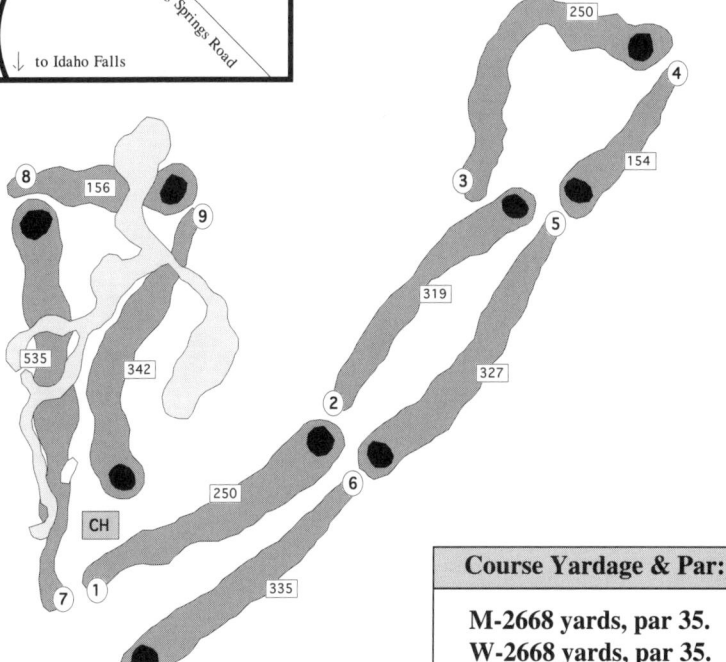

Course Yardage & Par:
M-2668 yards, par 35.
W-2668 yards, par 35.

Jefferson Hills Golf Course (public, 18 hole course)

4074 East 500 North; Rigby, Idaho 83442
Phone: (208) 745-6492. **Fax:** none. **Internet:** none.
Pro: Gerald Simonson, PGA. **Superintendent:** Mike Rice.
Rating/Slope: C 68.0/115; M 66.7/112; W 66.4/114. **Course record:** 28.
Green fees: W/D $14.50/$11; W/E $15.50/$12; VISA, M/C, AMEX, DIS.
Power cart: $17/$8.50. **Pull cart:** $2. **Trail fee:** $8.50/$4.25.
Reservation policy: yes, non stockholders please call 2 days in advance.
Winter condition: the golf course is closed during the winter months.
Terrain: flat (easy walking course). **Tees:** all grass. **Spikes:** soft spikes only.
Services: club rentals, lessons, snack bar, restaurant, lounge, beer, wine, pop,
pro shop, putting & chipping greens, club memberships, driving range.
Comments: excellent 18 hole track where a natural stream comes into play on
six holes. Fairways are wide with large landing areas. Greens are very flat.

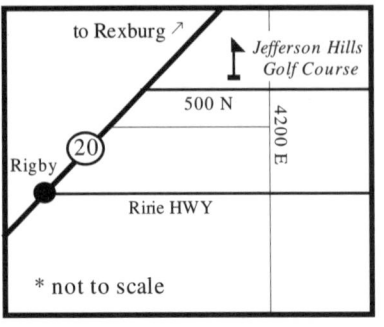

Directions: from Highway 20 exit at the Jefferson Hills/North Rigby exit. Turn right (eastbound) off the exit. Proceed eastbound for 1 mile to the golf course. Look for signs that are posted.

Course Yardage & Par:
C-6133 yards, par 70.
M-5884 yards par 70.
W-5032 yards par 70.

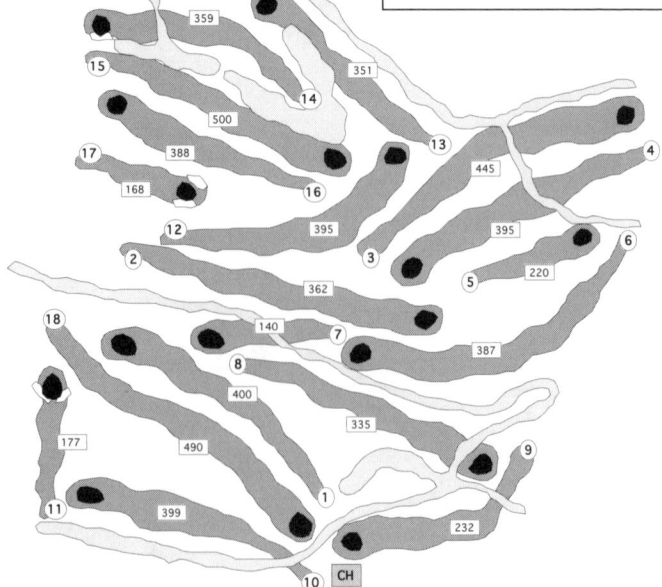

Jerome Country Club (semi-private, 18 hole course)

679 Golf Course Road; P.O. Box 484; Jerome, Idaho 83338
Phone: (208) 324-5281. Fax: none. Internet: none.
Pro: John E. Peterson, PGA. Superintendent: to be determined.
Rating/Slope: C 68.8/106; M 67.0/102; W 71.2/114. **Course record:** 60.
Green fees: W/D $30; W/E $30; no special rates; M/C, VISA.
Power cart: $20/$10. **Pull cart:** $5. **Trail fee:** not allowed.
Reservation policy: non members may make tee times 3 days in advance.
Winter condition: the golf course is closed from December 1st to March 1st.
Terrain: flat, some hills. **Tees:** all grass. **Spikes:** soft spikes only.
Services: rentals, lessons, snack bar, restaurant, lounge, beer, wine, liquor, beverages, pro shop, putting & chipping greens, driving range.
Comments: flat, easy walking golf course. Greens and fairways are kept in excellent condition throughout the peak season. The course features large, well bunkered greens and water coming into play on five holes. Excellent course.

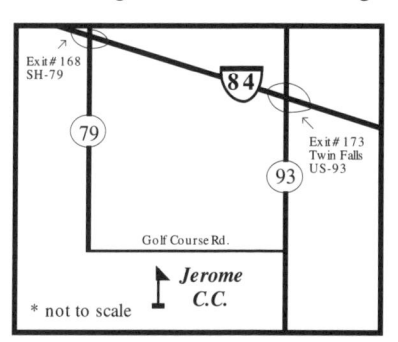

Directions: from I-84 take exit #173 (Hwy 93) and proceed southbound on Hwy 93 to Golf Course Road. Turn westbound on Golf Course Road. The golf course is located 4.1 miles ahead. Signs are posted along the way.

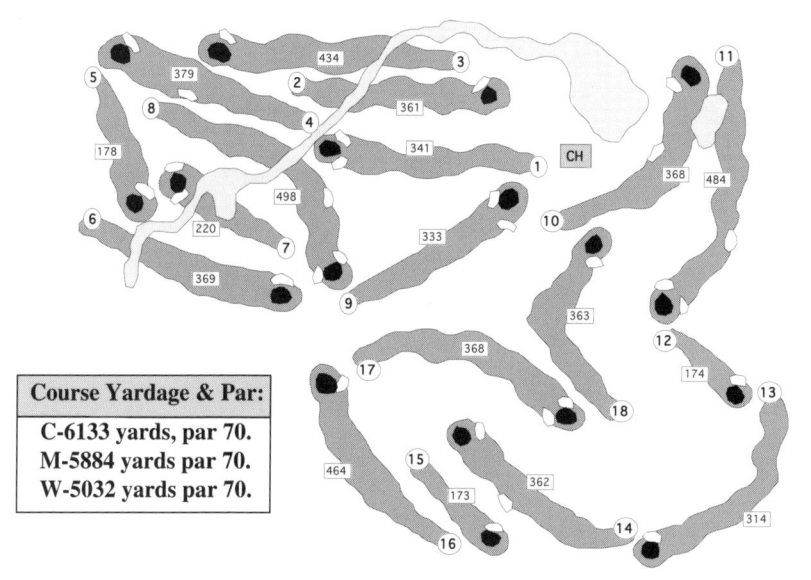

Course Yardage & Par:
C-6133 yards, par 70.
M-5884 yards par 70.
W-5032 yards par 70.

Juniper Hills Country Club (private, 18 hole course)

6600 South Bannock Highway; Pocatello, Idaho 83204
Phone: (208) 233-0269. Fax: none. Internet: none.
Pro: Rick Deacon, PGA. Superintendent: Joe Mullett.
Rating/Slope: C 68.1/119; M 66.7/116; W 68.2/114. **Course record:** 67.
Green fees: private club, members & guests only; limited reciprocation.
Power cart: private club. **Pull cart:** private club. **Trail fee:** not allowed.
Reservation policy: private club, members & guests only. Public play is
allowed on Mondays only. Please call the pro shop for advance tee times.
Winter condition: the golf course is closed from November to February.
Terrain: flat, some hills. **Tees:** all grass. **Spikes:** soft spikes preferred.
Services: club rentals, lessons, snack bar, beer, wine, lounge, showers, lockers,
beverages, putting & chipping greens, driving range, tennis courts, pool, sauna.
Comments: this golf course has many lateral water hazards and sand bunkers to
challenge your game. This course plays much longer than the yardage indicates.

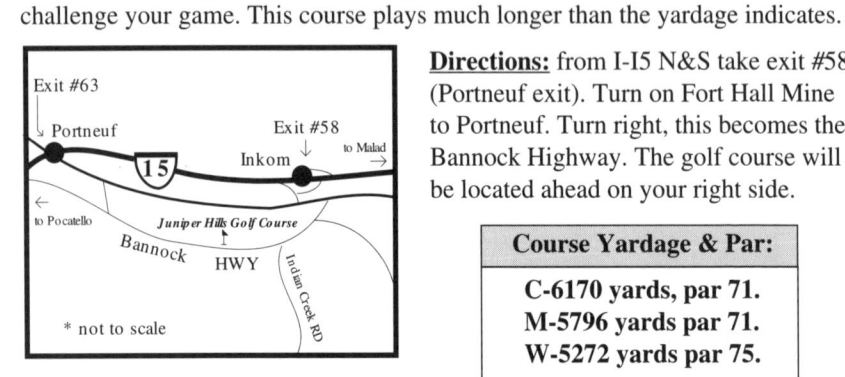

Directions: from I-I5 N&S take exit #58
(Portneuf exit). Turn on Fort Hall Mine
to Portneuf. Turn right, this becomes the
Bannock Highway. The golf course will
be located ahead on your right side.

Course Yardage & Par:
C-6170 yards, par 71.
M-5796 yards par 71.
W-5272 yards par 75.

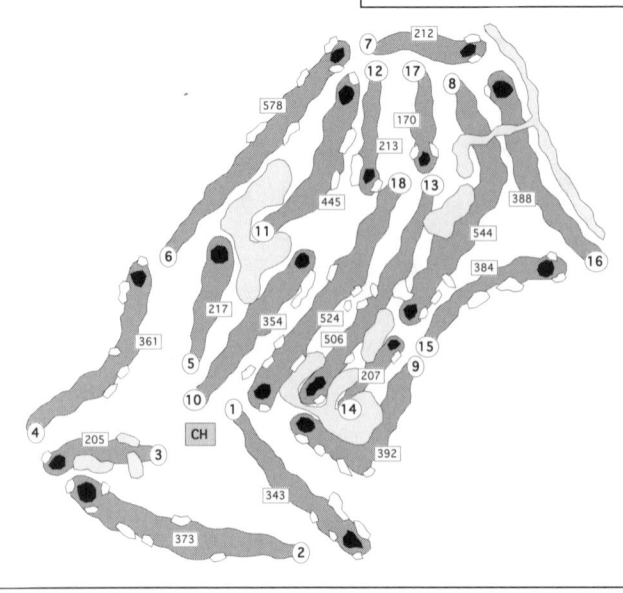

Krystal Lake Golf Course (public, 9 hole executive course)

1275 North 900; Shelley, Idaho 83274
Phone: (208) 357-7329. **Fax:** none. **Internet:** none.
Pro: none. **Superintendent:** none.
Rating/Slope: the golf course is not rated. **Course record:** 25.
Green fees: $9/$6 all week long; no special rates; no credit cards.
Power cart: not available. **Pull cart:** $1. **Trail fee:** not available.
Reservation policy: not needed, times are on a first come first served basis.
Winter condition: the golf course is closed during inclement weather.
Terrain: relatively flat with some hills. **Tees:** grass. **Spikes:** no policy.
Services: the golf course has very limited services, some vending machines.
Comments: this short course is perfect for a family outing. The golf course
is wide open with very few hazards. Great course for the beginner golfer.

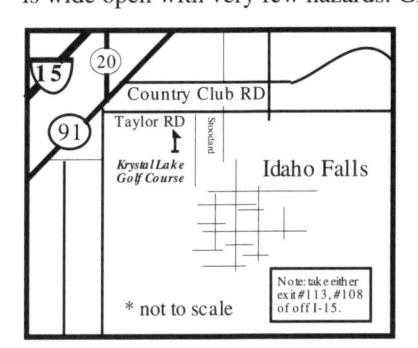

Directions: from Hwy 91 turn eastbound
on Taylor Road. Proceed to North 900.
At North 900 turn southbound to the golf
course. Look for signs marking your way
to the golf course.

Course Yardage & Par:
M-1563 yards, par 29.
W-1563 yards, par 29.

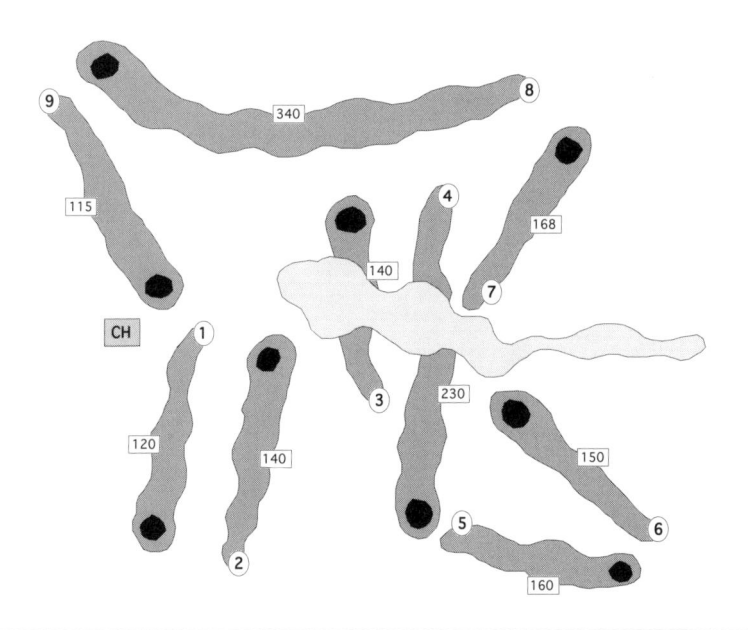

Lewiston Golf & Country Club (private, 18 hole course)

3985 Country Club Drive; Lewiston, Idaho 83501
Phone(208) 746-2801. Fax: (208) 746-7994. Internet: none.
Pro: Erik Nielsen, PGA. Superintendent: Paul McCarthy.
Rating/Slope: C 71.9/125; M 70.3/124; W 72.5/119. **Course record:** 62.
Green fees: private club; reciprocates; M/C, VISA (for merchandise only).
Power cart: private club. **Pull cart:** private club. **Trail fee:** not allowed.
Reservation policy: private club, members & guests of members only.
Winter condition: the golf course is open all year long, weather permitting.
Terrain: relatively hilly. **Tees:** all grass. **Spikes:** soft spikes required.
Services: club rentals, lessons, restaurant, lounge, beer, wine, liquor, pro shop, lockers, showers, driving range, putting & chipping greens, club memberships.
Comments: well kept private course. Greens and fairways are always kept in excellent condition. This fairly long golf course can be a bear to score on.

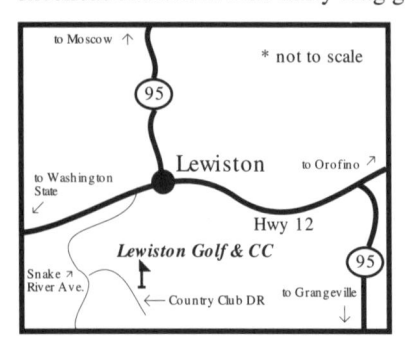

Directions: from Hwy 95 N&S take the Snake River Avenue exit. Head south to Country Club Drive. Take left on Country Club Drive. Proceed to the golf course.

Course Yardage & Par:
C-6689 yards, par 72.
M-6376 yards, par 72.
W-5798 yards, par 73.

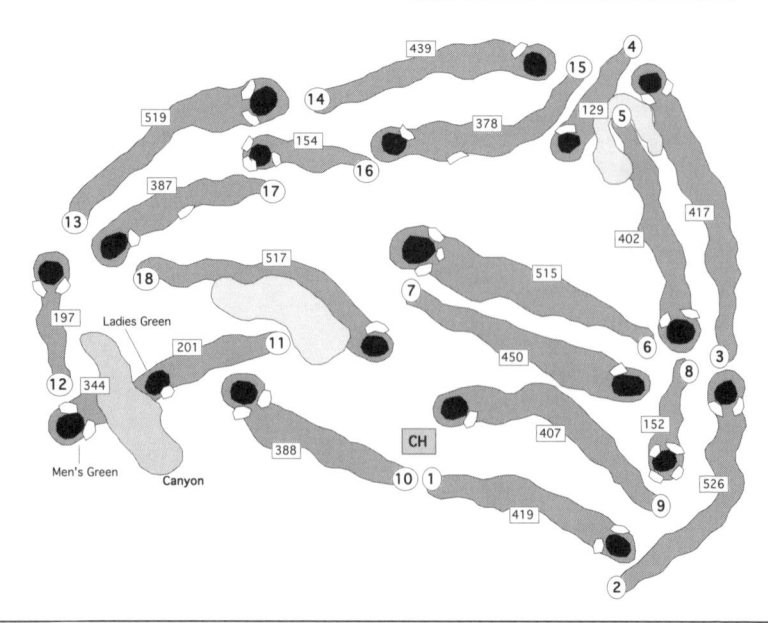

Links Golf Club, The (semi-private, 18 hole course)

6400 N. Chase Road; Post Falls, Idaho 83854
Phone: (208) 777-7611. Fax: (208) 777-8811. Internet: none.
Pro/Manager: Kent Hochberger, PGA. Superintendent: unavailable.
Rating/Slope: the golf course has not yet been rated. **Course record:** N/A.
Green fees: W/D $30/$24; W/E $44/$36; the course will have a grand opening
special offering rates of $27 for 18 holes and $18 for 9 holes all week long.
This special should last for about 2-3 months; VISA, M/C, AMEX, DIS.
Power cart: $20/$12. **Pull cart:** $4. **Trail fee:** personal carts not allowed.
Reservation policy: you may call up to 30 days in advance for tee times.
Winter condition: the golf course is closed from late October to early March.
Terrain: flat, (easy walking). **Tees:** all grass. **Spikes:** soft spikes required.
Services: club rentals, lessons, beer, wine, liquor, lounge, snack bar, pro shop,
lockers, driving range, beverage cart, outdoor patio barbeque, putting green.
Comments: new golf course that is slated to open up May 1st of 2000. The
course will feature a unique par of 73. The 9th hole is a par 6 (this could be the
longest hole in the northwest). The course itself is a links style layout featuring
long, fast fairways and greens. Windy conditions may persist. Worth a trip.

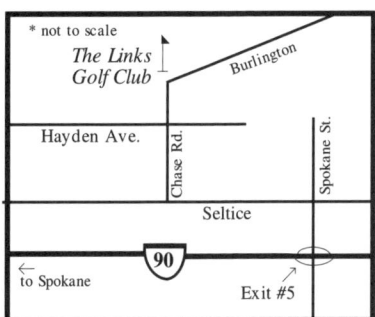

Directions: from I-90 E&W take exit
#5 (Spokane Street). Turn north on
Spokane until you reach Seltice where
you will turn left. Proceed on Seltice to
Chase Rd. turn right on Chase Rd.
Proceed for 3.6 miles on Chase Rd. to
the golf course on your left.

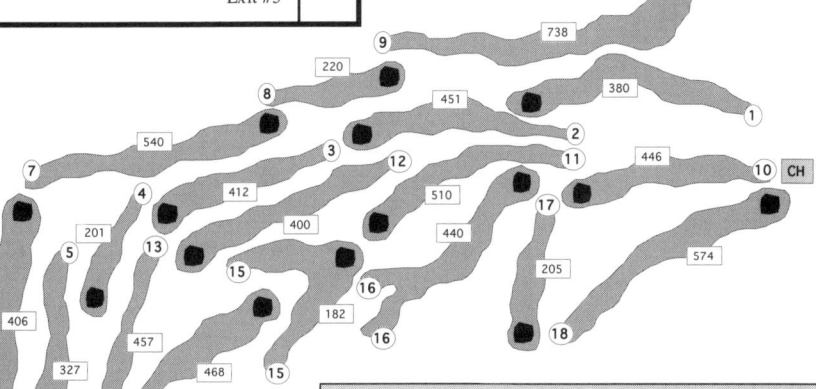

Course Yardage & Par:
T-7357 yards, par 73. C-6898 yards, par 73.
M-6143 yards par 73. W-5598 yards par 71.

McCall Golf Course (public, 27 hole course)

878 Reedy Lane; P.O. Box 1545; McCall, Idaho 83638
Phone: (208) 634-7200. Fax: none. Internet: none.
Pro: Carl Hoss, PGA. Superintendent: Charlie Denham.
Rating/slope: M 69.0/117; W 68.7/118 (Aspen Tees). **Course record:** 67.
Green fees: W/D $23/$12; W/E $27/$14; VISA, M/C, AMEX.
Power cart: $20/$11. **Pull cart:** $3/$2. **Trail fee:** personal carts not allowed.
Reservation policy: please call up to 1 week in advance after 6:00 am.
Winter condition: the golf course is closed from mid-November to April.
Terrain: flat with rolling hills. **Tees:** grass. **Spikes:** soft spikes only.
Services: club rentals, lessons, lounge, restaurant, beer, wine, liquor, pro shop, beverages, driving range, putting & chipping greens, club memberships.
Comments: a lovely resort golf course in a mountain setting with many tall evergreen trees bordering the fairways. Greens are small and can be very hard to hold. Do not let the lack of yardage fool you. This great course is a must play.

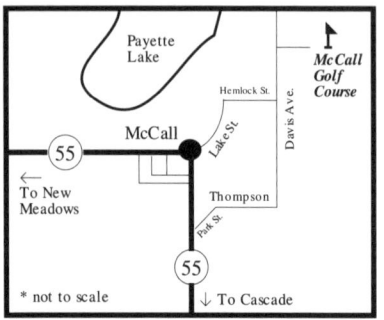

Directions: from Highway 55S turn left on Thompson. Proceed to Davis and turn left. Travel to Reedy where you will turn right and follow to the course (from Hwy 55N turn right on Thompson). Watch for green & white signs posted along the way.

Course Yardage & Par:
C-6227 yards, par 71.
M-5861 yards, par 71.
W-5421 yards, par 73.

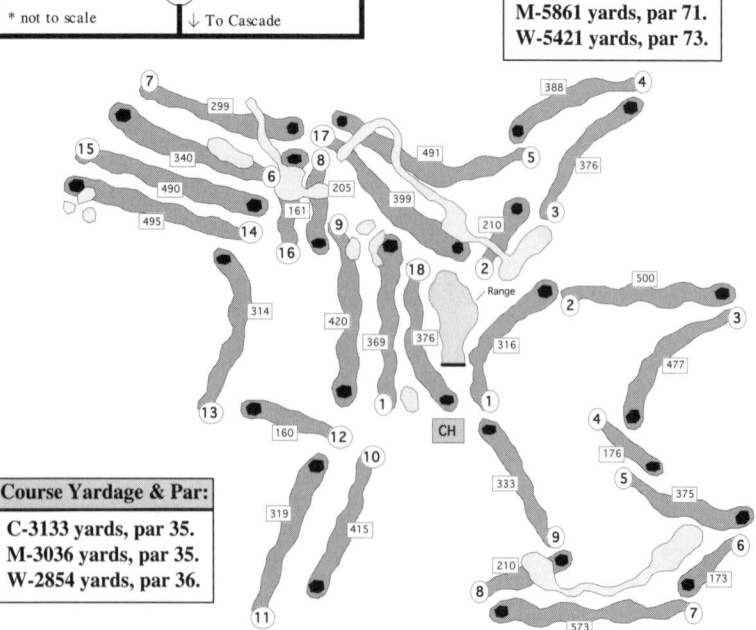

Course Yardage & Par:
C-3133 yards, par 35.
M-3036 yards, par 35.
W-2854 yards, par 36.

Meadow Creek Golf & Field Club (semi-private, 18 hole course)

Physical address: One Meadow Creek Court; New Meadows, Idaho 83654
Mailing address: Drawer #C; New Meadows, Idaho 83654
Phone: (208) 347-2164. **Fax:** none. **Internet:** none.
Pro: Lew Golde, PGA. **Superintendent:** Steve McCarley.
Rating/Slope: C 71.0/130; M 68.9/125; W 68.2/124. **Course record:** 66.
Green fees: $30/$22 all week long; M/C, VISA, AMEX , DIS.
Power cart: $22/$16. **Pull cart:** $4. **Trail fee:** personal carts not allowed.
Reservation policy: no limit. Unaccompained guests are allowed after 1 pm.
Winter condition: the course is closed from October 15th to mid April or May.
Terrain: flat to very hilly. **Tees:** all grass. **Spikes:** soft spikes only.
Services: club rentals, lessons, snack bar, restaurant, lounge, beer, wine, liquor, beverages, pro shop, lockers, showers, driving range, putting & chipping greens.
Comments: very scenic, mountainous terrain. Four Diamond restaurant. On site lodging and pool. This facility is worth a special trip if you are in the area.

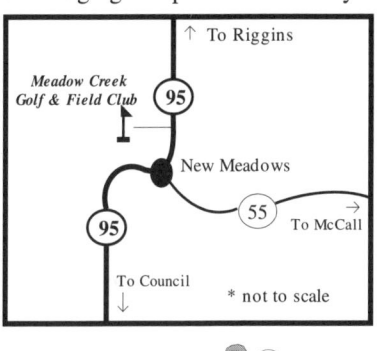

Directions: the golf course is located on Highway 95, 2 miles north of the town of New Meadows, Idaho. The Main entrance to the course is at Hwy 95 and the 45th parallel. Look for signs along the way.

Course Yardage & Par:
C-6587 yards, par 72.
M-6164 yards par 72.
W-5005 yards par 72.

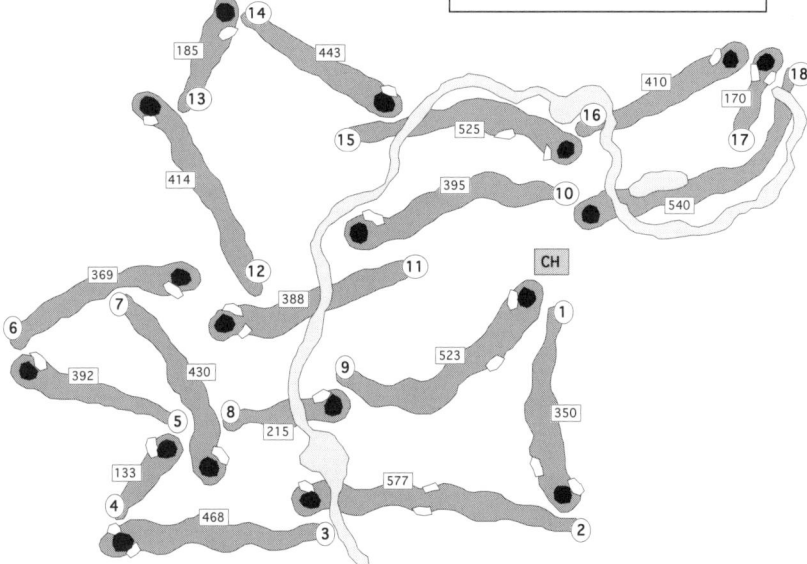

Midas Golf Course (public, 9 hole executive course)

7145 Garfield Bay Road; Sagle, Idaho 83860
Phone: (208) 263-1087. **Fax:** none. **Internet:** none.
Manager: Bill Daly. **Superintendent:** Bill Daly.
Rating/Slope: the golf course is not rated. **Course record:** 26.
Green fees: $7 for 9 holes all week long; no credit cards are accepted.
Power cart: not available. **Pull cart:** $2. **Trail fee:** not allowed.
Reservation policy: none needed, times are on a first come first served basis.
Winter condition: closed during the winter months. November to March.
Terrain: flat, some hills. **Tees:** grass & mats. **Spikes:** no policy.
Services: the golf course has no services.
Comments: the golf course check in is at the Anchor Gas & Grocery Store. The golf course is very rustic in nature. Greens and fairways are on the rough side.

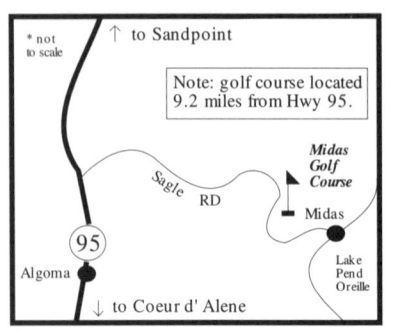

Directions: from Hwy 95 turn east on Sagle Road to Garfield Bay. Travel approximately 9.2 miles to the course. The Anchor Gas & Grocery Store will be on the left hand side of the road.

Course Yardage & Par:
M-1121 yards, par 29.
W-1121 yards, par 29.

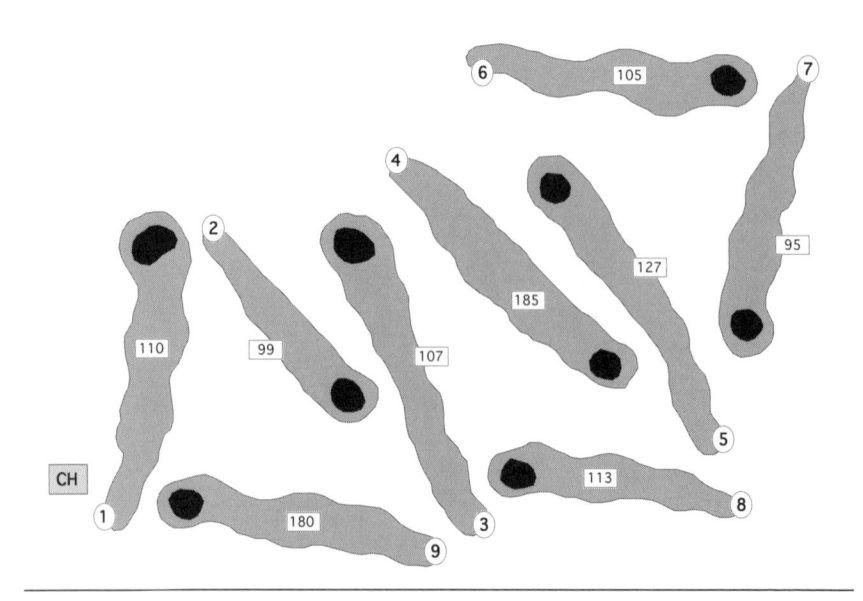

Mirror Lake Golf Course (public, 9 hole course)

Highway 95; P.O. Box 3040; Bonners Ferry, Idaho 83805
Phone: (208) 267-5314. Fax: none. Internet: none.
Manager: Chad Dietz. Superintendent: none.
Rating/Slope: M 68.3/121; W 70.4/128. **Course record:** 33.
Green fees: $18/$12 all week long; no special rates; M/C, VISA.
Power cart: $20/$10. **Pull cart:** $2. **Trail fee:** $4 for personal carts.
Reservation policy: yes, please call up to 2 weeks in advance for tee-times.
Winter condition: the course is closed from November 1st to March or April.
Terrain: flat, some hills. **Tees:** all grass. **Spikes:** soft spikes preferred.
Services: club rentals, snack bar, beer, wine, lessons, pro shop, driving range.
Comments: plush, well kept nine hole golf course. Friendly staff to serve you.
The course plays fairly wide open with sand and water in play.

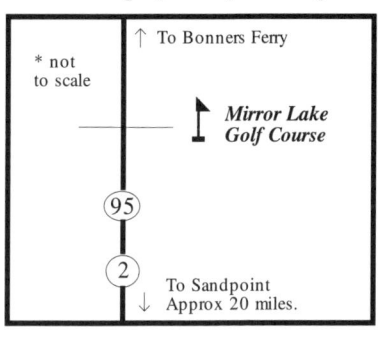

Directions: the golf course is located just 2 miles south of Bonners Ferry, Idaho in the Kootenai Valley. From I-90 E&W exit at Hwy 95 in Coeur d' Alene. Proceed northbound on Hwy 95 through Sandpoint and beyond. The course is 30 miles south of the Canadian border. Look for signs.

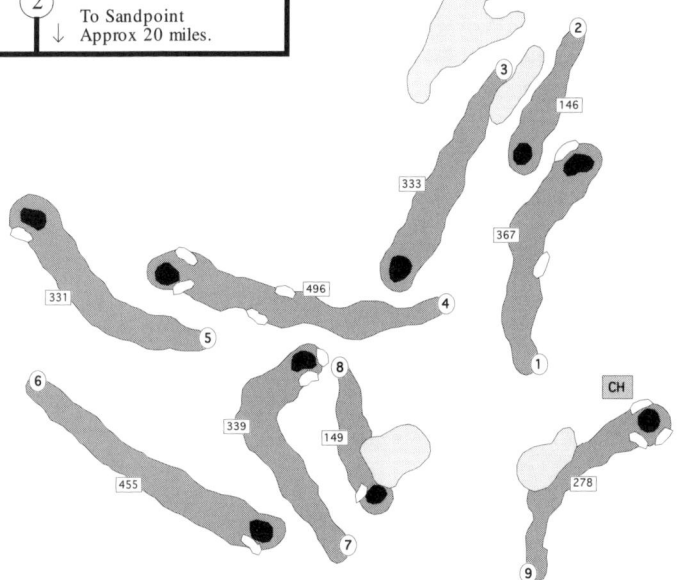

Course Yardage & Par:
M-2885 yards, par 36. M-5905 yards, par 72.
W-2563 yards, par 36. W-5307 yards, par 72.

Montpelier Golf Course (public, 9 hole course)

2110 Boise Street; Montpelier, Idaho 83254
Phone: (208) 847-1981. Fax: none. Internet: none.
Pro: Rick Deacon, PGA. Superintendent: Rick Deacon.
Rating/Slope: C 68.3/111; M 67.0/108; W 67.6/116. **Course record:** 63.
Green fees: weekdays $12; weekends $18; VISA, M/C, AMEX.
Power cart: $18/$9. **Pull cart:** $2/$1.50. **Trail fee:** personal carts not allowed.
Reservation policy: yes, please call 7 days in advance for your tee-times.
Winter condition: the golf course closed from October 15th to April 15th.
Terrain: flat, some hills. **Tees:** all grass. **Spikes:** no spike policy.
Services: club rentals, lessons, snack bar, pro shop, driving range, putting green.
Comments: bent grass greens. Good, quality course which is easy to get on. The golf course plays longer than the yardage, leaving you long irons into greens.

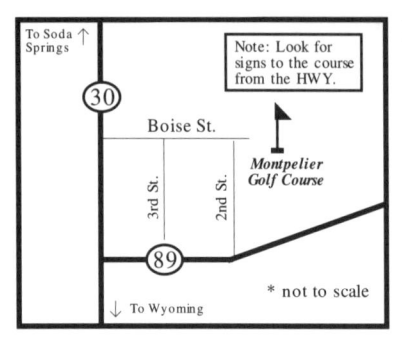

Directions: from I-15 N&S take exit #47 (Hwy 30). Proceed on Hwy 30 to Soda Springs. Proceed out of Soda Springs on Hwy 30 to Montpelier (26.3 miles). When in Montpelier the golf course is located 1 block off the junction's of Hwy 89 and Hwy 30. Look for signs at your turn.

Course Yardage & Par:
C-3357 yards par 36.
M-3172 yards, par 36.
W-2992 yards, par 36.

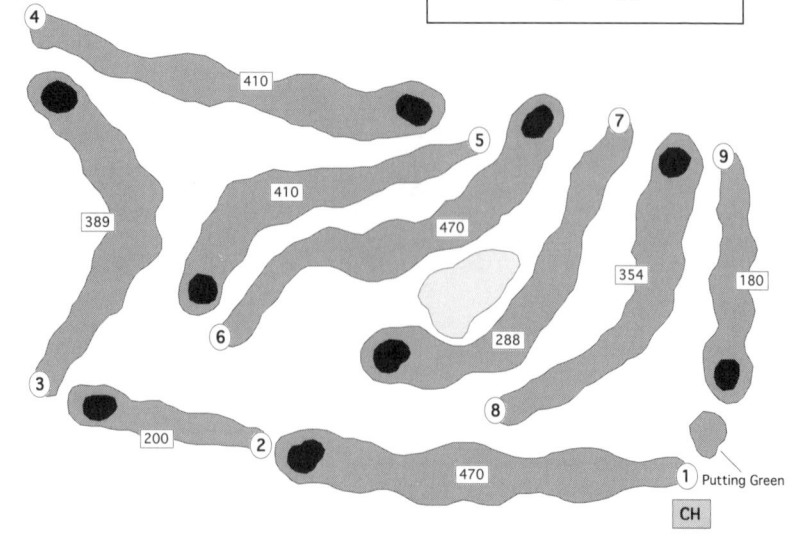

Moscow Elks Golf Club (private, 9 hole course)

3300 Highway 8; Moscow, Idaho 83843
Phone: (208) 882-3015. Fax: (208) 882-2577. Internet: none.
Manager: Jack Cluff. Superintendent: Jack Cluff.
Rating/Slope: M 70.3/116; W 72.8/126. **Course record:** 63.
Green fees: private club, Elks and guests only; no credit cards.
Power cart: private club. **Pull cart:** private club. **Trail fee:** not available.
Reservation policy: private club members and guests of members only.
Winter condition: the golf course is closed from November 1st to April 1st.
Terrain: flat, some hills. **Tees:** all grass. **Spikes:** soft spikes only.
Services: club rentals, lessons, snack bar, restaurant, lounge, beer, wine, liquor, beverages, pro shop, lockers, showers, putting & chipping greens, driving range.
Comments: friendly staff, tree lined fairways and great greens are the trademark of this private 9 hole track. The course can play very long from the men's tees.

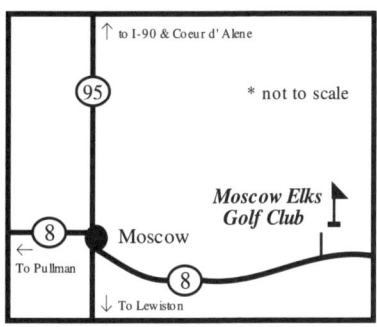

Directions: the golf course is located 3 miles out of Moscow, Idaho on Hwy 8. Turn east at the intersection of Hwy's 95 and Hwy 8. Proceed for for 2.5 miles to the main gate. Look for a sign posted.

Course Yardage & Par:
M-3139 yards, par 35.
W-2885 yards, par 37.
Dual tees for 18 holes:
M-6445 yards, par 72.
W-5758 yards, par 74.

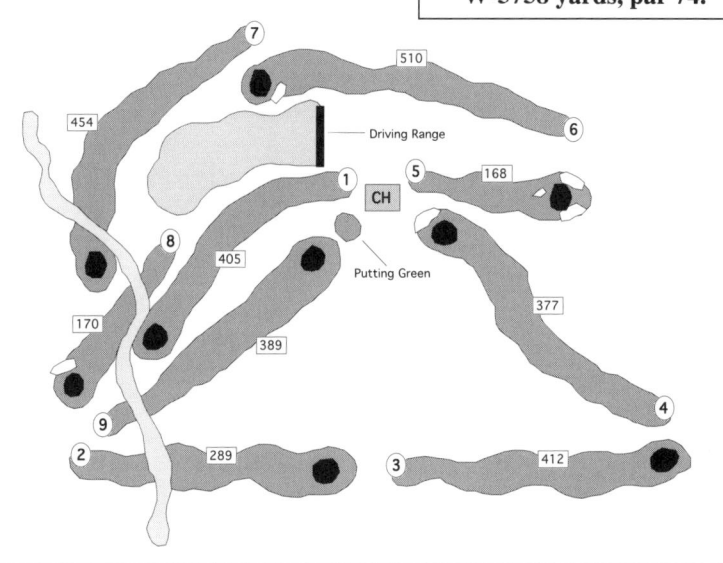

Oregon Trail Country Club (semi-private, 9 hole course)

2525 Highway 30; P.O. Box 567; Soda Springs, Idaho 83276
Phone: (208) 547-2204. Fax: none. Internet: none.
Pro: Ray Donaldson, PGA. Superintendent: unavailable.
Rating/Slope: C 69.9/114; M 67.6/112; W 69.2/114. **Course record:** 66.
Green fees: $15.70 all week long; no special rates; no credit cards.
Power cart: $16. **Pull cart:** $3/$2. **Trail fee:** personal carts not allowed.
Reservation policy: please call for reservation policy for public play.
Winter condition: the golf course is closed from November 1st to March 1st.
Terrain: flat (easy walking). **Tees:** all grass. **Spikes:** soft spikes preferred.
Services: club rentals, lessons, restaurant, snack bar, pro shop, driving range.
Comments: the golf course is located on the Alexander Reservoir. The course is flat with some trees and a few bunkers to contend with. This area of southeastern Idaho is quite historic and scenic. Excellent off the beaten track golf course.

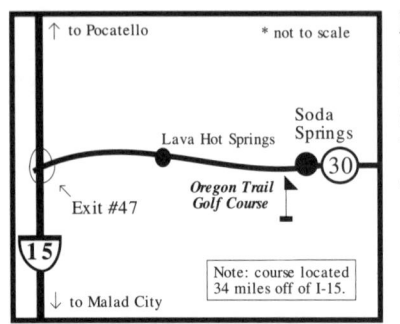

Directions: from I-15 N&S take exit #47 (Hwy 30). Proceed on Hwy 30 to Soda Springs. The golf course is located in Soda Springs right off of Highway 30. You will see the course on the west side of town and south of the highway.

Course Yardage & Par:
M-3017 yards, par 36.
W-2700 yards, par 36.
<u>Dual tees for 18 holes:</u>
M-6279 yards, par 72.
W-5400 yards, par 72.

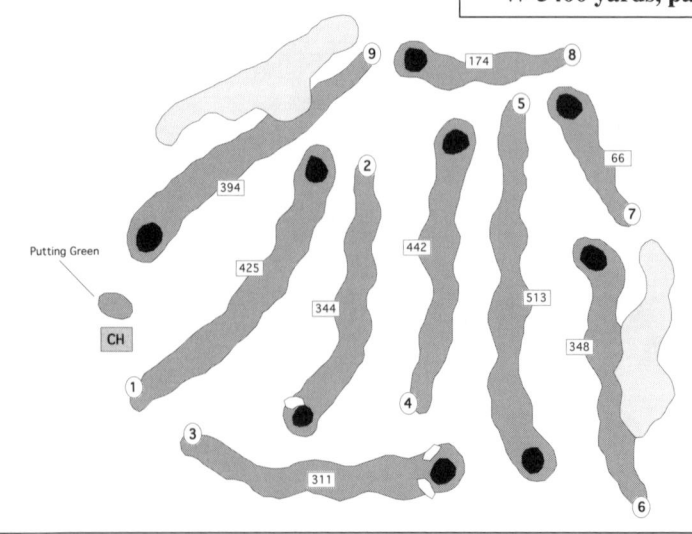

Orofino Golf & Country Club (semi-private, 9 hole course)

3430 Highway 12; Orofino, Idaho 83544
Phone: (208) 476-3117. Fax: none. Internet: none.
Manager: Steve Ballard. Superintendent: Steve Ballard.
Rating/Slope: M 65.7/110; W 68.2/113. **Course record:** 65.
Green fees: $16/$11 all week long; Jr. rates; M/C, VISA, AMEX.
Power cart: $18/$9. **Pull cart:** $2. **Trail fee:** $5 for personal carts.
Reservation policy: no restriction on tee times. First come first served.
Winter condition: the golf course is closed from November 1st to March 1st.
Terrain: relatively hilly. **Tees:** all grass. **Spikes:** soft spikes preferred.
Services: club rentals, restaurant, beer, wine, pop, pro shop, club memberships.
Comments: beautiful nine hole course in a very scenic area of Idaho. The golf course plays much longer than the yardage indicates because of the hilly terrain. The greens are large with few hazards fronting them. Excellent public course.

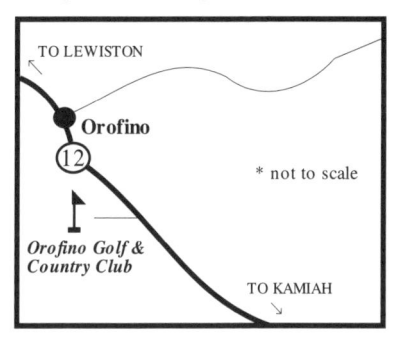

Directions: the golf course is located 3 miles east of Orofino on Highway 12. From the city of Orofino, proceed on Hwy 12 eastbound for 2.3 miles. from this point look for a sign marking your turn to the golf course.

Course Yardage & Par:
M-2696 yards, par 35.
W-2491 yards, par 37.
Dual tees for 18 holes:
M~5415 yards, par 72.
W-4952 yards, par 74.

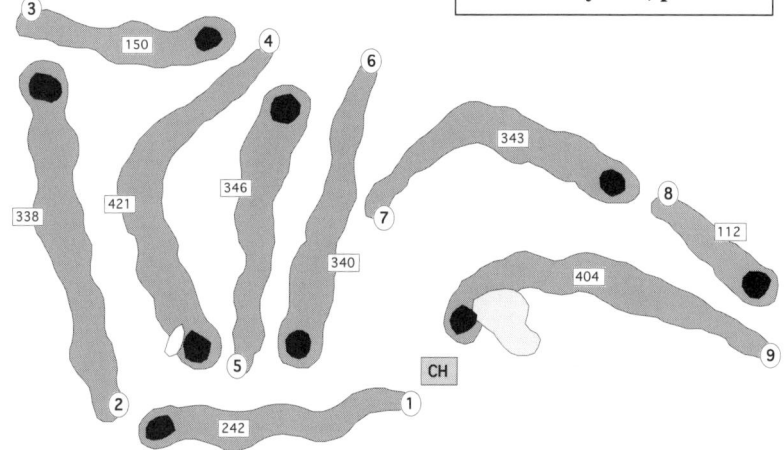

Pinecrest Municipal Golf Course (public, 18 hole course)

701 East Elva Street; Idaho Falls, Idaho 83401
Phone: (208) 529-1485. Fax: (208) 529-1113. Internet: none.
Pro: Tim Reinke, PGA. Superintendent: Keith Pugmire.
Rating/Slope: M 69.0/110; W 73.2/121. **Course record:** 62.
Green fees: W/D $15.50/$12; W/E $16.50/$13; M/C, VISA.
Power cart: $15/$8. **Pull cart:** $1.50. **Trail fee:** personal carts not allowed.
Reservation policy: yes, please call 1 day in advance for tee-times.
Winter condition: golf course is closed from November 15th to March 1st.
Terrain: flat, some hills. **Tees:** all grass. **Spikes:** soft spikes required.
Services: club rentals, lessons, snack bar, beer, pop, pro shop, putting green.
Comments: this public golf course can play very tough. Small greens that are
hard to hold and trees lining the fairways make this course a real challenge.

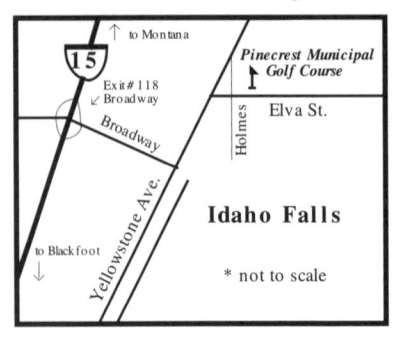

Directions: from I-15 in Idaho Falls, take
exit #118 (Broadway). Turn right and go
to Yellowstone Avenue. Turn left on
Yellowstone. Follow this to Elva Street.
Turn right on Elva Street to the course.
Look for signs posted at your turn.

Course Yardage & Par:
M-6356 yards, par 70.
W-6092 yards, par 77.

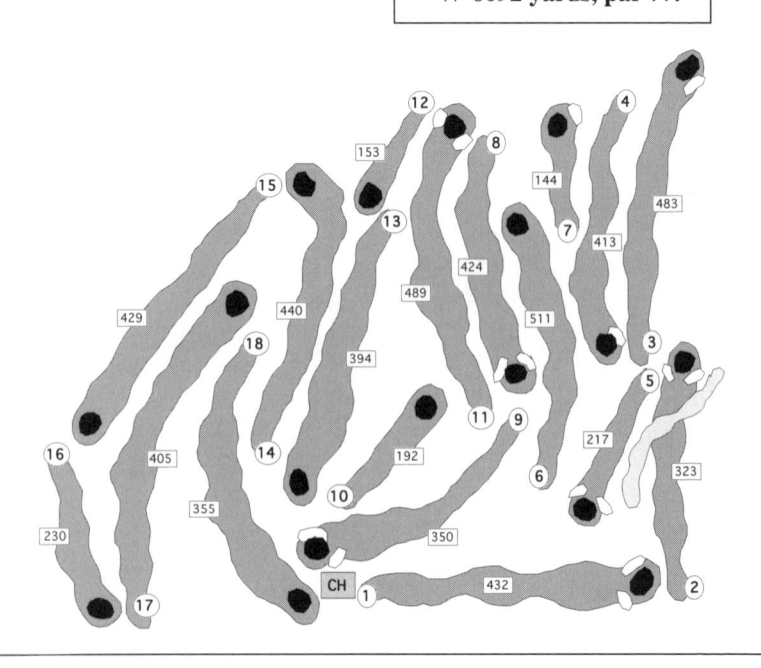

Pinehurst Golf Course (public, 9 hole course)

Country Club Lane; P.O. Box 998; Pinehurst, Idaho 83837
Phone: (208) 682-2013. Fax: (208) 784-5081. Internet: none.
Manager/Pro: Stan Edwards, PGA. Superintendent: Stan Edwards.
Rating/Slope: M 67.9/112; W 70.6/115. **Course record:** 63.
Green fees: $18/$12; all day rate $25; Jr. & Sr. rates; M/C, VISA, AMEX.
Power cart: $20/$10. **Pull cart:** $2.50. **Trail fee:** $3 for personal carts.
Reservation policy: please call 1 day in advance for all your tee-times.
Winter condition: the golf course is closed November thru February or March.
Terrain: flat (easy walking). **Tees:** all grass. **Spikes:** soft spikes preferred.
Services: club rentals, lessons, restaurant, lounge, beer, wine, beverages, liquor, pro shop, putting and chipping greens, driving range, club memberships.
Comments: 2 sets of tees for 18 hole play. Course has very small greens and is well trapped. Excellent nine hole track that can test any level of golfer.

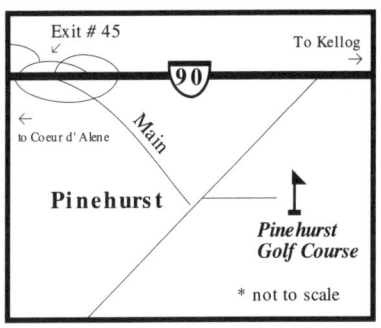

Directions: I-90 E&W take exit #45, go into the city center of Pinehurst. At the four way stop make a left. The golf course will be located ahead. Look for signs marking your way to the course.

Course Yardage & Par:
M-3026 yards, par 36.
W-2826 yards, par 37.
Dual tees for 18 holes:
M-5988 yards, par 72.
W-5503 yards, par 74.

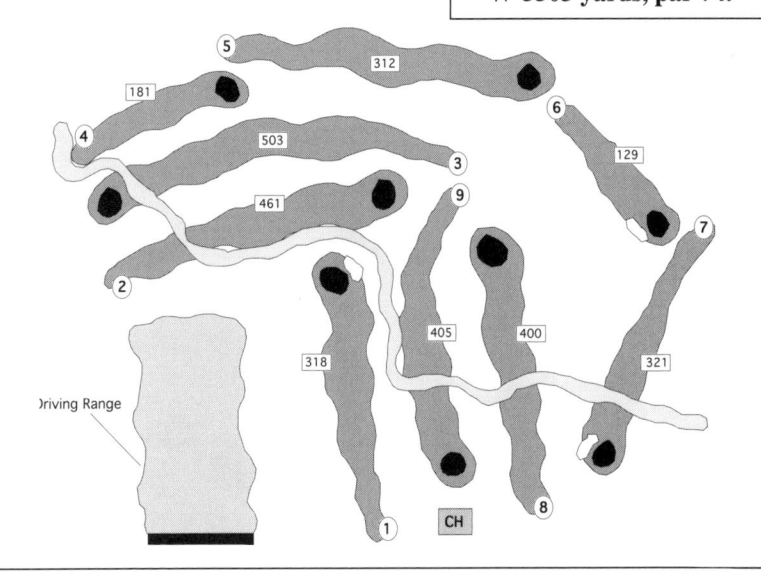

Pierce Park Greens (public, 9 hole par 3 course)

5812 N. Pierce Park Lane; Boise, Idaho 83703
Phone: (208) 853-3302. **Fax:** (208) 853-6701. **Internet:** none.
Pro: Kevin Burton, PGA. **Superintendent:** Dennis Labrum.
Rating/Slope: the golf course is not rated. **Course record:** 23.
Green fees: $11/$8 all week long; no credit cards.
Power cart: none. **Pull cart.** $2. **Trail fee:** personal carts not allowed.
Reservation policy: tee times are on a first come first served basis.
Winter condition: the golf course is closed December thru February.
Terrain: flat (easy walking). **Tees:** all grass. **Spikes:** soft spikes required.
Services: club rentals, lessons, pro shop, putting/chipping green, driving range.
Comments: new 9 hole course that opened in May of 1999. The course has a
laid back, friendly family atmosphere. The course is in great shape and offers
fun and challenging golf to all abilities. Perhaps the best driving range in the
Treasure Valley can be found at Pierce Park. Great place to practice your game.

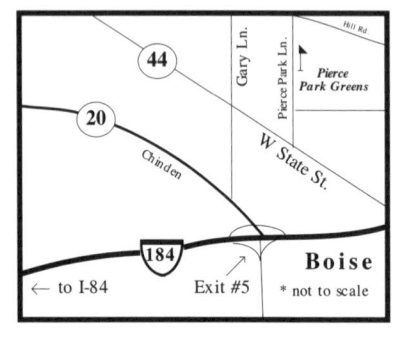

Directions: the golf course is located in
northwest Boise between Hill Road and
State Street. From I-184 E&W Proceed to
2.6 miles and exit at Farview Ave. exit.
Keep left at the fork in the ramp. Turn left
onto Garden St. Turn left on Main St.
Proceed to Hwy 20 west to Garden City/
Fairgrounds. Merge onto Chinden Blvd.
Hwy 20. Turn right onto Glenwood St.
Proceed to W State St. turn right. Proceed
to Pierce Park Lane turn left to course.

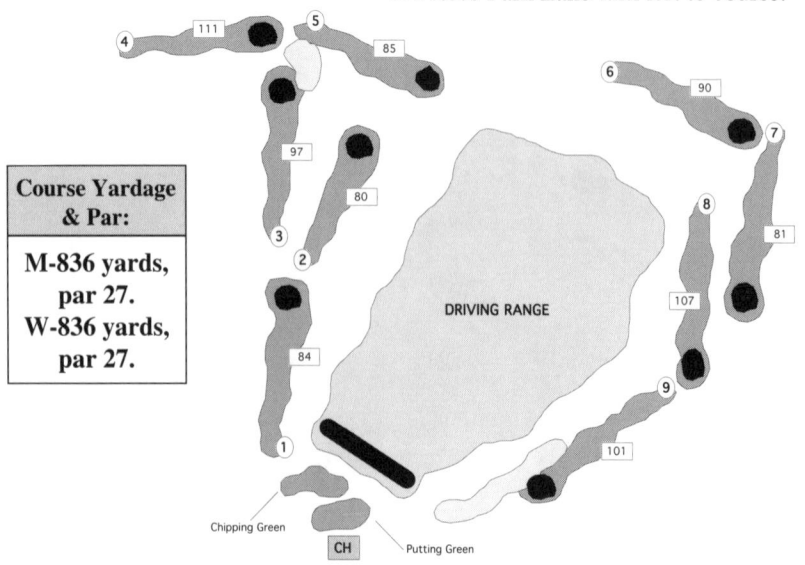

Course Yardage & Par:

M-836 yards, par 27.
W-836 yards, par 27.

DRIVING RANGE

Chipping Green

Putting Green

Plantation Golf Club, The (private, 18 hole course)
6515 West State Street; Boise, Idaho 83703
Phone: (208) 853-4440. Fax: (208) 853-4721. Internet: americangolf.com
Pro: Jim Empey, PGA. Superintendent: Jim Bodnar.
Rating/Slope: C 68.6/115; M 67.1/110; W 64.1/104. **Course record:** 62.
Green fees: private club members & guests only; reciprocates; M/C, VISA.
Power cart: private club. **Pull cart:** private club. **Trail fee:** private club.
Reservation policy: private club members & guests of members only.
Winter condition: the golf course is closed during the winter months.
Terrain: flat (easy walking course). **Tees:** grass. **Spikes:** soft spikes only.
Services: club rentals, lessons, snack bar, restaurant, lounge, beer, wine, liquor, pro shop, lockers, showers, putting & chipping greens, club memberships.
Comments: built in 1935 The Plantation Golf Club is one of the oldest courses in the state of Idaho. This is a beautiful golf course situated along the Boise River and is challenging to every level of golfer. Excellent private facility.

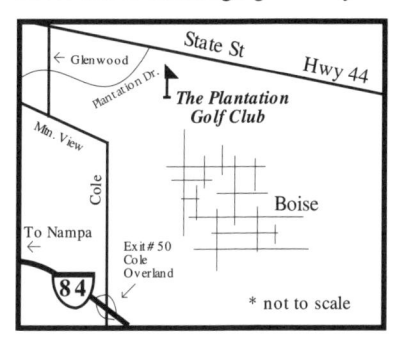

Directions: from I-84 take exit #50 (Cole). Proceed north on Cole and it will blend into Mountain View. Go until you reach Glenwood. Turn right on Glenwood. Proceed to State St. Turn right on State St. The course is located on your right hand side.

Course Yardage & Par:
C-6308 yards par 71.
M-5957 yards, par 71.
W-5256 yards, par 72.

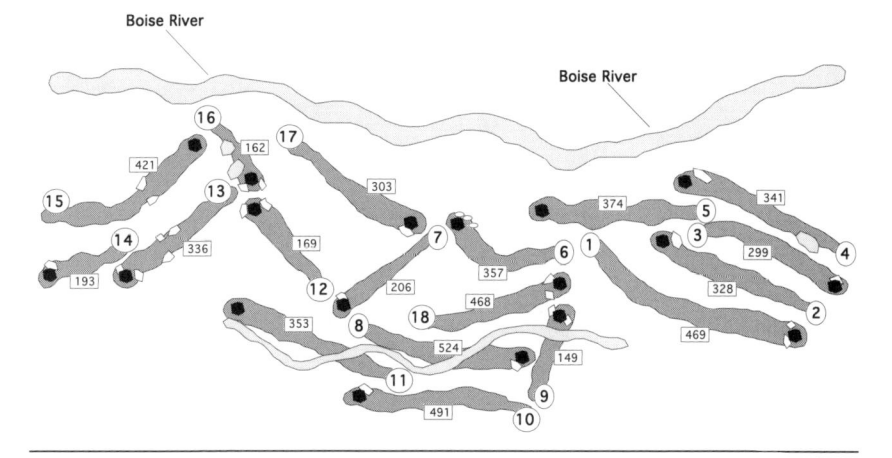

Pleasant Valley Golf Course (semi-private, 9 hole course)

3195 North 3504 East; Kimberly, Idaho 83341
Phone: (208) 423-5800. Fax: none. Internet: none.
Pro/Manager: Al Rohweder, PGA. **Superintendent:** Carl Feldhusen.
Rating/Slope: M 63.0/97; W 64.4/96. **Course record:** 60.
Green fees: $16/$8 all week; twilight rates offered; M/C, VISA.
Power cart: $15/$9. **Pull cart.** $2. **Trail fee:** $8/$6 for personal carts.
Reservation policy: please call 7 days in advance for all your tee-times.
Winter condition: the golf course is closed November thru February or March.
Terrain: flat (easy walking). **Tees:** all grass. **Spikes:** soft spikes preferred.
Services: club rentals, lessons, pro shop, putting/chipping green, driving range.
Comments: new 9 hole course that is just south of Twin Falls Idaho. The course features flat terrain that is easy to walk. Greens are small to medium in size and can be hard to hold. The golf course is selling real estate around the golf course.

Directions: the golf course is located approximately 5 1/2 miles south of Kimberly, Idaho. From I-84 E&W take exit #182 (Hwy 50). Turn right on Hwy 50. Proceed on Hwy 50 for 4.6 miles to Hwy 30. Turn left on Hwy 30. Hwy 30 becomes Main St. Stay straight on Main St. which becomes 3500 East Rd. The golf course is located on the left side.

Course Yardage & Par:
M-2847 yards, par 33.
W-2362 yards, par 33.

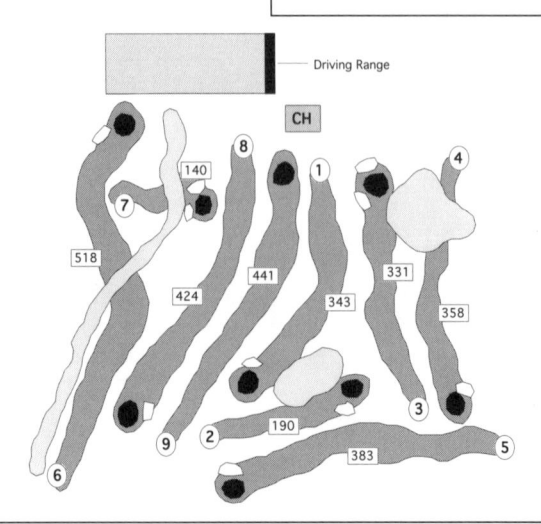

Ponderosa Golf Course (public, 9 hole par 3 course)

320 Minidoka Avenue; Burley, Idaho 83318
Phone: (208) 679-5730. Fax: (208) 679-0565. Internet: none.
Manager: Earl Simpson. Superintendent: Dan Simpson.
Rating/Slope: the golf course is not rated. **Course record:** 22.
Green fees: $12/$7.50 all week long; Sr. rates (weekdays only); M/C, VISA.
Power cart: $6 per 9 holes. **Pull cart:** $2. **Trail fee:** $5 per 9 holes.
Reservation policy: not needed. Tee-times are on a first come first served basis.
Winter conditioned: the golf course is closed from November to March.
Terrain: flat, some hills. **Tees:** all grass. **Spikes:** soft spikes only.
Services: club rentals, vending machines, snacks, putting & chipping green.
Comments: fair par 3 tract that is great fun for the whole family. This course is perfect for the first time or beginner golfer. The golf course has a wide variety of whole lengths giving the golfer a chance to use every club in their bags.

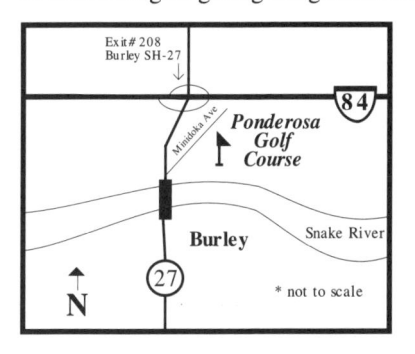

Directions: from I-84 E&W take exit #208 (Hwy 27) in Burley, Idaho. Proceed south off the exit to the golf course on your left. Look for signs that are posted at your turn to the course.

Course Yardage & Par:
M-1250 yards, par 27.
W-1250 yards, par 27.

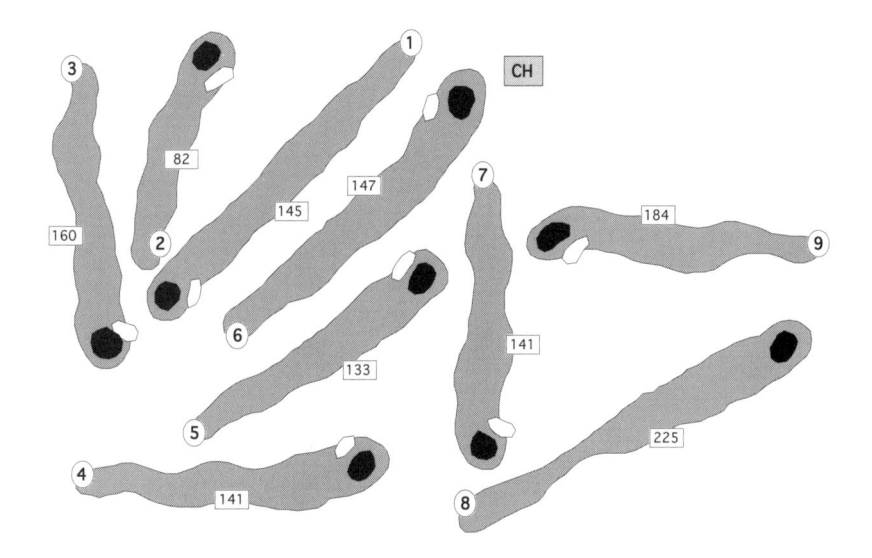

Ponderosa Springs Golf Course (public, 9 hole par 3 course)

2814 Galena Drive; Coeur d'Alene, Idaho 83814

Phone: (208) 664-1101. **Fax:** none. **Internet:** none.

Pro: Dean Fotis, PGA. **Superintendent:** Alex Lynch.

Rating/Slope: the golf course is not rated. **Course record:** 23.

Green fees: W/D $13/$8; W/E $3/$8; Jr. & Sr. rates (M-F); no credit cards.

Power cart: not available. **Pull cart:** $2. **Trail fee:** personal carts not allowed.

Reservation policy: not needed. Tee-times are on a first come first served basis.

Winter condition: the golf course is closed from November 1st to March 15th.

Terrain: flat, some hills. **Tees:** all grass. **Spikes:** no policy.

Services: club rentals, lessons, beer, wine, liquor, pop, lounge, putting green.

Comments: tough par 3 course with holes ranging from 91-165 yards. A pond comes into play on many of the holes giving the golfer a challenge on many approach shots. If you are looking for a change of pace try Ponderosa Springs.

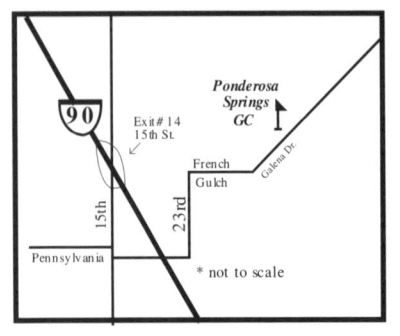

Directions: I-90 E&W take 15th St. exit. Go south on 15th to Pennsylvania East on Pennsylvania to 23rd. North on 23rd to French Gulch Road. Then turn on French Gulch to the golf course. Look for signs.

Course Yardage & Par:
M-1211 yards, par 27.
W-1110 yards, par 27.

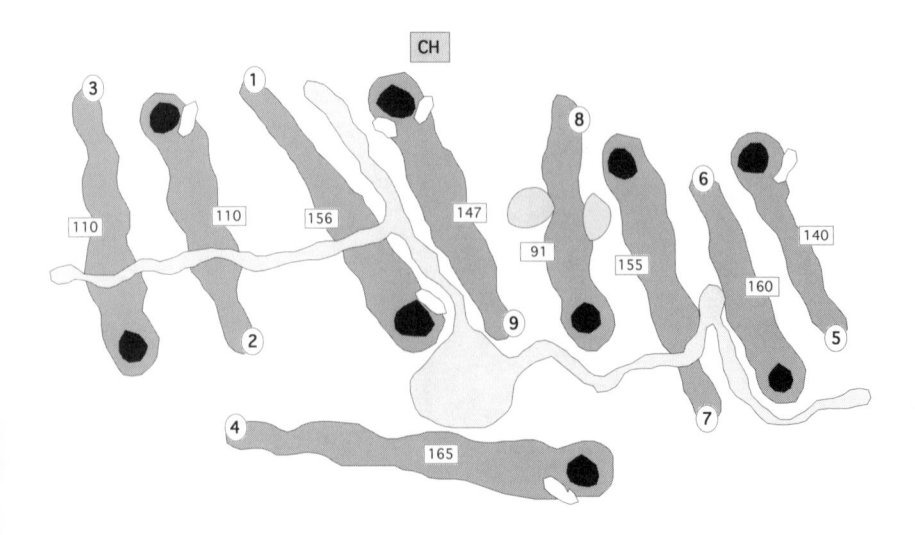

Prairie Falls Golf Club (public, 9 hole course)

3200 North Spokane Street; Post Falls, Idaho 83854
Phone: (208) 457-0210. **Fax:** (208) 773-6883. **Internet:** prairiefallsgc@aol.com
Pro: Tim Morton, PGA. **Superintendent:** Marcus Curry.
Rating/Slope: C 70.2/118; M 68.4/113; M 66.6/109; W 70.0/119. **Record:** 66.
Green fees: $17/$12 all week long; VISA, M/C, AMEX, DISCOVER.
Power cart: $20/$12. **Pull cart:** $3. **Trail fee:** $5 for personal carts.
Reservation policy: you may call up to 7 days in advance for tee times.
Winter condition: the golf course is closed from December to early February.
Terrain: flat, some hills. **Tees:** all grass. **Spikes:** soft spikes required.
Services: club rentals, lessons, beer, wine, snack bar, pro shop, driving range.
Comments: new golf course that opened in 1997. The golf course will start
construction on the back 9 in spring of 2000. Expected completion date is
spring 2001. Good public course that features well kept fairways and greens.

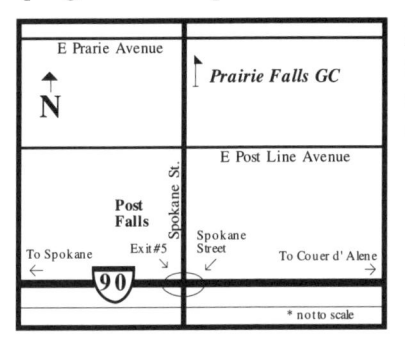

Directions: from I-90 E&W take exit #5
(Spokane Street). Turn north on Spokane
and proceed for 5 miles to the golf course
on your right hand side.

Course Yardage & Par:
C-3299 yards, par 36.
M-3106 yards, par 36.
M-2910 yards, par 36.
W-2727 yards, par 36.

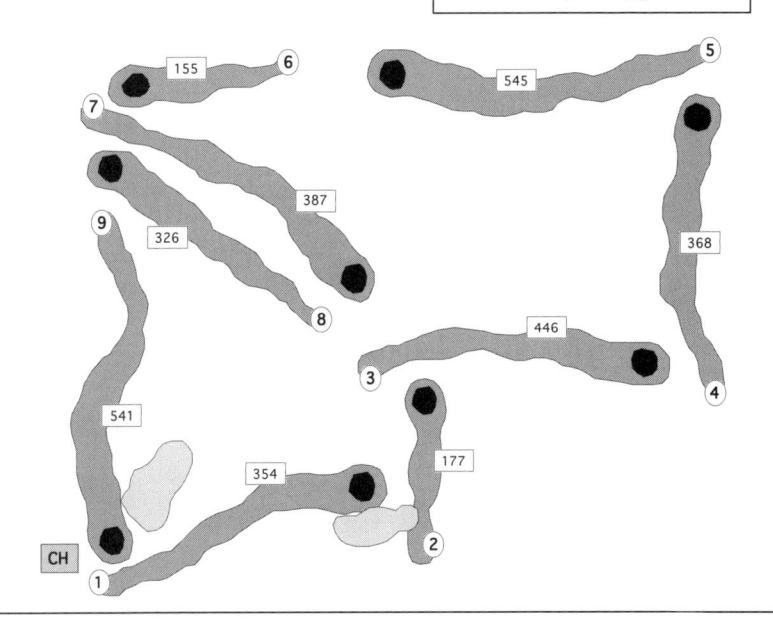

Preston Golf & Country Club (semi-private, 9 hole course)

1215 N 800 East; Preston, Idaho 83263
Phone: (208) 852-2408. Fax: none. Internet: none.
Pro: Matt Sickler, PGA. Superintendent: unavailable.
Rating/Slope: C 68.0/114; M 67.2/112; W 69.1/116. **Course record:** 31.
Green fees: W/D $12/$6; W/E $16/$8; play cards available; VISA, M/C.
Power cart: $18/$9. **Pull cart:** $2/$1. **Trail fee:** $2.50 for personal carts.
Reservation policy: yes, for weekends and holidays. Call 1 week in advance.
Winter condition: the golf course is closed from November 1st to March 1st.
Terrain: flat (easy walking course). **Tees:** all grass. **Spikes:** no policy.
Services: club rentals, snack bar, beer, pro shop, driving range, putting green.
Comments: this course is flat and easy to walk. Greens are medium in size and
have bunkers fronting most of them. The terrain usually gives the golfer a decent
lie from the fairway. Very friendly course that is fun for all.

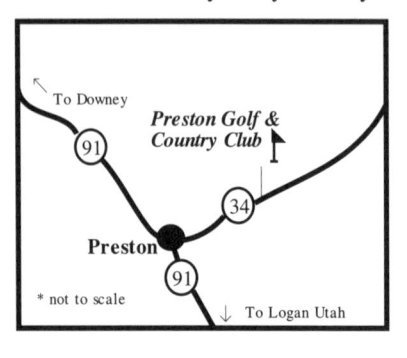

Directions: the golf course is located 1
mile northeast of Preston on Hwy 34.
From the city of Preston proceed north on
Hwy 36. The golf course can be seen from
the highway. Look for signs indicating
your turn to the golf course.

Course Yardage & Par:
M-3126 yards, par 36.
W-2896 yards, par 36.

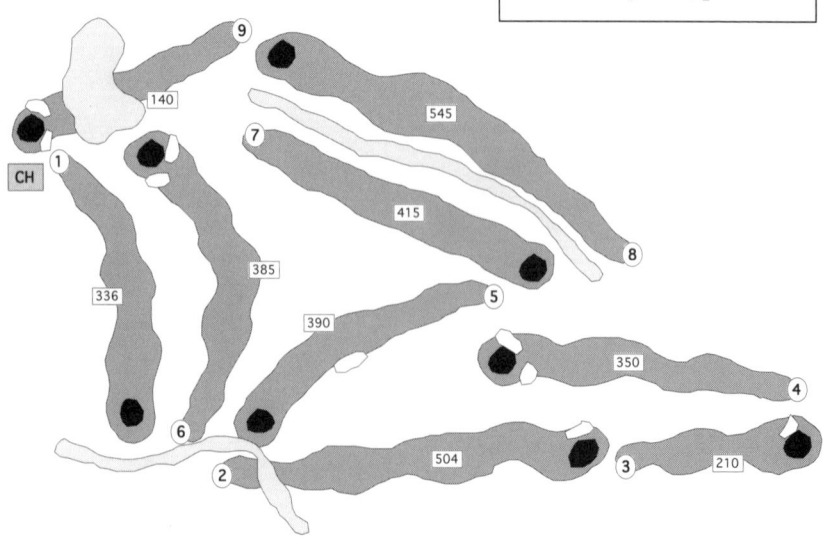

Priest Lake Golf Course (public, 9 hole course)

HCR 5-Box 151; off Highway 57; Priest Lake, Idaho 83856
Phone: (208) 443-2525. Fax: none. Internet: none.
Pro: teaching pro in summer. Superintendent: none.
Rating/Slope: M 69.2/118; W 70.0/115. **Course record:** 32.
Green fees: $20/$15 all week long; no special rates; M/C, VISA.
Power cart: $20/$15. **Pull cart:** $3. **Trail fee:** $3 for personal carts.
Reservation policy: yes, usually available same day. No maximum time limit.
Winter condition: the golf course is closed during the winter months.
Terrain: flat, some hills. **Tees:** all grass. **Spikes:** no policy.
Services: club rentals, restaurant, lounge, beer, wine, liquor, snack bar, pro shop, driving range, putting green. **Comments:** excellent well conditioned golf course. The golf course is surrounded by trees with water coming into play on many holes. The facility will be expanding to 18 holes in July of 2001.

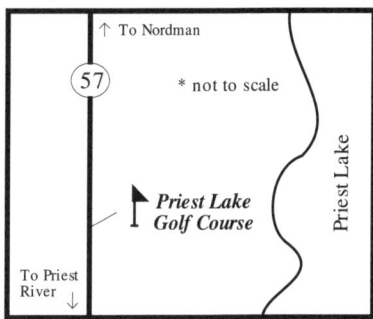

Directions: the golf course is located on Highway 57, 26 miles north of the city of Priest River, Idaho. Look for signs.

Course Yardage & Par:
M-3097 yards par 36.
W-2696 yards par 36.

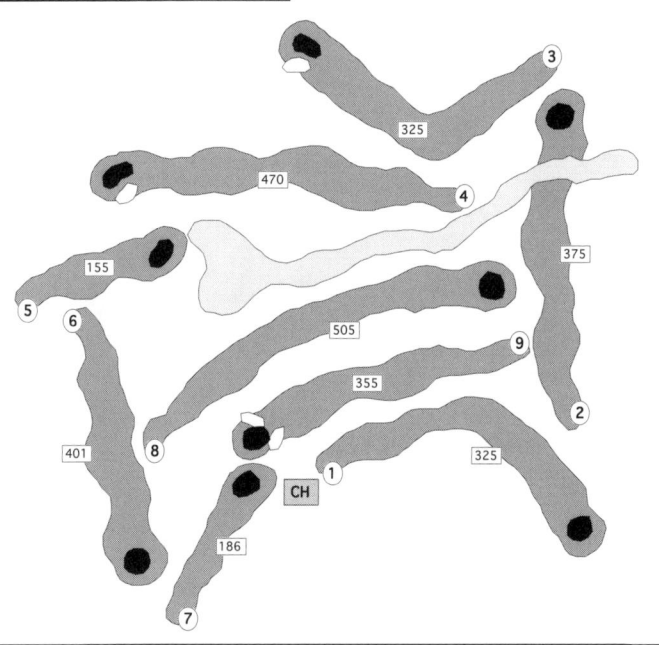

Purple Sage Golf Course (public, 18 hole course)

15192 Purple Sage Road; P.O. Box 1211; Caldwell, Idaho 83605
Phone: (208) 459-2223. Fax: none. Internet: none.
Pro: John Watson, PGA. Superintendent: Gordon Crockett.
Rating/Slope: C 70.8/123; M 68.8/117; W 69.2/114. **Course record:** 67.
Green fees: W/D $14/$l0; W/E $16; twilight rates W/E's $10; M/C, VISA.
Power cart: $18/$10. **Pull cart:** $3/$1.50. **Trail fee:** $8.25 for personal carts.
Reservation policy: yes, call 1 day in advance for Monday thru Thursday times
fimes. Call on Wednesday for your Friday, Saturday, Sunday & holiday times.
Winter condition: the golf course is closed from December 1st to March 1st.
Terrain: flat (easy walking). **Tees:** grass. **Spikes:** soft spikes required.
Services: club rentals, lessons, snack bar, restaurant, beer, wine, beverages,
lockers, driving range, putting & chipping greens, club memberships.
Comments: course voted one of Idaho's best in Golf Digest 1989. 5 time host
course for the Idaho State Open Championship. If you are ever in the area of
Caldwell be sure to stop in and play. This facility is worth a special trip.

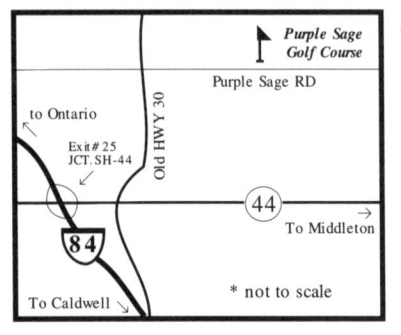

Directions: from I 84 E&W take exit #25 (Hwy 44). Proceed east off the exit. At Old Hwy 30 turn north. Proceed on Old Hwy 30 to Purple Sage Road. Turn right on Purple Sage Road. Proceed ahead to the golf course on your left hand side.

Course Yardage & Par:
C-6718 yards, par 71.
M-6308 yards, par 71.
W-5307 yards, par 72.

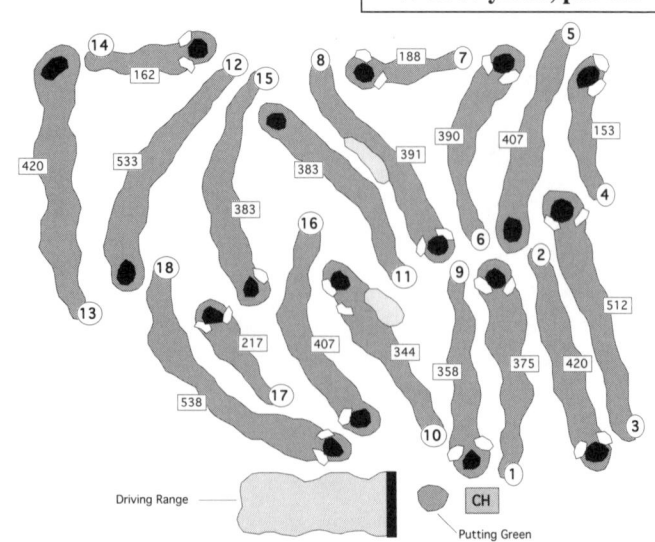

Quail Hollow Golf Club (semi-private, 18 hole course)

4520 North 36th; Boise, Idaho 83703
Phone: (208) 344-7807. Fax: (208) 344-7824. Internet: none.
Pro: Matt Ennis, PGA. Superintendent: Kevin Orr.
Rating/Slope: C 68.0/129; M 65.5/123; W 65.0/115. **Course record:** 62.
Green fees: W/D $22/$15; W/E $27/$15; winter rates; Jr./Sr. rates; M/C, VISA.
Power cart: $18/$9. **Pull cart:** complimentary. **Trail fee:** not allowed.
Reservation policy: yes, please call 5 days in advance for your tee-times.
Winter condition: the golf course is open all year long. Damp conditions.
Terrain: relatively hilly. **Tees:** all grass. **Spikes:** soft spikes required.
Services: club rentals, lessons, snack bar, restaurant, lounge, beer, wine,
pro shop, driving range, putting and chipping greens, club memberships.
Comments: very nice golfing facility that was opened in 1981. The course has
well bunkered greens and water coming into play on nearly half the holes. Not a
overly long course but very challenging. Worth a trip if in the Boise area.

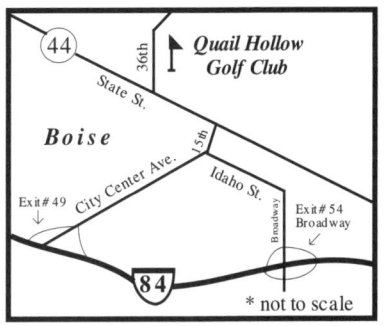

Directions: from I-84 E&W take I-184 to the Boise city center. Proceed to the Curtis exit. Turn north off the exit. Follow Curtis to Chinden Blvd. it turns into Veterans Memorial Parkway. Proceed on this until you get to State St. it turns into North 36th. Proceed on N 36th to the course. Look for signs.

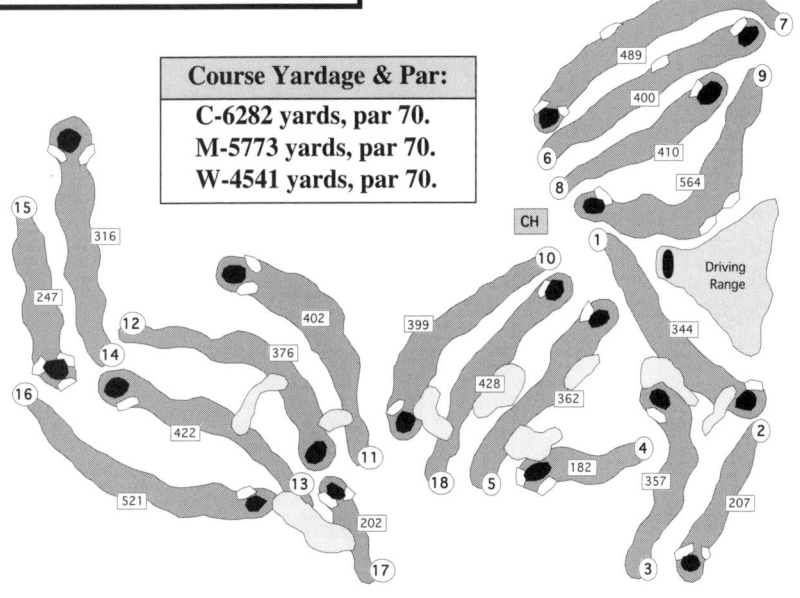

Course Yardage & Par:

C-6282 yards, par 70.
M-5773 yards, par 70.
W-4541 yards, par 70.

Ranch Club Golf Course (public, 9 hole course)

Highway 2; P.O. Box 430; Priest River, Idaho 83856
Phone: (208) 448-1731. Fax: none. Internet: ranchclub@povn.com
Managers: Bill Tait & Dennis Napier.
Rating/Slope: M 63.2/94; W 66.0/98. **Course record:** 60.
Green fees: $15/$10 all week; spring & fall rates; M/C, VISA.
Power cart: $16/$9. **Pull cart:** $2. **Trail fee:** none.
Reservation policy: yes, please call in advance for a tee time. No time limit.
Winter condition: the golf course is closed from November 1st to March 1st.
Terrain: flat, some hills. **Tees:** all grass. **Spikes:** soft spikes only.
Services: club rentals, lessons, snack bar, restaurant, lounge, beer, wine, liquor, pro shop, putting green. **Comments:** Greens are medium sized and have bunkers guarding your approach shots. This well maintained course is a great place to bring the family for a golf outing. Very friendly staff and atmosphere.

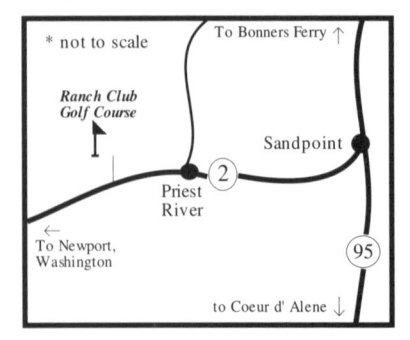

Directions: the golf course is located on Highway 2 between Newport Washington and Priest River, Idaho. From Highway 2 you will turn left into the driveway to the golf course, one mile west of Priest River. Look for signs posted at your turn to the Priest River golf course.

Course Yardage & Par:
M-2530 yards, par 33.
W-2464 yards, par 36.

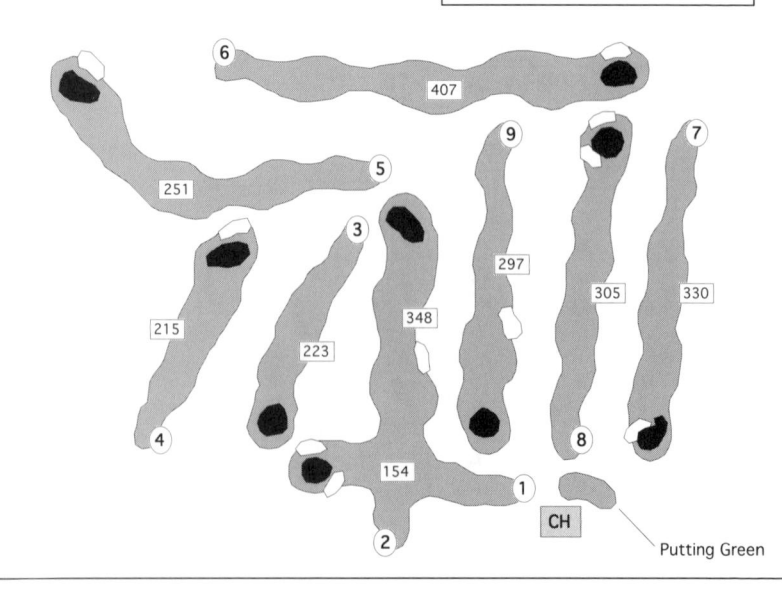

Rexburg Municipal Golf Course (public, 9 hole course)

South Airport Road; P.O. Box 408; Rexburg, Idaho 83440
Phone: (208) 359-3037. Fax: none. Internet: none.
Pro: Duffy McFarland, PGA. Superintendent: unavailable.
Rating/Slope: C 68.0/109; M 65.7/105; W 70.5/111. **Course record:** 63.
Green fees: $12/$7.50 all week long; VISA, M/C; Jr. & Sr. rates.
Power cart: $15/$7.50. **Pull cart:** $2. **Trail fee:** personal carts are not allowed.
Reservation policy: yes, please call up to 2 days in advance for your tee-times.
Winter condition: closed from November to March depending on the weather.
Terrain: flat (easy walking). **Tees:** all grass. **Spikes:** soft spikes preferred.
Services: club rentals, lessons, snack bar, pro shop, putting & chipping green.
Comments: this course is primarily flat but beware of the runway where it is
easy to go out of bounds and add strokes to your game. Fair conditioned course.

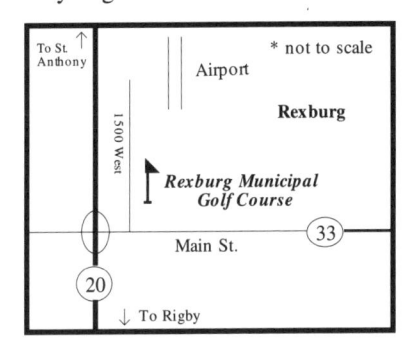

Directions: from I-15 N&S take exit
#119 to Highway 20 east. Proceed on
Hwy 20 northeast to Rexburg. Take the
exit to Highway 33, east to Rexburg,
Idaho. Take the immediate left on 1500
West to the golf course on your right.
Look for signs on the highway marking
your turn to the golf course.

Course Yardage & Par:
C-3159 yards, par 35.
M-2891 yards, par 35.
W-2773 yards, par 35.

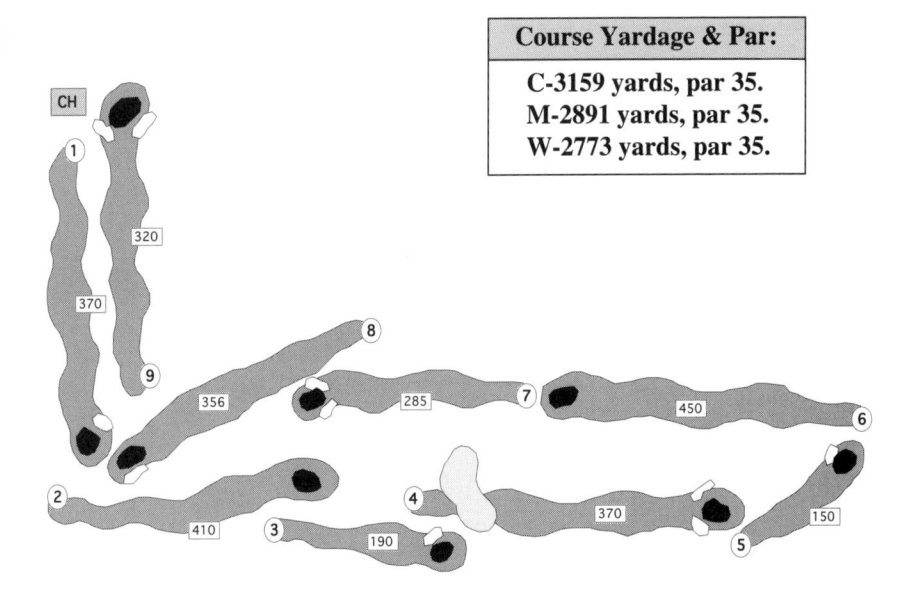

Ridgecrest Golf Club (public, 18 hole course, 9 hole executive)

3730 Ridgecrest Drive; Nampa, Idaho 83687
Phone: (208) 468-9073. **Fax:** (208) 466-9627. **Internet:** www.ridgecrestgolf.com
Pro: James Brown, PGA. **Superintendent:** Charlie Denham.
Rating/Slope: T 72.0/125; C 69.6/119; M 67.2/113; W 68.8/120. **Record:** 65.
Green fees: (M-Th) $120; (Fri./Sat./Sun./Hol.) $23; Jr. rates $12.
Green fees executive course: $11 all week long; season passes; M/C, VISA.
Power cart: $10 per person. **Pull cart:** $3. **Trail fee:** $7 for personal carts.
Reservation policy: yes, please call up to 2 days in advance for your tee-times.
Winter condition: the course is open all year long, depending on the weather.
Terrain: flat, rolling hills. **Tees:** all grass. **Spikes:** soft spikes only.
Services: club rentals, lessons, snack bar, pro shop, beer, wine, putting &
chipping greens, practice bunker, driving range, full service clubhouse.
Comments: set in the rolling corn fields, this links style course is one of the best
facilities in the state of Idaho. Stretching nearly 6900 yards from the back tees
the regulation course will test you at every turn. A must play if in the area.

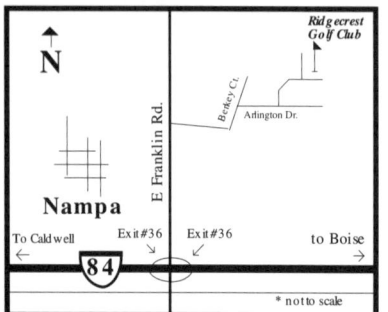

Directions: from I-84 E&W take exit #36
(E Franklin Road). Proceed northbound
off the freeway on Franklin Blvd. The
golf course is located just off Franklin
Blvd. on the right hand side of the road.

Course Yardage & Par:
C-6836 yards, par 72.
M-6330 yards, par 72.
W-5836 yards, par 72.

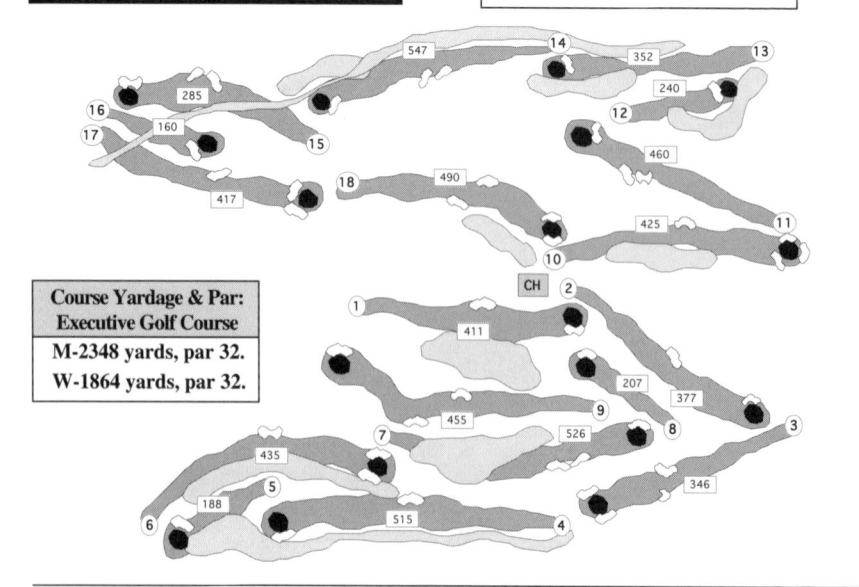

Course Yardage & Par: Executive Golf Course
M-2348 yards, par 32.
W-1864 yards, par 32.

Rimrock Golf Course (public, 9 hole par 3 course)
North 21600 Highway 95; Athol, Idaho 83801
Phone: (208) 762-5054. Fax: none. Internet: none.
Owner: John Veylupek. Superintendent: John Veylupek.
Rating/Slope: the golf course is not rated. **Course record:** 24.
Green fees: $12/$7 all week long; no credit cards accepted.
Power cart: $6 per 9 holes. **Pull cart:** $1. **Trail fee:** none.
Winter condition: the golf course is open all year long, weather permitting.
Terrain: flat (easy walking). **Tees:** all grass tees. **Spikes:** soft spikes preferred.
Services: pop, coffee, snack bar, beer, putting & chipping greens, driving range.
Comments: 9 hole par 3 golf course that opened in August of 1993. This
course is very friendly and a great place to bring the entire family to for a golf
outing. Great on course driving range and putting green for those practicing.

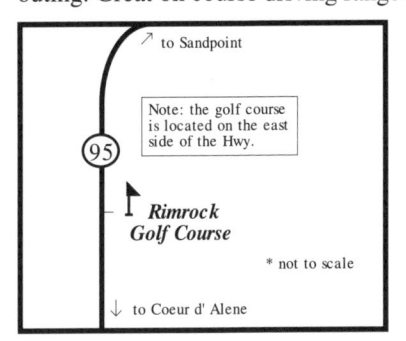

Directions: the golf course is located 3
miles south of the Silverwood Theme
Park on the east side of US Highway
95. Look for a sign posted at your turn.

Course Yardage & Par:
M-1269 yards, par 27.
W-1269 yards, par 28.

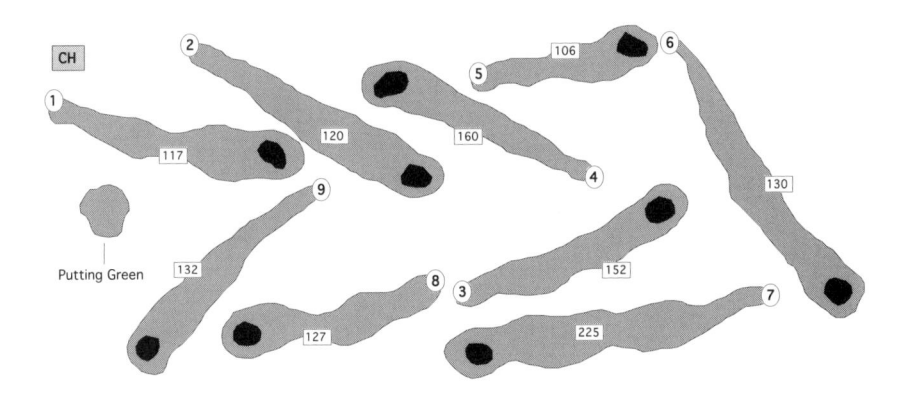

River Bend Golf Course (public, 18 hole course)

18539 Fish Road; Wilder, Idaho 83676
Phone: (208) 482-7169. **Fax:** (208) 482-7196. **Internet:** none.
Owner: Joe Bidegarita. **Superintendent:** Joe Bidegarita.
Rating/Slope: C 69.4/113; M 67.0/108; W 70.2/117. **Course record:** N/A.
Green fees: $16/$11 all week long; Sr. rates; VISA, M/C, DIS.
Power cart: $18/$10. **Pull cart:** $3/$2. **Trail fee:** $5 for personal carts.
Reservation policy: please call 6 days in advance for your tee times.
Winter condition: the golf course is closed from November 1st to March 1st.
Terrain: flat, rolling terrain. **Tees:** all grass. **Spikes:** soft spikes only.
Services: club rentals, snack bar, beer, pro shop, driving range, putting green.
Comments: good public track that is a favorite with the local golfers. River Bend features medium size greens plenty of sand and water coming into play on numerous holes. Great course to spend the day in a low key golfing atmosphere.

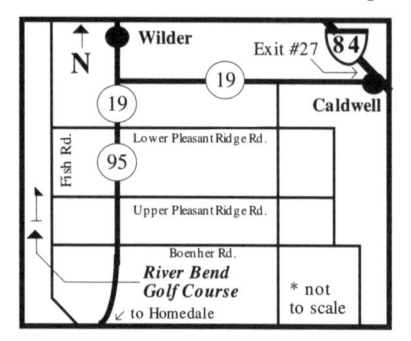

Directions: from I-84 E&W take exit #27 (Hwy 19). Proceed westbound on Hwy 19 toward Wilder. When you reach Hwy 95 turn south (left). Proceed southbound until you reach Bohner Road. Turn right on Bohner Road. Follow until the road stops at the "T" turn right. The course is located ahead on your left hand side. Look for signs that are posted.

Course Yardage & Par:
C-6432 yards, par 72.
M-5960 yards, par 72.
W-5092 yards, par 72.

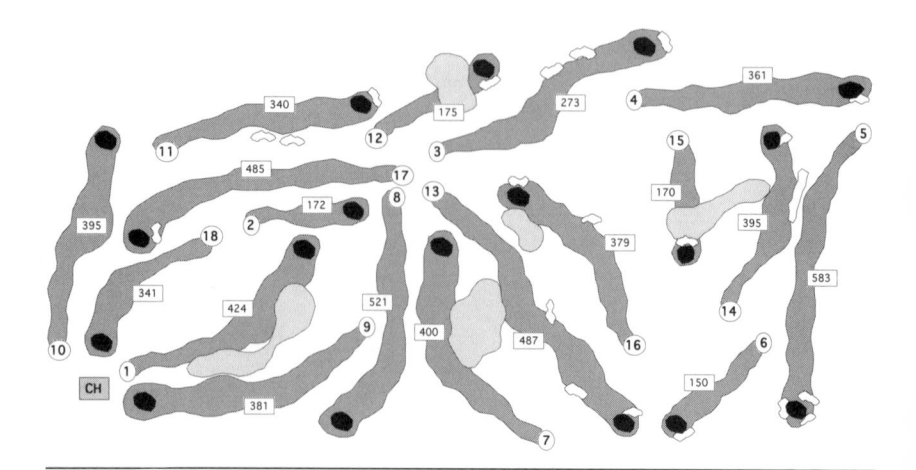

River Park Golf Course (public, 9 hole executive course)

717 Capital Avenue; P.O. Box 252; MacKay, Idaho 83251
Phone: (208) 588-2296. Fax: none. Internet: none.
Manager: Mike Marinac. Superintendent: Mike Marinac.
Rating/Slope: C 63.5/106; M 63.0/105; W 64.3/101. **Course record:** 29.
Green fees: $11/$7 all week long; no special rates; VISA, M/C.
Power cart: $14/$7. **Pull cart:** $2. **Trail fee:** personal carts not allowed.
Reservation policy: yes, please call up to 2 days in advance for tee-times.
Winter condition: the golf course is closed from November 1st to March 1st.
Terrain: flat (easy walking). **Tees:** all grass. **Tees:** no policy.
Services: RV park, club rentals, putting green, snacks, pop, vending machines.
Comments: this is a fun course to take the family to when doing some camping
or vacationing in central Idaho. Relatively few hazards and flat fairways make
this a great course to learn on. The course is in fair condition during the season.

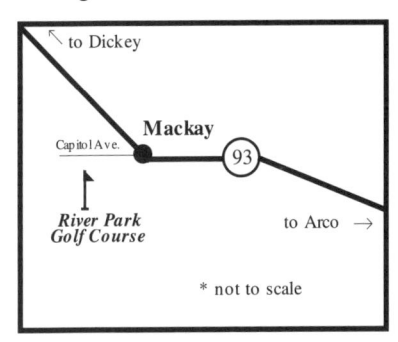

Directions: from Highway 93 turn west
on Capital Avenue to the clubhouse and
entrance on your left hand side.

Course Yardage & Par:
C-5138 yards, par 31.
M-5028 yards, par 31.
W-5484 yards, par 31.

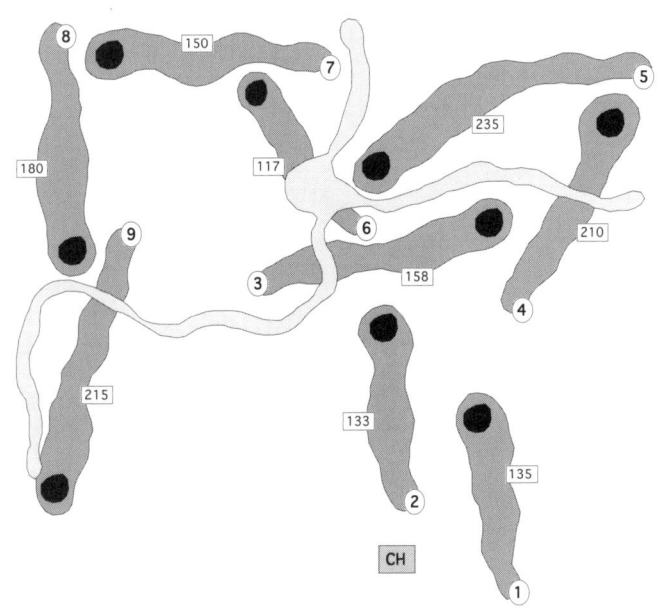

Riverside Golf Course (public, 18 hole course)

3500 Bannock Highway; P.O. Box 1061; Pocatello, Idaho 83204
Phone: (208) 232-9515. Fax: (208) 323-0130. Internet: none.
Director of Golf: Denny Howell, PGA. Pro: Bobby Howell, PGA.
Superintendent: Dan Harting. Course record: 61.
Rating/Slope: C 69.1/115; M 67.6/111; W 70.8/120.
Green fees: W/D $16/$12; W/E $17/$13; M/C, VISA.
Power cart: $19/$10.50. **Pull cart:** $2. **Trail fee:** $8.50 for personal carts.
Reservation policy: call Thursday for the weekend. Call 1 day ahead for W/D's.
Winter condition: the course is closed from November 1st to February 15th.
Terrain: flat (easy walking). **Tees:** all grass. **Spikes:** soft spikes preferred.
Services: club rentals, lessons, snack bar, restuarant, beer, coolers, pro shop, beverages, driving range, putting & chipping greens, memberships available.
Comments: flat terrain makes this course easy to walk and fun for any golfer. Well conditioned golf course that plays longer than the yardage indicates.

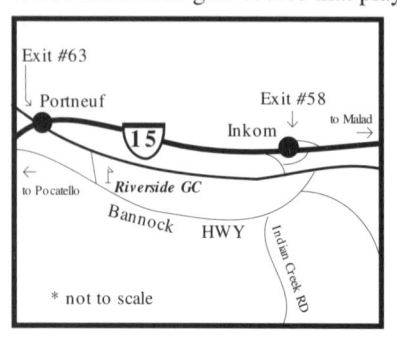

Directions: I-86/I-15 N&S (the course is at the junctions of these freeways) take the Clark Street exit. Follow Clark Street to 4th. Turn left on 4th to Benton. Turn Right on Benton to Arthur. Left on Arthur. The course is approximately 2.5 miles ahead.

Course Yardage & Par:
C-6357 yards, par 71.
M-6001 yards, par 71.
W-5710 yards par 74.

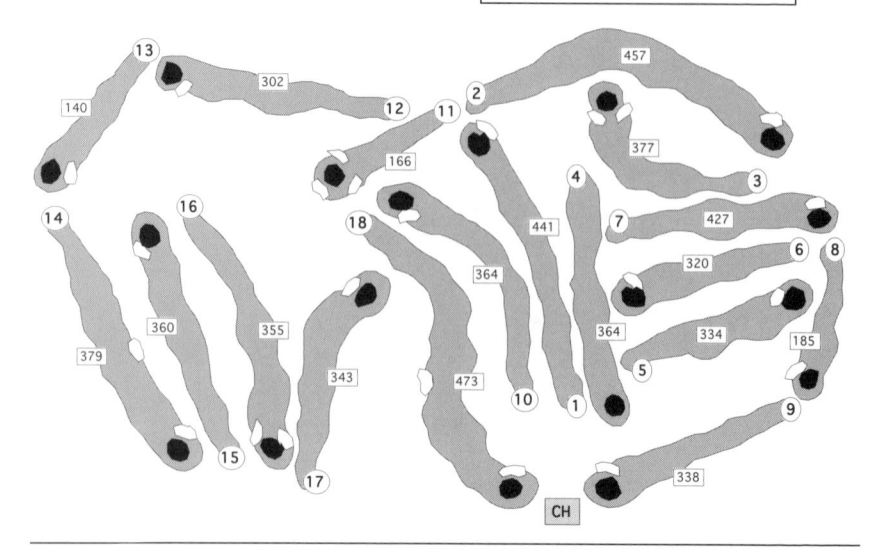

Rolling Hills Golf Course (public, 9 hole course)

50 West Indianhead Road; Weiser, Idaho 83672
Phone: (208) 549-0456. Fax: (208) 549-2460. Internet: none.
Manager: Debbie Mendiguren. Superintendent: Steve Hausman.
Rating/Slope: M 68.0/113; W 73.7/124. **Course record:** 28.
Green fees: $15/$12 all week long; Jr. & Sr. rates; M/C, VISA, DIS.
Power cart: $18/$10. **Pull cart:** $5/$3. **Trail fee:** $5 for personal carts.
Reservation policy: call ahead for weekend & holiday tee-times. No time limit.
Winter condition: the golf course is open all year long. Damp conditions.
Terrian: flat, some hills. **Tees:** all grass. **Spikes:** soft spikes required.
Services: club rentals, snack bar, restaurant, lounge, beer, wine, liquor, pro shop, beverages, snack bar, putting green, driving range, club memberships.
Comments: challenging nine hole course with sand and water. The course is tree lined and can play much longer than the yardage indicates. Good public track that plans to expand to 18 holes sometime in late summer 2000 or 2001.

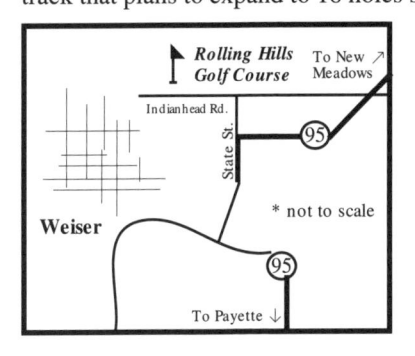

Directions: from I-84 E&W take exit #3 (Hwy 95). Proceed north on Hwy 95 for 21.7 miles. Once in Weiser take State Street through town. Look for the truck route. Proceed to Indianhead Rd. and turn left. Continue to the top of the hill. Look for signs posting the way.

Course Yardage & Par:
M-3081 yards, par 36.
W-2981 yards, par 36.
Dual tees for 18 holes:
M-6122 yards, par 72.
W-5958 yards, par 74.

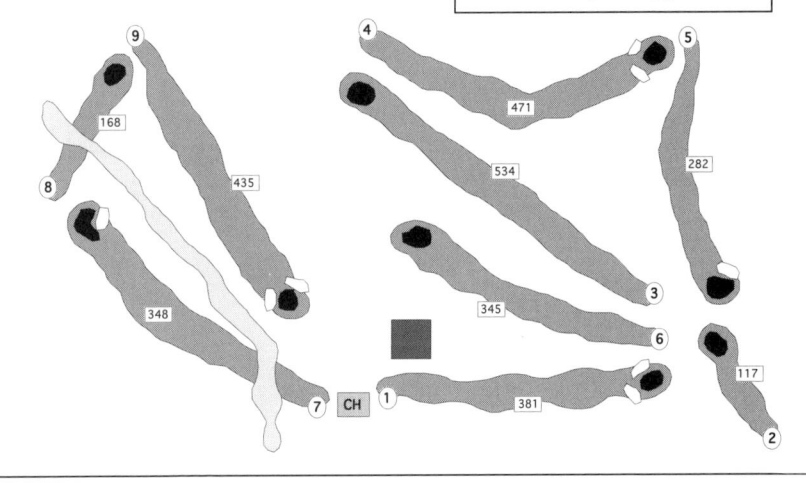

Rupert Country Club (private, 9 hole course)

200 West 85th South; Rupert, Idaho 83350
Phone: (208) 436-9168. Fax: (208) 436-9168. Internet: none.
Pro: Bob Lantz, PGA. Superintendent: Brian Sprague.
Rating/Slope: M 68.0/113; W 73.7/124. **Course record:** 63.
Green fees: private club, members & guests of members only; no credit cards.
Power cart: private club. **Pull cart:** private club. **Trail fee:** not allowed.
Reservation policy: none; private club, members & guests of members only.
Winter condition: the golf course is closed from November 1st to February 1st.
Terrain: flat (easy walking). **Tees:** all grass. **Spikes:** soft spikes only.
Services: club rentals, lessons, snack bar, beer, wine, lounge, driving range.
Comments: this course will allow some outside play, call ahead for restrictions.
The golf course is very flat but there are trees and bunkers to catch errant shots.

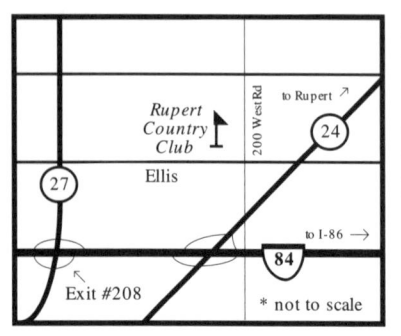

Directions: exit I-84 E&W at exit #208 to Hwy 27. Follow to the town of Paul. Turn right at Ellis. This becomes 100 S. At 200 West turn left The golf course entrance will be immediately on your left hand side. Look for signs that are posted.

Course Yardage & Par:
M-3204 yards, par 36.
W-2857 yards, par 37.
Dual tees for 18 holes:
M-6423 yards, par 71.
W-5816 yards, par 74.

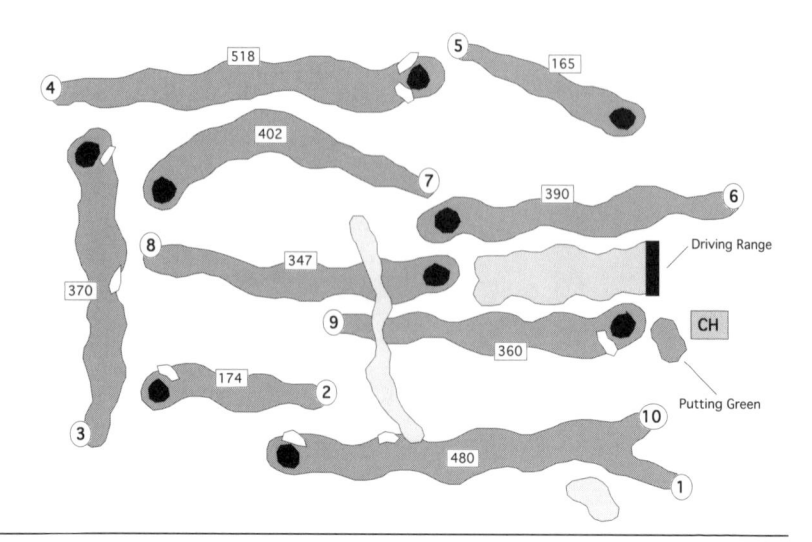

Sage Lakes Golf Course (public, 18 hole course)

100 East 65 North; Idaho Falls, Idaho 83401
Phone: (208) 528-5535. Fax: (208) 528-5542. Internet: none.
Pro: Galen E. Denning, PGA. Superintendent: Deren Bowman.
Rating/Slope: C 70.4/115; M 67.5/108; W 66.4/109. **Course record:** 64.
Green fees: $15/$10 all week long; Sr. rates; M/C, VISA, DIS.
Power cart: $15/$8. **Pull cart:** $2/$1. **Trail fee:** personal carts not allowed.
Reservation policy: please call up to 1 day in advance for your tee-time.
Winter condition: the golf course is closed from November 1st to February 1st.
Terrain: flat, some hills. **Tees:** all grass. **Spikes:** soft spikes required.
Services: club rentals, lessons, snack bar, beer, wine, pro shop, driving range.
Comments: the golf course is nicely mounded and has many water hazards to contend with. If you are in the area this is certainly a facility you should visit.

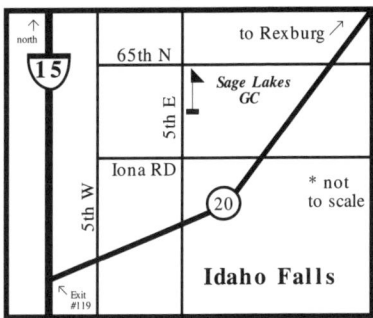

Course Yardage & Par:
C-6738 yards, par 70.
M-5973 yards, par 70.
W-5068 yards, par 70.

Directions: from Highway 20 exit for Riverside Dr/City Center. Turn right on Freemont (at the end of the exit). This becomes 5th W (E. River Road). Travel approximately 1.8 miles and turn right on 65 N. (Tower Road). Proceed .4 miles to the course on your right. Look for signs.

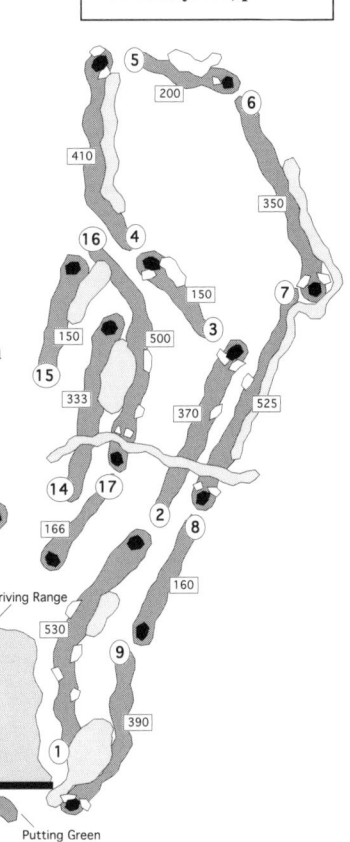

Saint Maries Golf Course (public, 9 hole course)

Route 4 Box 6; 909 Main Street; Saint Maries, Idaho 83861
Phone: (208) 245-3842. Fax: none. Internet: none.
Manager: Dave Hanley. Superintendent: Dave Kendall.
Rating/Slope: M 66.7/111; W 67.6/112. **Course record:** 19 (nine holes).
Green fees: W/D $15/$10; W/E $17/$12; Jr. rates; no credit cards.
Power cart: $19/$10. **Pull cart:** $2.50. **Trail fee:** $3 for personal carts.
Reservation policy: yes accepted. Please call 1 day in advance for tee-times.
Winter condition: the golf course is closed from November 1st to April 1st.
Terrain: relatively hilly. **Tees:** all grass. **Spikes:** no spike policy.
Services: club rentals, snack bar, restaurant, lounge, beer, wine, liquor, pro shop.
Comments: the golf course is very challenging. Sand traps, trees and lakes
come into play on several holes. Great course if want to get in a quick 9 holes.

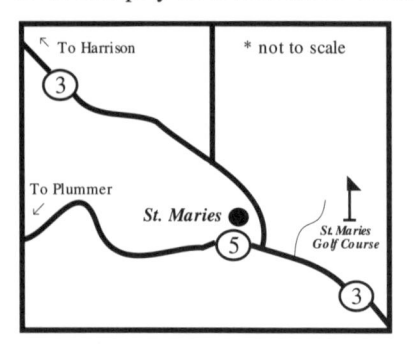

Directions: the golf course is located
60 miles east of Spokane Washington.
From I-90 E&W take exit #34 (Hwy 3).
Proceed on Hwy 3 southbound to St.
Maries. The turn off for the golf
course is 1 mile east of the town of St.
Maries on Highway 3. Look for signs.

Course Yardage & Par:
M-2644 yards, par 35.
W-2226 yards, par 35.
Dual tees for 18 holes:
M-5411 yards, par 70.
W-4870 yards, par 70.

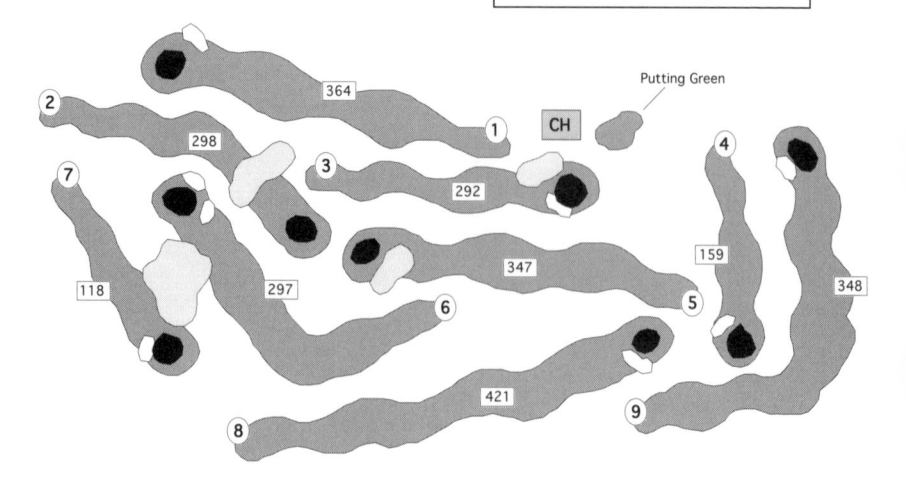

Salmon Valley Golf Course (public, 9 hole course)

Highway 28; P.O. Box 550; Salmon, Idaho 83467
Phone: (208) 756-4734. Fax: (208) 756-4734. Internet: none.
Pro: Shane Warriner, PGA. Superintendent: Larry Watkins.
Rating/Slope: M 69.0/117; W 71.3/122. **Course record:** 65.
Green fees: W/D $14/$9; W/E $15/$10; all week long; VISA, MC.
Power cart: $18/$9. **Pull cart:** $2. **Trail fee:** $5 for personal carts.
Reservation policy: not necessary. Times are on a first come first served basis.
Winter condition: the golf course is closed in winter. November to March.
Terrain: flat, some hills. **Tees:** all grass. **Spikes:** soft spikes preferred.
Services: club rentals, lessons, lounge, restaurant, beer, wine, liquor, pro
shop, beverages, driving range, putting & chipping greens, club memberships.
Comments: this course is primarily flat but does have some lateral and regular
water hazards to contend with. The course has dual tees for a full 18 hole round.

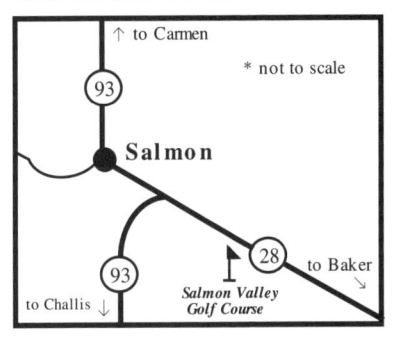

Directions: the golf course is located
right off Hwy 28 in Salmon, Idaho. Look
for a sign marking your turn to the course.

Course Yardage & Par:
M-3168 yards, par 36.
W-2778 yards, par 37.
Dual tees for 18 holes:
M-6434 yards, par 72.
W-5638 yards, par 74.

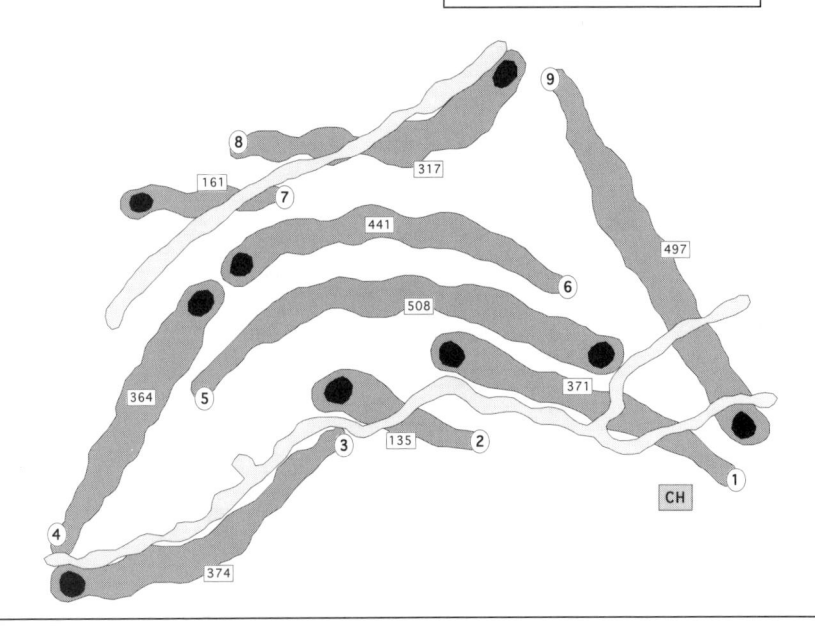

Sand Creek Golf Course (public, 18 hole course)

5200 South Hackman Road; Idaho Falls, Idaho 83405
Phone: (208) 529-1115. **Fax:** none. **Internet:** none.
Pro: John Graham, PGA. **Superintendent:** J. Schwarzenberger.
Rating/Slope: C 70.4/115; M 68.8/112; W 71.1/118. **Course record:** 63.
Green fees: W/D $12.50/$9; W/E $13.50/$10; Jr. & Sr. rates; VISA, M/C.
Power cart: $15/$7.50. **Pull cart:** $2. **Trail fee:** personal carts not allowed.
Reservation policy: yes, please call 1 day in advance for all your tee-times.
Winter condition: the course is closed from November 1st to February 15th.
Terrain: flat (easy walking). **Tees:** all grass. **Spikes:** soft spikes preferred.
Services: club rentals, lessons, snack bar, beer, wine, beverages, pro shop,
driving range, putting & chipping greens, club memberships, season passes.
Comments: well kept municipal golf course that can play very long from the
back tees. Greens are large and water comes into play on nearly every hole on
the course. One of the best public golf courses in the Idaho Falls area.

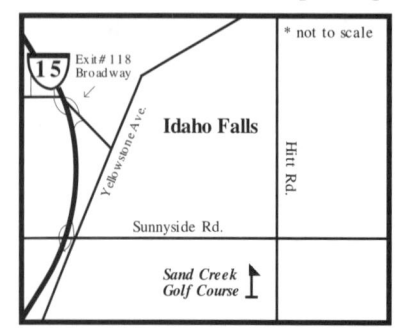

Directions: I-15 exit at Sunnyside Road.
East on Sunnyside Rd. to Hitt Road. Turn
right on Hitt Road. Proceed 3/4 mile to the
golf course. Look for signs to the course.

Course Yardage & Par:
C-6703 yards, par 72.
M-6374 yards, par 72.
W-5785 yards, par 74.

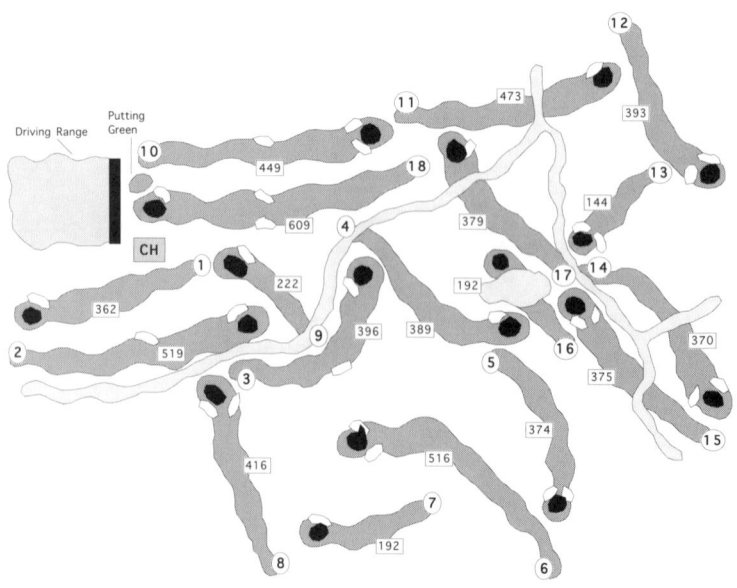

Sandpoint Elks Golf Course (public, 9 hole course)

Highway 200 East; P.O. Box 338; Sandpoint, Idaho 83864
Phone: (208) 263-4321. Fax: none. Internet: none.
Manager: Tom Tharpe. Superintendent: Tom Tharpe.
Rating/Slope: M 65.8/109; W 71.0/112. **Course record:** 60.
Green fees: $15/$10 all week long; Jr. & Sr. rates; M/C, VISA.
Power cart: $20/$10. **Pull cart:** $2. **Trail fee:** $4 for personal carts.
Reservation policy: no policy on advance tee times. First come first served.
Winter condition: the golf course is closed from November 1st to April 1st.
Terrain: flat (easy walking). **Tees:** all grass. **Spikes:** soft spikes preferred.
Services: club rentals, lessons, snack bar, restaurant, lounge, beer, wine, liquor, beverages, pro shop, lockers, chipping & putting greens, club memberships.
Comments: course is easy to walk. 2 sets of tees for a different look for 18 holes. Course gets alot of play in the summer so be sure to get there early.

Directions: the golf course is located on Highway 200E, 1/2 mile north of the Highway 95 turn off. The course is at the outskirts of town. Look for signs marking your way to the golf course.

Course Yardage & Par:
M-2897 yards, par 35.
W-2790 yards, par 35.
Dual tees for 18 holes:
M-5701 yards, par 70.
W-5452 yards, par 70.

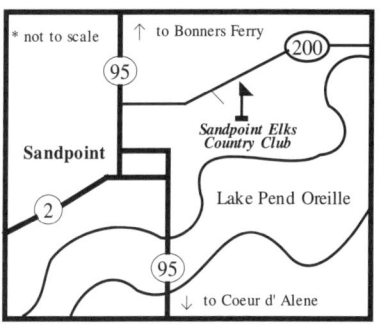

Scotch Pines Golf Course (public, 18 hole course)

10610 Scotch Pines Road; Payette, Idaho 83661
Phone: (208) 642-1829. Fax: (208) 642-1892. Internet: none.
Pro: Alan Morrison, PGA. Superintendent: Eric McCormick.
Rating/Slope: C 69.4/111; M 67.9/108; W 70.3/116. **Course record:** 63.
Green fees: $20/$14 all week long; Jr. & Sr. rates; M/C, VISA.
Power cart $20/$10. **Pull cart:** $2. **Trail fee:** $5.25 for personal carts.
Reseration policy: yes, please call 2 days in advance for your tee times.
Winter condition: the golf course is closed from November to February.
Terrain: flat, some rolling hills. **Tees:** all grass. **Spikes:** soft spikes only.
Services: club rentals, lessons, snack bar, restaurant, lounge, beer, wine, liquor,
beverages, pro shop, driving range, putting & chipping green, club memberships.
Comments: Challenging course will that will test your skill of shot making.
Fair conditioned public course that gets alot of play during the peak season.
The layout sports medium to large sized greens that are fronted by bunkers.

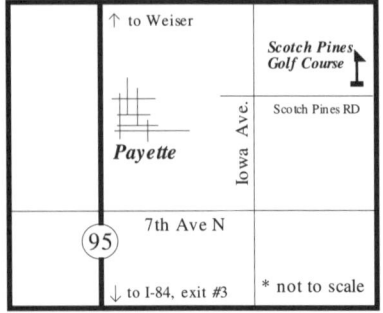

Directions: from Boise and I-84 E&W take exit #3 to Hwy 95. Proceed north on Hwy 95. When you reach 7th Ave. N turn eastbound. Proceed on 7th Ave. N for approximately 1 mile. Then turn north on Iowa for 2 miles. When you reach Scotch Pines Road take a right and follow to the golf course. Look for signs.

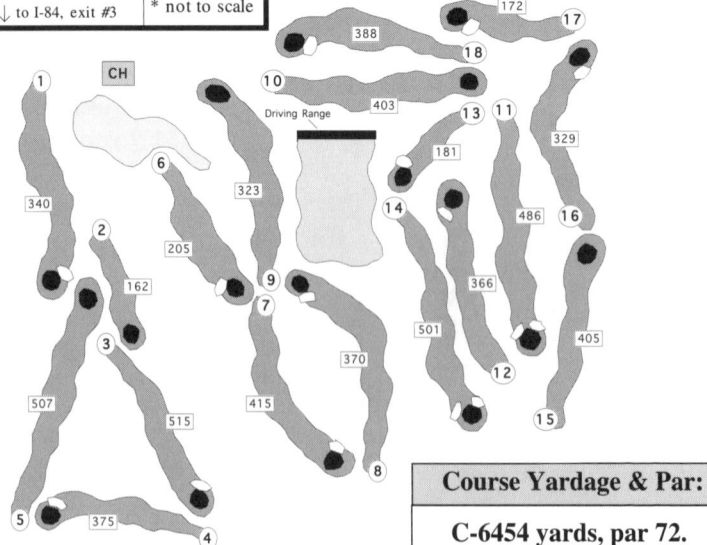

Course Yardage & Par:

C-6454 yards, par 72.
M-6087 yards, par 72.
W-5586 yards, par 72.

Shadow Valley Golf Course (public, 18 hole course)

Route 1 Highway 55; Boise, Idaho 83703
Phone: (208) 939-6699. Fax: (208) 939-9658. Internet: none.
Pro: Bud Sower, PGA. Superintendent: Victor Waffner.
Rating/Slope: C 69.6/118; M 68.6/116; W 70.6/117. **Course record:** 65.
Green fees: Monday thru Thursday $21/$14; Friday thru Sunday $30/$16;
Junior & Senior rates available; winter rates; M/C, VISA, AMEX, DIS.
Power cart: $14 per person. **Pull cart:** $2. **Trail fee:** $10 for personal carts.
Reservation policy: yes, please call 5 days in advance for your tee times.
Winter condition: good, the golf course is closed during bad weather.
Terrain: flat, some hills. **Tees:** grass. **Spikes:** soft spikes only.
Services: club rentals, lessons, snack bar, lounge, beer, pro shop, driving range.
Comments: sporty golf course that's fun to play. The golf course is anything
but boring. Excellent golf course to play if in the Boise area. Worth a trip.

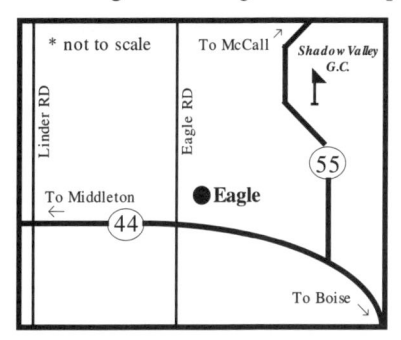

Directions: from Boise go westbound
on Highway 44 then north for 5 miles
on Highway 55 to the golf course. The
golf course is located on Highway 55.
Look for signs posted at your turn.

Course Yardage & Par:
C-6433 yards, par 72.
M-6119 yards, par 72.
W-5394 yards, par 72.

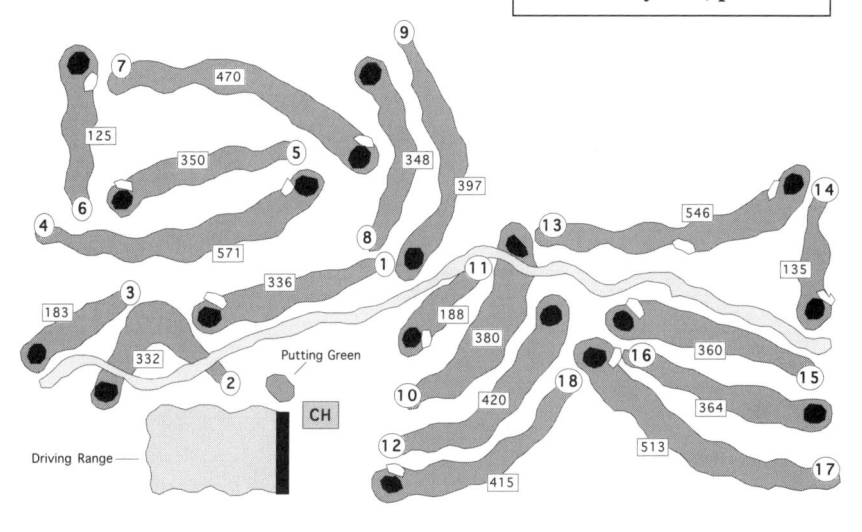

Shamrock Golf Course (public, 9 hole par 3 course)
1801 Wildwood Street; Boise, Idaho 83704
Phone: (208) 327-0780. Fax: none. Internet: none.
Pro: none. Superintendent: none.
Rating/Slope: the golf course is not rated. **Course record:** 24.
Green fees: $8 all week long; no special rates; no credit cards.
Power cart: not available. **Pull cart:** $2. **Trail fee:** personal carts not allowed.
Reservation policy: advance reservations not required. First come first served.
Winter condition: the golf course is closed during the winter months.
Terrain: flat (easy walking). **Tees:** all grass. **Spikes:** no policy.
Services: club rentals, pro shop, mini golf, driving range, lessons, pop, snacks.
Comments: great on course pro shop and golf learning center. Good course for those wanting a change of pace. Bring the first time golfer or youngster.

Directions: from I-84 E&W take the Eagle Road exit (#46). Proceed north on Eagle Road to Fairview Avenue. Turn right on Fairview Avenue. Proceed to the golf course on your left hand side ofthe road. Look for signs that are posted.

Course Yardage & Par:
M-1207 yards, par 27.
W-1207 yards, par 27.

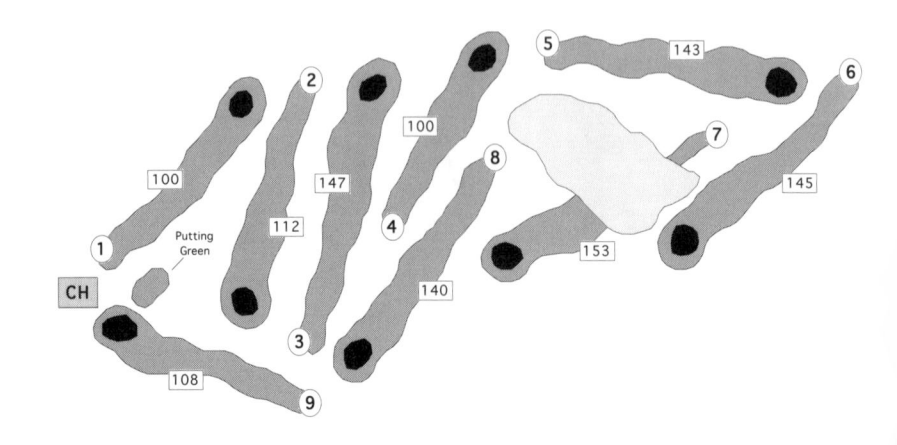

Shoshone Golf & Tennis Club (semi-private, 9 hole course)
Gold Run Mountain; P.O. Box 629; Osburn, Idaho 83849
Phone: (208) 784-0161. Fax: none. Internet: none.
Pro: Wayne "Sano" Haldi. Superintendent: unavailable.
Rating/Slope: M 69.3/119; W 73.1/128. **Course record:** 64.
Green fees: W/D $18/$12; W/E $21/$13; Jr. rates; M/C, VISA.
Power cart: $22/$11. **Pull cart:** $2. **Trail fee:** $3 for personal carts.
Reservation policy: yes, please call 7 days in advance for your tee-times.
Winter condition: the course is closed from November 1st to March 15th.
Terrain: relatively hilly. **Tees:** all grass. **Spikes:** soft spikes preferred.
Services: club rentals, lessons, snack bar, restaurant, lounge, beer, wine, liquor, beverages, pro shop, lockers, showers, driving range, putting & chipping greens.
Comments: water and sand come into play on some holes. The golf course is located on a mountain top in a very picturesque setting. Good public track.

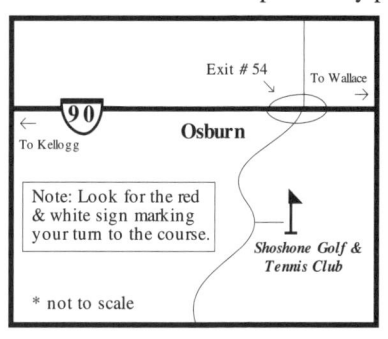

Directions: from I-90 E&W take exit #54. The golf course is located 1.5 miles off freeway. Look for a sign to the golf course from the freeway.

Course Yardage & Par:
M-3176 yards, par 36.
W-2991 yards, par 37.
Dual tees for 18 holes:
M-6270 yards, par 72.
W-5959 yards, par 74.

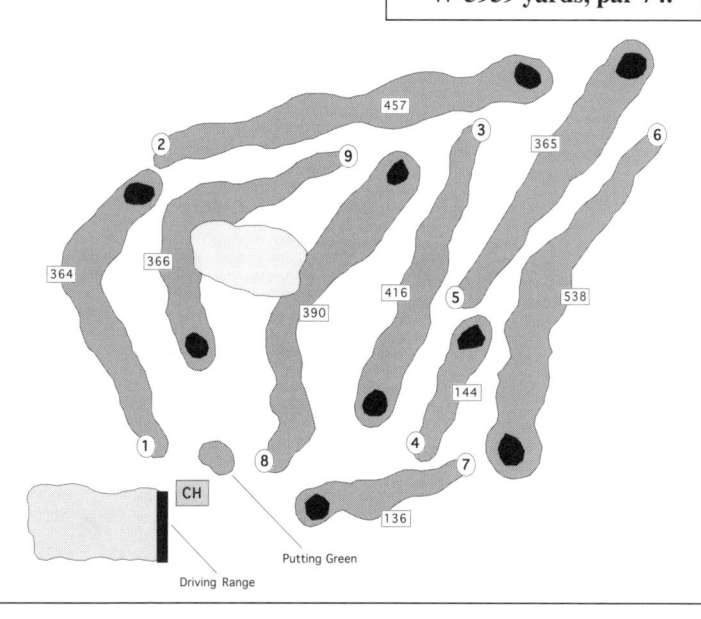

Silver Sage Golf Course (private-military, 18 hole course)

366 SVS/SVRG; #4109; Mountain Home AFB, Idaho 83647
Phone: (208) 828-6559. Fax: (208) 828-6317. Internet: none.
Manager: Ray Newman. Superintendent: John Mills.
Rating/Slope: M 70.5/116; W 70/108. **Course record:** 64.
Green fees: military and their guests, sliding scale according to rank.
Power cart: private club. **Pull cart:** private club. **Trail fee:** private club.
Reservation policy: none needed. Military and their guests only.
Winter condition: the golf course is closed during the winter months.
Terrain: flat (easy walking). **Tees:** all grass. **Spikes:** soft spikes required.
Services: club rentals, lessons, snack bar, beer, wine, pro shop, driving range.
Comments: this course is one of the longest tracks in the state of Idaho. Many mature trees line the fairways and generous sized sand bunkers are strategically placed to catch your errant shots. Great course that is a must play if you can.

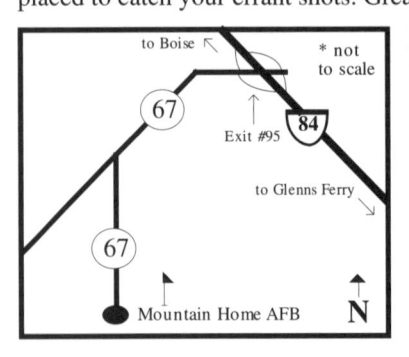

Directions: from I-84 take the exit for Exit #95 Idaho 67 (Grandview Road) in Mountain Home. Take the south cutoff on Idaho 67, the road ends at the military base where the course is located.

Course Yardage & Par:
C-6759 yards, par 72.
M-6533 yards, par 72.
W-5630 yards, par 74.

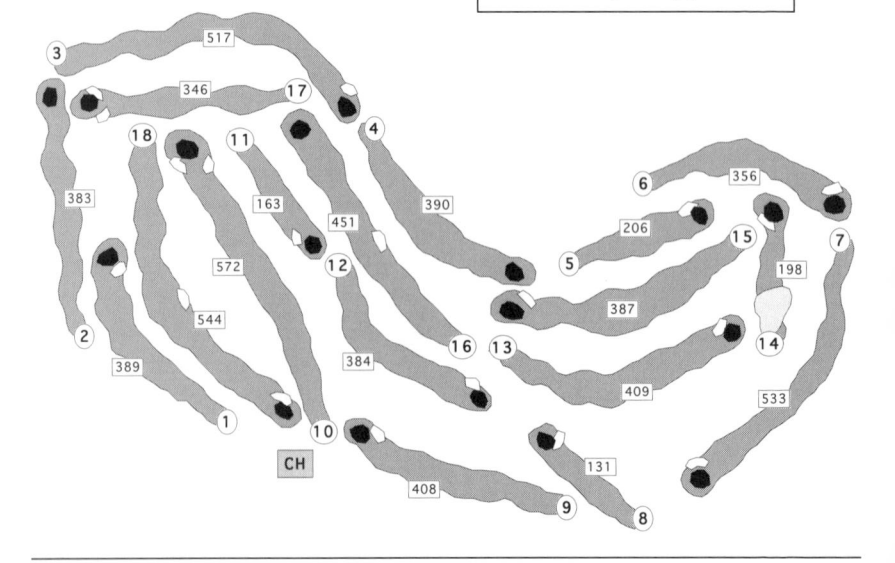

Soldier Mountain Ranch & Resort (public, 9 hole course)

400 West & 660 N; P.O. Box 279; Fairfield, Idaho 83327
Phone: (208) 764-2506. Fax: none. Internet: none.
Manager: Sheryl Anderson. Superintendent: Sheryl Anderson.
Rating/Slope: M 70.5/124; W 70.9/113. Course record: 32 (9 holes).
Green fees: $16/$12 all week long; no special rates; M/C, VISA.
Power cart: $15/$10. **Pull cart:** $3. **Trail fee:** no charge.
Reservation policy: not necessary. Times are on a first come first served basis.
Winter condition: the golf course is closed from November to March.
Terrain: flat, some hills. **Tees:** all grass. **Spikes:** soft spikes preferred.
Services: club rentals, lounge, restaurant, beer, wine, liquor, small pro shop.
Comments: this is a peaceful resort course located in the foothills at the base of Soldier Mountain. The resort also offers tennis, hot tubs, swimming, home cooked meals in the main lodge and 19 separate guest houses all with kitchens.

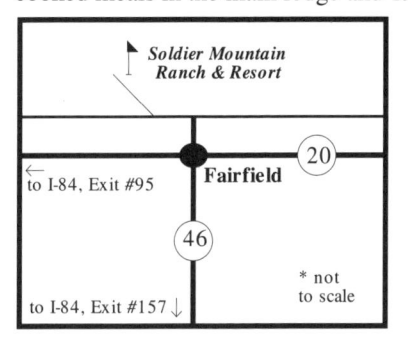

Directions: from I-84 E&W take exit #95 (Hwy 20). Proceed toward Fairfield on Hwy 20. From Highway 20 turn on Shaw Road. Travel north 2 miles to Baseline. Turn left. When Baseline T's turn left. Proceed .25 miles and turn right at the sign, the resort is located at the end of the road. The resort is located 6.5 miles NW of Fairfield.

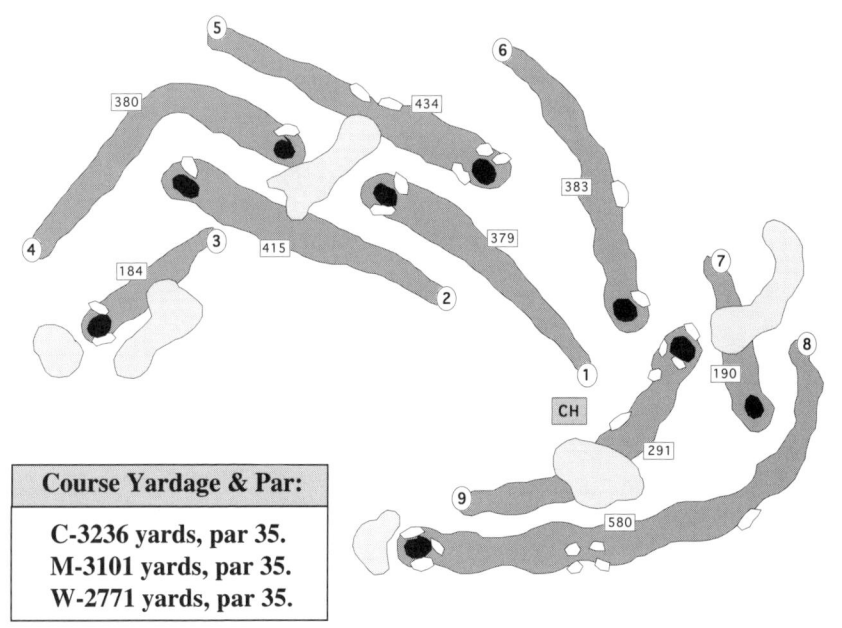

Course Yardage & Par:

C-3236 yards, par 35.
M-3101 yards, par 35.
W-2771 yards, par 35.

Spurwing Country Club (private, 18 hole course)

6800 North Spurwing Way; Meridian, Idaho 83642
Phone: (208) 884-4445. Fax: (208) 887-9967. Internet: www.spurwing.com
Pro: Jay M. Frank, PGA. Superintendent: Jerry Troy.
Rating/slope: T 73.1/120; C 70.9/113; M 69.5/111; W 70.2/117. **Record:** 65.
Green fees: private club, members & guests only.
Power cart: private club. **Pull cart:** private club. **Trail fee:** private club.
Reservation policy: private club members & guests of members only.
Winter condition: the golf course is closed during inclement weather.
Terrain: some hills. **Tees:** all grass. **Spikes:** soft spikes only.
Services: club rentals, lessons, snack bar, restaurant, lounge, beer, wine, liquor, pop, pro shop, driving range, putting & chipping greens, club memberships.
Comments: Spurwing is one of the finest private courses in the state of Idaho. The course features expansive meadows, lakes and streams. Greens are large and are bordered by 30 green side bunkers and huge berms. Great course.

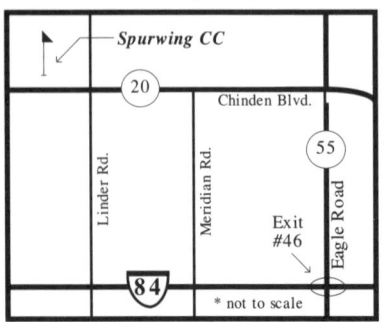

Directions: the golf course is located off of Chinden Boulevard in Meridian Idaho. From I-84 E&W take exit #46 (Eagle Rd., Hwy 55). Proceed northbound off the exit on Hwy 55 to Chinden Blvd. Turn left on Chinden. Proceed on Chinden until you reach the corners of Linder Rd. and Chinden Blvd. where the course is located.

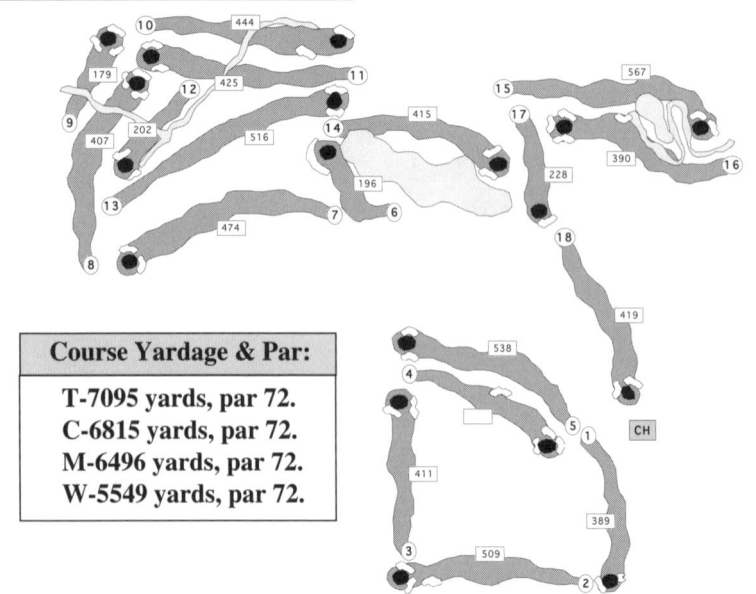

Course Yardage & Par:
T-7095 yards, par 72.
C-6815 yards, par 72.
M-6496 yards, par 72.
W-5549 yards, par 72.

Stoneridge Country Club (semi-private, 18 hole course)

1 Blanchard Road; P.O. Box 277; Blanchard, Idaho 83804
Phone: (208) 437-4682. Fax: none. Internet: none.
Pro: Doug Phares, PGA. Superintendent: Tom Brown.
Rating/Slope: C 71.4/127; M 69.4/123; W 72.4/126. **Course record:** 64.
Green fees: $20/$15 all week long; Jr & Sr rates; M/C, VISA.
Power cart: $23/$13. **Pull cart:** $3.50. **Trail fee:** $5 for personal carts.
Reservation policy: yes, please call 7 days in advance for your tee times.
Winter condition: the course is closed from November 1st to March 1st.
Terrain: relatively hilly. **Tees:** grass. **Spikes:** soft spikes preferred.
Services: club rentals, lessons, snack bar, restaurant, lounge, beer, wine, liquor, pop, pro shop, driving range, putting & chipping greens, club memberships.
Comments: well kept grounds, excellent greens, beautiful flowers and great golf will be found at Stoneridge. Friendly course that will not disappoint.

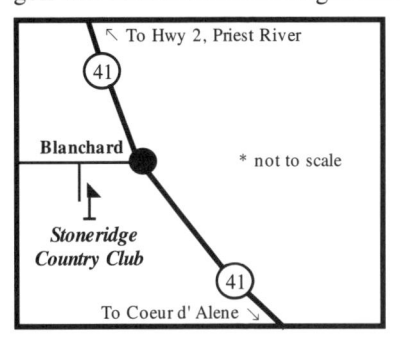

Directions: from I-90 E&W take exit #7 (Hwy 41). Proceed northbound on Hwy 41 to Blanchard, Idaho. The golf course is located 35 miles north of Coeur d'Alene, Idaho on Highway 41. Look for signs marking your way to the course.

Course Yardage & Par:
C-6522 yards, par 72.
M-6141 yards, par 72.
W-5678 yards, par 72.

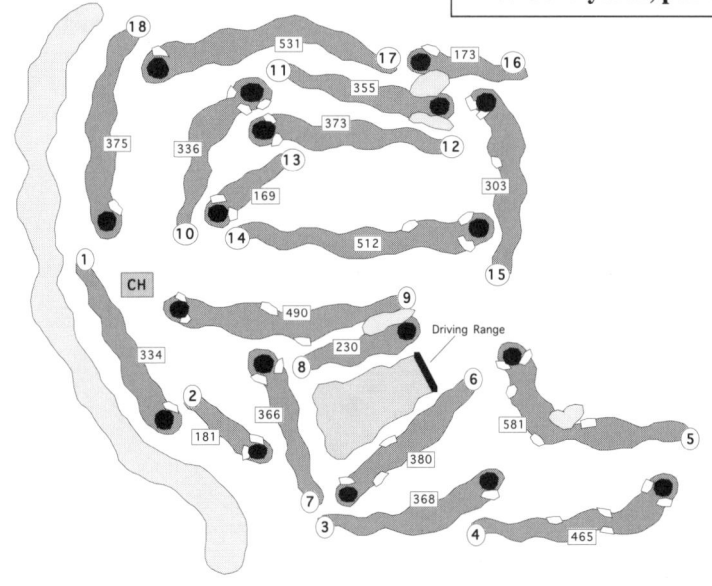

Sun Valley Resort Golf Course (resort, 18 hole course)

Highway 75 & Sun Valley Road; Sun Valley, Idaho 83353
Phone: (208) 622-2251. Fax: (208) 622-2236. Internet: www.sunvalley.com
Pro: Doyle Corbett, PGA. Superintendent: Ken Zimmerman.
Rating/Slope: C 71.4/126; M 68.9/120; W 68.5/116. **Course record:** 64.
Green fees: $92 (non guests); $80 (for guests); M/C, VISA, DIS, AMEX.
Power cart: $18/$12. **Pull cart:** none. **Trail fee:** not allowed.
Reservation policy: yes, call 30 days in advance, must confirm 2 days ahead.
Winter condition: the golf course is closed from November 1st to May 1st.
Terrain: relatively hilly. **Tees:** all grass. **Spikes:** soft spikes required.
Services: club rentals, lessons, snack bar, beer, wine, pro shop, driving range.
Comments: the golf course features elevated tees, tree lined fairways and well bunkered greens. This track will challenge the golfer at every turn. A very picturesque golf course and resort that is worth a long weekend or special trip.

Directions: from Hwy 75 N&S go into Ketchum, Idaho. Turn right at Sun Valley Road (first light). Proceed for 1 mile to the course. Look for signs posted along your way.

Sun Valley Resort Golf Course

Ketchum

Sun Valley Rd.

75

Elkhorn Rd.

* not to scale

Course Yardage & Par:
C-6565 yards, par 72.
M-6057 yards, par 72.
W-5241 yards, par 72.

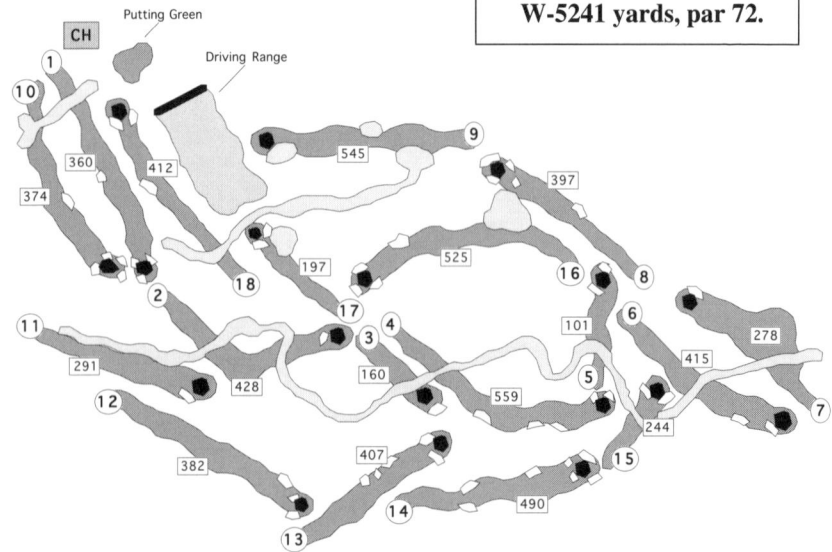

South Central Region

Sun Valley's Elkhorn Resort G.C. (semi-private , 18 hole course)
#1 Elkhorn Road; P.O. Box 6009; Sun Valley, Idaho 83354
Phone: 800-355-4676; (208) 622-4511. Fax: (208) 622-2236. Internet: none.
Pro: David Hardison, PGA. Superintendent: Ken Zimmerman.
Rating/Slope: C 71.4/133; M 68.9/120; W 68.5/116. **Course record:** 62.
Green fees: $98 all week long; no special rates; M/C, VISA, DIS, AMEX.
Power cart: included in green fee. **Pull cart:** none. **Trail fee:** not allowed.
Reservation policy: 2 weeks in advance for afternoon tee-times. 2 days for morning tee-times. You may make times any time with your hotel confirmation.
Winter condition: the golf course is closed during the winter months.
Terrain: flat, some big hills. **Tees:** all grass. **Spikes:** soft spikes only.
Services: club rentals, lessons, snack bar, restaurant, pro shop, driving range.
Comments: golf course rated in the top 75 resort courses by *Golf Digest* in 1989. This beautiful layout is also ranked in the top five golf courses in Idaho. This golf course and resort are worth a special trip for vacation or long weekend.

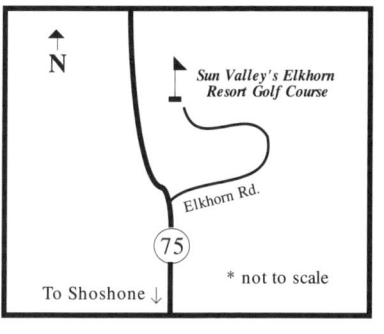

Directions: from Hwy 75 proceed eastbound on Elkhorn Road for 3.1 miles to the golf course. Look for signs marking your way to the resort and the golf course.

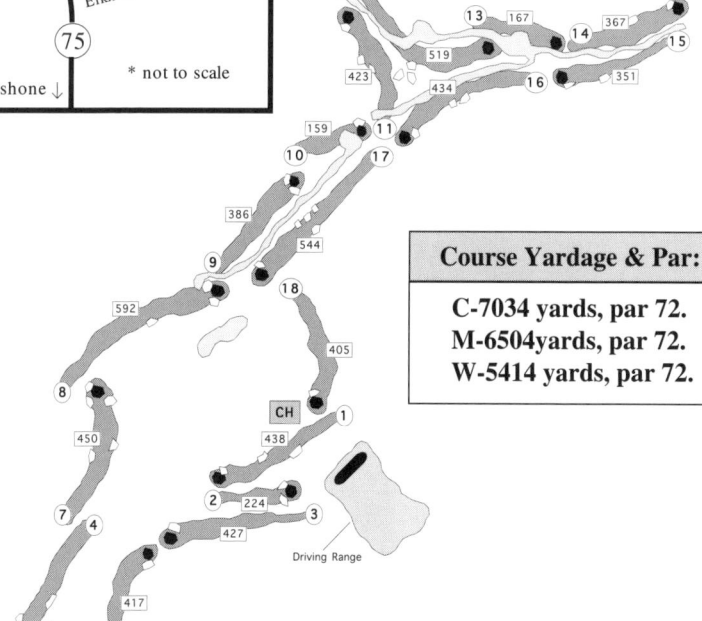

Course Yardage & Par:

C-7034 yards, par 72.
M-6504yards, par 72.
W-5414 yards, par 72.

Targhee Village Golf Course (public, 9 hole course)

Stateline & Golf Course Roads; P.O. Box 707; Driggs, Idaho 83422
Phone: (208) 354-8577. Fax: none. Internet: none.
Pro: teaching pro in season. Superintendent: unavailable.
Rating/Slope: M 68.5/115; W 67.2/115. Course record: 63.
Green fees: $10 all week long; no credit cards accepted.
Power cart: $8 per 9 holes. Pull cart: $2. Trail fee: not allowed.
Reservation policy: not needed unless you have a large group.
Winter condition: the golf course is closed from November 1st to May 1st.
Terrain: flat, some hills. Tees: all grass. Spikes: soft spikes preferred.
Services: club rentals, snack bar, putting green, driving range.
Comments: this course is located right on the Idaho Wyoming border with the golf course being in Wyoming. Greens are open in the front leaving the golfer with the ability to run the ball up to the hole. Fair conditioned public golf course.

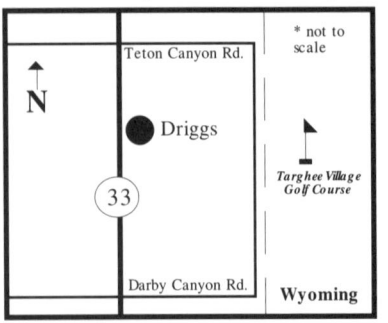

Directions: from Highway 33 take the exit for Driggs and travel eastbound to Stateline Road. The golf course is located on Stateline Road and Golf Course Road. Look for signs marking your turn.

Course Yardage & Par:
C-3193 yards, par 35.
M-2988 yards, par 35.
W-2659 yards, par 35.

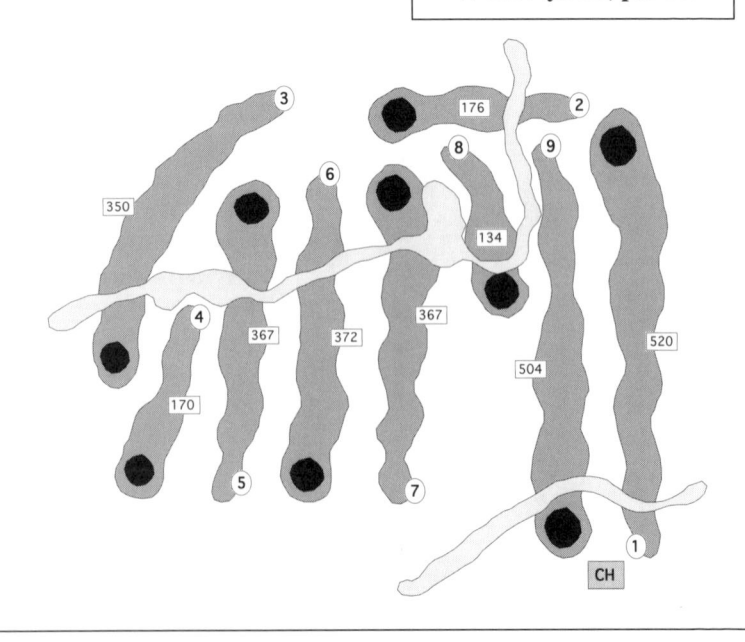

Terrace Lakes Resort Golf Course (semi-private, 18 hole course)

101 Holiday Drive; P.O. Box 4201; Garden Valley, Idaho 83622
Phone: (208) 462-3250. Fax: none. Internet: none.
Pro: Brent Fleshman, PGA. Superintendent: Eric Randall.
Rating/Slope: C 69.3/121; M 68.0/118; W 68.2/110. **Course record:** 66.
Green fees: Monday-Thur. $20; Fri.-Sunday & Holidays $30 (non members).
Power cart: $20/$10. **Pull cart:** $5. **Trail fee:** for club members only.
Reservation policy: please call in advance for all your tee-times.
Winter condition: the golf course is closed from November to March.
Terrain: relatively hilly. **Tees:** all grass. **Spikes:** soft spikes preferred.
Services: club rentals, restaurant, lounge, tennis courts, geothermal pool, motel.
Comments: this course is nestled in the mountains and provides some beautiful
views. Memberships available for those wanting a vacation spot. Call for details.
The course allows some outside play on a daily basis so be sure to call ahead.

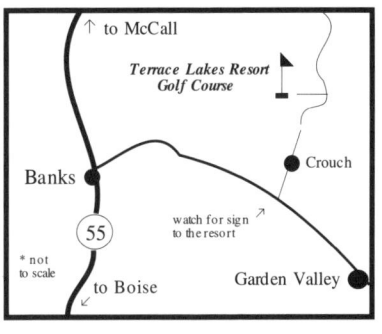

Directions: the golf course is located 40
miles north of Boise on Hwy 55 on your
way to Banks. Exit Hwy 55 at the Banks
Lowman Hwy traveling northeast. Go 8
miles and turn left at the Crouch turnoff.
The course is located 4 miles north of
Crouch, look for a rock sign indicating
the turn for the golf course.

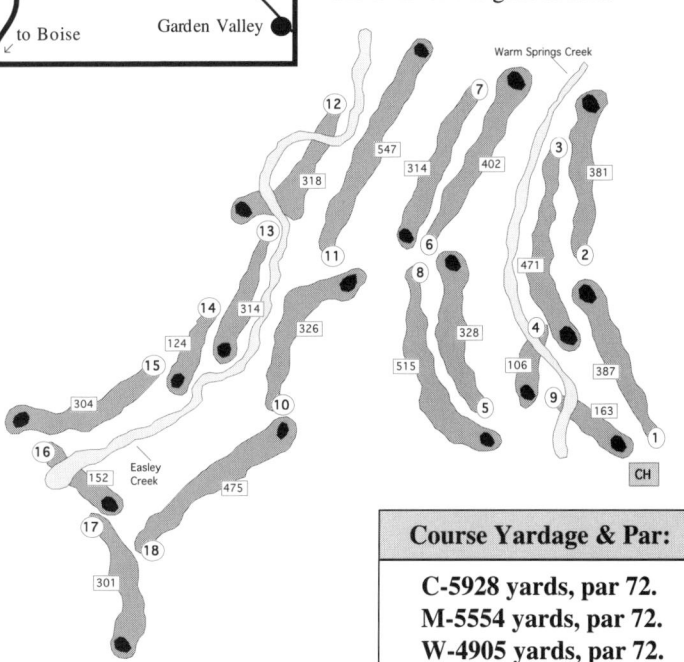

Course Yardage & Par:
C-5928 yards, par 72.
M-5554 yards, par 72.
W-4905 yards, par 72.

Teton Lakes Golf Course (public, 18 hole course)

1014 N 2000 W; Rexburg, Idaho 83440
Phone: (208) 359-3036. Fax: none. Internet: none.
Pro: Duffy McFarland, PGA. Superintendent: Darin Bowman.
Rating/Slope: C 69.4/119; M 66.6/112; W 68.6/121. **Course record:** 65.
Green fees: $12.50/$9.50 all week long; no special rates; VISA, M/C, DIS.
Power cart: $15/$7.50. **Pull cart:** $2. **Trail fee:** $7 for personal carts.
Reservation policy: yes call up to 2 days in advance for your tee-times.
Winter condition: the golf course is closed from November 1st to April 1st.
Terrain: flat, some hills. **Tees:** all grass. **Spikes:** soft spikes required.
Services: club rentals, lessons, restaurant, snack bar, beer, wine, beverages, showers, lockers, driving range, pro shop, putting green, club memberships.
Comments: this course is always kept in great shape. Fairways are flat with mounding around the perimeter. Greens are large with bunkers coming in play on several holes. The back nine has water so have a well stocked bag of balls.

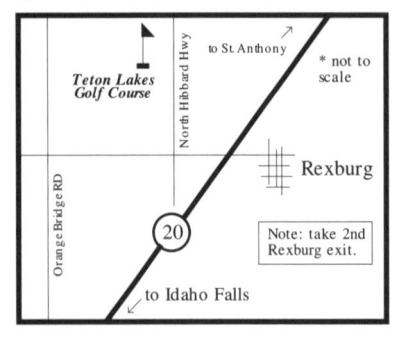

Directions: from Highway 20 North take the 2nd exit in Rexburg. Travel west for .5 miles and then turn north on N 3000W (Orange Bridge Road). Proceed 1 mile to the golf course which is located on the North Hibbard Highway (W 2000 N).

Course Yardage & Par:
C-6258 yards, par 71.
M-5768 yards, par 71.
W-5202 yards, par 71.

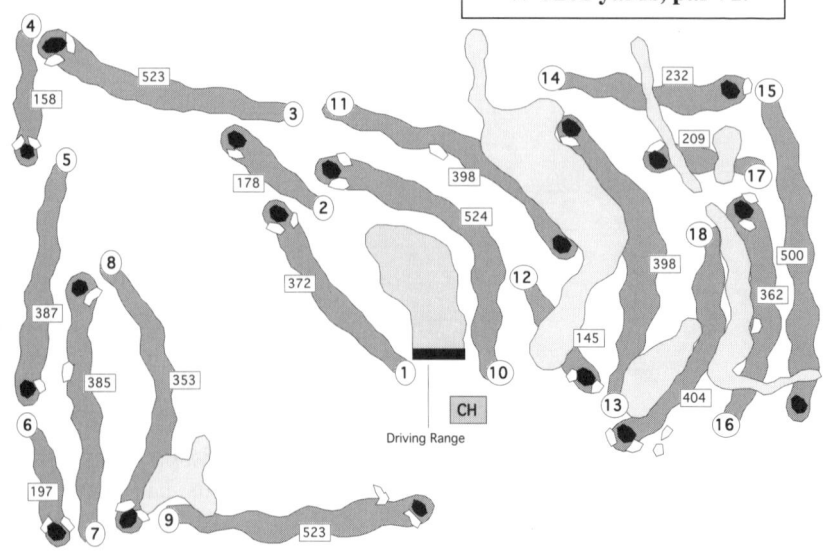

Thunder Canyon Golf Course (public, 9 hole course)

9898 East Merrick Road; Lava Hot Springs, Idaho 83246
Phone: (208) 776-5048. Fax: none. Internet: none.
Pro: Dick Andreasen, PGA. Superintendent: Dick Andreasen.
Rating/Slope: C 64.1/100; M 63.6/98; W 64.0/100. **Course record:** 58.
Green fees: W/D $11/$7; W/E $13/$8; no credit cards.
Power cart: $16/$8. **Pull cart:** $3/$2. **Trail fee:** $2 for personal carts.
Reservation policy: yes, please call 2 days in advance for all your tee times.
Winter condition: the golf course is closed from late October to April 1st.
Terrain: relatively hilly. **Tees:** all grass. **Spikes:** soft spikes preferred.
Services: club rentals, lessons, snack bar, beer, wine, liquor, pro shop.
Comments: this public course is surrounded by mountains and scenic views.
A stream crosses several holes and is a major factor on this nine hole course.

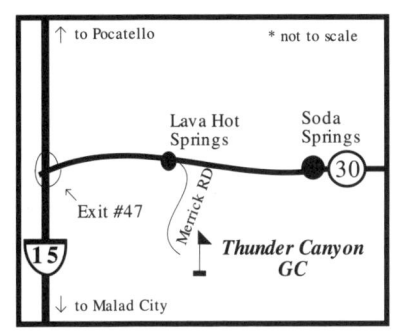

Directions: the golf course is located 12 miles west of the McCammon cutoff on Hwy US 91. Take Highway 30 to Lava Hot Springs. Turn west on Main Street to 4th Street. Turn left on 4th Street and continue 1.5 miles to the golf course.

Course Yardage & Par:
C-2905 yards, par 35.
M-2815 yards, par 35.
W-2397 yards, par 35.

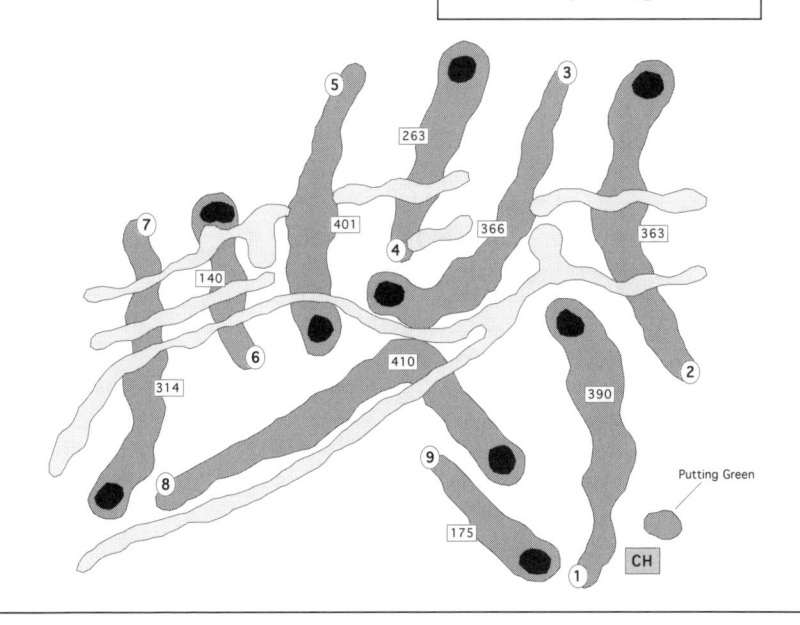

Twin Falls Municipal Golf Course (public, 18 hole course)

Grandview Drive; P.O. Box 1433; Twin Falls, Idaho 83301
Phone: (208) 733-3326. Fax: (208) 736-1514. Internet: none.
Pro: Mike Hamblin, PGA. Superintendent: Kevin Packard.
Rating/Slope: M 64.8/115; W 66.7/108. **Course record:** 58.
Green fees: W/D $12/$9; W/E & Holidays $14; Jr. & Sr. rates; M/C, VISA.
Power cart: $20/$10. **Pull cart:** $3. **Trail fee:** $9 for personal carts.
Reservation policy: call on Friday for W/E's & holidays. 1 day ahead for rest.
Winter condition: the golf course is closed from November to February.
Terrain: flat (easy walking). **Tees:** all grass. **Spikes:** soft spikes preferred.
Services: club rentals, lessons, snack bar, restaurant, beer, wine, pro shop,
lockers, driving range, putting & chipping greens, bunkers, club memberships.
Comments: well conditioned public golf course. The track is very easy to walk
and sports small, flat greens. Fairways are wide with generous landing areas.

Directions: I-84 E&W take the Twin
Falls exit #173. Follow into town on Blue
Lakes Boulevard. Turn right on Addison
Avenue proceed for 2 miles then turn left
on Grandview Drive to the golf course.

Course Yardage & Par:
M-5326 yards, par 68.
W-5067 yards, par 72.

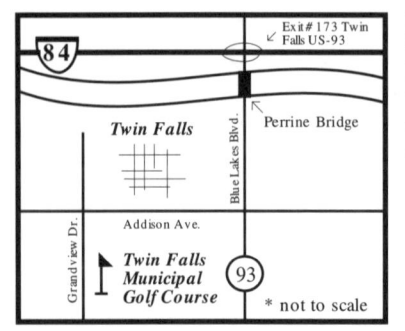

Driving Range

Twin Lakes Village (semi-private, 18 hole course)

2600 E Village Boulevard; Route 4 Box V-551; Rathdrum, Idaho 83858
Phone: (208) 687-1311. **Fax:** (208) 687-0999. **Internet:** none.
Pro: Steve Caruso, PGA. **Superintendent:** Terry Holt.
Rating/Slope: C 69.1/120; M 67.5/116; W 71.0/127. **Course record:** 65.
Green fees: $30/$18; Jr & Sr rates; winter rates; 10 play pass; M/C, VISA.
Power cart: $23/$12. **Pull cart:** $3. **Trail fee:** $5 for personal carts.
Reservation policy: yes, please call 1 week in advance for your tee-times.
Winter condition: the golf course is closed from November to April.
Terrain: flat, some hills. **Tees:** all grass. **Spikes:** soft spikes only.
Services: club rentals, lessons, snack bar, restaurant, lounge, beer, wine, liquor, pro shop, showers, putting & chipping greens, driving range, club memberships.
Comments: course is very wooded leaving the fairways narrow in spots. Eight beautiful ponds and lakes come into play. Excellent facility that is worth a trip.

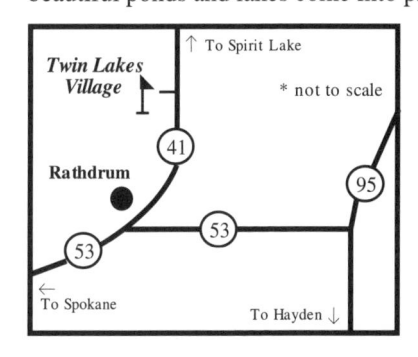

Directions: from I-90 E&W take exit #7 (Hwy 41) and head northbound for 12.6 miles. The golf course is located 4 miles north of Rathdrum Idaho on Hwy 41. Look for signs posted along the way to the course. The way is well marked.

Course Yardage & Par:
C-6158 yards, par 71.
M-5836 yards, par 71.
W-5362 yards, par 72.

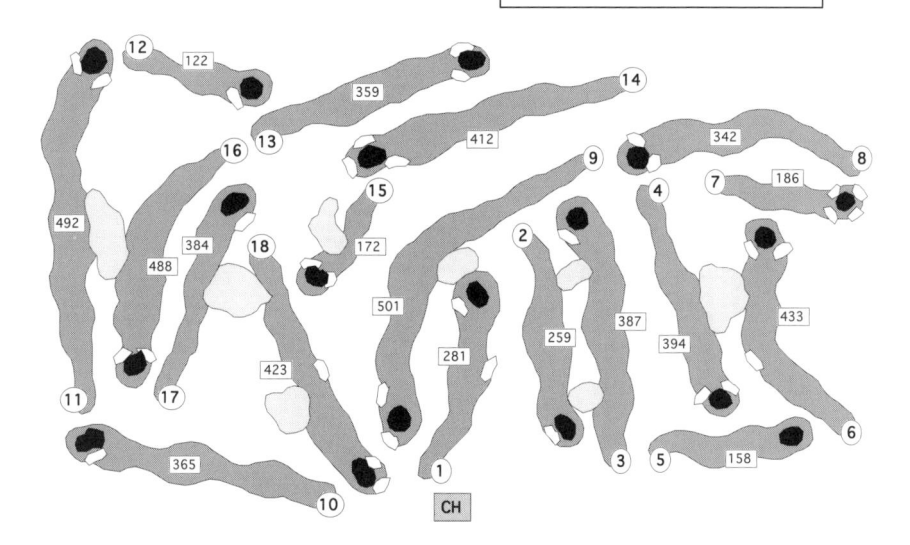

University of Idaho Golf Course (public, 18 hole course)

1215 Nez Perce Drive; Moscow, Idaho 83843
Phone: (208) 885-6171. **Fax:** (208) 885-0558. **Internet:** www.uidaho.edu/golf
Pro: Dawes Marlatt, PGA. **Superintendent:** Michael Snyder.
Rating/Slope: C 70.5/124; M 67.9/118; W 71.9/121. **Course record:** 64.
Green fees: W/D $18/$14; W/E $20; students & Sr. rates; M/C, VISA, DIS.
Power cart: $22/$12. **Pull cart:** $2.50. **Trali fee:** $5 for personal carts.
Reservation policy: yes, please call 1 week in advance for tee-times.
Winter condition: the golf course is closed from November 1st to March 1st.
Terrain: very hilly. **Tees:** all grass. **Spikes:** soft spikes required.
Services: club rentals, lessons, snack bar, lounge, beer, wine, liquor, pro shop,
lockers, driving range with target greens, putting & chipping greens.
Comments: tough windy conditions and hilly terrain put a premium on your
shot making. Good public golf course that can play very long from the back tees.

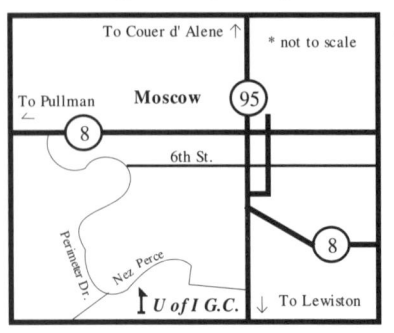

Directions: the golf course is located on
the west edge of the University of Idaho
campus. If going north or south on Hwy
95 turn west on 6th Street. Then turn left
at Perimeter Drive. The golf course will
be at the top of the hill. Look for signs.

Course Yardage & Par:
C-6637 yards, par 72.
M-6154 yards, par 72.
W-5770 yards, par 72.

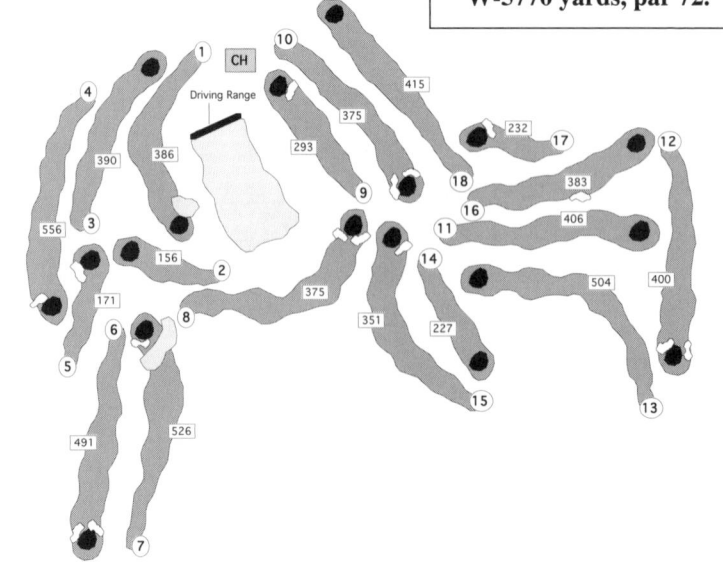

Valley Club, The (private, 18 hole course)

Mailing address: P.O. Box 252; Sun Valley, Idaho 83353
Physical address: 100 Club View Drive N; Hailey, Idaho 83333
Phone: (208) 788-5400. **Fax:** (208) 788-5702. **Internet: tvclub@micron.net**
Pro: Scott Syms, PGA. **Superintendent:** Stephen E. Maas.
Rating/Slope: T 72.6/128; C 68.4/115; M 66.9/111; W 69.1/118. **Record:** 66.
Green fees: private club members & guests of members only.
Power cart: private club. **Pull cart:** private club. **Trail fee:** not allowed.
Reservation policy: private club members & guests of members only.
Winter condition: closed during winter, approximately Nov. 1st - March 31st.
Terrain: flat, some hills. **Tees:** all grass. **Spikes:** soft spikes only.
Services: lessons, driving range, putting green, full service ammenities.
Comments: the course was co-designed by Hale Irwin and opened for play in 1996. Estate style homesites, tennis courts, and a swimming pool are among the amenities that are offered by this exclusive club. Beautiful private golf club.

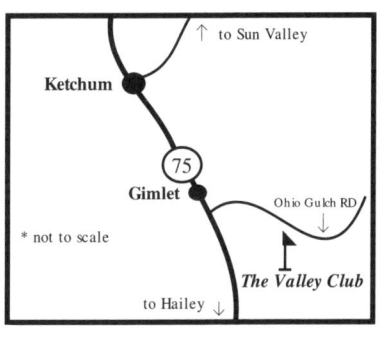

Directions: the golf course is located 4 miles north of Hailey, Idaho. From Hwy 75 turn eastbound on Ohio Gulch Road. Take the first right and proceed to the golf course.

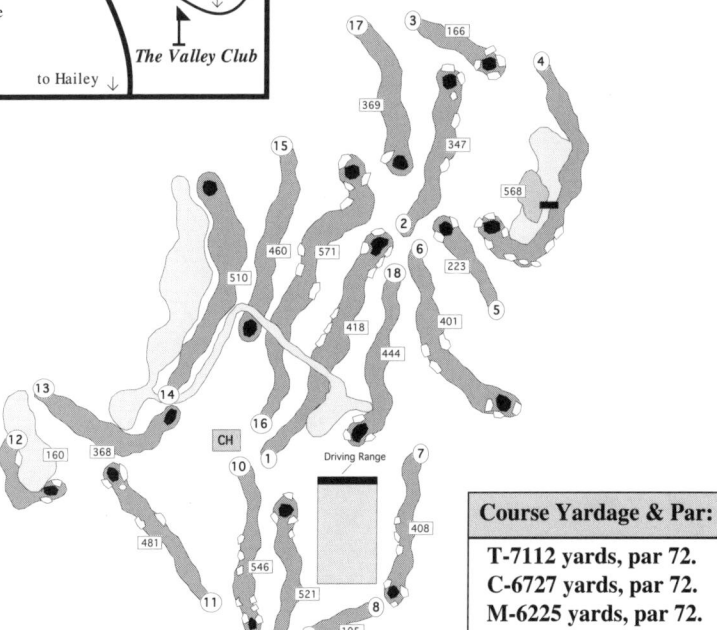

Course Yardage & Par:
T-7112 yards, par 72.
C-6727 yards, par 72.
M-6225 yards, par 72.
W-5843 yards, par 72.

Vineyard Greens Golf Course (public, 9 hole course)

795 West Madison; Glenns Ferry, Idaho 83623
Phone: (208) 366-2313. Fax: (208) 366-2458. Internet: none.
Owners: Roger & Nancy Jones. Manager: Rick Burke.
Rating/Slope: M 61.3/99; W 60.2/98. **Course record:** 61 (18 holes).
Green fees: W/D $16/$14; W/E $20/$12; no special rates; VISA, M/C.
Power cart: $16/$10. **Pull cart:** $3. **Trail fee:** $3 for personal carts.
Reservation policy: please call ahead. No time limit. A must on the weekends.
Winter condition: the golf course is open all year long, weather permitting.
Terrain: flat, some hills. **Tees:** all grass. **Spikes:** soft spikes required.
Services: club rentals, lounge, restaurant, beer, wine, pro shop, driving range.
Conunents: this course is uniquely situated at the Carmella Vineyards Winery.
Newer golf course that opened in 1993 is quickly becoming very popular with
the local crowd. Water and sand bunkers are the primary hazards.

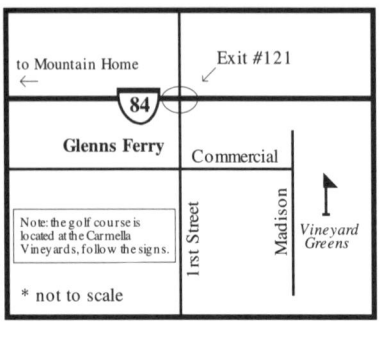

Directions: from I-84 E&W take exit #121 to Glenns Ferry. Follow 1st street to Commercial. Turn left on Commercial. Follow Commercial to your turn on Madison and the golf course. The clubhouse will be located on your left hand side. Watch for signs along the way.

Course Yardage & Par:
M-2214 yards, par 34.
W-2093 yards, par 34.

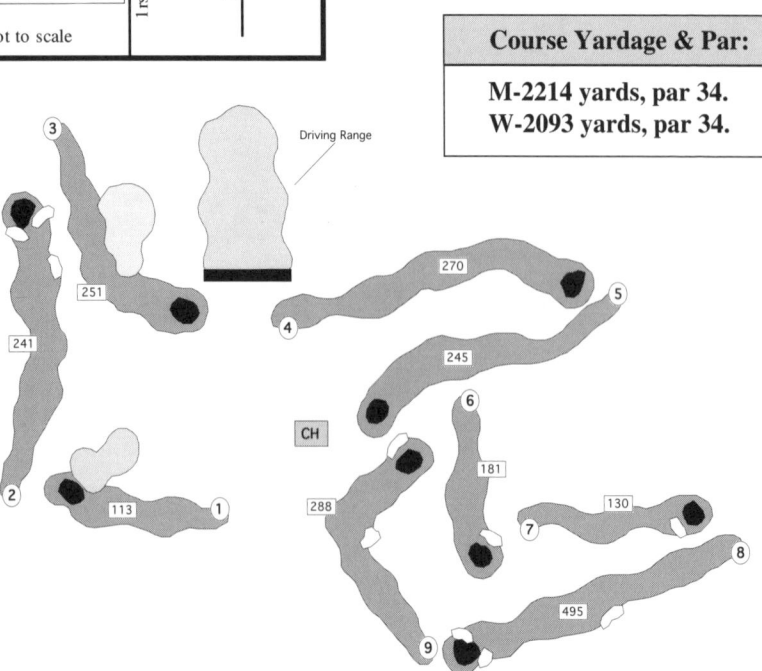

Warm Springs Golf Club (public, 18 hole course)

2495 Warm Springs Avenue; Boise, Idaho 83712
Phone: (208) 343-5661. Fax: (208) 343-5680. Internet: none.
Pro: Blake Mason, PGA. Superintendent: Lee Monroe.
Rating/Slope: C 70.1/117; M 68.7/114; W 70.7/117. **Course record:** 60.
Green fees: W/D $17; W/E $21; Sr. rates; winter rates; M/C, VISA.
Power cart: $18/$9. **Pull cart:** $2. **Trail fee:** $6 for personal carts.
Reservation policy: yes, please call 7 days in advance for your tee-times.
Winter condition: the golf course is open all year long, dry conditions.
Terrain: flat (easy walking). **Tees:** all grass. **Spikes:** soft spikes only.
Services: club rentals, lessons, snack bar, restaurant, beer, coolers, pro shop,
beverages, lockers, driving range, club memberships, putting & chipping greens.
Comments: friendly golf course that has a very courteous staff to serve you.
Well maintained facility that is worth a trip. Course is flat and easy to walk.

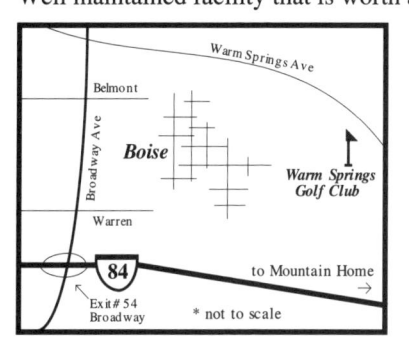

Directions: from I-84 exit at Broadway.
Go north on Broadway to Warm
Springs Avenue. East on Warm Springs
to the golf course approximately 2 miles
ahead. Watch for signs that are posted.

Course Yardage & Par:
C-6708 yards, par 72.
M-6281 yards, par 72.
W-5659 yards, par 72.

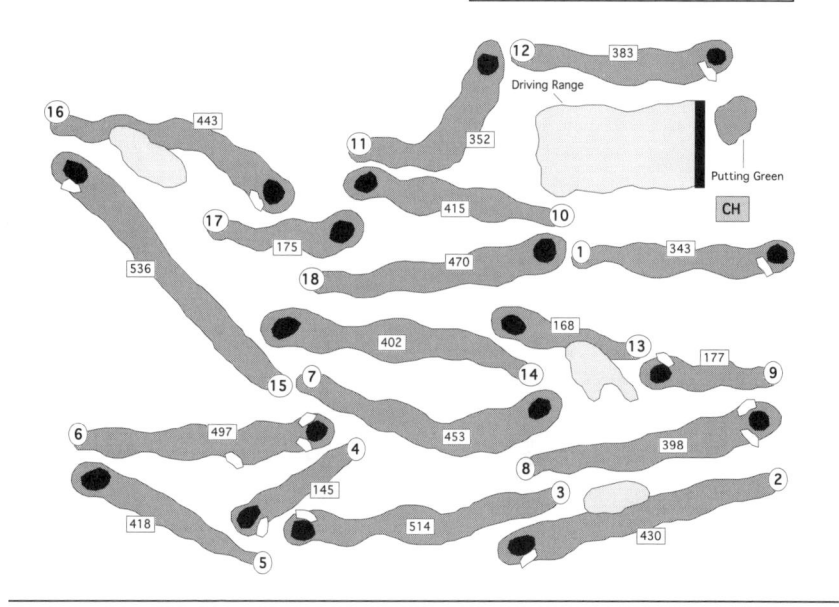

Warm Springs Golf Course (public, 9 hole course)

1801 Warm Springs Road; P.O. Box 1234; Ketchum, Idaho 83340
Phone: (208) 726-3715. Fax: none. Internet: none.
Owner/Manager: Patrick Simpson. Superintendent: Patrick Simpson.
Rating/Slope: M 69.3/111; W 71.5/119. **Course record:** 31(9 holes).
Green fees: $24/$18 rates for June 1st through Labor Day weekend; May and September through mid October golf all day for $18; M/C, VISA, AMEX.
Power cart: $22/$11. **Pull cart:** $2.50. **Trail fee:** personal carts not allowed.
Reservation policy: one day in advance for 4-somes, larger groups more notice.
Winter condition: the golf course is closed from mid October to May 1st.
Terrain: flat, 1 hill. **Tees:** all grass. **Spikes:** soft spikes preferred.
Services: club rentals, lessons, restaurant, snack bar, beer, pop, beverages, pro shop, lockers, driving net, tennis courts, putting & chipping greens.
Comments: natural alpine setting that offers spectacular views of the surrounding countryside. Beautiful summer golf course. A river runs along one side of the course and a forest on the other. Great course for the entire family.

Directions: from downtown Ketchum (at the stop light) travel 3 blocks north, to second stop light. Turn left at the fork in the road. Continue out Warm Springs Road for 1 mile to the course on the left.

Course Yardage & Par:
M-2604 yards, par 35.
W-2458 yards, par 39.
Dual tees for 18 holes:
M-5294 yards, par 70.
W-5062 yards, par 78.

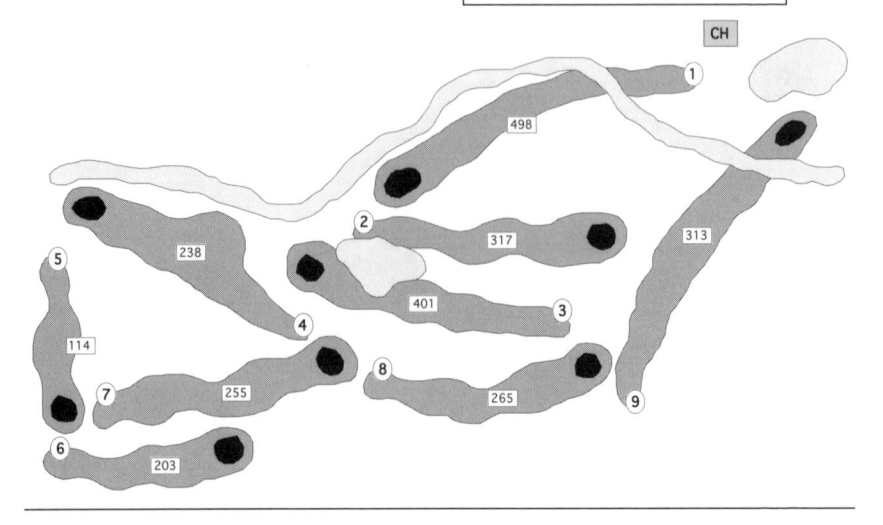

Desert Winds Golfing Range
3910 W 6th S; Mountain Home, Idaho 83647
(208) 587-6099. Pro: seasonal pro.
Hours: seasonal hours. **Lights:** no.
Covered: yes. **Putting & chipping:** yes.
Services: lessons, club repair, pro shop,
snacks, putting & chipping green, gift shop.
Directions: the driving range is located just off of
Hwy 67. The range is located on your right hand as
you are traveling west. **R1; Map 2; Grid G3**

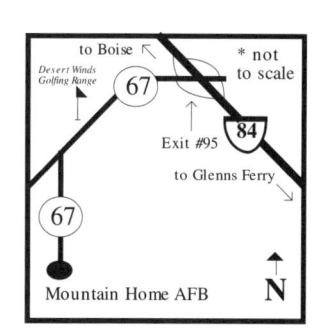

Divotz Discount Golf & Range
11350 Franklin Road; Boise, Idaho 83709
(208) 323-1135. Pro: Bob Campbell.
Hours: seasonal hours. **Lights:** no.
Covered: no. **Putting & chipping:** yes.
Services: lessons, pro shop, snack bar, club rentals.
Directions: from I-84 E&W take the Eagle Road
Exit (Hwy 55). Proceed north to Fairview. Turn
right on Fairview. The range will be on your right.
R2; Map 2; Grid E2

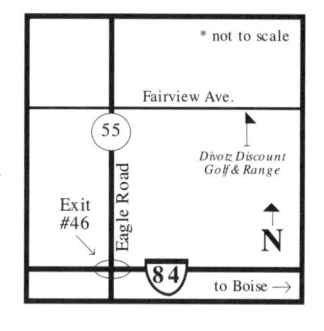

Farm City Driving Range
510 North 21st; Caldwell, Idaho 83605
(208) 455-1967. Pro: Jon Stein, PGA
Hours: seasonal hours. **Lights:** no.
Covered: yes. **Putting & chipping:** yes.
Services: lessons, club repair, pro shop, sand
bunker, snacks, custom clubs.
Directions: from Hwy 95 turn west on Prairie
Avenue. Travel for .4 miles to the range on your
left hand side. **R3; Map 1; Grid C1**

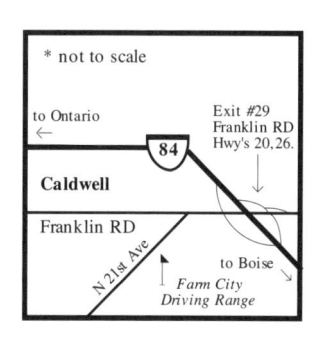

Golf Shack, The
17801 11th Ave. N; Nampa, Idaho 83687
(208) 465-0505. Pro: John Wallace.
Hours: seasonal hours. **Lights:** no.
Covered: no. **Putting & chipping:** yes.
Services: lessons, club repair, pro shop.
Directions: from I-84 E&W take exit #38 (Can-
Ada Road). Proceed north on Can-Ada Rd. Take
right on Ustick. Proceed to 11th Ave N. Turn left,
range is in the left. **R4; Map 2; Grid E2**

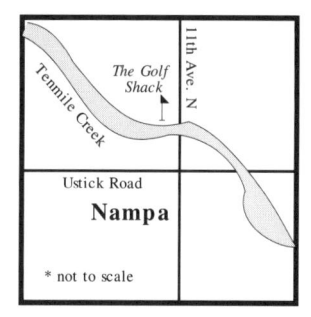

Green Links Driving Range
10436 Hwy 44; Middleton, Idaho 83644
(208) 585-9217. Pro: J. Howard Todd.
Hours: seasonal hours. **Lights:** yes.
Covered: no. **Putting & chipping:** yes.
Services: lessons, club repair, pro shop,
snacks, custom club fitting.
Directions: from I-84 E&W take exit #25 (Hwy
44). Proceed eastbound on Hwy 44 to Middleton.
Range will be on your left. **R5; Map 2; Grid E1**

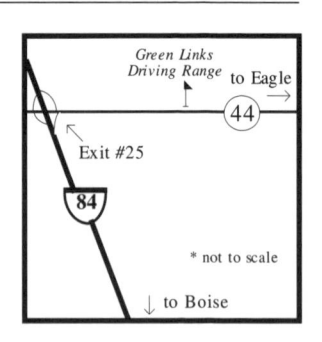

Outback Golf Park
1665 Pocatello Creek Rd; Pocatello, Idaho 83201
(208) 234-0612. Pro: seasonal pro.
Hours: seasonal hours. **Lights:** yes.
Covered: no. **Putting & chipping:** no.
Services: pro shop, snack bar, mini golf.
Directions: from I-15 take the Pocatello Creek
Road exit. Keep left at the fork in the ramp. Turn
left on Pocatello Creek Rd. Proceed to the range.
R6; Map 4; Grid F2

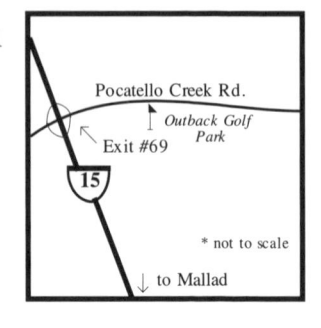

Swing Scene
1825 Highway 16; Emmett, Idaho 83617
(208) 365-4999. Pro: seasonal pro.
Hours: seasonal hours. **Lights:** no.
Covered: no. **Putting & chipping:** yes.
Services: lessons, restaurant.
Directions: from I-84 E&W take Eagle Road exit.
Proceed on Hwy 55 to Hwy 44. Turn left on Hwy
44. Proceed to Hwy 16 north to Emmett. Range is
located on the left. **R7; Map 2; Grid E2**

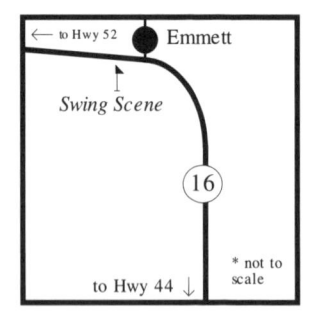

Art's Golf Shop
23786 Winterhawk Drive; Caldwell, Idaho; (208) 459-6011
Services: club repair, custom clubs, club refinishing

Bartlett's Golf Service
1771 North Wildwood; Boise, Idaho; (208) 322-5827
Services: club repair, custom clubs, club refinishing, pro shop, swing analyzer.

Bartlett's Golf Service
1116 Garrity Blvd.; Nampa, Idaho; (208) 465-9966
Services: club repair, custom clubs, club refinishing, pro shop, swing analyzer.

Boise Golf Works
2320 Madison Avenue; Boise, Idaho; (208) 336-9985
Services: club repair, custom clubs, club refinishing.

Caddy Shack
1100 West Prairie Avenue; Hayden Lake, Idaho; (208) 762-7275
Services: virtual indoor golf facility.

CJ's Golf Club Repair Shop
129 Valley Drive; Idaho Falls, Idaho; (208) 523-4031
Services: custom clubs.

Chubs Golf Club Repair
14919 Chancery Drive; Caldwell, Idaho; (208) 454-8815
Services: club repair.

Duffers Golf Cart Service
1313 E Best Avenue, Coeur d' Alene, Idaho; (208) 666-0338
Services: golf cart sales and service.

Fred Schimdt's Golf Cart Sales
1713 13th Avenue; Lewiston, Idaho; (208) 743-3964
Services: golf cart sales and service.

Full Swing Golf, INC
1009 West Main; Boise, Idaho; (208)336-6998
Services: indoor golf facility.

Golf Car Country
760 N Ralstin Street; Meridian, Idaho; (208) 898-0171
Services: golf cart sales and service.

Golf Depot
1439 Elk Creek Drive; Idaho Falls, Idaho; (208) 529-2078
Services: club repair, custom clubs, club refinishing, pro shop.

Golf Magic
2250 E State Street; Eagle, Idaho; (208) 939-0609
Services: club repair, custom clubs.

Golf Shoppe, The
7141 Overland Road; Boise, Idaho; (208) 375-1122
Services: club repair, custom fitting, pro shop.

Golf USA
799 Cheney Drive #1; Twin Falls, Idaho; (208) 736-8866
Services: discount pro shop, brand name clubs, retail store.

Gordon's Golf
1628 Syringa Street; Pocatello, Idaho; (208) 233-5030
Services: club repair, custom fitting, pro shop.

Hayden Golf Cars
1675 W Appleway Avenue #C; Coeur d' Alene, Idaho; (208) 769-7000
Services: golf cart sales and service.

Hole in One Golf Shop, The
5593 N Citadel Way; Boise, Idaho; (208) 336-1028
Services: complete club services.

Idaho Par Golf
2079 E 17th Street (Grand Teton Plaza); Idaho Falls, Idaho; (208) 523-6766
Services: complete club services, pro shop.

Kountry Klub Golf
448 Colonial Loop; Blackfoot, Idaho; (208) 785-2850
Services: complete golf club services.

Las Vegas Discount Golf & Tennis
5226 Overland Road; Boise, Idaho; (208) 345-4140
Services: club repair, custom fitting, full service pro shop, swing analyzer.

Lowe's Golf Center
6848 Goverment Way #111; Hayden Lake, Idaho; (208) 762-4653
Services: club repair, custom fitting, full service pro shop.

Mitchells Discount Golf
1675 W. Appleway Avenue #B; Coeur d'Alene, Idaho; (208) 667-5363
Services: club repair, custom fitting.

Mulligans Golf Club & Repair
1302 Leta; Boise, Idaho; (208) 344-9519
Services: club refinishing, reshafting, custom clubs.

Nevada Bobs/From Tee to Green
8011 Fairview; Boise, Idaho; (208) 377-4996 or 1-800-446-5343
Services: club repair, club refinishing, full service pro shop.

Northwest Golf
2417 12th Avenue; Lewiston, Idaho; (208) 743-8774
Services: club repairs, club regripping.

Par-Time Golf
West 296 Sunset Avenue #8, Hwy 95; Coeur d'Alene, Idaho; (208) 765-6876
Services: club repair, custom fitting, pro shop, indoor driving range.

Par-Time Golf
1926 19th Avenue; Lewston, Idaho; (208) 746-2928
Services: club repair, custom fitting, pro shop, indoor driving range.

Paradise Golf Accessories
8025 Track Road; Nampa, Idaho; (208) 468-8898
Services: retail golf shop.

Ron's Car & Sport
2732 Pole Line Road; Pocatello, Idaho; (208) 232-0202
Services: golf cart repair, sales.

Ron's Golf Cart Repair
872 Filer Avenue West; Twin Falls, Idaho; (208) 733-6710
Services: golf cart repair.

Stan's Golf Cars
4540 W State Street; Boise, Idaho; (208) 336-1736
Services: golf cart sales and service.

Urie's Golf Carts
443 Overland Avenue W; Hansen, Idaho; (208) 423-4566
Services: golf cart repair, golf cart sales.

Valley Golf Cars
805 Snake River Avenue; Lewiston, Idaho; (208) 746-6264
Services: golf cart repair, golf cart sales.

Vano's Professional Golf of Idaho
2097 Candleridge Drive; Twin Falls, Idaho; (208) 733-6577
Services: professional golf services.

Aberdeen: Hazard Creek Golf Course
American Falls: American Falls Golf Course
Ashton: Aspen Acres Golf Club
Athol: Rimrock Golf Course
Blanchard: Stoneridge Country Club
Blackfoot: Blackfoot Golf Course
Boise: Boise Ranch Golf Course, Crane Creek Country Club, Divotz Discount Golf & Range, Foxtail Golf Course, Golf & Recreation Club, Hillcrest Country Club, Indian Lake Golf Course, Pierce Park Greens, The Plantation Golf Club, Quail Hollow Golf Club, Shadow Valley Golf Course, Shamrock Golf Course, Spurwing Country Club, Warm Springs Golf Club
Bonners Ferry: Mirror Lake Golf Course
Buhl: Clear Lake Country Club
Burley: Burley City Municipal Golf Course, Ponderosa Golf Course
Caldwell: Fairview Municipal Golf Course, Farm City Driving Range, Purple Sage Golf Course
Cascade: Cascade Golf Course
Challis: Challis Centennial Golf Course
Coeur d'Alene: Coeur d'Alene Golf Club, The Coeur d'Alene Resort Golf Course, Ponderosa Springs Golf Course
Council: Council Mountain Golf Course
Driggs: Targhee Village Golf Course
Eagle: Banbury Golf Club, Eagle Hills Golf Course
Emmett: Gem County Golf Course, Swing Scene
Fairfield: Soldier Mountain Rach & Resort
Fish Haven: Bear Lake West Golf Course
Garden Valley: Terrace Lakes Resort Golf Course
Glenns Ferry: Vineyard Greens Golf Course
Gooding: Gooding Country Club
Grace: Central Links Golf Course
Grangeville: Grangeville Country Club
Hayden Lake: Avondale Golf Course, Hayden Lake Country Club
Idaho Falls: Idaho Falls Country Club, Pinecrest Municipal Golf Course, Sage Lakes Golf Course, Sand Creek Golf Course
Island Park: Island Park Village Golf Course
Jerome: 93 Golf Ranch, Jerome Country Club
Ketchum: Bigwood, The Valley Club, Warm Springs G.C.
Kimberly: Pleasant Valley Golf Course
Lava Hot Springs: Thunder Canyon Golf Course
Lewiston: Bryden Canyon Golf Course, Lewiston Golf & Country Club
Mackay: River Park Golf Course
McCall: McCall Golf Course
Meridian: Cherry Lane Golf Club, Foxtail Golf Course
Middleton: Green Links Driving Range

Montpelier: Montpelier Golf Course
Moscow: Moscow Elks Golf Club, University of Idaho Golf Course.
Mountain Home: Desert Canyon Golf Course, Desert Winds Golfing Range,
Silver Sage Golf Course
Nampa: Broadmore Country Club, Centennial Golf Course, The Golf Shack,
Ridgecrest Golf Club,
New Meadows: Meadow Creek Golf & Field Club
Orofino: Orofino Golf & Country Club
Osburn: Shoshone Golf & Tennis Club
Payette: Scotch Pines Golf Course
Pinehurst: Pinehurst Golf Course
Pocatello: Highland Golf Course, Juniper Hills Country Club,
Outback Golf Park, Riverside Golf Course.
Post Falls: The Highlands Golf & Country Club, The Links Golf Club,
Prairie Falls Golf Club
Preston: Preston Golf & Country Club
Priest Lake: Priest Lake Golf Course
Priest River: Ranch Club Golf Course
Rathdrum: Twin Lakes VIllage
Rexburg: Rexburg Municipal Golf Course, Teton Lakes Golf Course
Rigby: Jefferson Hills Golf Course
Ririe: Heise Hills Golf Course
Rupert: Rupert Country Club
Sagle: Midas Golf Course
Saint Maries: Saint Maries Golf Course
Saint Anthony: Fremont County Golf Course
Salmon: Salmon Valley Golf Course
Sandpoint: Hidden Lakes Golf Resort, Sandpoint Elks Golf Course
Shelley: Krystal Lake Golf Course
Soda Springs: Oregon Trail Country Club
Sun Valley: Bigwood Golf Course, Sun Valley Resort Golf Course,
Sun Valley's Elkhorn Resort Golf Course, The Valley Club, Warm Springs
Golf Course (see Ketchum for additional listings)
Twin Falls: Blue Lakes Country Club, Candleridge Golf Course, Canyon
Springs Golf Course, Twin Falls Municipal Golf Course
Weiser: Rolling Hills Golf Course
Wilder: River Bend Golf Course

Idaho State Regional Map

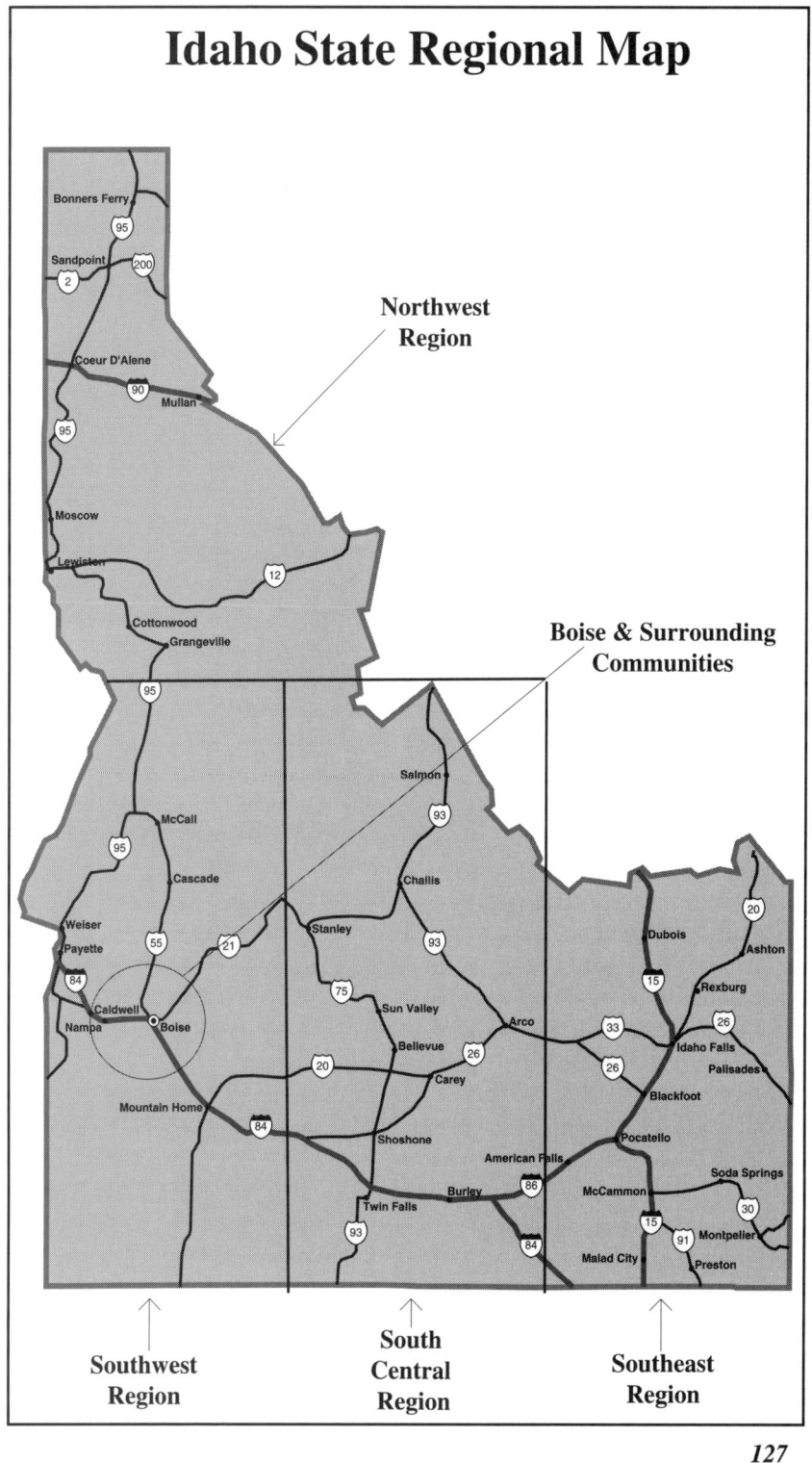

Northwest Region

Boise & Surrounding Communities

Southwest Region

South Central Region

Southeast Region

Boise & Surrounding Communities

Banbury Golf Club
Boise Ranch Golf Course
Broadmore Country Club
Centennial Golf Course
Cherry Lane Golf Club
Crane Creek Country Club
Divotz Discount Golf & Range
Eagle Hills Golf Course
Fairview Municipal Golf Course
Farm City Driving Range
Foxtail Golf Course
Golf & Recreation Club
Golf Shack, The
Green Links Driving Range
Hillcrest Country Club
Indian Lake Golf Course
Pierce Park Greens
Plantation Golf Club, The
Purple Sage Golf Course
Quail Hollow Golf Club
Ridgecrest Golf Club
Shadow Valley Golf Course
Shamrock Golf Course
Spurwing Country Club
Warm Springs Golf Club

Northwest Region

Avondale Golf Course
Bryden Canyon Golf Course
Coeur d' Alene Golf Club
Coeur d' Alene Resort Golf Course, The
Grangeville Country Club
Hayden Lake Country Club
Hidden Lakes Golf Resort
Highlands Golf & Country Club, The
Lewiston Golf & Country Club
Links Golf Club, The
Midas Golf Course
Mirror Lake Golf Course
Moscow Elks Golf Club
Orofino Golf & Country Club

Pinehurst Golf Course
Ponderosa Springs Golf Course
Prairie Falls Golf Club
Priest Lake Golf Course
Ranch Club Golf Course
Rimrock Golf Course
Saint Maries Golf Course
Twin Lakes Village
University of Idaho Golf Course
Sandpoint Elks Golf Course
Shoshone Golf & Tennis Club
Stoneridge Country Club

South Central Region

93 Golf Ranch
Bigwood Golf Course
Blue Lakes Country Club
Burley City Municipal Golf Course
Candleridge Golf Course
Canyon Springs Golf Course
Cascade Golf Course
Challis Centennial Golf Course
Clear Lake Country Club
Gooding Country Club
Jerome Country Club
Pleasant Valley Golf Course
Ponderosa Golf Course
River Park Golf Course
Rupert Country Club
Salmon Valley Golf Course
Soldier Mountain Ranch & Resort
Sun Valley Resort Golf Course
Sun Valley's Elkhorn Resort Golf Course
Twin Falls Municipal Golf Course
Valley Club, The
Warm Springs Golf Course

Southeast Region

American Falls Golf Course
Aspen Acres Golf Club
Bear Lake West Golf Course
Blackfoot Golf Course
Central Links Golf Course
Fremont County Golf Course
Hazard Creek Golf Course
Heise Hills Golf Course
Highland Golf Course
Idaho Falls Country Club
Island Park Village Golf Course
Jefferson Hills Golf Course
Juniper Hills Country Club
Krystal Lake Golf Course
Montpelier Golf Course
Oregon Trail Country Club
Outback Golf Park
Pinecrest Municipal Golf Course
Preston Golf & Country Club
Rexburg Municipal Golf Course
Riverside Golf Course
Sage Lakes Golf Course
Sand Creek Golf Course
Targhee Village Golf Course
Teton Lakes Golf Course
Thunder Canyon Golf Course

Southwest Region

Council Mountain Golf Course
Desert Canyon Golf Course
Desert Winds Golfing Range
Gem County Golf Course
McCall Golf Course
Meadow Creek Golf & Field Club
River Bend Golf Course
Rolling Hills Golf Course
Scotch Pines Golf Course
Silver Sage Golf Course
Swing Scene
Terrace Lakes Resort Golf Course
Vineyard Greens Golf Course

Montana
State
Golf
Facilities
Section

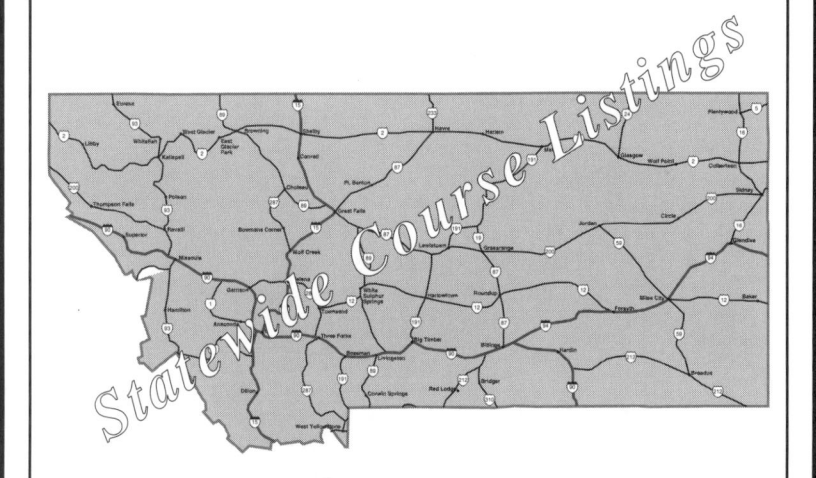

Statewide Course Listings

MAC Productions

Golf Guides Since 1986

Map 1

① Denotes approximate Golf Course Location.

Numbers on map correspond with golf course page numbers. R before a number represents range.

Grid→ ↓	1	2	3	4

Fortine — 187

② 148 Libby

93

West Glacier — 167 ② 2

89 Browning

Whitefish — 224, 198, 194, 223, 193, R1, 146

188 Columbia Falls

166 East Glacier

210 Thompson Falls

Kalispell

Creston

158 Bigfork

Montana

203 Plains

St. Regis

220

200

Polson — 205

93

191 Ronan

157 Seely Lake

149 Superior

Idaho

Frenchtown — 176

Missoula

Missoula: 173 180 182 192 221

199

90

226 Stevensville

1

D

93

169 Hamilton

E

N
W ← → E
S

Montana

F

Salmon

Idaho

93

G

* not to scale

Map 2

① Denotes approximate Golf Course Location.

Numbers on map correspond with golf course page numbers. R before a number represents range.

Grid→	1	2	3	4

* not to scale

N
W ← → E
S

A

Cut Bank (155)

Shelby (186)

(2)

Chester

Conrad (206)

Power

Fort Benton (87) (216)

B

Choteau (151)

Fairfield (170) (89)

(287)

(15) (160) **Great Falls**

(87)

C

Montana

Wolf Creek

(89)

Great Falls Area
(138) (189) (212) (R2)

D

(143) (165) (168) **Helena**

(15)

Deer Lodge (156)

(287)

Townsend (195)

(12)

White Sulfur Springs

E

(1)
(162) (137)
Anaconda (196)

(147) (172) **Butte**

(90)

(171) Three Forks

Big Timber (197)

Bozeman
(211) (145)
(222) (154) (183) Livingston

F

Ennis (184)

(142) Big Sky

(287)

Montana

Dillon (141)

(15)

G

Wyoming

Idaho

Map 3

*not to scale

Grid → | **1** | **2** | **3** | **4**

A
233
140 Havre
150 Chinook
2 Harlem
217 Saco
2

B
185 Malta
191
Montana

C
191 Lewistown
201 176
19
Grass Range
200

D
191
175 Harlowton
87
12
202 Roundup
12

E
12
94
Columbus
218
181
94 Laurel
Billings
Huntley
206
164 Hardin

Billings Area
144 152 161 172
178 200 227

F
139
209 Red Lodge
212
Montana
90

G
Wyoming

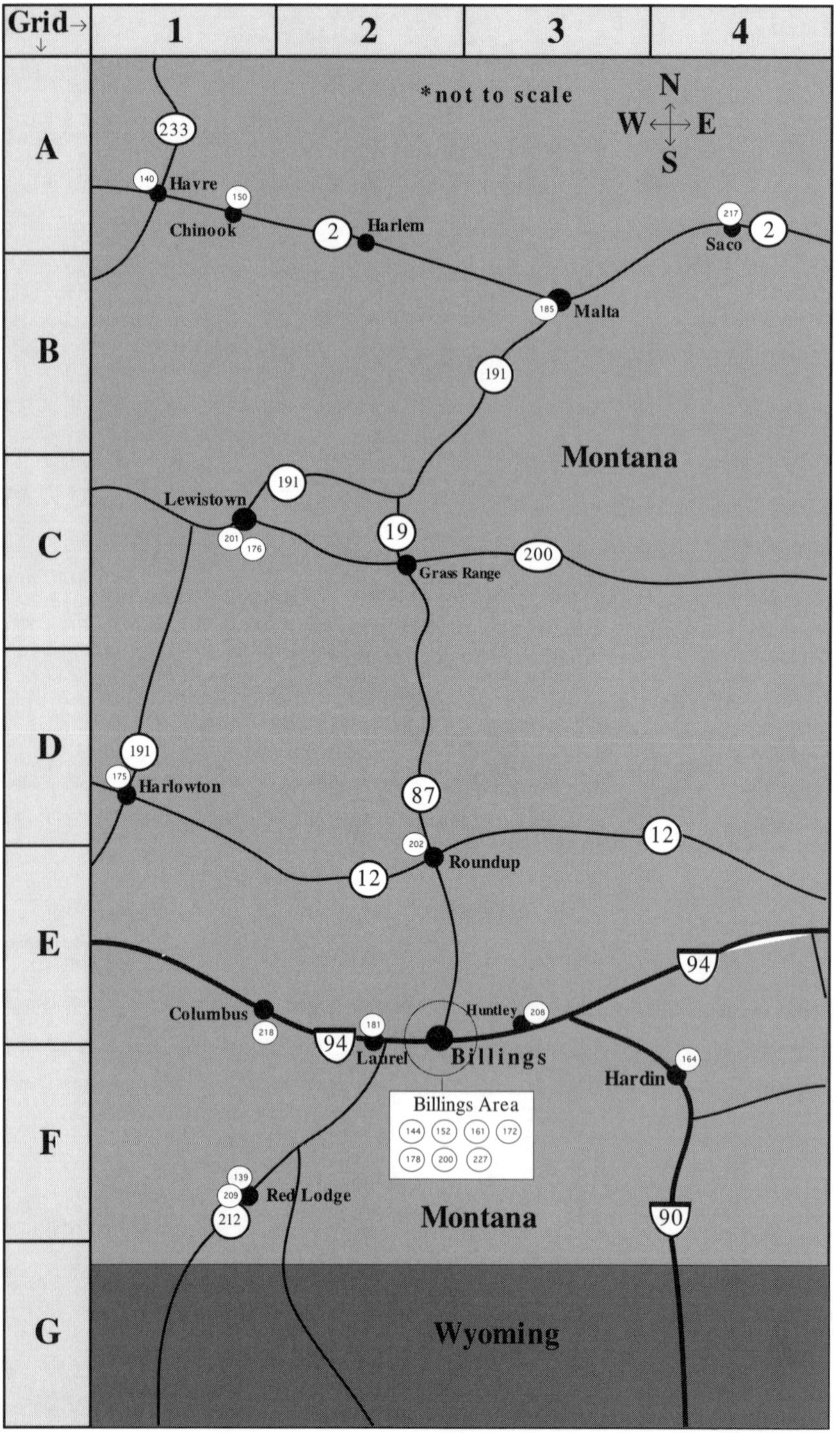

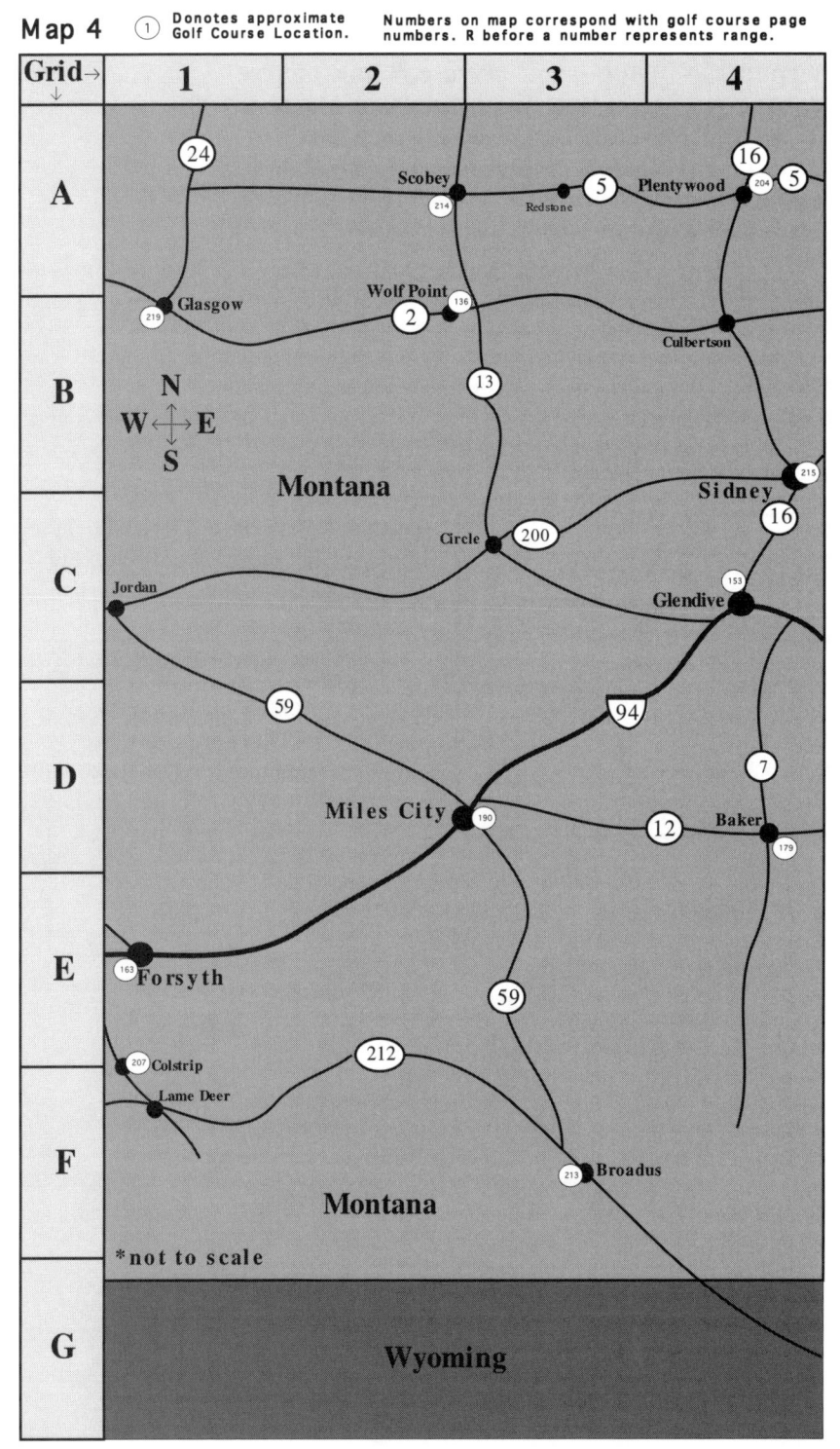

Map 4 ① Donotes approximate Golf Course Location. Numbers on map correspond with golf course page numbers. R before a number represents range.

Airport Golf Club (semi-private, 9 hole course)
P.O. Box 116; east of Wolf Point; Wolf Point, Montana 59201
Phone: (406) 653-2161. Fax: none. Internet: none.
Manager: C. Fromdahl. Superintendent: unavailable.
Rating/Slope: the golf course is not rated . **Course record:** 65 (18 holes).
Green fees: Weekdays $14/$9; Weekends $16/$11; M/C, VISA.
Power cart: $18/$9. **Pull cart:** $2. **Trail fee:** personal carts are not allowed.
Reservation policy: call in advance for your tee times. No time limit.
Winter condition: the golf course is closed during inclement weather.
Terrain: flat (easy walking). **Tees:** all grass. **Spikes:** soft spikes preferred.
Services: club rentals, snack bar, beer, beverages, putting green.
Comments: the golf course is quite flat and easy to walk. A nice country course which plays fairly wide open, great for seniors and familys. The clubhouse opens at 8:00 a.m. daily. Dual tees are available for a full 18 hole round of golf.

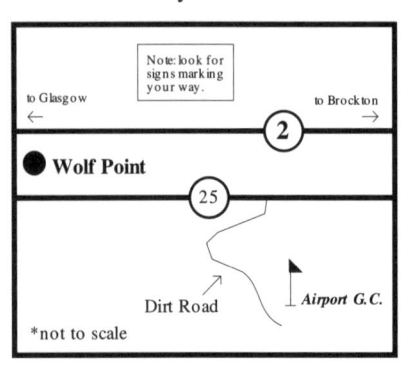

Directions: the course is located right off Montana Highway 25 east of Wolf Point right next to the airport. Look for signs.

Course Yardage & Par:
M-3267 yards, par 36.
W-2720 yards, par 36.
Dual tees for 18 holes:
M-6499 yards, par 72.
W-5360 yards, par 72.

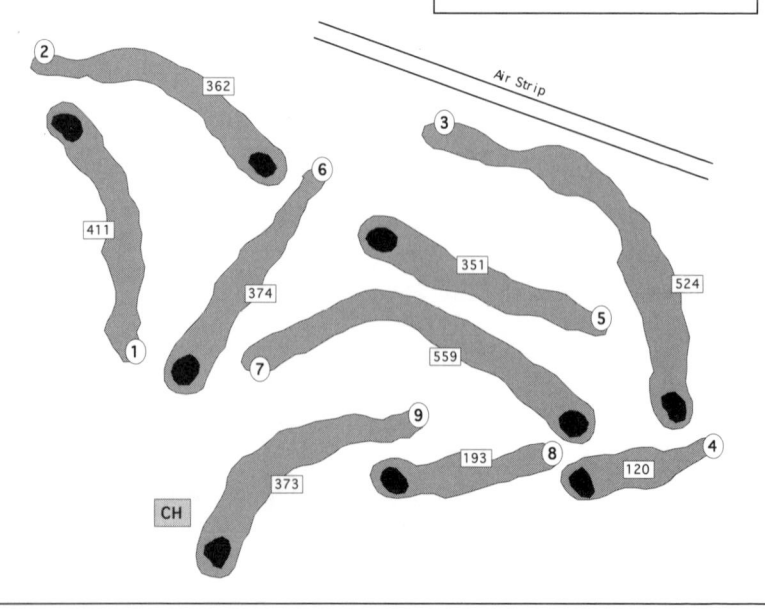

Anaconda Country Club (semi-private, 9 hole course)

P.O. Box 1351; 1302 West 4th; Anaconda, Montana 59711
Phone: (406) 797-3220. Fax: none. Internet: none.
Pro: Mark Torney, PGA. Superintendent: Fred Girard.
Rating/Slope: M 67.8/108; W 69.7/110. **Course record:** 63.
Green fees: Weekdays $18/$12; Weekends $18/$12; M/C, VISA, AMEX.
Power cart: $18/$10. **Pull cart:** $3. **Trail fee:** personal carts not allowed.
Reservation policy: please call in advance for your tee times. No time limit.
Winter condition: the golf course is closed from November 1st to March 1st.
Terrain: flat (easy walking). **Tees:** grass. **Spikes:** soft spikes preferred.
Services: club rentals, snack bar, beer, wine, liquor, pro shop, lockers, lessons,
beverages, driving range, putting & chipping greens, club memberships.
Comments: the course is very flat with some tree lined fairways. The Anaconda
smokestack (worlds largest smokestack) is your backdrop in the skyline. Dual tees
are available for a full 18 hole round. Please call for daily public play policy.

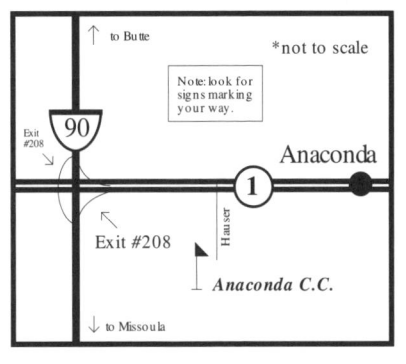

Directions: from I-90 take exit #208 for
Anaconda (Montana Highway 1). Turn
right on Hauser which leads directly to
the golf course entrance 1.1 miles ahead.
Note: The golf course is located east of
Anaconda. Watch for the green & white
sign marking your turn to the golf course.

Course Yardage & Par:
M-3020 yards, par 35.
W-2701 yards, par 37.
Dual tees for 18 holes:
M-6223 yards, par 71.
W-5545 yards, par 73.

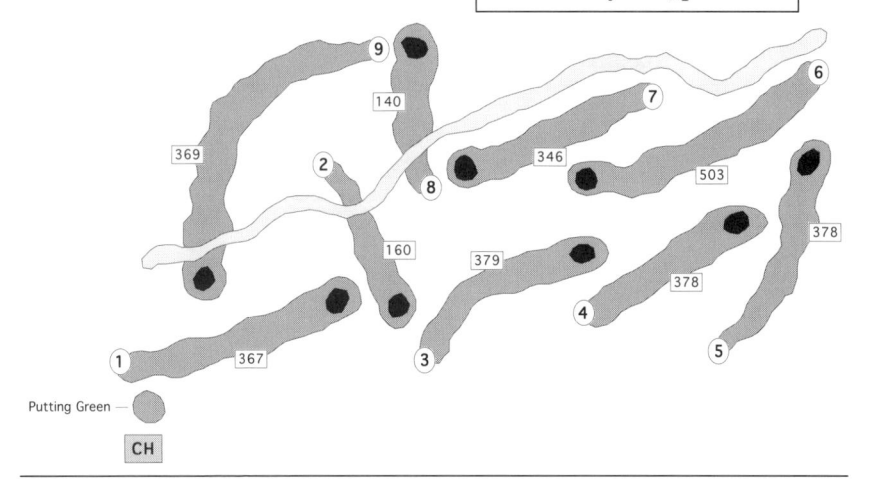

Anaconda Hills Golf Course (public, 18 hole course)

24th Street & Smelter Avenue; P.O. Box 5021; Great Falls, Montana, 59403
Phone: (406) 761-8459. Fax: none. Internet: none.
Pro: Michael E. Burrall, PGA. Superintendent: unavailable.
Rating/Slope: T 66.2/115; C 64.5/111; M 62.3/108; W 62.8/101. Record: 67.
Green fees: W/D $20/$14; W/E $20; Jr. rates $10; M/C, VISA.
Power cart: $18/$11. Pull cart: $2.50. Trail fee: call course for policy.
Reservation policy: call 2 days in advance for your tee times.
Winter condition: the golf course is closed during inclement weather.
Terrain: very hilly. Tees: all grass tees. Spikes: soft spikes preferred.
Services: club rentals, snack bar, pop, small pro shop, lessons, driving range.
Comments: course is located on a hill above the river so you have some river views. The course offers challenging terrain due to the hill it sits on. A very nice driving range is on site for those wanting "pound the ball" after their round.

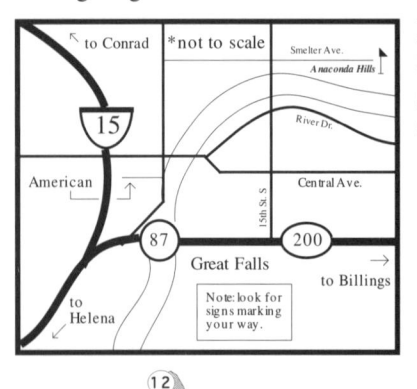

Directions: from Highway 87 turn on Smelter Avenue. Proceed .5 miles to the golf course entrance located straight ahead. Look for signs that are posted.

Course Yardage & Par:
T-5666 yards, par 69.
C-5271 yards, par 69.
M-4829 yards, par 67.
W-4332 yards, par 66.

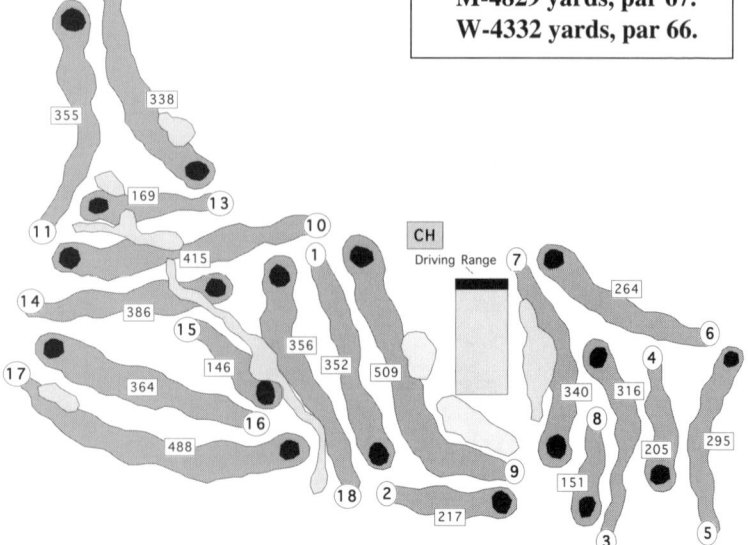

Beartooth Golf & Country Club (public, 9 hole course)
off Hwy 139; Red Lodge, Montana, 59068
Phone: (406) 446-3938. **Fax: none. Internet: none.**
Manager/Pro: none. Superintendent: none.
Rating/Slope: the golf course is not rated. **Course record:** 34 (9 holes).
Green fees: Weekdays $6; Weekends $6; no credit cards.
Power cart: not available. **Pull cart:** not available. **Trail fee:** no charge.
Reservation policy: none needed. Tee-times are on a first come first served basis.
Winter condition: the golf course is closed from mid-November to mid-April.
Terrain: flat, some slight hills. **Tees:** all grass. **Spikes:** no spike policy.
Services: very limited services. The clubhouse is very primitive in nature.
Comments: this 9 hole course is touted as the "oldest continuously played golf course in Montana." The course setting is beautiful, below the ski area in Red Lodge, however, of the many golf courses we have visited this is certainly one of the most rustic. You might want to play Beartooth just to say "you survived it".

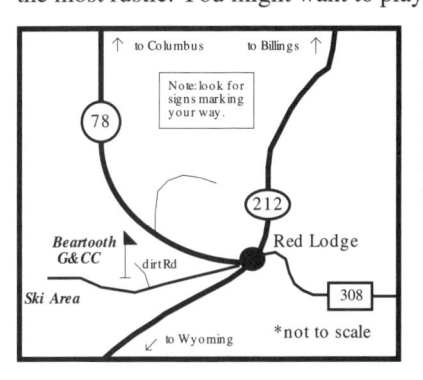

Directions: the golf course is located on the road to the Palisades Campground which is just south of downtown Red Lodge. The way is not well marked. The streets do not have names nor is there any signs indicating the route you must take.

Course Yardage & Par:
M-3120 yards, par 36.
W-3120 yards, par 41.

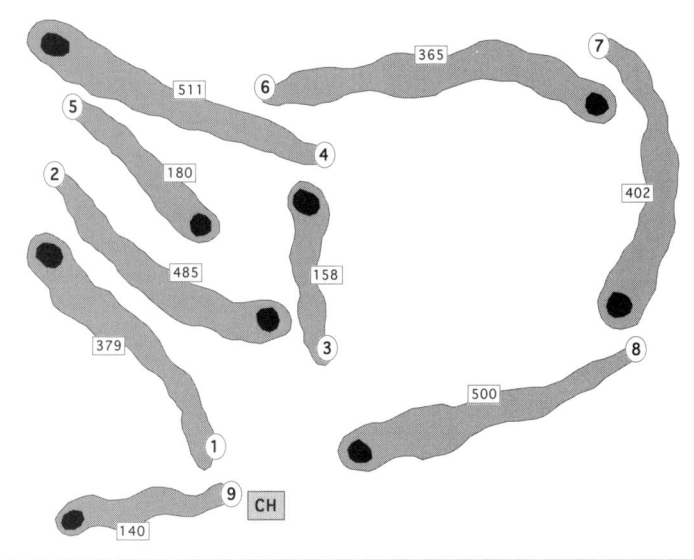

Beaver Creek Golf Course (semi-private, 9 hole course)

Highway 2 West; P.O. Box 350; Havre, Montana 59716
Phone: (406) 265-4201 or (208) 265-7861. **Fax:** none. **Internet:** none.
Pro: Doug Sheppard. Superintendent: unavailable.
Rating/Slope: M 69.1/113; W 71.6/117. **Course record:** 67.
Green fees: W/D $17/$10; W/E $17/$10; Jr. & Sr. rates; M/C, VISA.
Power cart: $20/$10. **Pull cart:** $2.50. **Trail fee:** personal carts not allowed.
Reservation policy: please call 2 days in advance for your tee times.
Winter condition: the golf course is closed from November 1st- March 1st.
Terrain: flat (easy walking). **Tees:** all grass. **Spikes:** soft spikes preferred.
Services: club rentals, snack bar, beer, wine, beverages, pro shop, lessons.
Comments: the course is easy to walk as it is very flat, with bunkers guarding most greens. There are also dual tees so you can play a full 18 hole round of golf. You usually can walk on during the week without any advance tee-time.

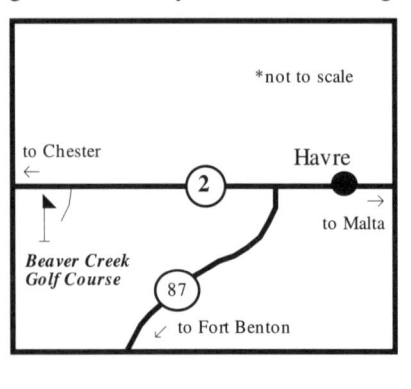

Directions: the golf course is located 3 miles west of downtown Havre on Hwy 2. From Hwy 87 turn west on Hwy 2. The course is .9 miles ahead on your left. Look for a sign posted at your turn.

Course Yardage & Par:
M-3192 yards, par 36.
W-2889 yards, par 38.
<u>Dual tees for 18 holes:</u>
M-6346 yards, par 72.
W-5776 yards, par 76.

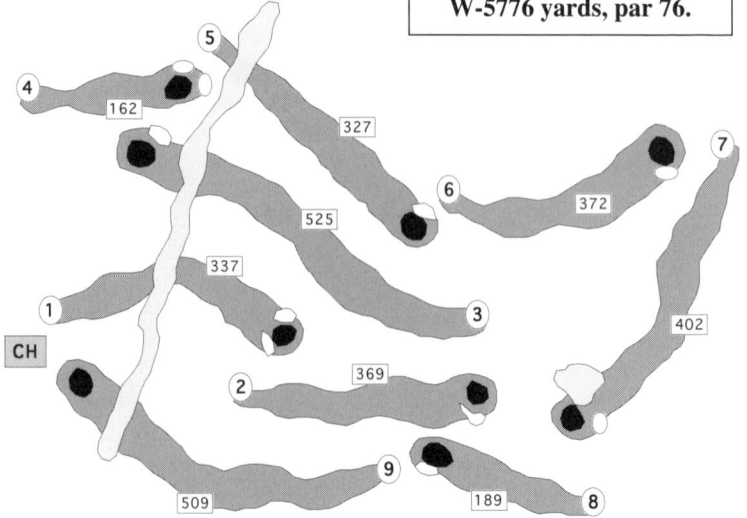

Beaverhead Golf Course (semi-private, 9 hole course)

1200 State Highway 41; P.O. Box 426; Dillon, Montana 59725
Phone: (406) 683-9933. Fax: none. Internet: none.
Manager/Superintendent: Greg Morstein.
Rating/Slope: M 68.4/116; W 69.6/123. **Course record:** 62.
Green fees: W/D $16/$10; W/E $16/$10; M/C, VISA.
Power cart: $16/$9. **Pull cart:** $2. **Trail fee:** $7 for personal carts.
Reservation policy: call 1 week in advance for your tee times.
Winter condition: the golf course is closed from mid-October thru mid-March.
Terrain: flat (easy walking). **Tees:** all grass. **Spikes:** soft spikes preferred.
Services: club rentals, snack bar, beer, wine, pop, pro shop, putting green.
Comments: the course is very flat and easy to walk with few hazards. Dillon is set in a valley surrounded by mountains which afford a beautiful view while playing a round of golf. Dual tees are available for those wanting a full round.

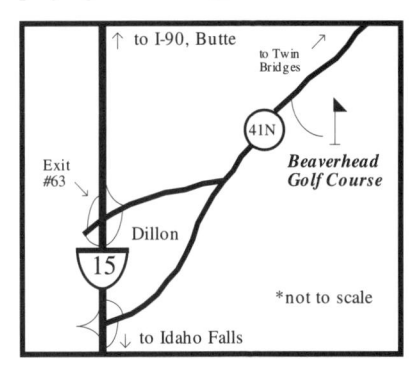

Directions: from I-15 take exit #63. Proceed north on Highway 41N right off of the exit and proceed .3 miles to the course entrance located on your right.

Course Yardage & Par:
M-3220 yards, par 36.
W-2861 yards, par 37.
Dual tees for 18 holes:
M-6344 yards, par 72.
W-5814 yards, par 74.

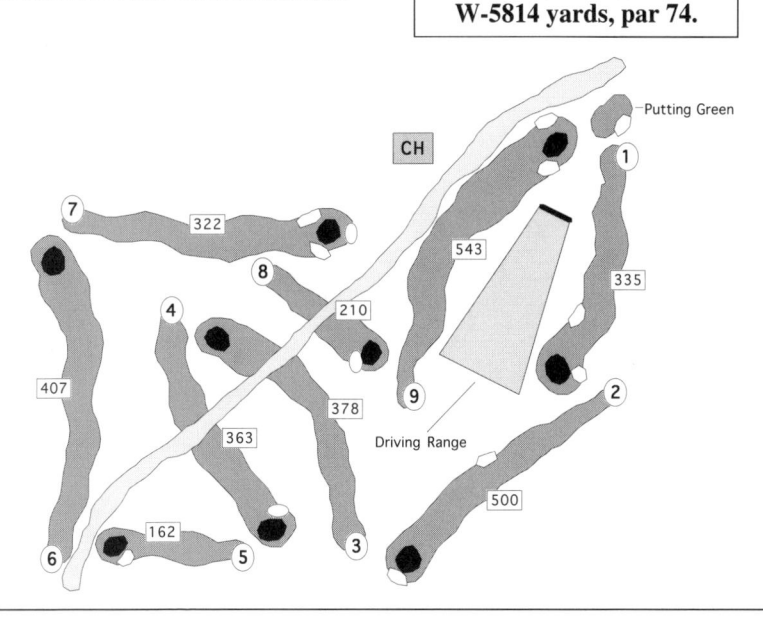

Big Sky Golf Club (resort, 18 hole course)

2100 Black Otter Road; P.O. Box 160001; Big Sky, Montana 59716
Phone: (406) 995-4706. Fax: none. Internet: none.
Pro: Terry Mumey, PGA. Superintendet: unavailable.
Rating/Slope: C 69.0/111; M 66.0/105; W 67.4/104. **Course record:** 67.
Green fees: W/D $35/$27; W/E $35/$27; M/C, VISA, AMEX, DIS.
Power cart: $22/$16. **Pull cart:** $3. **Trail fee:** personal carts not allowed.
Reservation policy: call 2 weeks in advance for all your tee times.
Winter condition: the golf course is closed from November 1st to mid-April.
Terrain: flat (easy walking). **Tees:** all grass. **Spikes:** soft spikes required.
Services: club rentals, snack bar, restaurant, beer, wine, liquor, pro shop,
showers, lessons, driving range, putting & chipping greens, club memberships.
Comments: this resort offers an Arnold Palmer designed layout in a spectacular
setting along the Gallatin River. Resort has full amenities for the whole family.

Directions: the course is located in Big
Sky Meadow Village at the Big Sky
Resort in Big Sky, Montana. From
Highway 64 turn right on Black Otter.
Proceed for 1/2 mile then turn left to the
clubhouse and pro shop. Look for signs.

*not to scale

to Bozeman ↑

Big Sky
Golf Club

Big Sky

64

191

Note: look for
signs marking
your way.

to West Yellowstone ↓

Course Yardage & Par:
C-6748 yards, par 72.
M-6115 yards, par 72.
W-5374 yards, par 72.

Bill Roberts Municipal Golf Course (public, 18 hole course)

2201 N. Benton Avenue; Helena, Montana 59604
Phone: (406) 442-2191. Fax: none. Internet: none.
Pro: Dale Newell, PGA. Superintendent: unavailable.
Rating/Slope: C 71.2/117; M 69.1/115; M 68.5/113; W 65.8/107. **Record:** 65.
Green fees: W/D $20/$12; W/E $20/$12; Jr. & Sr. rates; M/C, VISA.
Power cart: $22/$11. **Pull cart:** $2. **Trail fee:** $9 for personal carts.
Reservation policy: 1 day in advance for weekdays, on Thursdays for weekends.
Winter condition: the course is closed from December 1st to February 28th.
Terrain: flat, some hills. **Tees:** all grass. **Spikes:** soft spikes preferred.
Services: club rentals, snack bar, beer, wine, lessons, pro shop, driving range.
Comments: the course is very challenging with some recent remodeling to lakes and sandtraps. A nice municipal golf course located in the heart of the city.

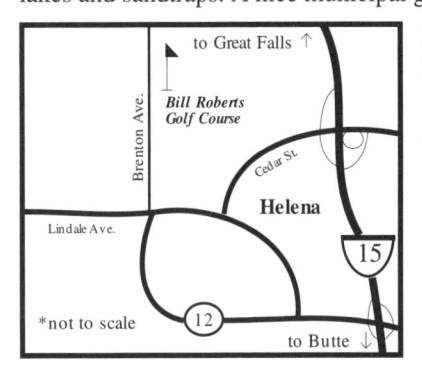

Directions: the course is located just north of Carroll College on Benton Avenue, follow the signs to the college. From I-15 exit at Cedar Street. Proceed to Lindale Ave. Turn right. Proceed to Benton Avenue. Course is on the right.

Course Yardage & Par:
C-6782 yards, par 72.
M-6391yards, par 72.
M-5612 yards, par 72.
W-4700 yards, par 72.

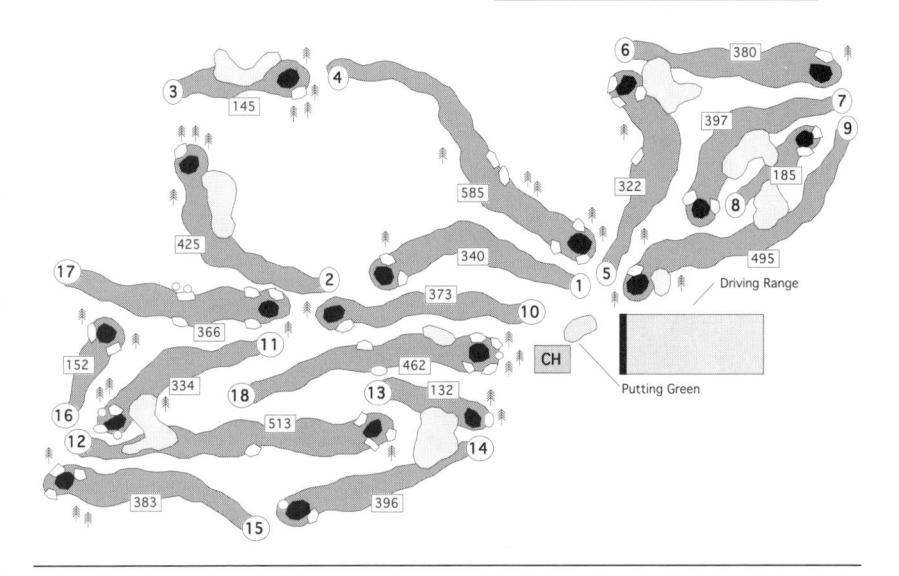

Briarwood, The (private, 18 hole course)
3429 Briarwood Boulevard; Billings, Montana 59101
Phone: (406) 248-2702. **Fax:** none. **Internet:** none.
Pro: Bob Eames, PGA. **Superintendent:** Jerry Aisenbrey.
Rating/Slope: T 73.0/132; C 71.6/128; M 69.8/126; W 70.1/120. **Record:** 67.
Green fees: private course. Members and guests of members only; reciprocates.
Power cart: private club. **Pull cart:** private club. **Trail fee:** private club.
Reservation policy: call in advance for tee times. Members have priority times.
Winter condition: the golf course is open weather permitting.
Terrain: flat, some steep hills. **Tees:** all grass. **Spikes:** not in use.
Services: club rentals, snack bar, restaurant, beer, wine, liquor, pop, pro shop, lockers, showers, lessons, driving range, putting green, club memberships.
Comments: the course offers two distinct nines. The front 9 winds around Blue Creek. The back 9 is surrounded by native stands of pine and juniper. Excellent private golf course that will challenge you at every turn.

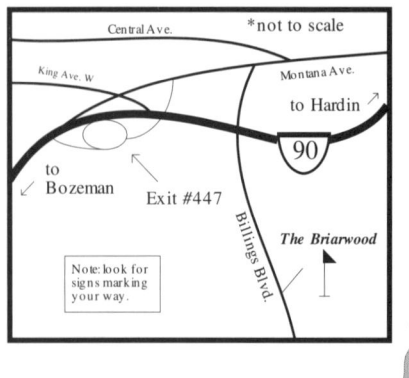

Directions: from I-90 take exit #447 and proceed south on Billings Boulevard to the Briarwood entrance on your left hand side. The course entrance is located approximately 3 miles from I-90. Look for signs that are posted on the route.

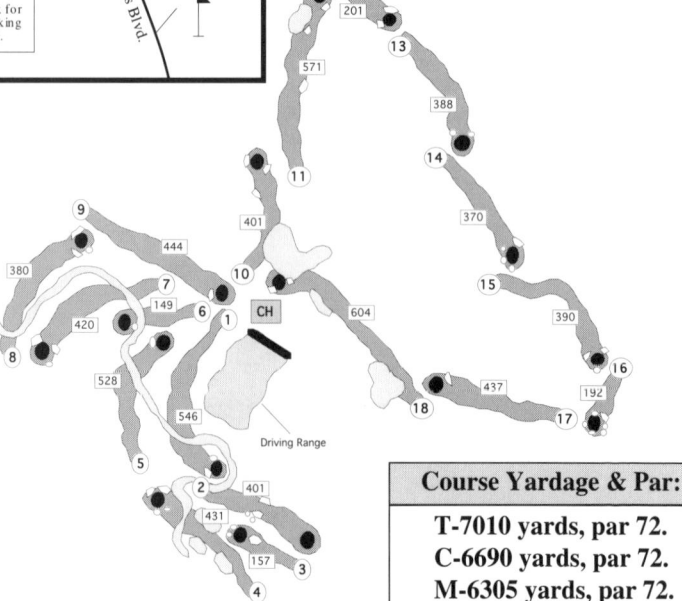

Course Yardage & Par:
T-7010 yards, par 72.
C-6690 yards, par 72.
M-6305 yards, par 72.
W-5436 yards, par 74.

Bridger Creek (public, 18 hole course)

2710 McIllhattan Road; Bozeman, Montana 59715
Phone: (406) 586-2333. Fax: (406) 586-9797. Internet: none.
Pro: Mark Holiday, PGA. Superintendent: Dane Gamble.
Rating/Slope: C 69.9/119; M 67.5/115; W 66.2/112. **Course record:** 66.
Green fees: M-Th $24/$14; Fri.-Sun. $26/$15; M/C, VISA.
Power cart: $20/$12. **Pull cart:** $2/$3. **Trail fee:** $20/$12.
Reservation policy: please call up to 30 days in advance for all your tee times.
Winter condition: the golf course is closed during inclement weather.
Terrain: flat, some hills. **Tees:** all grass. **Spikes:** spft spikes required.
Services: club rentals, pro shop, lessons, snack bar, driving range, putting green.
Comments: this fantastic course was recently voted by *Golf Digest* as "One of the 10 best golf courses you can play in the state of Montana". A beautiful creek, old growth cottonwoods and great greens make this course a must play.

Directions: from I-90 exit at 7th Avenue. Proceed on 7th north to Griffin Drive and turn right. At Rouse, take the veer left to Bridger Drive. Proceed to Storymill Road and turn left to the golf course located ahead on your right hand side.

Course Yardage & Par:

C-6511 yards, par 71.
M-6017 yards, par 71.
W-4902 yards, par 71.

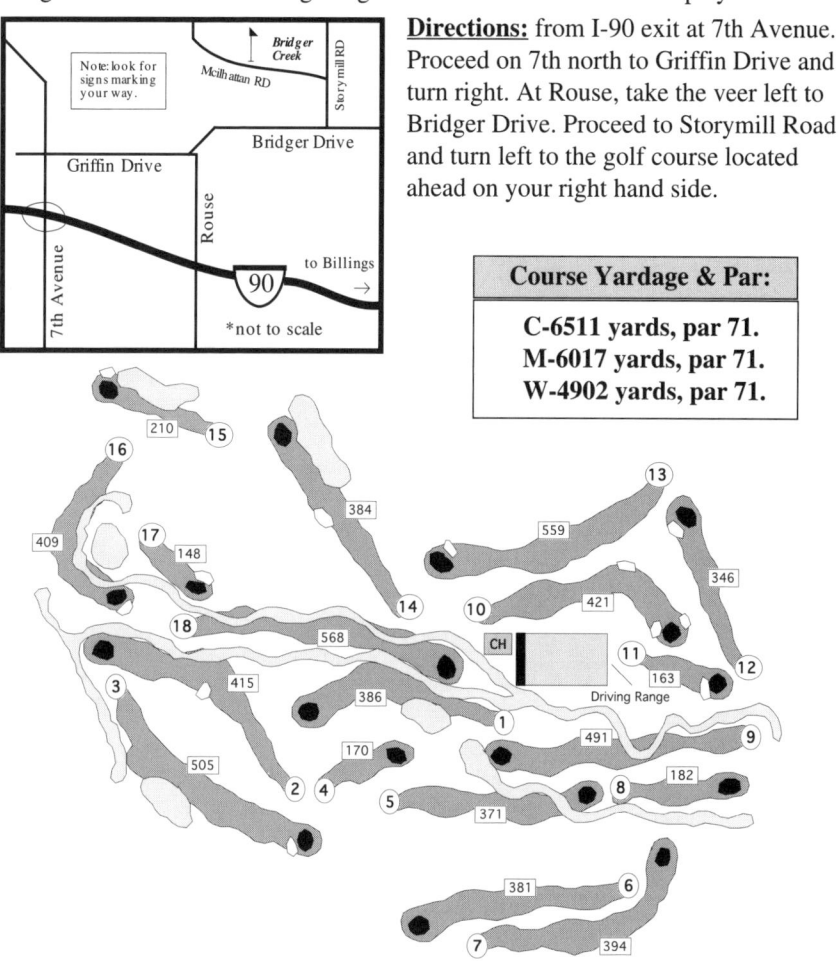

Buffalo Hill Golf Club (public, 27 hole course)

1176 North Main Street; P.O. Box 1116; Kalispell, Montana, 59901
Phone: (406) 756-4530. Fax: none. Internet: none.
Pro: Dave Broeder, PGA. Superintendent: Pat Meeker.
Rating/Slope: C 71.4/131; M 70.2/128; W 70.3/125. **Course record:** 67.
Green fees Championship Course: $36; twilight rates; M/C, VISA.
Greens fees Cameron Course: $18; twilight rates M/C, VISA
Power cart: $24/$12. **Pull cart:** $3/$2. **Trail fee:** not allowed.
Reservation policy: please call 3 days in advance for all your tee times.
Winter condition: the golf course is closed during inclement weather.
Terrain: flat, some hills. **Tees:** all grass. **Spikes:** soft spikes only.
Services: club rentals, pro shop, lessons, snack bar, driving range, putting green.
Comments: great golf course that is a test for any level of golfer. The fairways
are tree-lined and greens are well bunkered. This facility is simply fantastic.

Directions: from Hwy 93N exit in North
Kalispel at N Main St. Go for .6 miles to
the course on left. From 93S turn east on
Wyoming. Proceed .2 miles to N Main St.

Course Yardage & Par:

C-6525 yards, par 72.
M-6247 yards, par 72.
W-5258 yards, par 74.

Championship Course

Course Yardage & Par:

M-3001 yards, par 35.
W-2950 yards, par 38.

Cameron Course

"Cameron Nine"

"Championship Course"

Butte Country Club (private, 18 hole course)

3400 Elizabeth Warren Avenue; P.O. Box 3465; Butte, Montana 59702
Phone: (406) 494-3383. Fax: none. Internet: none.
Pro: Bryan Morgan, PGA. Superintendent: unavailable.
Rating/Slope: C 68.8/116; M 67.5/113; W 69.4/112. **Course record:** 66.
Green fees: private club members & guests only; M/C, VISA.
Power cart: private club. **Pull cart:** private club. **Trail fee:** private club.
Reservation policy: private club members & guests of members only.
Winter condition: the golf course is closed during the winter months.
Terrain: flat (easy walking). **Tees:** all grass. **Spikes:** soft spikes only.
Services: club rentals, lessons, snack bar, beer, wine, liquor, restaurant, beverages, putting & chipping green, pro shop, club memberships. **Comments:** the course is flat and easy to walk. This private country club is challenging for all levels of Greens are large in size with a stream coming in play on several holes.

Directions: from I-90/I-15 in Butte take exit #228. Proceed south on Continental Drive to Elizabeth Warren Avenue. Turn right on Elizabeth Warren for .5 miles to the golf course entrance on your left hand side of the street.

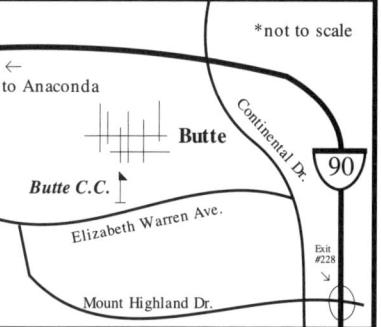

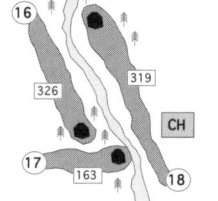

Course Yardage & Par:

C-6343 yards, par 70.
M-6055 yards, par 70.
W-5424 yards, par 71.

Cabinet View Country Club (public, 9 hole course)

378 Cabinet View Country Club Rd.; P.O. Box 1062; Libby, Montana 59923
Phone: (406) 293-7332. Fax: none. Internet: none.
Pro: Keith Johnson, PGA. Superintendent: Steve Richard.
Rating/Slope: M 68.5/112; W 69.4/113. **Course record:** 65.
Green fees: W/D $19/$12; W/E $20/$12; Jr. & Sr. rates; M/C, VISA.
Power cart: $18/$10. **Pull cart:** $3/$2. **Trail fee:** $5 for personal carts.
Reservation policy: you may call in advance for your tee-times. No time limit.
Winter condition: the golf course is closed from November 1st to mid-March.
Terrain: flat, 2 small hills. **Tees:** all grass. **Spikes:** soft spikes preferred.
Services: club rentals, snack bar, pro shop, lounge, lessons, lockers, beer, wine, beverages, liquor, driving range, putting & chipping greens, club memberships.
Comments: good public golf course that is surrounded by beautiful countryside. The fairways are tree-lined and can be narrow in spots. Greens are large and have few undulations to them. Very friendly golf course that will be worth a trip.

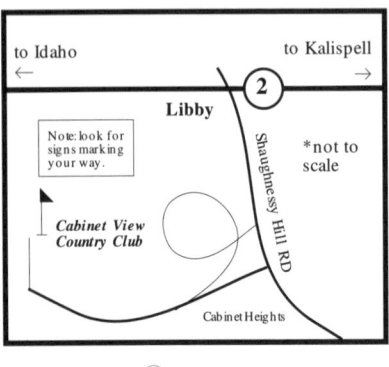

Directions: from Highway 2S in Libby, Montana turn westbound on Shaughnessy Hill Road. Follow this for 1.2 miles to the course. Look for signs marking your turn.

Course Yardage & Par:
M-3105 yards, par 36.
W-2722 yards, par 36.
Dual tees for 18 holes:
M-6341 yards, par 72.
W-5508 yards, par 72.

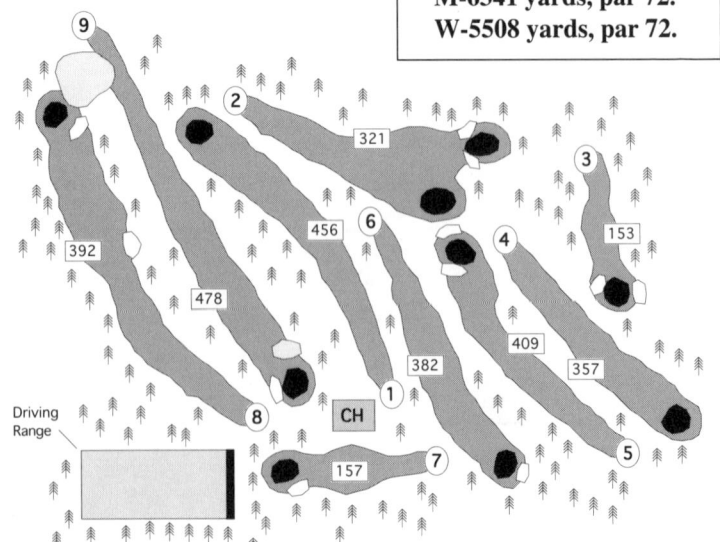

Cedar Creek Golf Course (public, 9 hole par 3 course)

10 Wadsworth Lane; P.O. Box 567; Superior, Montana 59872
Phone: (406) 822-4443. Fax: none. Internet: none.
Manager: Bernie Anderson. Superintendent: unavailable.
Rating/Slope: the golf course is not rated. **Course record:** 25.
Green fees: W/D $7; W/E $7; no special rates; VISA, M/C.
Power cart: $12/$7. **Pull cart:** $2/$1. **Trail fee:** call for policy.
Reservation policy: course is on a first come first served basis.
Winter condition: the golf course is closed from November to March.
Terrain: flat (easy walking). **Tees:** all grass. **Spikes:** soft spikes preferred.
Services: club rentals, snack bar, small pro shop, putting green.
Comments: newer course that opened in spring of 1996. The course features
bent grass greens with water coming into play on several holes. Fairways are
tree-lined and narrow. The course is selling homesites around this 9 hole track.

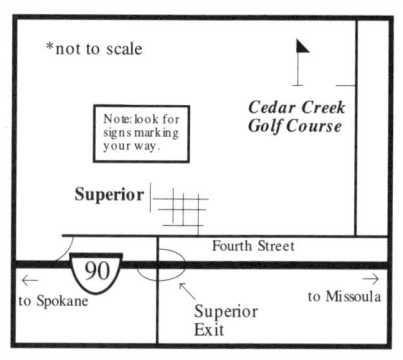

Directions: from I-90 E&W take the
Superior Montana exit. Exit to Fourth
Street. Head eastbound on Fourth Street
and turn left at the golf course sign some
4 blocks ahead. Look for signs.

Course Yardage & Par:
M-1401 yards, par 27.
W-1202 yards, par 27.

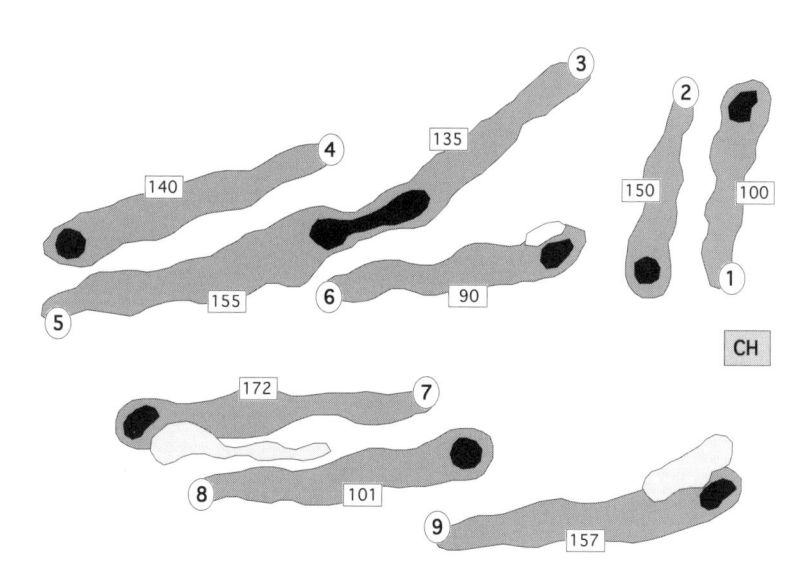

Chinook Golf & Country Club (public, 9 hole course)

Highway 2; P.O. Box 146; Chinook, Montana 59523
Phone: (406) 357-2244. Fax: none. Internet: none.
Manager: J. Munson. Superintendent: J. Munson.
Rating/Slope: the golf course is not rated. **Course record:** 34 (9 holes).
Green fees: W/D $12/$9; W/E $12/$9; no credit cards.
Power cart: not available. **Pull cart:** $2. **Trail fee:** $3 for personal carts.
Reservation policy: advance reservations are not required or needed.
Winter condition: the golf course is closed from November 1st to March 1st.
Terrain: flat, some hills. **Tees:** all grass. **Spikes:** soft spikes preferred.
Services: limited services for the golfer. Course is sometimes on the honor box.
Comments: this nine hole course has undergone some revisions in the last few
years. The course now sports new grass greens and some additonal mounding
around these surfaces. Fairways are wide open leaving lots of room off the tee.

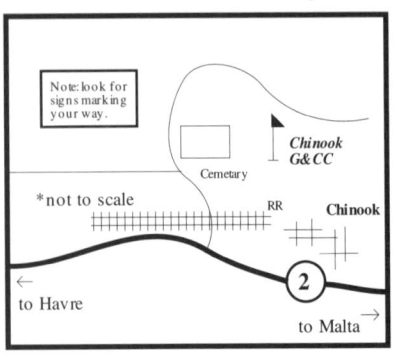

Directions: from Highway 2 turn E&W
northbound .3 miles west of the town
of Chinook. Watch for signs (green &
white) to the golf course. Proceed over
the railroad tracks and follow 1.3 miles
to the golf course.

Course Yardage & Par:
M-3130 yards, par 36.
W-3130 yards, par 36.

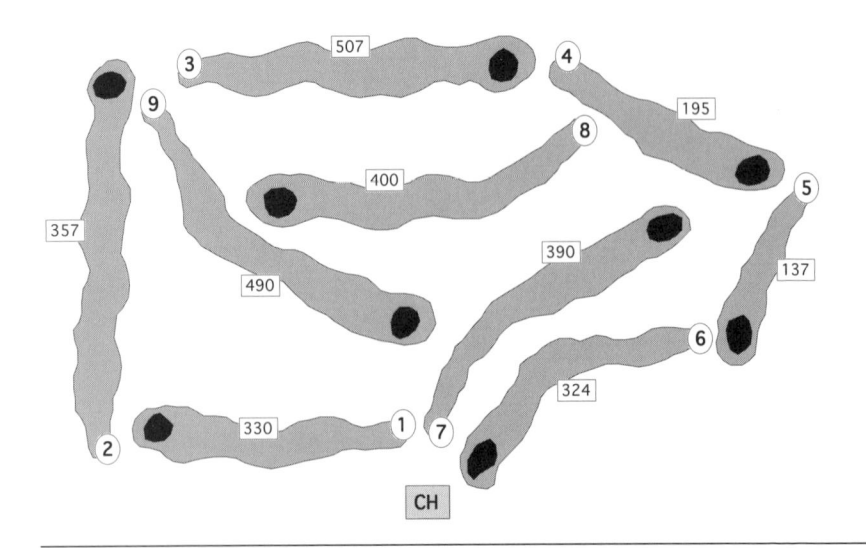

Choteau Country Club (public, 9 hole course)

Aiport Road; P.O. Box 804; Choteau, Montana 59422
Phone: (406) 466-2020. Fax: none. Internet: none.
Manager: Susie Durocher. Superintendent: Tim Hill.
Rating/Slope: C 67.9/97; M 66.0/94; W 68.8/109. **Course record:** 32 (9 holes).
Green fees: W/D $15/$9; W/E $18/$11; M/C, VISA, AMEX.
Power cart: $18/$10. **Pull cart:** $2. **Trail fee:** $5 for personal carts.
Reservation policy: please call 1 week in advance for your tee time.
Winter condition: course is open weather permitting. Uses temporary greens.
Terrain: flat (easy walking). **Tees:** all grass. **Spikes:** soft spikes required.
Services: club rentals, beer, wine, beverages, snack bar, limited pro shop, driving range, putting green. **Comments:** this course is very flat and easy to walk. Located next to the Choteau airport the course offers the golfer views of the surrounding valley and countryside. The course offers full service amenities.

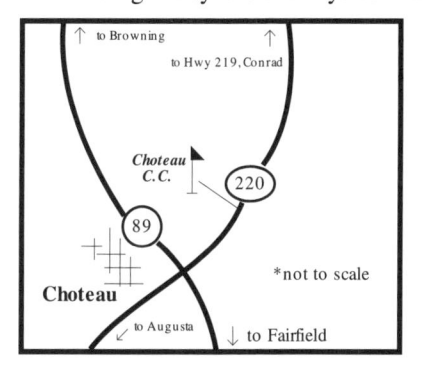

Directions: from Highway 220 in the town of Choteau exit on Airport Road and follow this road to the golf course. The course is located east of Choteau Montana. Look for signs along your way.

Course Yardage & Par:
C-3105 yards, par 35.
M-2904 yards, par 35.
W-2612 yards, par 36.

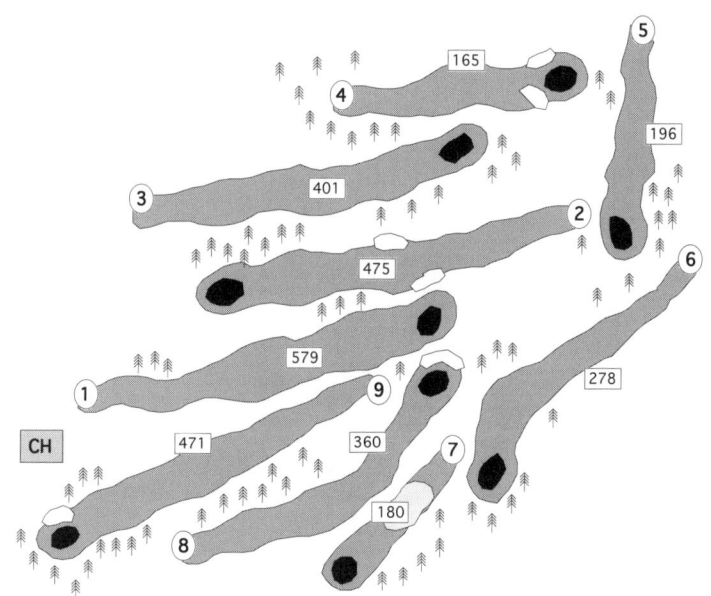

Circle Inn Golf Links (public, 9 hole par 3 course)

1029 Main Street; Billings, Montana 59105
Phone: (406) 248-4202. **Fax:** none. **Internet:** none.
Manager: A. Steffinch. **Superintendent:** A. Steffinch.
Rating/Slope: the golf course is not rated. **Course record:** 24.
Green fees: $6 all week long; $7 all day rate; Jr. & Sr. rates; M/C, VISA.
Power cart: not available. **Pull cart:** $2. **Trail fee:** personal carts not allowed.
Reservation policy: advance reservations are not required. Just show up.
Winter condition: the course is open all year long, weather permitting.
Terrain: flat (easy walking). **Tees:** all grass. **Spikes:** no policy.
Services: club rentals, beer, wine, beverages, snack bar, liquor, casino.
Comments: this course is very flat and easy to walk. This par 3 track has little in the way of hazards to contend with. Greens are very small leaving the golfer with a great deal of chipping if you have difficulty off the tee. Good beginner course.

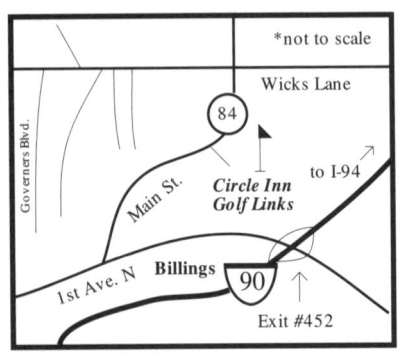

Directions: from I-90 take exit #452. Proceed west to 1st Avenue N. Turn right Main Street the course is located on the east side of the Highway. Look for the Casino sign.

Course Yardage & Par:
M-789 yards, par 27.
W-789 yards, par 27.

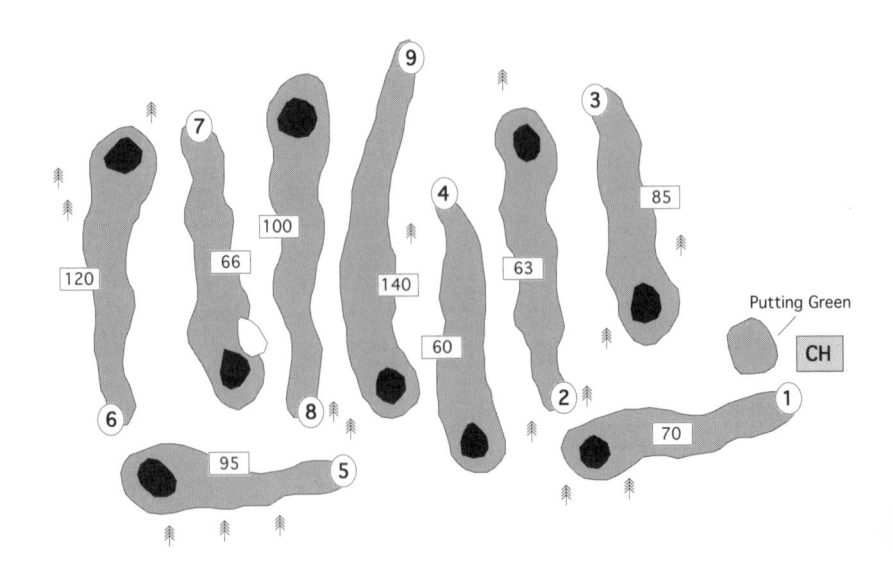

Cottonwood Country Club (public. 9 hole course)
Country Club Road; P.O. Box 317; Glendive, Montana 59330
Phone: (406) 365-8797. Fax: none. Internet: none.
Pro/Manager: Scott McPherson, PGA. Superintendent: Scott McPherson.
Rating/Slope: C 66.7/102; M 65.7/100; W 66.8/102. **Course record:** 66.
Green fees: W/D $15/$12; W/E $15/$12; Jr. & Sr. rates; M/C, VISA, AMEX.
Power cart: $23/$12. **Pull cart:** $2. **Trail fee:** $5 for personal carts.
Reservation policy: please call 1 week in advance for your tee time.
Winter condition: the golf course is closed from November1st to April 1st.
Terrain: flat, some hills. **Tees:** all grass. **Spikes:** soft spikes required.
Services: club rentals, beer, wine, beverages, snack bar, liquor, restaurant,
pro shop, driving range, putting & chipping greens, club memberships.
Comments: fair public course that can play much longer than the yardage would
indicate. Greens are large in size with few undulations. Fairways are wide giving
you generous landing area's from the tee. Give it a try if you are out this way.

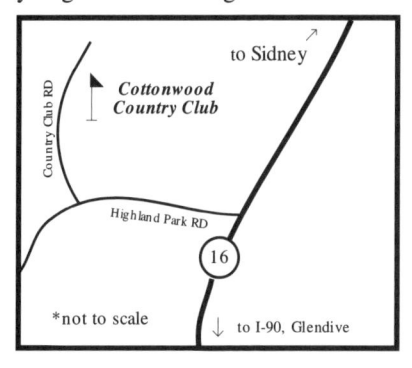

Directions: from Highway 16 in
northeast Glendive exit onto Highland
Park Road. Follow Highland Park Road
for .7 miles to Country Club Road where
you will turn right. Follow Country Club
Road .5 miles to the golf course. Look
for signs that are posted along the way.

Course Yardage & Par:
C-3286 yards, par 36.
M-3151 yards, par 36.
W-3018 yards, par 40.

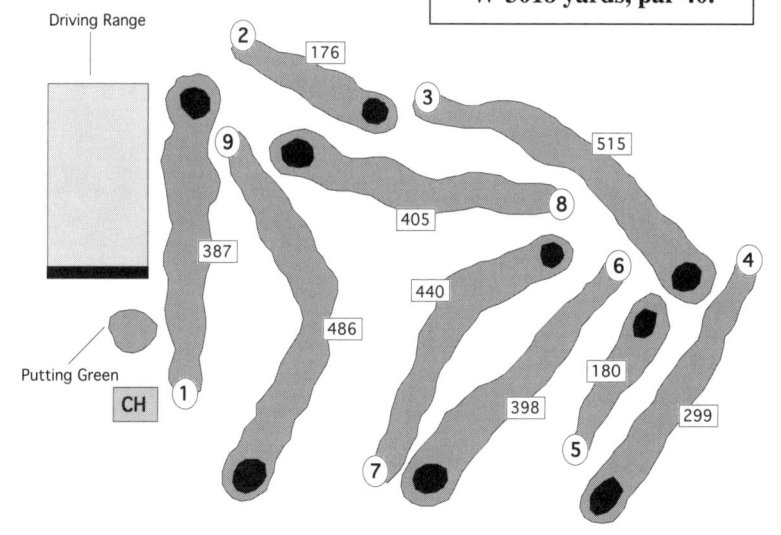

Cottonwood Hills Golf Course (public, 18 hole & 9 hole Exc.)

8955 River Road; P.O. Box 454; Bozeman, Montana 59715
Phone: (406) 587-1118. **Fax:** none. **Internet:** none.
Pro: Bill Larson, PGA. **Superintendent:** unavailable.
Rating/Slope: T 70.1/119; C 68.7/115; M 66.8/112; W 67.9/110. **Record:** 65.
Green fees: W/D $24/$16; W/E $24/$16; Jr. rates; M/C, VISA.
Green fees executive course: W/D $8; W/E $8; no special rates; M/C, VISA.
Power cart: $18/$12. **Pull cart:** $2. **Trail fee:** personal carts not allowed.
Reservation policy: you may call two days in advance for your tee-times.
Winter condition: the golf course is closed from November to February.
Terrain: flat, some hills. **Tees:** all grass. **Spikes:** soft spikes preferred.
Services: club rentals, snack bar, pro shop, lockers, lessons, driving range.
Comments: season passes are available at this challenging golf course. A good variety of holes will require you to use every club in the bag. The executive course sports a par of 29 and is fun for the entire family. Good public course.

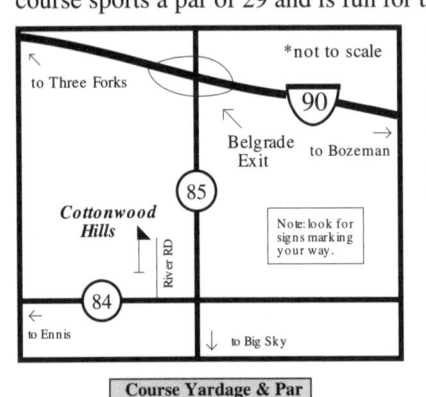

Directions: from I-90 take the Belgrade exit (Hwy 85). Proceed south on this. Proceed until (7 miles) you reach a four way stop. Turn west (Norris Rd.). Go on Norris for 1.3 miles to River Rd. Turn right on River Rd. to the course.

Course Yardage & Par:
T-6677 yards, par 70.
C-6356 yards, par 70.
M-5947 yards, par 70.
W-5186 yards, par 71.

Course Yardage & Par Executive Course:
M-1181 yards, par 29.

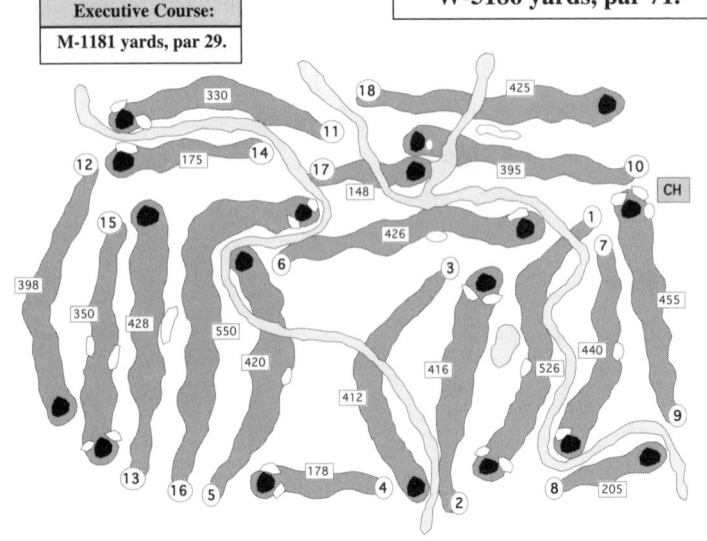

Cut Bank Golf & Country Club (public, 9 hole course)

59 Golf Course Road North; Cut Bank, Montana 59427
Phone: (406) 873-2574. **Fax:** none. **Internet:** none.
Pro: Brad Forbis. **Superintendent:** Brad Forbis.
Rating/Slope: M 66/106; W 70/110. **Course record:** 29 (9 holes).
Green fees: Weekdays $12; Weekends $12; M/C, VISA, AMEX.
Power cart: $16/$10. **Pull cart:** $2. **Trail fee:** personal carts not allowed.
Reservation policy: you may call 7 days in advance for tee times.
Winter condition: the course is closed from November to March.
Terrain: flat, some hills. **Tees:** grass. **Spikes:** soft spikes preferred.
Services: club rentals, snack bar, beer, wine, pro shop, lessons, driving range, putting & chipping greens, club memberships. **Comments:** the course is fairly wide open with few hazards to contend with except for water on three holes. Dual tees available for a full 18 hole round, giving variety between your nines.

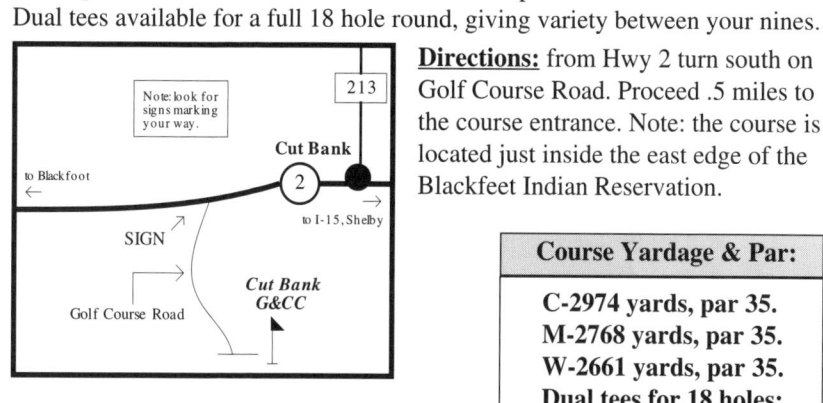

Directions: from Hwy 2 turn south on Golf Course Road. Proceed .5 miles to the course entrance. Note: the course is located just inside the east edge of the Blackfeet Indian Reservation.

Course Yardage & Par:
C-2974 yards, par 35.
M-2768 yards, par 35.
W-2661 yards, par 35.
<u>Dual tees for 18 holes:</u>
C-5948 yards, par 70.
M-5536 yards, par 70.
W-5322 yards, par 70.

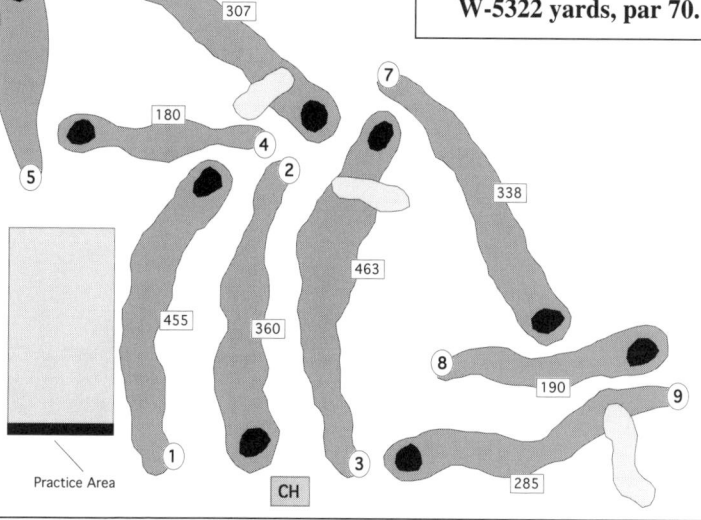

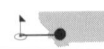

Deer Lodge Golf Club (public, 9 hole course)

Highway 10; P.O. Box 254; Deer Lodge, Montana 59722
Phone: (406) 846-1625. Fax: none. Internet: none.
Manager: Pat Johnson. Superintendent: Pat Johnson.
Rating/Slope: M 67.8/101; W 68.4/102. **Course record:** 65.
Green fees: Weekdays $15/$10; Weekends $15/$10; M/C, VISA.
Power cart: $15/$9. **Pull cart:** $2.50/$1.50. **Trail fee:** $5 for personal carts.
Reservation policy: none needed. Times are on a first come first served basis.
Winter condition: the golf course is closed from November 1st to March 15th.
Terrain: flat, some hills. **Tees:** all grass. **Spikes:** no spike policy.
Services: club rentals, lounge, restaurant, beer, wine, liquor, pro shop, driving range, putting green, club memberships. **Comments:** the course sports small undulating greens which make it tough to score on. Other features include some creeks, ponds, brush and large trees (no sand bunkers). Fair public golf course.

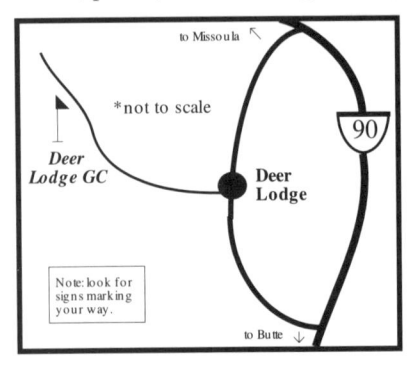

Directions: the golf course is located right off Highway 10 in Deer Lodge. Look for signs indicating your turn to the course. The way is well marked.

Course Yardage & Par:
M-3200 yards, par 36.
W-2749 yards, par 36.
Dual tees for 18 holes:
M-6400 yards, par 72.
W-5498 yards, par 72.

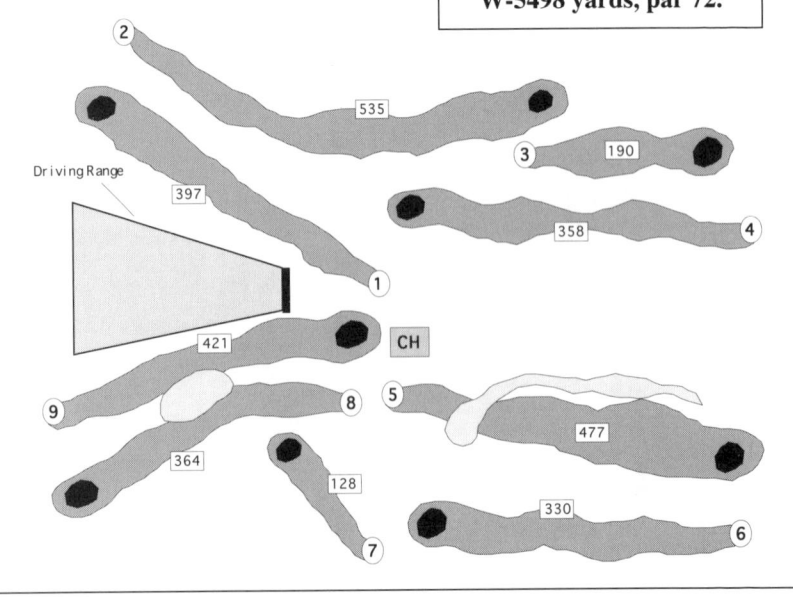

Double Arrow Golf Resort (resort, 9 hole course)

Highway 83; Seeley Lake, Montana 59868
Phone: (406) 677-3247. Fax: none. Internet: none.
Pro: Ed Bezanson, PGA. Superintendent: Jeff Marlatt.
Rating/Slope: C 68.9/119; M 67.2/116; W 68.1/118. **Course record:** 67.
Green fees: W/D $22/$13; W/E $22/$13; no special rates; M/C, VISA.
Power cart: $20/$10. **Pull cart:** $3/$2. **Trail fee:** personal carts not allowed.
Reservation policy: please call in advance for tee times. 2 weeks maximum.
Winter condition: the golf course is closed from November to March.
Terrain: flat, some hills. **Tees:** all grass. **Spikes:** soft spikes preferred.
Services: club rentals, pro shop, lessons, putting/chipping green, driving range.
Comments: this course offers challenging golf in a spectacular mountain setting.
Ponderosa pines line many of the rolling fairways and hole 6 has an island green.

Directions: from Highway 83 turn into the Seeley Lake Lodge and Resort just south of Seeley Lake on Double Arrow Road. At the "Y" veer left to the course entrance and pro shop. Look for signs.

to Swan Lake

Double Arrow Golf Resort

Seeley Lake

*not to scale

Double Arrow Road

83

Note: look for signs marking your way.

to Hwy 200, Missoula

Course Yardage & Par:
C-3167 yards, par 36.
M-2970 yards, par 36.
W-2526 yards, par 36.
Dual tees for 18 holes:
C-6334 yards, par 72.
M-5940 yards, par 72.
W-5052 yards, par 72.

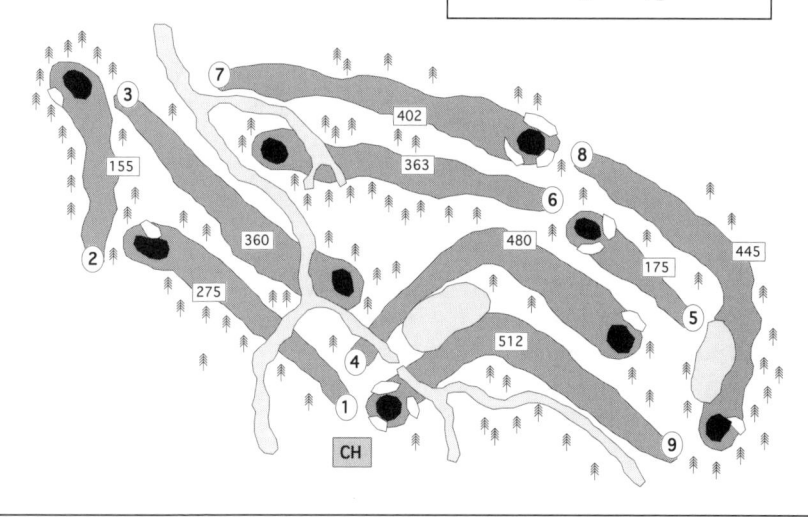

Eagle Bend Golf Club (27 hole resort course)

Physical address: 279 Eagle Bend Drive; Bigfork, Montana 59911
Mailing address: P.O. Box 1257; Bigfork, Montana 59911
Phone: (800) 255-5641 or (406) 837-7310. **Fax:** none. **Internet:** www.golfmt.com
Pro: Gary Shepherd, Jr., PGA. **Superintendent:** Larry Newlin.
Rating/Slope: please see ratings below. **Course record:** C-65; M-63.
Green fees: March-June 22/September 18th-November $32/$20 (off season);
June 23-September 17 $50/$27 (peak); Jr./Sr. rates; M/C, VISA, AMEX, DIS.
Power cart: $14/$9 per person. **Pull cart:** $4/$2.50. **Trail fee:** not allowed.
Reservation policy: please call 3 days in advance. Credit card is required.
Winter condition: the golf course is closed from November to March.
Terrain: rolling hills, mounding. **Tees:** all grass. **Spikes:** soft spikes only.
Services: club rentals, snack bar, practice facility, restaurant with full service
bar, pro shop, lessons, driving range, marina. Proper golf attire is required.
Comments: rated as one of the nation's top 50 courses by *Golf Digest* in 1990
this course offers golf at it's finest. Originally designed by William Hull in 1988,
this course offers plush, well groomed fairways, rolling terrain and the finest
greens in the Flathead Valley. In 1995 Jack Nicklaus designed an additional 9
holes making this 27 hole resort a must play on your next golfing vacation.

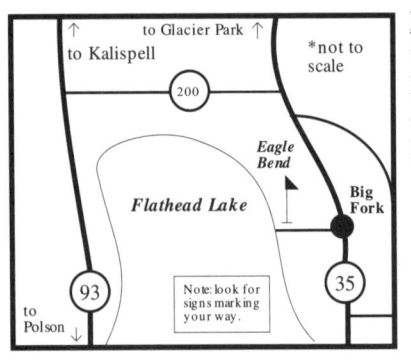

Directions: the golf course is located just
west of Highway 35 at the north end of
Flathead Lake. Take Holt Road to the
course entrance which will be on your
left. Look for signs along your way.

***course yardage on
the following page.**

Course Ratings & Slope:

Lake Course:
C 71.9/124; M 69.3/119; Mixed 70.6/121; W 68.9/120.

Ridge/Nicklaus Course:
C 71.2/121; M 69.9/117; W 70.1/119.

Course Yardage & Par:

C-6724 yards, par 72.
M-6189 yards, par 72.
W-5429 yards, par 72.
(Ridge/Nicklaus Course)

Ridge Course

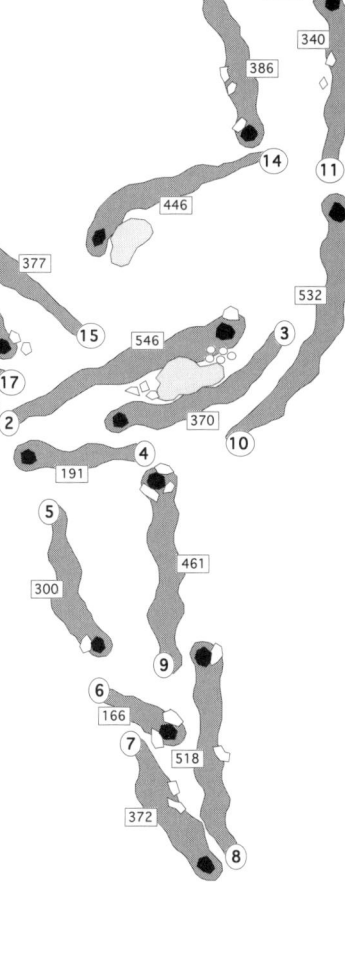

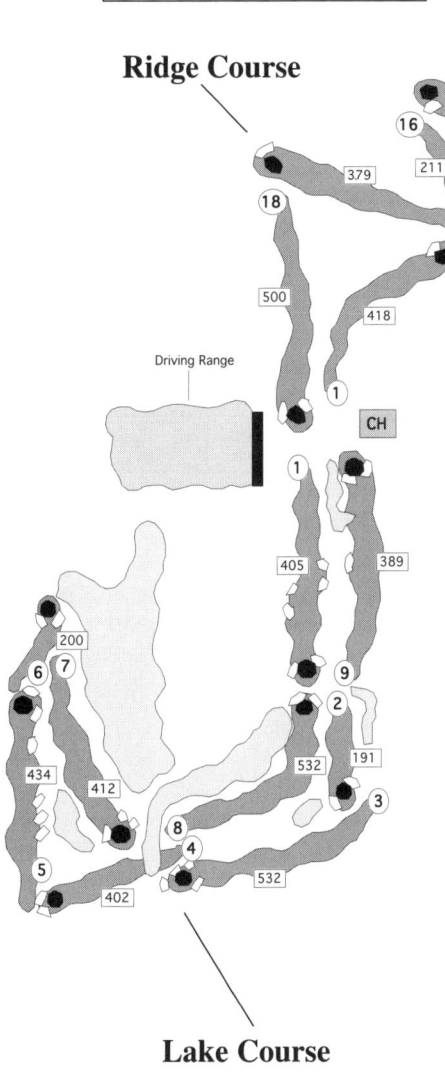

Driving Range

CH

Lake Course

Course Yardage & Par:

C-6854 yards, par 72.
M-6250 yards, par 72.
Mixed-6622 yards, par 72.
W-5148 yards, par 72.
(Lake Course)

Emerald Greens (public, 18 hole executive course)

1100 American Avenue SW; Great Falls, Montana 59404
Phone: (406) 453-4844. Fax: none. Internet: none.
Manager: G. L. Bass. Superintendent: unavailable.
Rating/Slope: the course is not rated. **Course record:** 59.
Green fees: W/D $14/$8.50; W/E $14/$8.50; M/C, VISA.
Power cart: $15/$9. **Pull cart:** $2. **Trail fee:** $10 for personal carts.
Reservation policy: you may call 7 days in advance for all your tee times.
Winter condition: the golf course is open in winter on temporary greens.
Terrain: flat, some hills. **Tees:** all grass. **Spikes:** no spike policy.
Services: club rentals, limited services for the golfer, putting green.
Comments: an easy walking course located in the city. A great place to take the kids to teach them to play. The course is fairly wide open with few hazards.

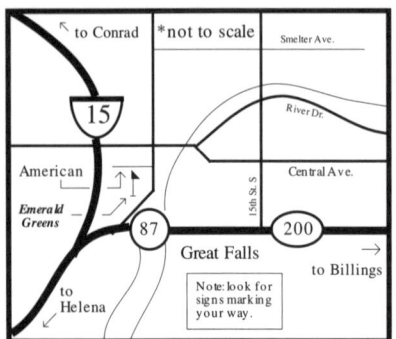

Directions: from Highway 15 exit on 6th Street SW. Proceed to American Avenue. Turn left. Proceed to the course entrance which is .3 miles ahead.

Course Yardage & Par:
M-3879 yards, par 61.
W-3796 yards, par 61.

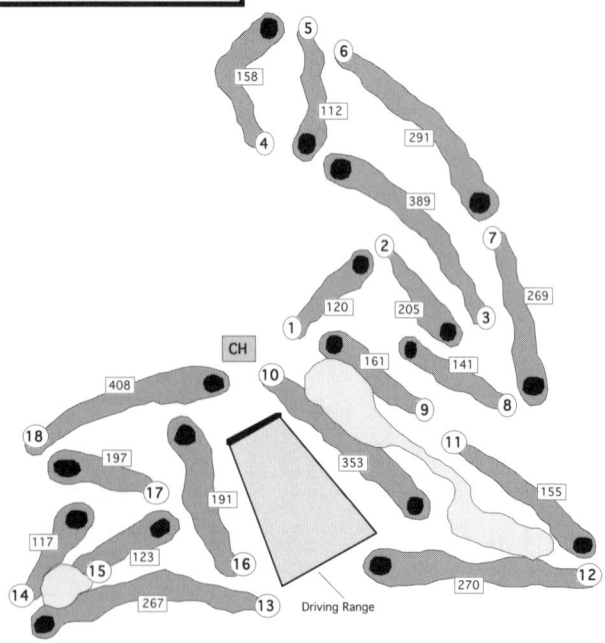

Exchange City Par-3 Golf Course (public, 18 hole par course)

19th St. W & Central Avenue; P.O. Box 20564; Billings, Montana 59102
Phone: (406) 652-2553. Fax: none. Internet: none.
Pro: Rob Jerhoff, PGA. Superintendent: Mark Walker.
Rating/Slope: M 69/51.3; W 69/51.3. **Course record:** 49.
Green fees: Weekdays $10/$7; Weekends $10/$7; M/C, VISA.
Power cart: $14/$8. **Pull cart:** $2. **Trail fee:** personal carts not allowed.
Reservation policy: please call 7 days in advance for your tee times.
Winter condition: the golf course is closed from November 1st to mid-March.
Terrain: flat, some hills. **Tees:** all grass. **Spikes:** soft spikes only.
Services: club rentals, snack bar, pro shop, lessons, driving range, putting green.
Comments: a friendly golf course great to practice your iron play on. The golf course is well maintained and offers 5 ponds, numerous sand traps and tree-lined fairways to challenge golfers of any level. Great course for a change of pace.

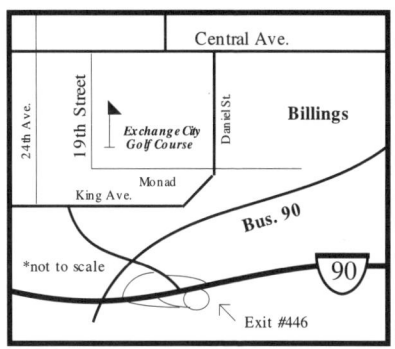

Directions: the golf course is located in the western section of Billings Montana. From downtown Billings take Division Street (becomes Central Avenue). Proceed on Central Avenue to the golf course. Look for the golf course at the intersections of 19th St. and Central Ave.

Course Yardage & Par:
C-2805 yards, par 54.
M-2799 yards, par 54.
W-2307 yards, par 54.

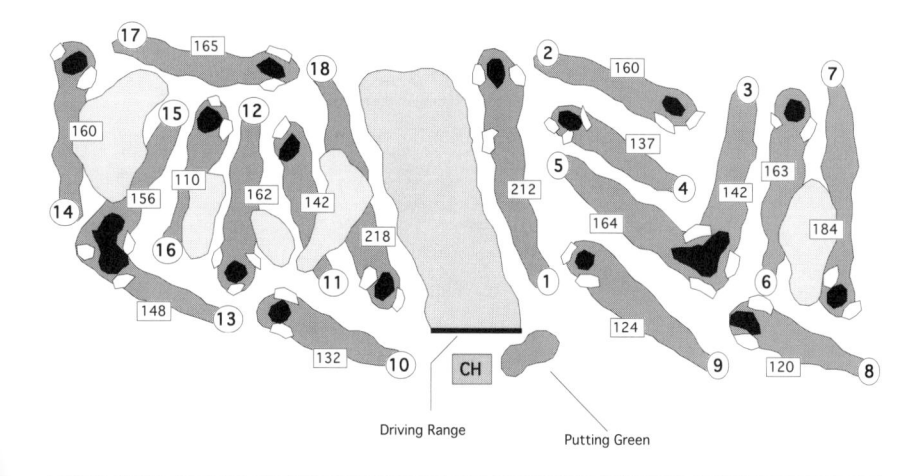

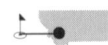

Fairmont Hot Springs Resort (18 hole resort course)

1500 Fairmont Road; Fairmont, Montana 59711
Phone: (406) 797-3241. **Fax:** none. **Internet:** none.
Manager: Ed Henrich. **Superintendent:** unavailable.
Rating/Slope: M 69.5/109; W 70.1/120. **Course record:** 65.
Green fees: W/D $27/$18; W/E $33/$22; M/C, VISA.
Power cart: $24/$16. **Pull cart:** $3.50. **Trail fee:** $25 for personal carts.
Reservation policy: you may call up to two weeks in advance for tee-times.
Winter condition: the golf course is closed from November to April.
Terrain: flat, some hills. **Tees:** all grass. **Spikes:** soft spikes only.
Services: club rentals, snack bar, restaurant, beer, wine, liquor, pro shop, lessons, driving range, tennis courts, RV hookups, full resort amennities.
Comments: "FUNTASTIC," the course has the longest hole in Montana, a 649 yard par 5 and the largest green in Montana on hole no. 3, par 3, a 10,000 square foot putting surface. The backdrop for your play is mountainous although the course itself is fairly wide open. This resort and course is worth a special trip.

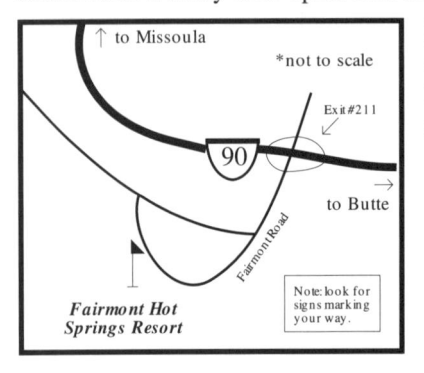

Directions: from I-90 E&W take exit #211. Proceed 3 miles west on Fairmont Road to the resort. Look for signs to the resort and golf course.

Course Yardage & Par:
M-6741 yards, par 72.
W-5921 yards, par 72.

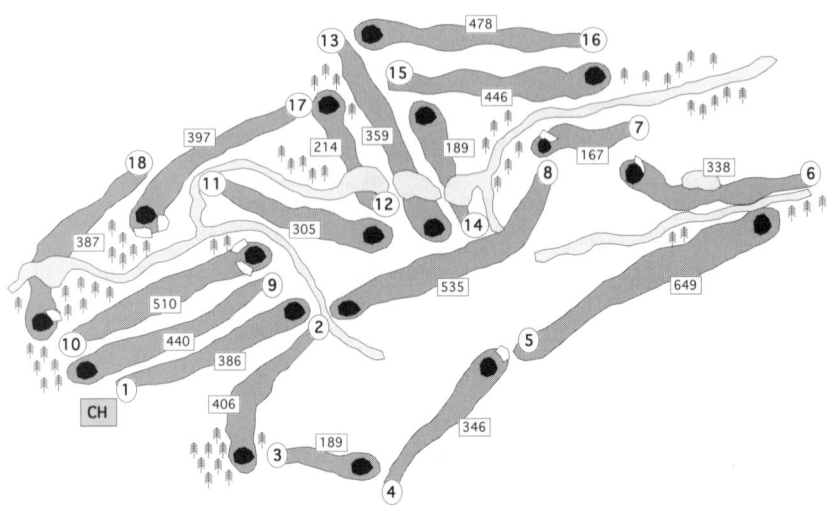

Forsyth Country Club (public, 9 hole course)

Frontage Road; P.O. Box 191; Forsyth, Montana 59327
Phone: (406) 356-7710. Fax: none. Internet: none.
Manager: Wanda Dowlin. Superintendent: none.
Rating/Slope: M 67.9/106; W 70.2/108. **Course record:** 67 (18 holes).
Green fees: W/D $18/$9; W/E $20/$12; M/C, VISA, AMEX, DIS.
Power cart: $16/$9. **Pull cart:** $1. **Trail fee:** personal carts not allowed.
Reservation policy: call in advance for tee times. No time limit on Tee-times.
Winter condition: the golf course is closed from November 1st to mid-March.
Terrain: flat, some hills. **Tees:** all grass. **Spikes:** soft spikes preferred.
Services: club rentals, snack bar, beer, wine, liquor, beverages, small pro shop.
Comments: dual tees are available for a full 18 hole variety at this 9 hole course.
Most fairways are tree-line although the trees have not reached maturity. Greens
are large in size with few undulations. Relaxing golf in a quiet country setting.

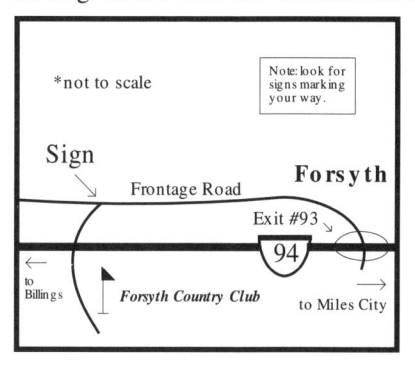

Directions: from I-94 take exit 93 for
Forsyth. Proceed over the freeway and
turn left on Frontage Road. Proceed 1.4
miles where you turn left under I-94.
Look for a red sign indicating your turn
(there is no street name). Proceed .4
miles to the course which will be on
your right side.

Course Yardage & Par:

M-3028 yards, par 36.
W-2780 yards, par 36.
Dual tees for 18 holes:
M-5913 yards, par 71.
W-5534 yards, par 72.

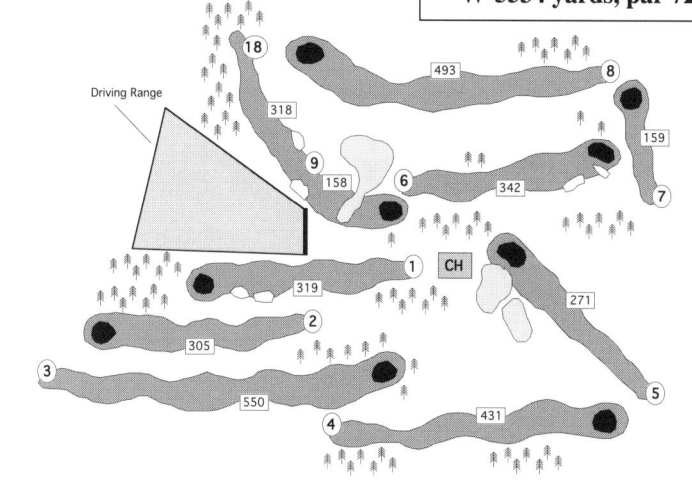

Fort Custer Golf Club (public, 9 hole course)

Highway 47; P.O. Box 316; Hardin, Montana 59034
Phone: (406) 665-2597. Fax: none. Internet: none.
Manager: J. Koebbe. Superintendent: J. Koebbe.
Rating/Slope: M 68.2/102; W 67.4/101. **Course record:** 67.
Green fees: W/D $13; W/E $13; Jr. and Sr. rates; M/C, VISA.
Power cart: $12/$8. **Pull cart:** $2. **Trail fee:** personal carts are not allowed.
Reservation policy: please call in advance for all your tee times.
Winter condition: the golf course is closed from November 15th to March 15th.
Terrain: flat (easy walking). **Tees:** all grass. **Spikes:** no spike policy.
Services: club rentals, snack bar, beer, wine, small pro shop, driving range.
Comments: be sure to visit the monument at the battleground where Custer's last stand took place to round out you day after golf. The course here offers dual tees, 3 ponds and some tree-lined fairways to challenge your skill. Good track.

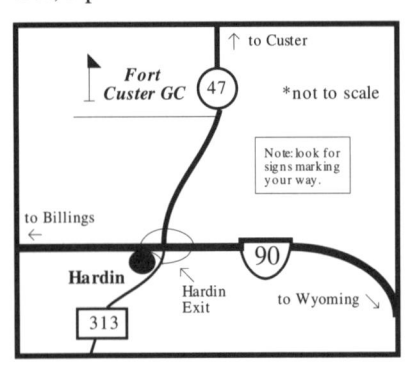

Directions: the course is located on Hwy 47. Proceed north of Hardin approximately 2.5 miles on Highway 47 to your turn to the golf course. Look for the sign marking your left hand turn. Proceed .4 miles to the course on your right,.

Course Yardage & Par:
M-3179 yards, par 36.
W-2755 yards, par 36.
Dual tees for 18 holes:
M-6448 yards, par 72.
W-5555 yards, par 72.

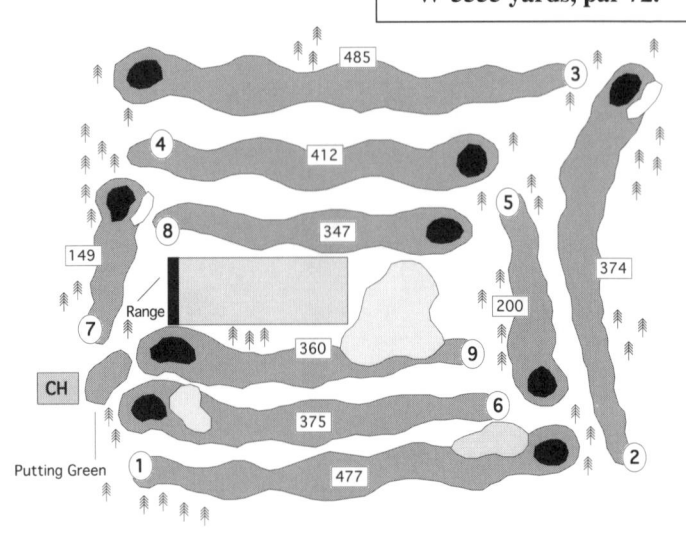

Fox Ridge Golf Course (public, 18 hole reg. & 18 hole par 3)
4020 Lake Helena Drive; Helena, Montana 59601
Phone: (406) 227-8304. Fax: none. Internet: none.
Pro: Lance M. Newman. Superintendent: unavailable.
Rating/Slope: C 69.7/114; M 69.5/110; W 70.2/115. **Course record:** 67.
Green fees: W/D $18/$11; W/E $18/$18; M/C, VISA.
Green fees for the par 3 course: $12/$7 all week long; M/C, VISA.
Power cart: $18/$11. **Pull cart:** $2/$1. **Trail fee:** $5 for personal carts.
Reservation policy: you may call 7 days in advance for a tee time.
Winter condition: the golf course is closed from December to February.
Terrain: flat, some hills. **Tees:** all grass. **Spikes:** soft spikes required.
Services: club rentals, snack bar, beer, wine, pro shop, lessons, driving range.
Comments: newer golf course that features numerous ponds and bunkers. The
facility also features a par 3 golf course that is fun for the whole family.

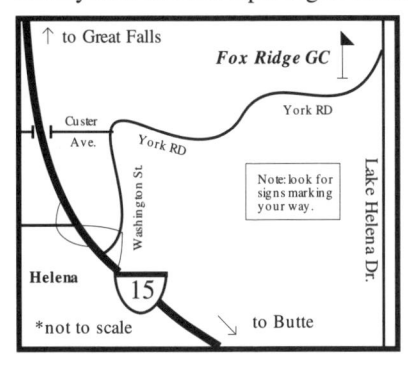

Directions: the course is located 7 miles
past the airport off of I-15. From I-15
take the Cedar Street exit. Proceed to
Custer and turn right. Proceed to York,
turn left. Proceed to the golf course.

Course Yardage & Par:
M-6301 yards, par 72.
M-5988 yards, par 72.
W-5921 yards, par 72.

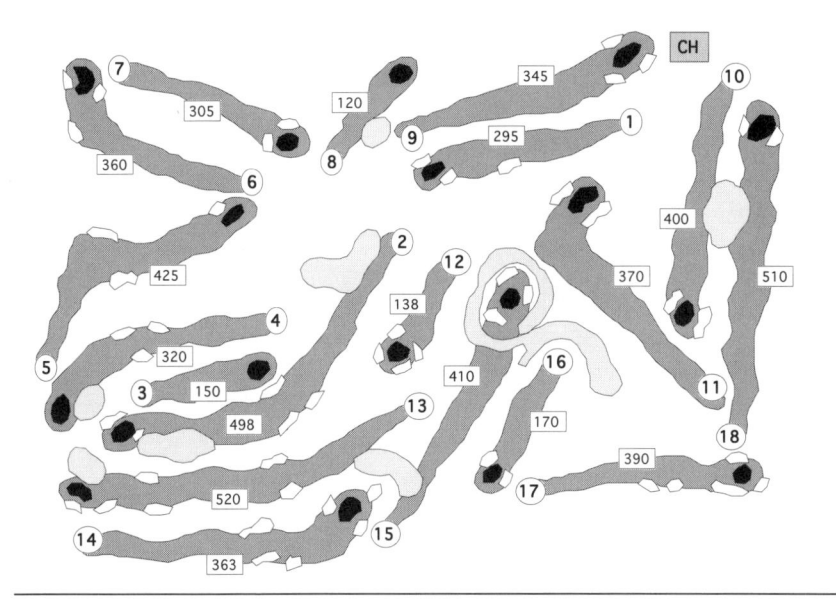

Glacier Park Golf Course (public, 9 hole course)

Highway's 49 & 2; East Glacier, Montana 59434
Phone: (406) 226-9311. **Fax:** none. **Internet:** none.
Manager: J. Martinson. **Superintendent:** unavailable.
Rating/Slope: the golf course is not rated. **Course record:** 33 (9 holes).
Green fees: W/D $20/$12; W/E $20/$12; twilight rates; M/C, VISA.
Power cart: $16/$9. **Pull cart:** $2. **Trail fee:** $6 for personal carts.
Reservation policy: please call in advance for your tee times. No time limit.
Winter condition: the golf course is closed from mid-October to late April.
Terrain: flat, some hills. **Tees:** all grass. **Spikes:** soft spikes preferred.
Services: club rentals, snack bar, pro shop, housing at the Glacier Park Lodge.
Comments: a great vacation spot for the whole family. Glacier National Park is
one of the most beautiful in the nation. If you will be staying a while check into
the family pass for the course as it may be more economical. Good 9 hole track.

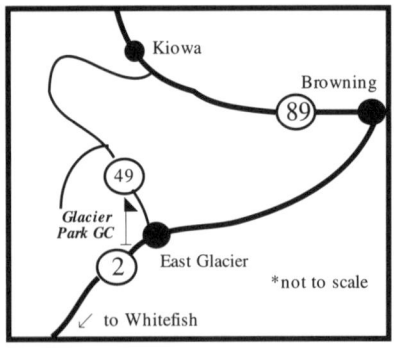

Directions: the entrance to the lodge is
right off Highway 49 at the junction for
Highway 2. Proceed northbound on
Highway 49 through the underpass of
the railroad tracks. Proceed to the lodge
where the clubhouse is located.

Course Yardage & Par:
M-3349 yards, par 36.
W-3349 yards, par 36.

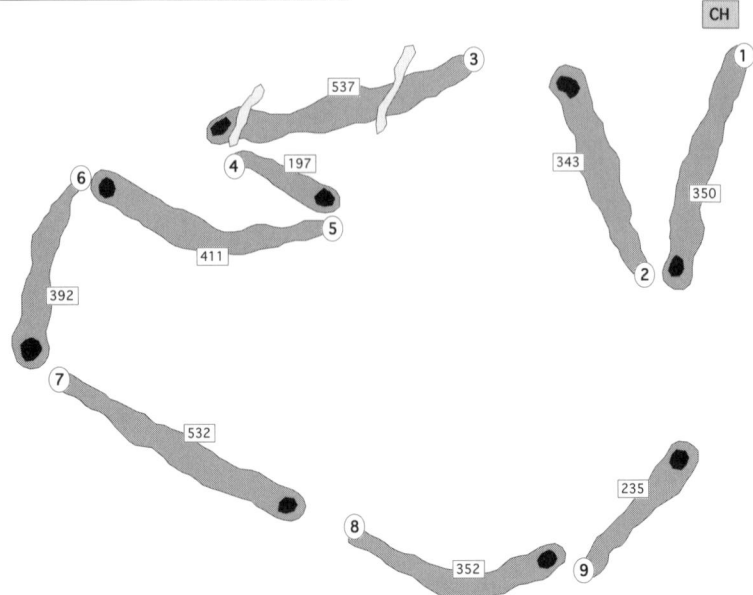

Glacier View Golf Club (public, 18 hole course)

River Bend Drive; P.O. Box 185; West Glacier, Montana 59936
Phone: (406) 888-5471. Fax: none. Internet: none.
Pro: Don Waller, PGA. Superintendent: Tom Ask.
Rating/Slope: M 64.1/88; W 64.6/96. **Course record:** 59.
Green fees: W/D $20/$12; W/E $20/$12; all day rates; M/C, VISA.
Power cart: $18/$10. **Pull cart:** $3/$2. **Trail fee:** personal carts not allowed.
Reservation policy: no restrictions, 7 days ahead is recommended in season.
Winter condition: the golf course is closed from October to late April.
Terrain: flat (easy walking). **Tees:** all grass. **Spikes:** soft spikes only.
Services: club rentals, snack bar, restaurant, beer, wine, liquor, pro shop, lessons, RV park. **Comments:** the course lies in a beautiful setting just outside Glacier National Park. Family oriented, the course is affordable and is in excellent condition in peak season. "Golf the Glacier and enjoy the view."

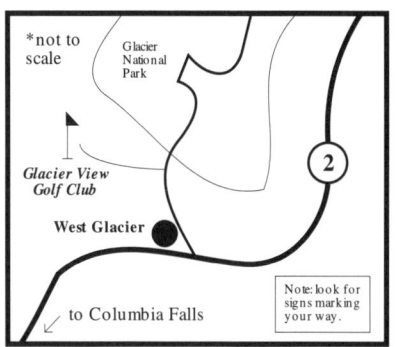

Directions: follow US Highway 2 east or west to Glacier National Park, then follow the signs to the golf course located 1 mile west of the town of West Glacier Montana.

Course Yardage & Par:
M-5105 yards, par 68.
W-4706 yards, par 68.

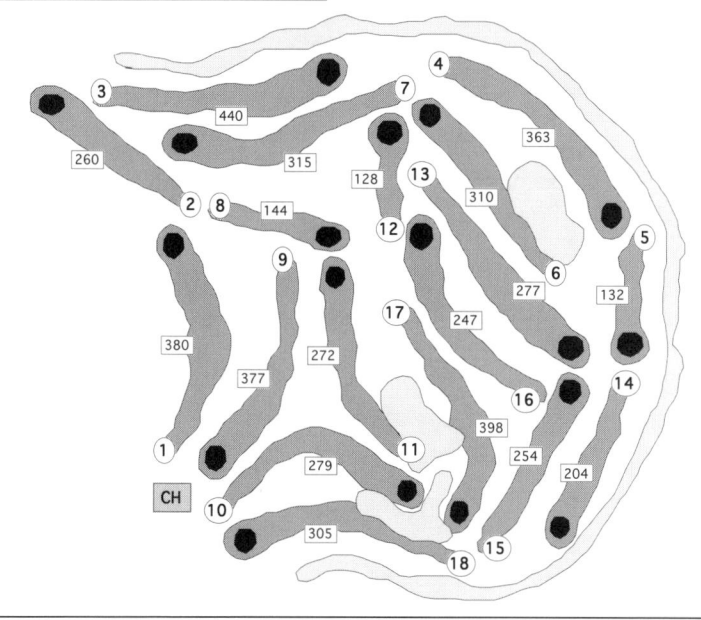

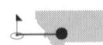

Green Meadow Country Club (private, 18 hole course)

2720 Country Club Avenue; P.O. Box 768; Helena, Montana 59601
Phone: (406) 442-1420. Fax: none. Internet: none.
Pro: Ray Hunthausen, PGA. Superintendent: unavailable.
Rating/Slope: C 70./122; M 68.6/118; W 73.7/125. **Course record:** 65.
Green fees: private club members & guests only; reciprocates.
Power cart: private club. **Pull cart:** private club. **Trail fee:** not allowed.
Reservation policy: private club members & guests of members only.
Winter condition: the golf course is closed from November to late March.
Terrain: flat, some hills. **Tees:** all grass. **Spikes:** soft spikes in summer.
Services: club rentals, lessons, beer, liquor, snack bar, full service private club, pro shop, lockers, driving range, putting & chipping greens, club memberships.
Comments: tough private golf course that sports lush tree-lined fairways and well bunkered greens. This is one of the finest courses in the state of Montana.

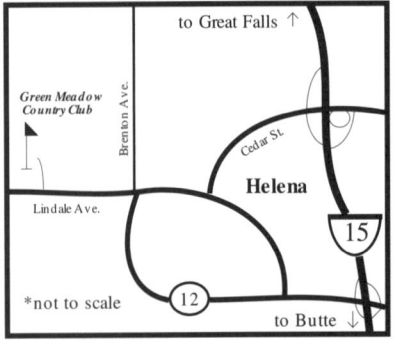

Directions: from Hwy 15 exit in Helena at exit 192B. Follow Hwy 12 through the city. First it turns north and is called Montana Avenue, then it will veer west and become Lindale Avenue, then Euclid Avenue. Turn right on Joslyn St. which is 3.7 miles from Hwy 15 exit. Follow Joslyn .1 mile and take an immediate left on Country Club Ave. Proceed .5 miles to the course entrance on your right.

Course Yardage & Par:
C-6434 yards, par 71.
M-6081 yards, par 71.
W-5495 yards, par 73.

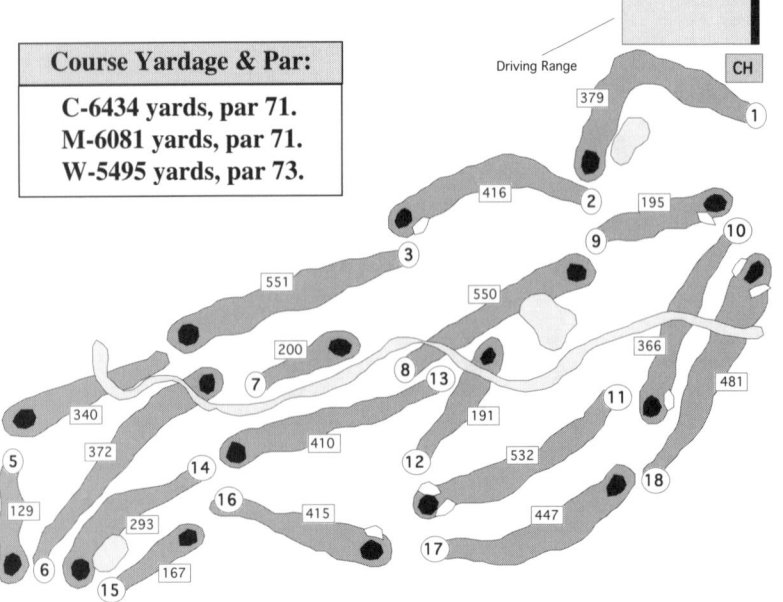

Hamilton Golf Club (public, 18 hole course)

1004 Country Club Lane; P.O Box 448; Hamilton, Montana 59840
Phone: (406) 363-4251. Fax: none. Internet: none.
Pro: Jason Lehtola. Superintendent: unavailable.
Rating/Slope: C 72.3/120; M 69.6/115; W 71.9/118. **Course record:** 66.
Green fees: W/D $24/$13; W/E $24/$13; M/C, VISA.
Power cart: $24/$12. **Pull cart:** $2/$1. **Trail fee:** $5 for personal carts.
Reservation policy: you may call 7 days in advance for all your tee-times.
Winter condition: the golf course is closed from November to March 15th.
Terrain: flat, some hills. **Tees:** all grass. **Spikes:** soft spikes only.
Services: club rentals, beer, snack bar, pro shop, driving range, putting green.
Comments: the golf course lies in the picturesque Bitterroot Valley and features
mature trees, small greens, numerous creeks and ponds which are all in play.

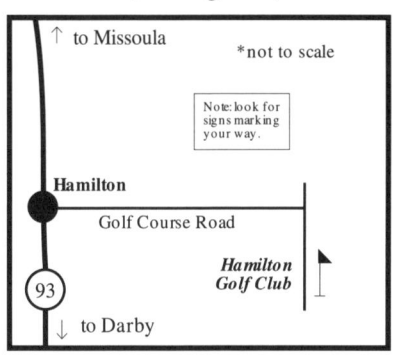

Directions: the golf course is located 3.5
miles east of Highway 93 in Hamilton.
From Highway 93 (1st Avenue) turn
eastbound on Golf Course Road for 3
miles to the golf course. Look for signs.

Course Yardage & Par:
C-6847 yards, par 72.
M-6545 yards, par 72.
W-5924 yards, par 73.

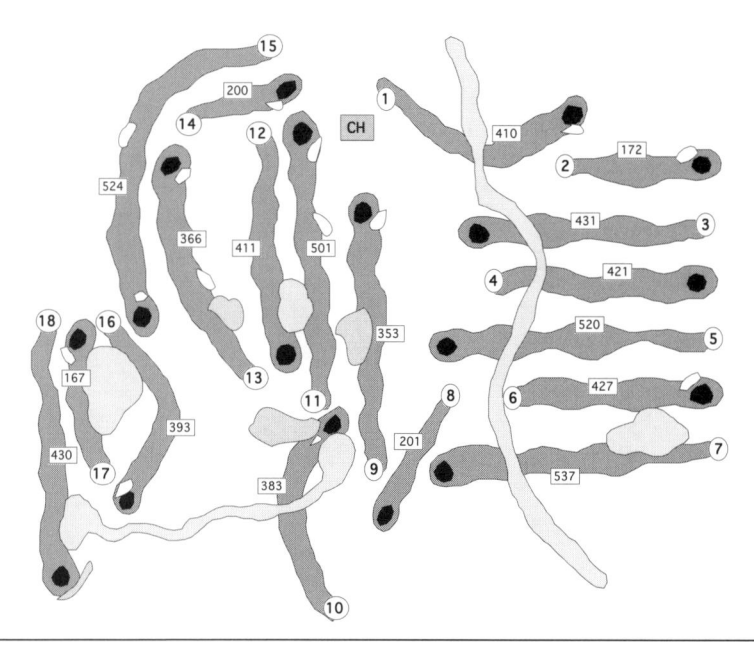

Harvest Hills Golf Course (public, 9 hole course)

Mailing address: 204 Fairfield, Montana 59436
Physical address: 1/2 mile south of Fairfield on US 89
Phone: (406) 467-2052. **Fax:** none. **Internet:** none.
Pro: none. **Manager:** none. **Superintendent:** none.
Rating/Slope: C 68.5/101; M 67.1/97; W 65.8/101. **Record:** 33 (9 holes).
Green fees: W/D $16/$10; W/E $20/$11; M/C, VISA.
Power cart: $17/$11. **Pull cart:** $2. **Trail fee:** $5 for personal carts.
Reservation policy: you may call up to 1 week in advance for tee times.
Winter condition: the course is open all year long. Temporary greens in winter.
Terrain: flat (easy walking). **Tees:** all grass. **Spikes:** soft spikes only.
Services: club rentals, lounge, snack bar, beer, wine, liquor, pro shop, range.
Comments: newer golf course that is challenging and a lot of fun to play. The layout has many dog legs and rough. Keep the ball in the fairway in order to score well. Great course for the beginner golfer. Very relaxed atmosphere.

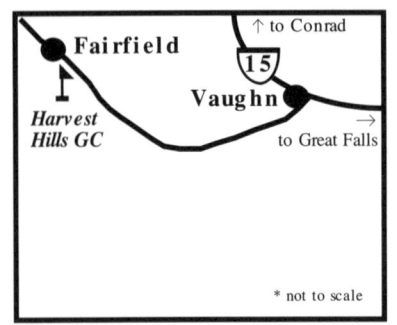

Directions: the golf course is located on US-89 on the west side of the highway just 1/2 mile south of the town of Fairfield or 35 miles northeast of Great Falls Montana.

Course Yardage & Par:
C-3229 yards, par 36.
M-3070 yards, par 36.
W-2542 yards, par 36.

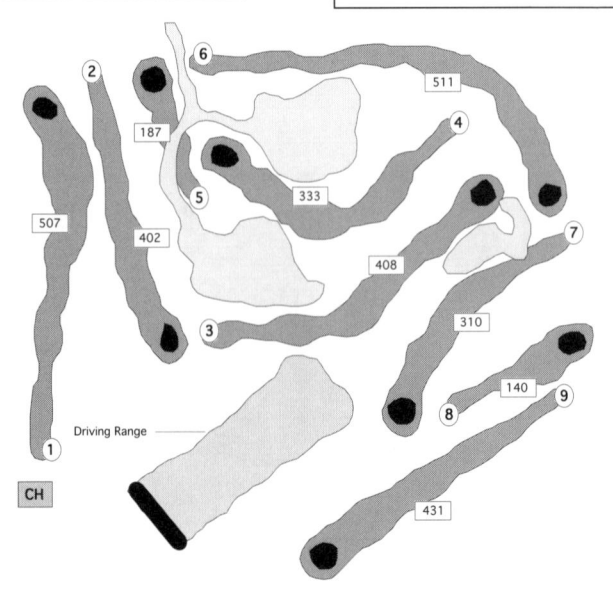

Headwaters Public Golf Course (public, 9 hole course)

225 7th Avenue East; Three Forks, Montana 59752
Phone: (406) 285-3700. **Fax:** none. **Internet:** none.
Manager: Van Schmidt. **Superintendent:** none.
Rating/Slope: C 68/113; M 67.1/112; W 67.7/107. **Course record:** 66.
Green fees: W/D $15/$10; W/E $16/$11; M/C, VISA.
Power cart: $16/$10. **Pull cart:** $2. **Trail fee:** $100 annual, $5 daily.
Reservation policy: you may call 1 week in advance for your tee-times.
Winter condition: the golf course is closed from November to March 15th.
Terrain: flat (easy walking). **Tees:** all grass. **Spikes:** soft spikes preferred.
Services: club rentals, snack bar, beer, wine, pro shop, driving range.
Comments: a challenging course with a lot of play. The course is very friendly, many beautiful ponds will challenge your skill. The pro shop is fully stocked for those wanting to do some shopping. Dual tees are available for a 18 hole round.

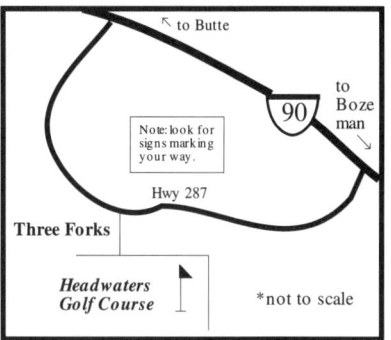

Directions: from I-90 take the exit at Three Forks. Upon entering Three Forks follow the highway into Main Street. Turn east off of Main at Cedar. Proceed to 7th Avenue, turn right. Proceed straight ahead on 7th to the golf course entrance.

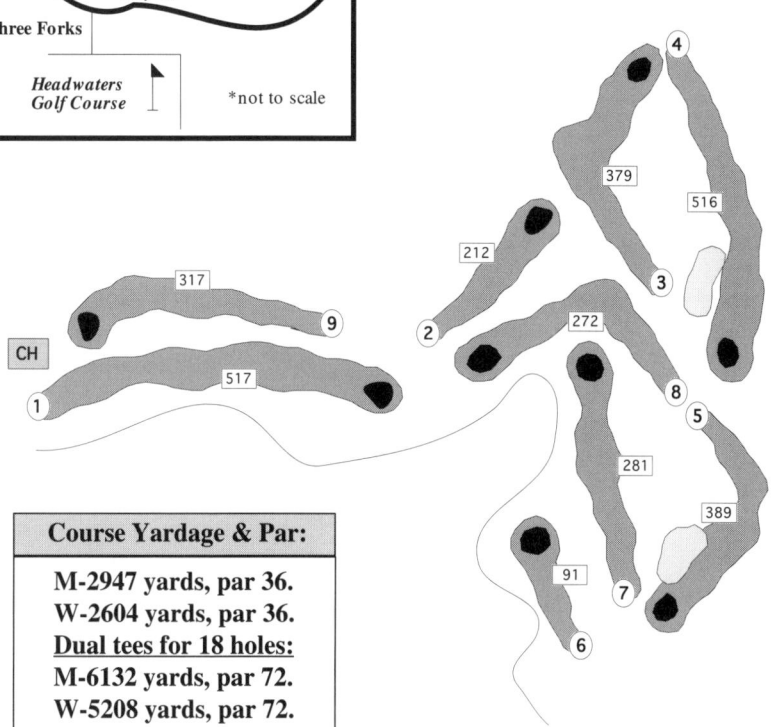

Course Yardage & Par:

M-2947 yards, par 36.
W-2604 yards, par 36.
Dual tees for 18 holes:
M-6132 yards, par 72.
W-5208 yards, par 72.

171

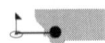

Highland View Golf Course (public, 18 hole & 9 hole par 3)

2903 Oregon Avenue; Butte, Montana 59701
Phone: (406) 494-7900. Fax: none. Internet: none.
Pro: Jack Crowley. Superintendent: unavailable.
Rating/Slope: M 67.2/102; W 69.5/106. **Course record:** 63.
Green fees: W/D $15/$10; W/E $15/$10; Jr. rates; M/C, VISA.
Power cart: $18/$10. **Pull cart:** $2. **Trail fee:** personal carts not allowed.
Reservation policy: you may call 1 week in advance for your tee times.
Winter condition: the golf course is closed from November to late March.
Terrain: flat, some hills. **Tees:** all grass. **Spikes:** soft spikes preferred.
Services: club rentals, snack bar, beverages, pro shop, lessons, putting greens.
Comments: a great course for the whole family. The golf course is very flat and wide open. Easy to walk, the track is great for the junior and senior golfer alike.

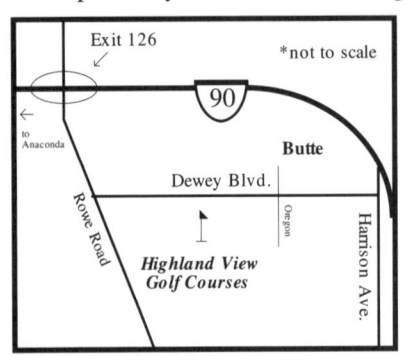

Directions: the golf course is located in Stodden Park at the intersection of Utah and Samson. From I-90/I-15 take exit #126, proceed south on Rowe (not marked except as Hwy 2). Proceed to Dewey Blvd and turn left. The turn for Dewey is 1.1 miles down Rowe. Proceed .4 miles to Utah and turn right.

Course Yardage & Par:
M-6249 yards, par 70.
W-5602 yards, par 71.

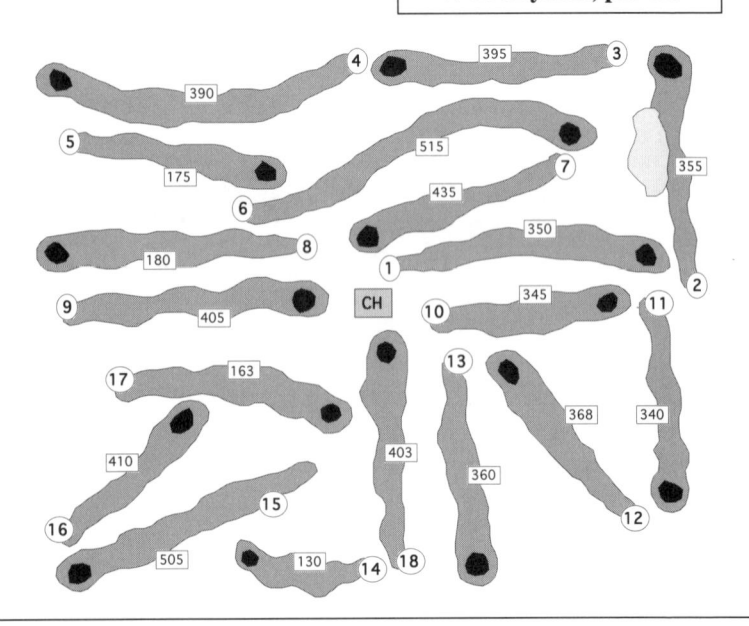

Highlands Golf Club, The (public, 9 hole course)
102 Ben Hogan Drive; Missoula, Montana 59803
Phone: (406) 728-7360. Fax: none. Internet: none.
Pro: Richard Hoffmaster, PGA. Superintendent: unavailable.
Rating/Slope: M 68.3/116; W 70.6/114. **Course record:** 63 (18 holes).
Green fees: W/D $22/$12; W/E $25/$15; M/C, VISA.
Power cart: $18/$9. **Pull cart:** $2. **Trail fee:** $7 for personal carts.
Reservation policy: you may call 7 days in advance for your tee times.
Winter condition: the golf course is closed from November to mid-March.
Terrain: flat, some hills. **Tees:** all grass. **Spikes:** soft spikes only.
Services: club rentals, snack bar, restaurant, beer, wine, pro shop, lessons.
Comments: the course offers dual tees. The lightning fast greens will challenge your putting skill. Fairways are mounded as in the Scottish tradition. Some of the fairways are lined with homes and have narrow landing area's. Good track.

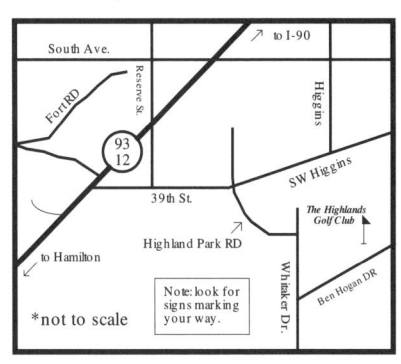

Directions: from Higgins Avenue turn onto Pattee Canyon Drive. Proceed to Whitaker where you will take a right. Proceed on Whitaker for 1.3 miles to the golf course on your left hand side.

Course Yardage & Par:
M-3200 yards, par 35.
W-2945 yards, par 37.
Dual tees for 18 holes:
M-6100 yards, par 69.
W-5550 yards, par 72.

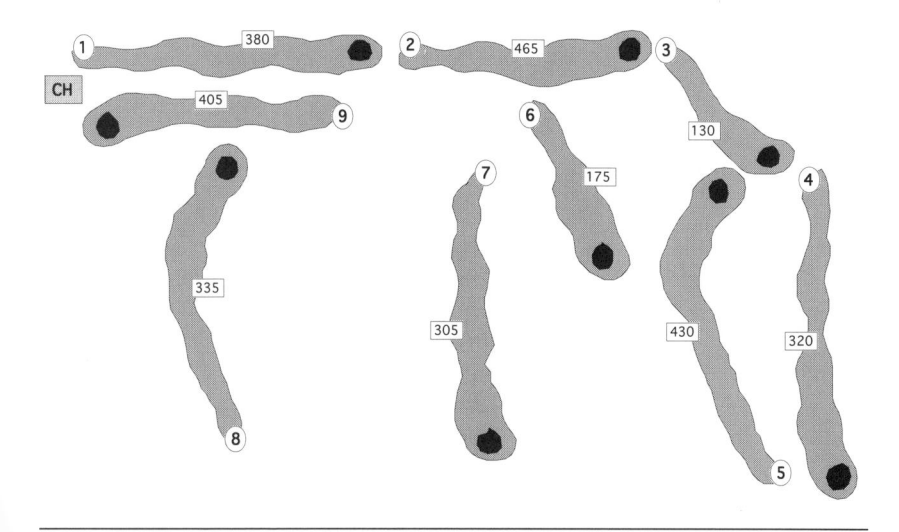

Hilands Golf Club (private, 9 hole course)

714 Poly Drive; Billings, Montana 59601
Phone: (406) 259-0419. **Fax:** none. **Internet:** none.
Pro: Rich Swarthout, PGA. **Superintendent:** unavailable.
Rating/Slope: M 68.6/118; W 71.5/118. **Course record:** 62.
Green fees: private club members & guests only; reciprocates.
Power cart: private club. **Pull cart:** private club. **Trail fee:** not allowed.
Reservation policy: private club members & guests of members only.
Winter condition: the golf course is open all year long, weather permitting.
Terrain: flat, some hills. **Tees:** all grass. **Spikes:** soft spikes preferred.
Services: club rentals, lessons, beer, liquor, snack bar, full service private club,
pro shop, lockers, driving range, putting & chipping green, club memberships.
Comments: dual tees are available at this private club. A stately old course
surrounded by mature foliage in a very established part of Billings. Great track.

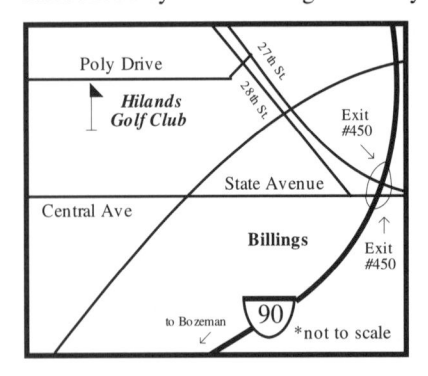

Directions: the golf course is located
in north central Billings on Poly Drive.

Course Yardage & Par:
M-3041 yards, par 35.
W-2791 yards, par 37.
Dual tees for 18 holes:
M-6042 yards, par 71.
W-5627 yards, par 74.

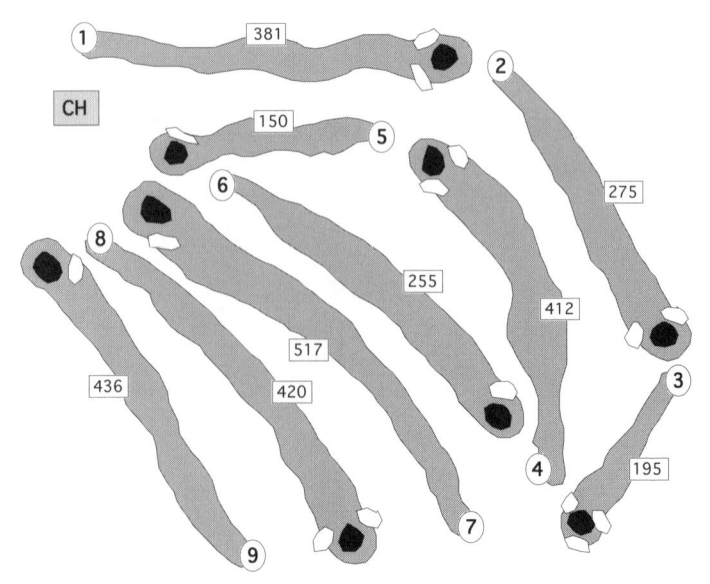

Jawbone Creek Country Club (public, 9 hole course)

Central Avenue; P.O. Box 765; Harlowton, Montana 59035
Phone: (406) 632-9960. Fax: none. Internet: none.
Manager: P. Elings. Superintendent: P. Elings.
Rating/Slope: M 70.0/108; W 72.1/108. Course record: 34 (9 holes).
Green fees: W/D $16/$9; W/E $16/$9; $15 all day rate; M/C, VISA.
Power cart: $16/$10. Pull cart: $2. Trail fee: $5 for personal carts.
Reservation policy: you may call 7 days in advance for your tee times.
Winter condition: the golf course is open all year long depending on weather.
Terrain: flat, some hills. Tees: all grass. Spikes: soft spikes preferred.
Services: club rentals, snacks, small pro shop, driving range, putting green.
Comments: good 9 hole course that offers the golfer a wide variety of lies from
the fairway. The course can play very long from the back tees giving the golfer
long irons into the medium size greens. If you need a golf fix try Jawbone Creek.

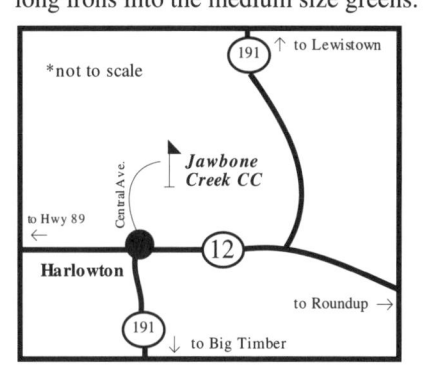

Directions: from Highway 191 in
downtown Harlowton turn northbound
on Central Avenue. Proceed on Central
Avenue up the hill to the golf course.
Look for signs along the way.

Course Yardage & Par:
M-3390 yards, par 36.
W-3203 yards, par 36.
Dual tees for 18 holes:
M-6593 yards, par 72.
W-5916 yards, par 72.

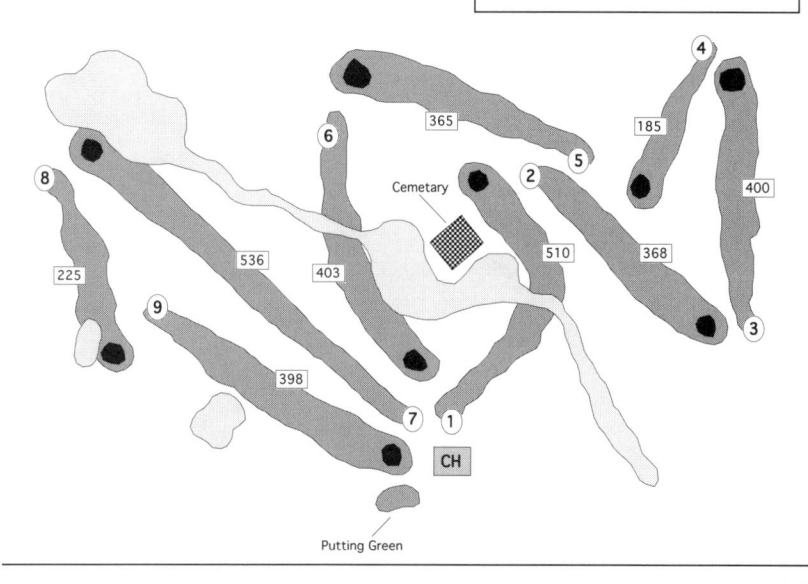

Judith Shadows Golf Course (public, 18 hole course)

End of Marcella Ave; P.O. Box 3506; Lewistown, Montana 59457
Phone: (406) 538-6062. Fax: (406) 538-6062. Internet: jsgc@tein.net
Pro: not available. Superintendent: not available.
Rating/Slope: C 70.4/120; M 70.2/117; W 69.8/116. **Course record:** 67.
Green fees: W/D $18/$10; W/E $18/$10; M/C, VISA.
Power cart: $14/$7. **Pull cart:** $3. **Trail fee:** $4 for personal carts.
Reservation policy: please call up to 30 days in advance for tee times.
Winter condition: the golf course is closed December thru March.
Terrain: relatively hilly. **Tees:** all grass. **Spikes:** soft spikes required.
Services: club rentals, snack bar, beverages, beer, driving range, putting green.
Comments: the Lewistown area has embraced this newer golf course. The track
is has received rave reviews for it's link style design. Water is the major factor
you will have to contend with as a creek runs through the entire layout.

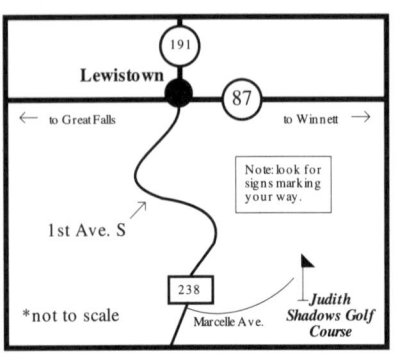

Directions: the golf course is northeast of
Lewistown off of Marcella Avenue. From
dowtown Lewistown take Hwy 87 east to
Marcella Avenue. Turn north on Marcella
Avenue. Proceed 1.2 miles to the course.

Course Yardage & Par:
C-6780 yards, par 72.
M-6151 yards, par 72.
W-5432 yards, par 72.

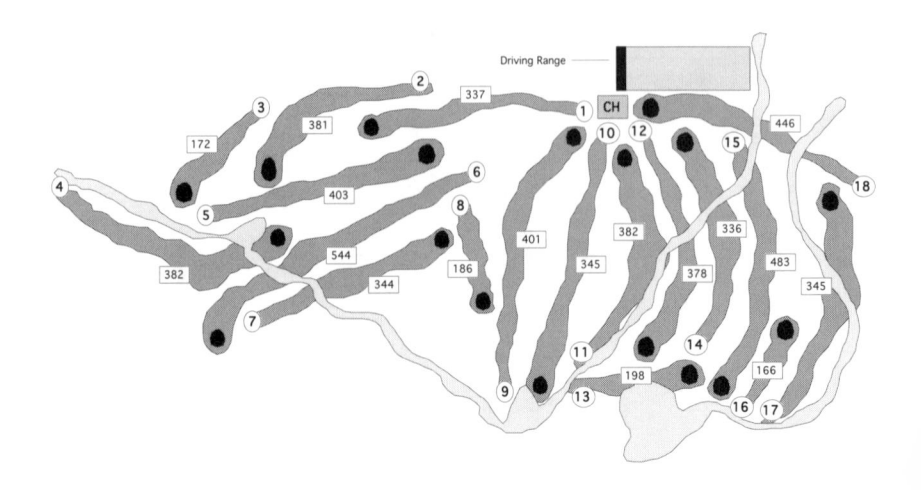

King Ranch Golf Course (public, 18 hole course)

Wild Goose Lane; P.O. Box 408; Frenchtown, Montana 59834
Phone: (406) 626-4000. **Fax:** none. **Internet:** none.
Pro: Chris Nowlen, PGA. **Superintendent:** unavailable.
Rating/Slope: C 70.6/118; M 69.0/113; W 66.8/107. **Course record:** 66.
Green fees: W/D $18/$10; W/E $20/$12; M/C, VISA.
Power cart: $18/$9. **Pull cart:** $2. **Trail fee:** $7 for personal carts.
Reservation policy: you may call 7 days in advance for your tee times.
Winter condition: the golf course is open all year long, weather permitting.
Terrain: flat (easy walking). **Tees:** all grass. **Spikes:** soft spikes required.
Services: club rentals, lessons, snack bar, pro shop, driving range, putting green.
Comments: good 18 hole course that was built on what was an old cattle ranch.
Greens are large in size giving the golfer an excellent target to shoot at. Water is
the major factor off the tee as well as on your approach shots. Worth a trip.

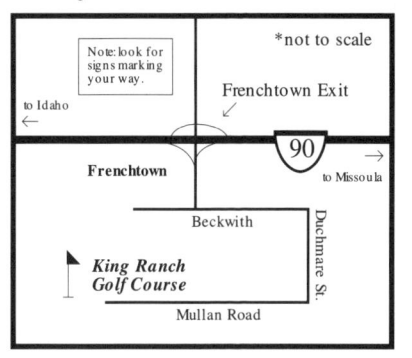

Directions: from I-90 E&W take exit #89. Go south to Frechtown. Proceed for .2 miles to Beckwith Road. Turn left to Ducharme where you will turn right. Travel to Mullan where you will turn right. Proceed on Mullan to the course.

Course Yardage & Par:
C-6858 yards, par 72.
M-6359 yards, par 72.
W-5482 yards, par 72.

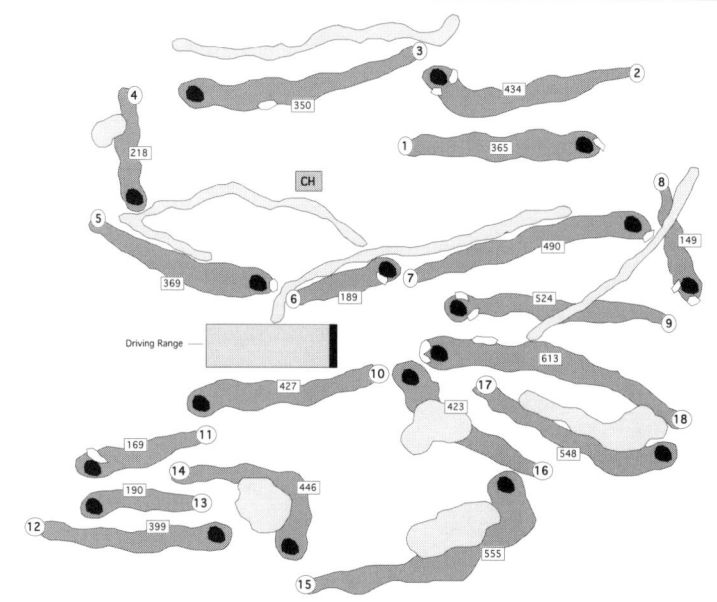

Lake Hills Golf Course (public, 18 hole course)

1930 Clubhouse Way; Billings, Montana 59105
Phone: (406) 252-9244. Fax: none. Internet: none.
Pro: Jon Wright, PGA. Superintendent: Kevin Bonk.
Rating/Slope: C 70.1/112; M 68.9/109; W 72.3/109. **Course record:** 58.
Green fees: W/D $17/$11; W/E $14; Jr., Sr. and twilight rates; M/C, VISA.
Power cart: $6/$10. **Pull cart:** $3. **Trail fee:** personal carts not allowed.
Reservation policy: call 3 days in advance or Thurs. for the following weekend.
Winter condition: the golf course is closed November 1st to March 1st.
Terrain: flat, some hills. **Tees:** all grass. **Spikes:** soft spikes only.
Services: club rentals, lessons, lounge, restaurant, beer, wine, showers, lockers,
pro shop, driving range, putting & chipping greens. **Comments:** this is a very
popular golf course in the summer months. The fairways are wide and primarily
straight. There are few hazards on the course other than one pond and a few sand
and grass bunkers which may challenge some of your apporach shots.

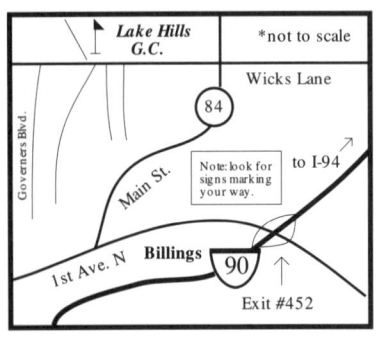

Directions: From I-90BUS (Main Street)
proceed north to Wicks Lane. Turn left on
Wicks Lane. Travel 1.2 miles to Lake
Hills. Turn right and proceed .4 miles up
to the course (stay right). Note: Watch for
the green and white signs to the course.

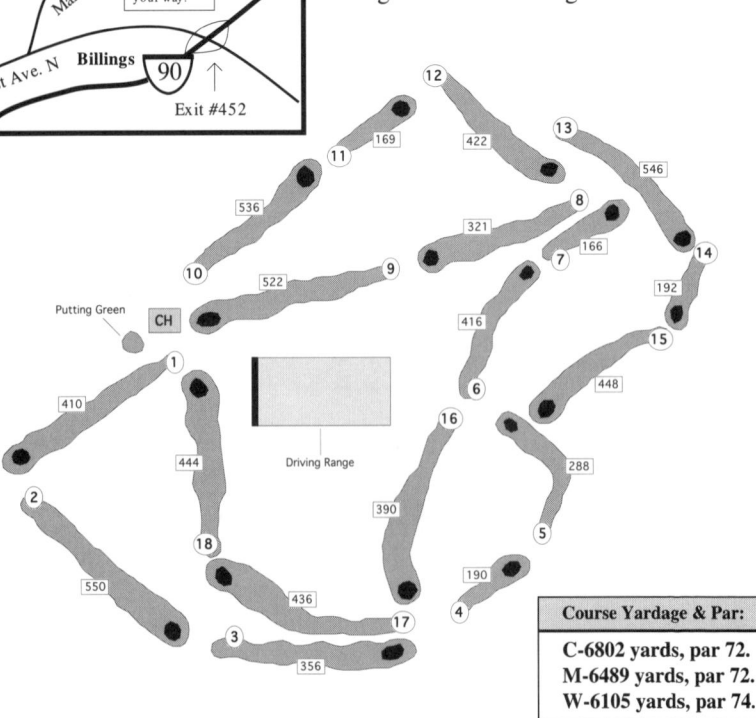

Course Yardage & Par:
C-6802 yards, par 72.
M-6489 yards, par 72.
W-6105 yards, par 74.

Lakeview Country Club (semi-private, 9 hole course)

P.O. Box 1274; Airport Road South; Baker, Montana 59313
Phone: (406) 778-3166. Fax: none. Internet: none.
Manager: Don Groshams. Superintendent: Don Groshams.
Rating/Slope: C 67.9/115; 66.8/112; W 69.3/117. **Course record:** 65.
Green fees: Weekdays $10; Weekends $12; no special rates; no credit cards.
Power cart: $6/$5. **Pull cart:** $2. **Trail fee:** personal carts not allowed.
Reservation policy: call 14 days in advance for all your weekend tee-times.
Winter condition: course is open all year long except during inclement weather.
Terrain: flat (easy walking). **Tees:** all grass. **Spikes:** soft spikes preferred.
Services: club rentals, snack bar, beer, wine, pop, pro shop, driving range.
Comments: the golf course is very wide open and flat which makes it great for beginners and seniors. One pond comes into play on holes 6 and 7 although this is one of the few hazards with which you will have to contend.

Directions: from Hwy 7 turn on Center Street. Proceed .2 miles to 3rd Street E. Turn right on 3rd Street E. The golf course is located .8 miles ahead on your left hand side. Look for signs indicating your turn.

Course Yardage & Par:
C-3330 yards, par 36.
M-2939 yards, par 36.
W-2533 yards, par 36.
<u>**Dual tees for 18 holes:**</u>
C-6660 yards, par 72.
M-5878 yards, par 72.
W-5066 yards, par 72.

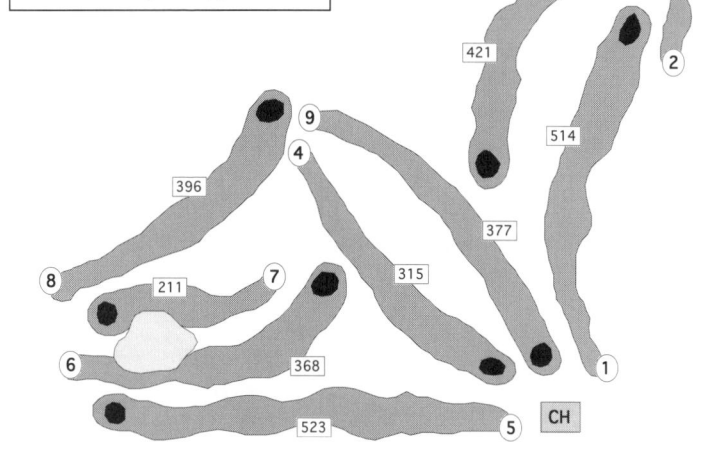

Larchmont Golf Course (public, 18 hole course)

3200 Old Fort Road; Missoula, Montana 59801
Phone: (406) 721-4416. Fax: none. Internet: none.
Pro: Bill Galiher, PGA. Superintendent: unavailable.
Rating/Slope: C 71.9/117; M 69.9/114; W 69.4/110. **Course record:** 65.
Green fees: Weekdays $16/$9; Weekends $18/$9; M/C, VISA, AMEX.
Power cart: $20/$10. Pull cart: $3/$2. **Trail fee:** personal carts not allowed.
Reservation policy: you may call 1 day in advance for all your tee times.
Winter condition: the golf course is closed November 1st to April 1st.
Terrain: flat (easy walking). **Tees:** all grass. **Spikes:** soft spikes only.
Services: club rentals, lessons, lounge, restaurant, beer, wine, pop, beverages, pro shop, driving range, putting and chipping greens, club memberships.
Comments: this course is host of the annual Montana Open. Reminiscent of a scottish links style course, deep grass bunkers surround many greens which are firm and hard to hold. Fairways are wide and fast. Good public golf course.

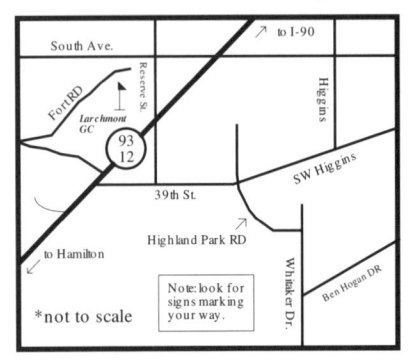

Directions: from I-90 take the Reserve Street exit. Proceed south on Reserve Street approximately 5 miles. At Old Hwy 93 turn right. Proceed to Post Siding Road and turn right. Travel .4 miles and turn right into the parking lot.

Course Yardage & Par:
C-7093 yards, par 72.
M-6688 yards, par 72.
W-5550 yards, par 72.

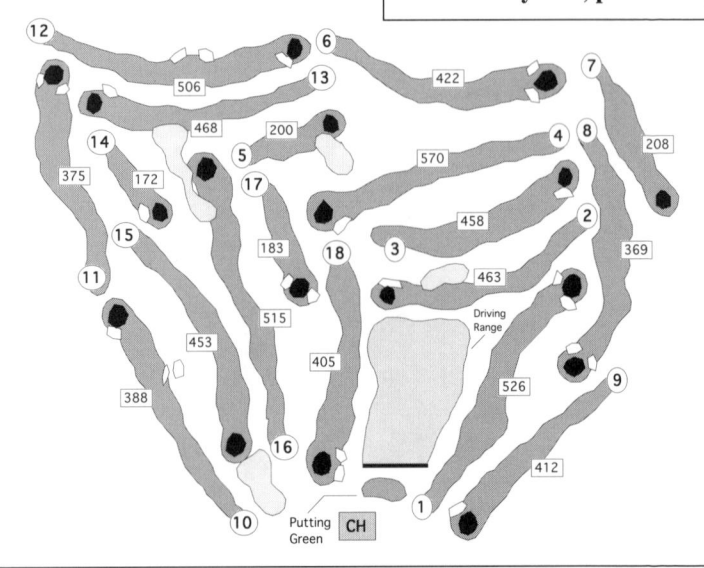

Laurel Golf Club (private, 18 hole course)

1020 Golf Course Road; P.O. Box 247; Laurel, Montana 59044
Phone: (406) 628-4504. Fax: none. Internet: none.
Pro: Tom Anderson, PGA. Superintendent: Joe Brinkel.
Rating/Slope: C 71.3/122; M 69.5/118; W 71.8/118. **Course record:** 64.
Green fees: private club members & guests of members only.
Power cart: private club. **Pull cart:** private club. **Trail fee:** not allowed.
Reservation policy: private club members & guests of members only.
Winter condition: the golf course is closed November 1st to late March.
Terrain: flat, some hills. **Tees:** all grass. **Spikes:** soft spikes only.
Services: club rentals, lessons, lounge, restaurant, beer, wine, pro shop, range.
Comments: this private club is the longest in Montana with two 470 yard par
4's, one on the front nine and one on the back. The combination of the length
and the hazards, both sand and water, make it tough to score on this golf course.

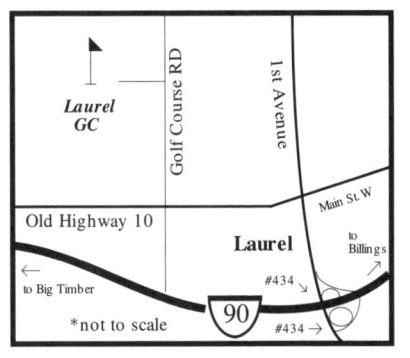

Directions: from I-90 take exit #434
and proceed north on 1st Avenue. Travel
.4 miles to Main Street W and turn left.
Proceed 1.4 miles to Golf Course Road
and turn right. Travel up Golf Course
Road .5 miles to the entrance on the left.

Course Yardage & Par:
C-6915 yards, par 72.
M-6537 yards, par 72.
W-5531 yards, par 72.

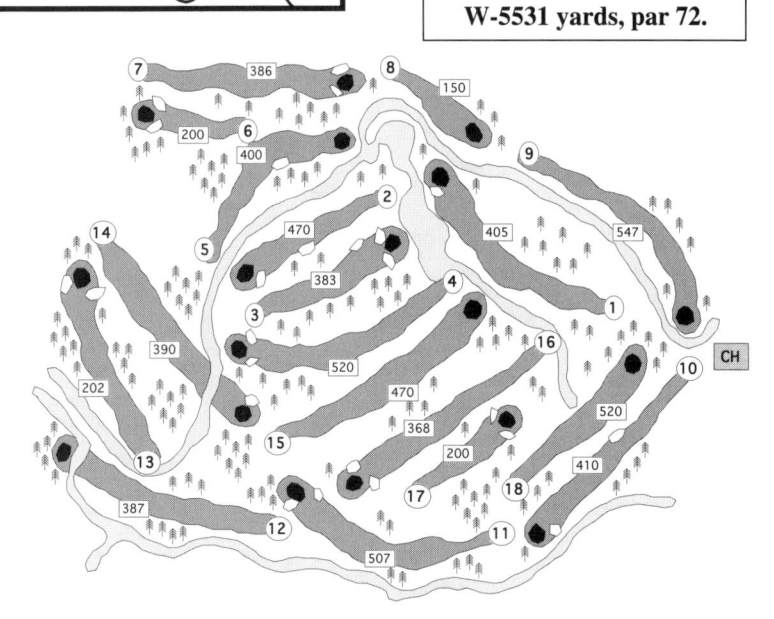

Linda Vista Public Golf Course (public, 9 hole executive course)

4915 Lower Miller Creek Road; Missoula, Montana 59801
Phone: (406) 251-3655. Fax: none. Internet: none.
Pro: John Galiher. Superintendent: unavailable.
Rating/Slope: C 55.7/85; M 53.8/81; W 54/77. **Course record:** 26 (9 holes).
Green fees: Weekdays $17; Weekends $19; M/C, VISA.
Power cart: $18/$9. **Pull cart:** $2. **Trail fee:** personal carts not allowed.
Reservation policy: call 14 days in advance for all your tee times.
Winter condition: the golf course is closed November 1st to March 1st.
Terrain: flat, some hills. **Tees:** all grass. **Spikes:** soft spikes only.
Services: club rentals, lessons, snack bar, pro shop, driving range, putting green.
Comments: the course opened in 1994 and is meticulously maintained. Several water hazards come into play which will test your shot making capability. The course is great for a family day on the golf course, it is a real treat to play. If you want a real change of pace try Linda Vista, you will not be disappointed.

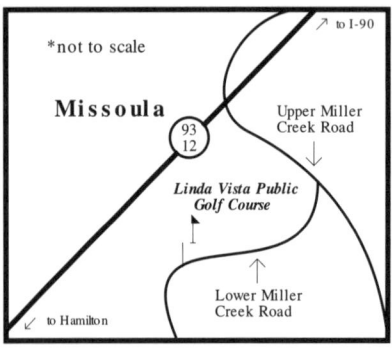

Directions: the course is located off of Hwy 93 South on Lower Miller Creek Road. Look for signs along the way.

Course Yardage & Par:
C-1745 yards, par 29.
M-1538 yards, par 29.
W-1333 yards, par 29.
Dual tees for 18 holes:
C-3490 yards, par 58.
M-3076 yards, par 58.
W-2666 yards, par 58.

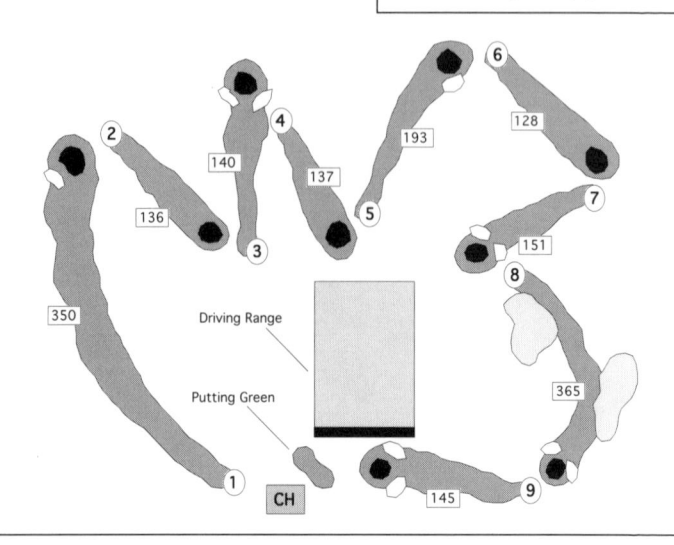

Livingston Golf & Country Club (semi-private, 9 hole course)

View Vista Drive; Livingston, Montana 59047
Phone: (406) 222-1031. Fax: none. Internet: none.
Pro: Scott Monroe, PGA. Superintendent: unavailable.
Rating/Slope: M 69.3/109; W 69.8/119. **Course record:** 64.
Green fees: W/D $19/$13; W/E $19/$13; M/C, VISA, AMEX.
Power cart: $16/$10. **Pull cart:** $1. **Trail fee:** personal carts not allowed.
Reservation policy: you may call up to 3 days in advance for tee-times.
Winter condition: the golf course is usually open in the winter months.
Terrain: flat (easy walking). **Tees:** all grass. **Spikes:** soft spikes preferred.
Services: club rentals, lessons, lounge, snack bar, beer, wine, liquor, pro shop,
driving range, putting green. **Comments:** small undualations in the greens make
putting a challenge. Surrounded by mountain ranges which include the "Sleeping
Giant" this course is located in a spectacular setting. The Yellowstone River
rushes by 3 holes. Dual tees are available for a different look on your second 9.

Directions: from I-90 take the Park
Street exit (the business loop) and
proceed to Main Street. Travel south on
Main Street approximately 3 miles to the
course which is near the high school.
Turn left beyond the school to the course.

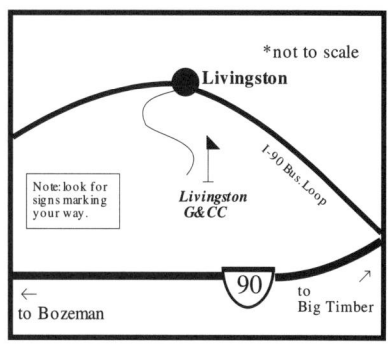

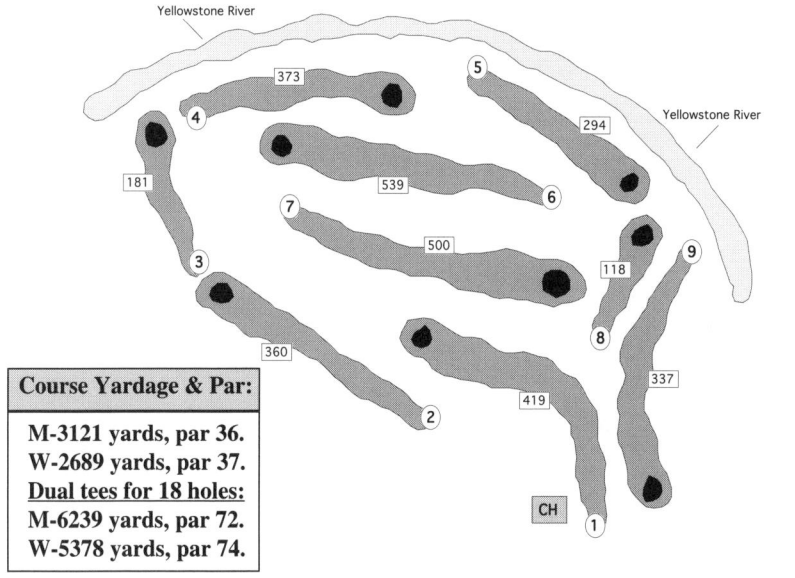

Course Yardage & Par:

M-3121 yards, par 36.
W-2689 yards, par 37.
<u>**Dual tees for 18 holes:**</u>
M-6239 yards, par 72.
W-5378 yards, par 74.

Madison Meadows Golf Course (public, 9 hole course)

Golf Course Drive; P.O. Box 522; Ennis, Montana 59729
Phone: (406) 682-7468. Fax: (406) 682-7468. Internet: none.
Pro: Brian James, PGA. Superintendent: unavailable.
Rating/Slope: C 35.2/47; M 34.9/43; W 33.6/46 (for 9 holes). **Record:** 31.
Green fees: W/D $18/$10; W/E $18/$10; Jr., Sr. & twilight rates; M/C, VISA.
Power cart: $8/$4. **Pull cart:** $2. **Trail fee:** personal carts not allowed.
Reservation policy: please call ahead for your tee times. No time limit.
Winter condition: the golf course is closed November 1st to March 1st.
Terrain: some hills. **Tees:** all grass. **Spikes:** soft spikes preferred.
Services: club rentals, lessons, snack bar, beer, wine, pro shop, putting green.
Comments: although mostly wide open this course will challenge your skill with it's rolling fairways, sidehill lies, and bunker placement. Greens are bent grass and firm. If you are in the area be sure to test your game at this course.

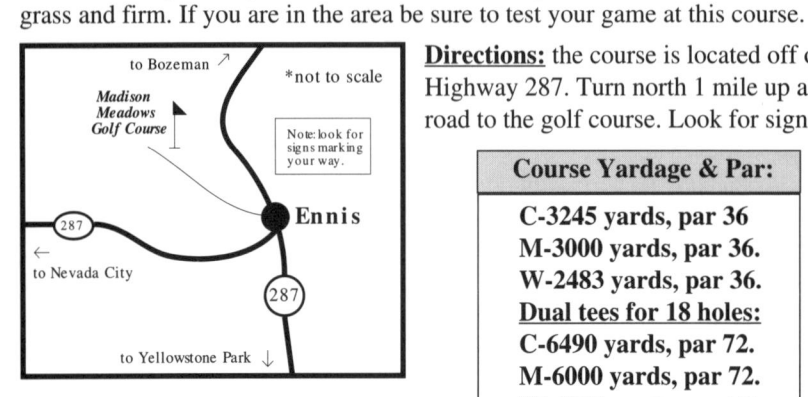

Directions: the course is located off of Highway 287. Turn north 1 mile up a dirt road to the golf course. Look for signs.

Course Yardage & Par:
C-3245 yards, par 36
M-3000 yards, par 36.
W-2483 yards, par 36.
Dual tees for 18 holes:
C-6490 yards, par 72.
M-6000 yards, par 72.
W-4966 yards, par 72.

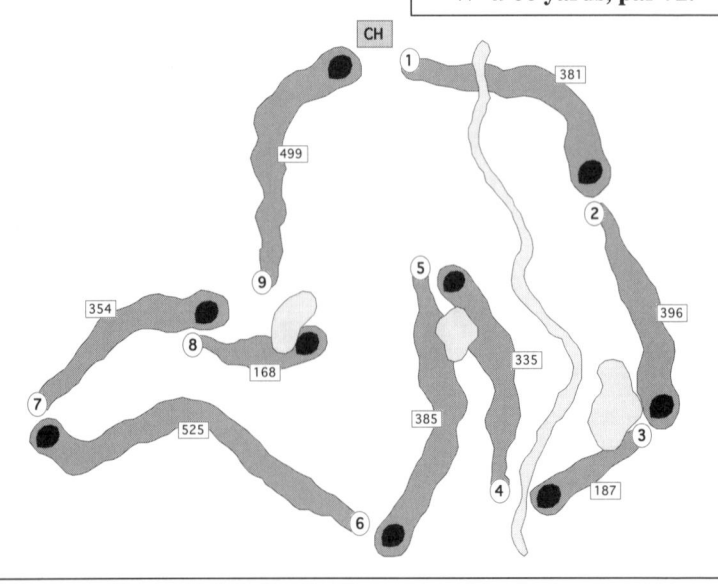

Marian Hills Country Club (public, 9 hole course)

100 Doral Lane; P.O. Box 1726; Malta, Montana 59538
Phone: no phone. **Fax:** none. **Internet:** none.
Pro: no pro. **Superintendent:** unavailable.
Rating/Slope: the golf course is not rated. **Course record:** 66 (18 holes).
Green fees: W/D \$20/\$10; W/E \$20/\$10; no special rates; no credit cards.
Power cart: \$18/\$10. **Pull cart:** \$2. **Trail fee:** \$8/\$4 for personal carts.
Reservation policy: tee times are on a first come first served basis.
Winter condition: the golf course is closed from November 1st to March 1st.
Terrain: relatively hilly. **Tees:** all grass. **Spikes:** no spike policy.
Services: pop machine, practice area. **Comments:** this track is considered one of the most difficult in the area, it is the largest 9 hole course in the state of Montana. Fairways are wide open but numerous water hazards make scoring difficult. While traveling through Montana stop in Malta and try Marian Hills.

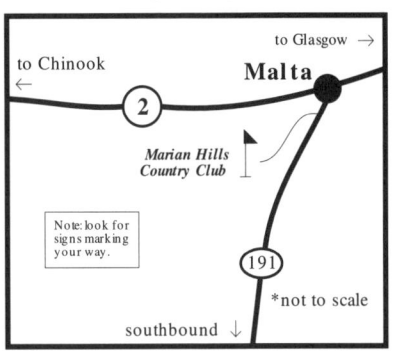

Directions: the golf course is located right off Highway 191 just south of downtown Malta. From Highway 2 turn south on Highway 191. The course is 1.4 miles ahead on your right hand side.

Course Yardage & Par:
M-3175 yards, par 36.
W-2770 yards, par 36.
Dual tees for 18 holes:
M-6600 yards, par 72.
W-5540 yards, par 72.

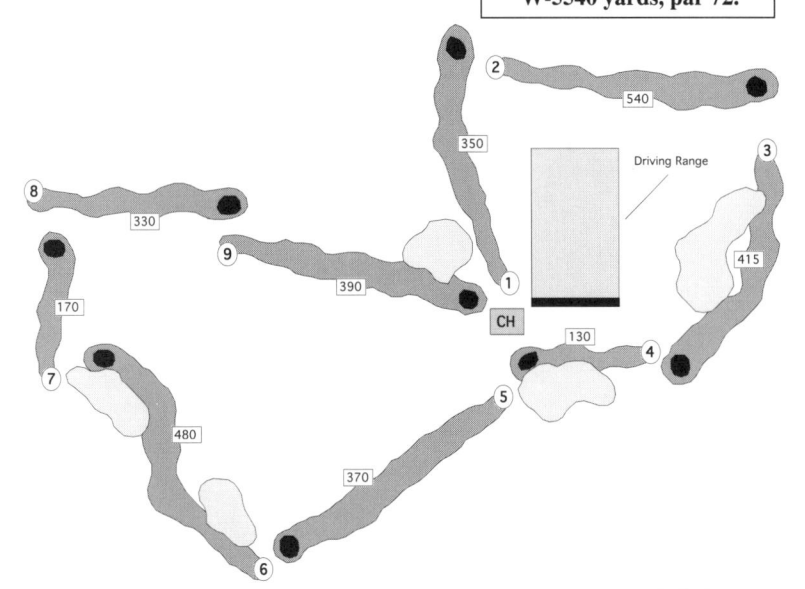

Marias Valley Golf & Country Club (public, 9 hole course)

Marias Valley Golf Course Road; P.O. Box 784; Shelby, Montana 59474
Phone: (406) 434-5940. **Fax:** none. **Internet:** none.
Pro: Joe Esh. **Superintendent:** unavailable.
Rating/Slope: M 68.9/118; W 71.3/118. **Course record:** 32 for 9 holes.
Green fees: W/D $22/$12; W/E $22/$12; Jr., Sr. and twilight rates; M/C, VISA.
Power cart: $22/$12. **Pull cart:** $2, all day. **Trail fee:** $8 for personal carts.
Reservation policy: 2 days in advance for tee times or 3 weeks for large groups.
Winter condition: the golf course is closed from November 1st to March 1st.
Terrain: flat (easy walking). **Tees:** all grass. **Spikes:** soft spikes preferred.
Services: club rentals, lessons, lounge, snack bar, beer, wine, liquor, pro shop, driving range, putting/chipping greens. **Comments:** one of the finest courses in northern Montana. Greens are very large which enable the course to utilize two pins on each green. This factor combined with two tee boxes on most holes gives the golfer looking to play eighteen holes a different look for the second nine.

Directions: from Highway 15 take exit #358. Proceed eastbound off the highway approximately .25 miles and turn left on the road which winds down into the valley. Look for signs marking your turn.

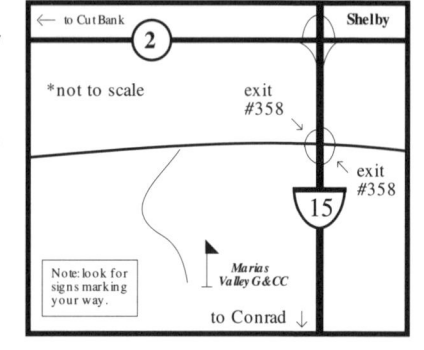

Course Yardage & Par:

M-3223 yards, par 36.
W-2816 yards, par 36.
Dual tees for 18 holes:
M-6496 yards, par 72.
W-5632 yards, par 72.

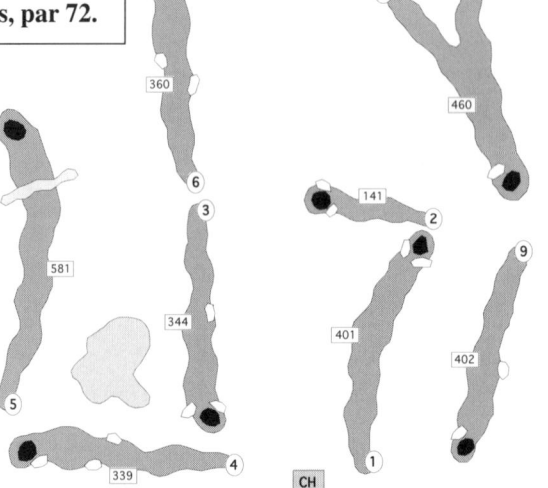

Meadow Creek Golf Course (public, 9 hole par 3 course)
1st Street South; P.O. Box 131; Fortine, Montana 59918
Phone: (406) 882-4474. Fax: none. Internet: none.
Managers: Jerry and Noreen Syth.
Rating/Slope: the golf course is not rated. **Course record:** 25.
Green fees: W/D $8; W/E $8; no credit cards.
Power cart: none. **Pull cart:** $1. **Trail fee:** personal carts not allowed.
Reservation policy: call ahead to check if tee times will be necessary.
Winter condition: the golf course is closed November 1st to March 1st.
Terrain: flat, some hills. **Tees:** all grass. **Spikes:** no spike policy.
Services: club rentals, steakhouse, beer, wine, liquor, casino, R.V. park.
Comments: a great course to take the family for the day, or just to practice your iron play on. R.V. parking is available for the overnighters. The course is easy to walk which makes it great for seniors and beginners as well. Be sure to stop at the steakhouse for lunch or dinner.

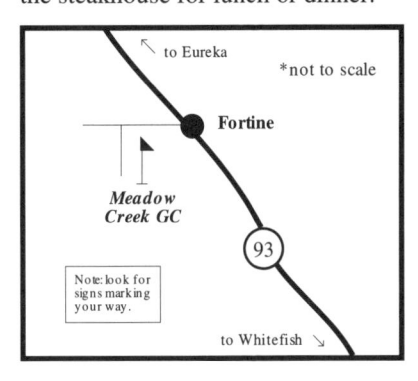

Directions: from Highway 93 exit westbound onto Meadow Creek Road. Proceed .3 miles and turn left. Follow this road to the course. Look for signs.

Course Yardage & Par:
M-1382 yards, par 27.
W-1382 yards, par 27.

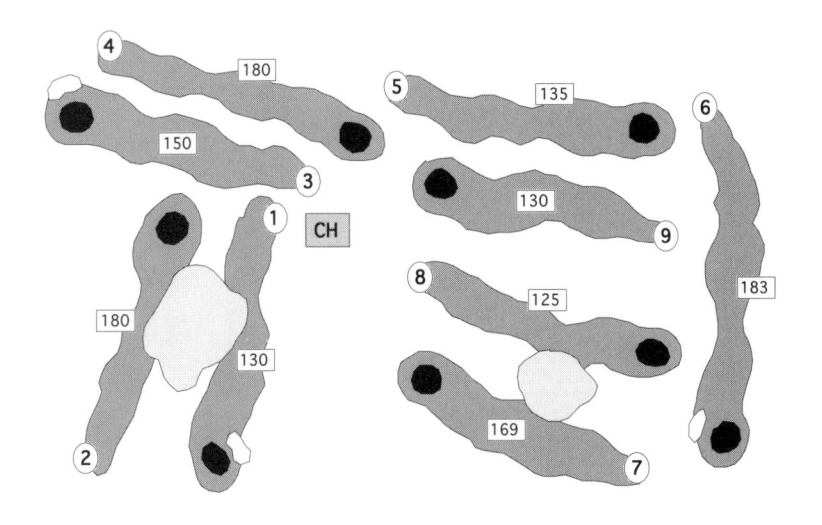

Meadow Lake Resort (18 hole resort course)

100 Saint Andrews Drive; Columbia Falls, Montana 59912
Phone: (406) 892-2111, 800-321-GOLF Internet: www.meadowlake.com
Pro: Kyle Long, PGA. Superintendent: unavailable.
Rating/Slope: T 71.3/118; C 70.2/126; M 69.1/123; W 69.9/122. **Record:** 66.
Green fees: W/D $45; W/E $45; twilight rates; M/C, VISA, AMEX.
Power cart: $26/$14. **Pull cart:** $3/$2. **Trail fee:** personal carts not allowed.
Reservation policy: please call in advance for your tee times.
Winter condition: the golf course is closed November 1st to April 1st.
Terrain: flat, some hills. **Tees:** all grass. **Spikes:** soft spikes required.
Services: club rentals, lessons, lounge, restaurant, beer, wine, pro shop, range.
Comments: tree lined fairways, numerous sand bunkers, and many water hazards make scoring on this beautiful resort course very difficult. Set in the spectacular Flathead Valley there are many activities available to do after golf.

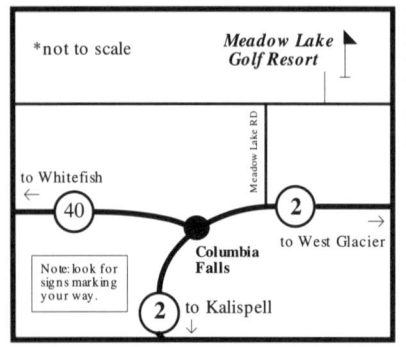

Directions: from Hwy 2 exit north on Meadow Lake Road (on the west side of town). Proceed 1.1 miles to the "T" in the road and turn left. The course entrance will be immediately on your right.

Course Yardage & Par:
C-6601 yards, par 71.
M-6303 yards, par 71.
W-5259 yards, par 72.

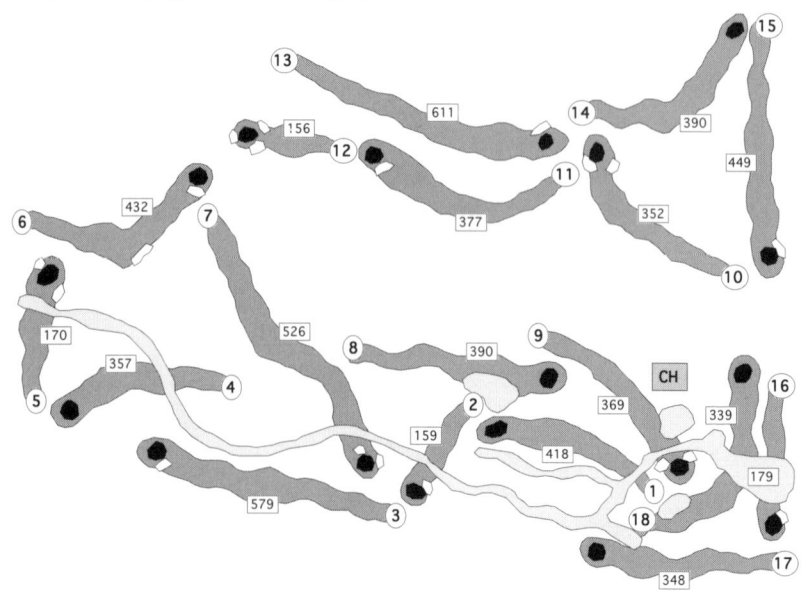

Meadow Lark Country Club (private, 18 hole course)

300 Country Club DR; Great Falls, Montana 59403
Phone: (406) 454-3553. Fax: (406) 454-2886. Internet: none.
Pro: Dudley S. Beard Jr., PGA Superintendent: Michael Saffel.
Rating/Slope: C 77./126; M 70.7/123; W 70.4/119. **Course record:** 63.
Greens fee: private club members & guests only; reciprocates.
Power cart: private club. **Pull cart:** private club. **Trail fee:** not allowed.
Reservation policy: private club members & guests of members only.
Winter condition: the course is typically closed November 1st to March 1st.
Terrain: flat, some hills. **Tees:** all grass. **Spikes:** soft spikes required.
Services: club rentals, lessons, beer, liquor, snack bar, full service private club,
pro shop, lockers, driving range, putting green, tennis courts, club memberships.
Comments: the course hosts many tournaments, it was the site of the 1994 U.S.
Girls Junior Championship. A tough private course that sports lush well kept
fairways and greens. The Missouri River runs alongside holes 15, 16, 17, and 18.

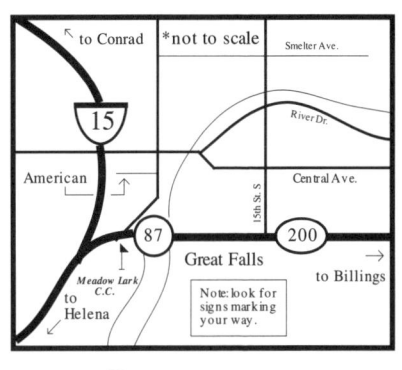

Directions: the course is located off of
10th Avenue South. Just west of the
Warden Bridge over the Missouri River.

Course Yardage & Par:
C-6932 yards, par 72.
M-6641 yards, par 72.
W-5555 yards, par 74.

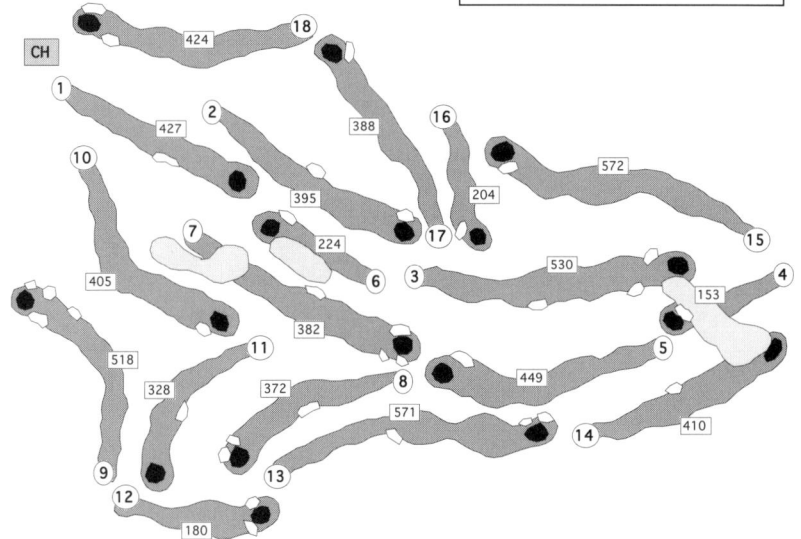

Miles City Town & Country Club (semi-private, 9 hole course)

4th & Eagle Street; P.O. Box 667; Miles City, Montana 59474
Phone: (406) 232-1500. Fax: none. Internet: none.
Pro: Patrick Stoltz, PGA. Superintendent: unavailable.
Rating/Slope: M 69.5/113; W 72.7/118. **Course record:** 31 for 9 holes.
Green fees: W/D $14/$10; W/E $18/$13; Jr., Sr. and twilight rates; M/C, VISA.
Power cart: $18/$9. **Pull cart:** $2. **Trail fee:** personal carts not allowed.
Reservation policy: please call up to 1 week in advance for tee-times.
Winter condition: the golf course is closed from December 1st to March 1st.
Terrain: flat, some hills. **Tees:** all grass. **Spikes:** soft spikes preferred.
Services: club rentals, lessons, lounge, snack bar, restaurant, beer, wine, liquor,
beverages, showers, lockers, pro shop, driving range, putting/chipping greens.
Comments: one of the finest public play golf courses in eastern Montana. Built
in 1957 the course fairways are lined with mature cottonwood trees. The
fairways are plush and well kept. Great course that will challenge any golfer.

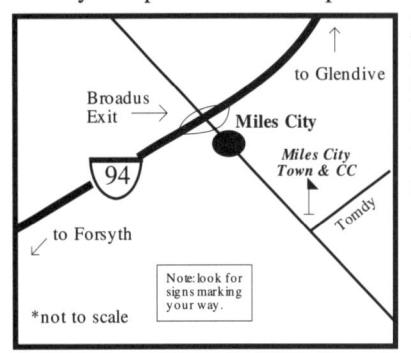

Directions: the golf course is located at
the southwest edge of Miles City. From I-
94 take the Broadus exit. Proceed toward
the town of Miles City. When you reach
Tomby turn left. Proceed for 1.5 miles to
the golf course entrance. Look for signs.

Course Yardage & Par:
M-3274 yards, par 36.
W-3115 yards, par 37.
Dual tees for 18 holes:
M-6576 yards, par 72.
W-6081 yards, par 74.

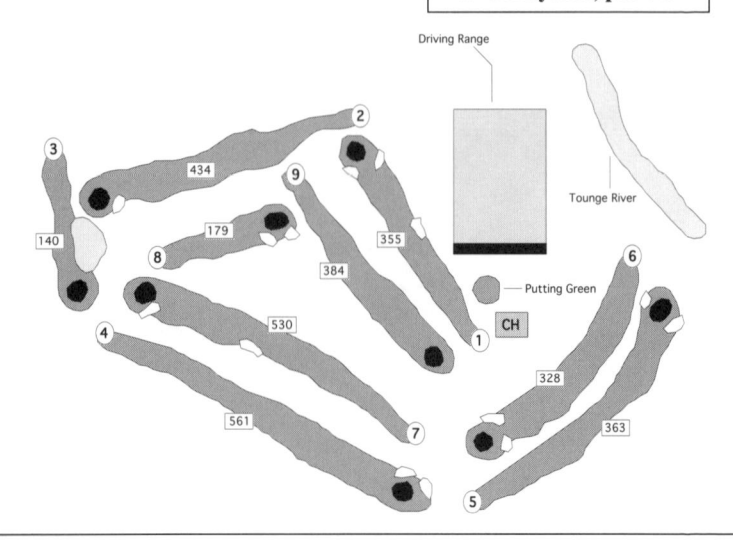

Mission Mountain Country Club (semi-private, 18 hole course)

640 Stagecoach Trail; Ronan, Montana 59864
Phone: (406) 676-4653. Fax: none. Internet: www.golfmontana.net
Pro: Marlin Hanson, PGA. Superintendent: Fred Skogen.
Rating/Slope: C 69.7/114; M 68.7/112; W 66.5/105. **Course record:** 67.
Green fees: W/D $29; W/E $29; no special rates; M/C, VISA.
Power cart: $23. **Pull cart:** $2. **Trail fee:** personal carts not allowed.
Reservation policy: 2 days in advance. Stockholders may call 5 days in advance.
Winter condition: the golf course is closed from November 1st to March 1st.
Terrain: flat, some hills. **Tees:** all grass. **Spikes:** soft spikes required.
Services: club rentals, lessons, lounge, snack bar, restaurant, beer, wine, showers,
lockers, pro shop, driving range, putting & chipping greens, club memberships.
Comments: the course went from 9 holes to 18 holes in 1992. Located at the
foot of the Mission Mountains this golf course is very scenic and wide open. The
track boasts havings some of the best kept fairways in the state of Montana.

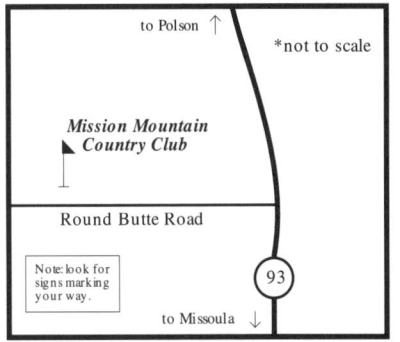

Directions: from Highway 93 exit
westbound on Round Butte Road in
Ronan. Proceed 2.6 miles to the course
entrance which will be on your right. The
clubhouse is .7 mi ahead. Look for signs.

Course Yardage & Par:
C-6478 yards, par 72.
M-6251 yards, par 72.
W-4888 yards, par 72.

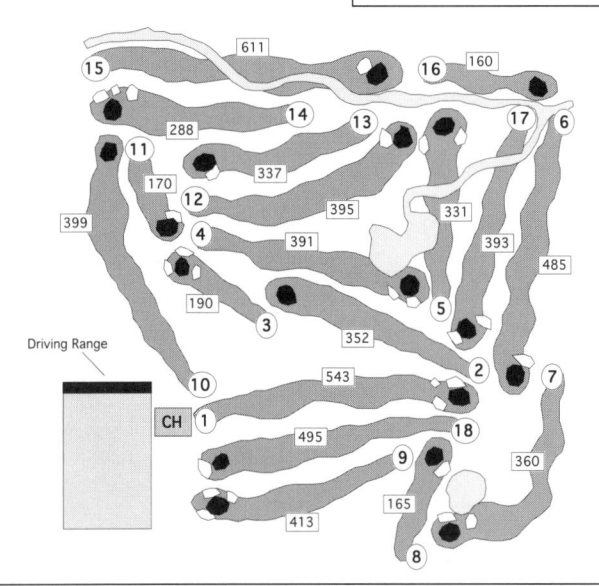

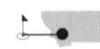

Missoula Country Club (private, 18 hole course)

3850 Old Hwy 93 South; Missoula, Montana 59801
Phone: (406) 251-2751. Fax: none. Internet: none.
Pro: Skip Koprivica, PGA. Superintendent: Jon Heselwood.
Rating/Slope: C 69.9/118; M 68.9/117; W 71.1/118. **Course record:** 64.
Green fees: private club members & guests only; reciprocates.
Power cart: private club. **Pull cart:** private club. **Trail fee:** not allowed.
Reservation policy: private club members & guests of members only.
Winter condition: the golf course is closed November 1st to March 1st.
Terrain: flat (easy walking). **Tees:** all grass. **Spikes:** soft spikes required.
Services: club rentals, lessons, beer, liquor, snack bar, full service private club, pro shop, lockers, driving range, putting & chipping greens, club memberships.
Comments: mature tree lined fairways characterize this very well conditioned course. The course is tight in places so out of bounds is often a hazard to beware of. A great private facility that offers relaxing golf in a very quiet setting.

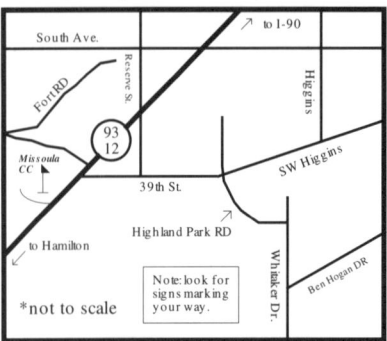

Directions: from I-90 E&W take the Reserve Street exit. Proceed on Reserve Street approximately 5 miles to Old 93 South. Turn right. Travel .5 miles to the course entrance on your right hand side.

Course Yardage & Par:
C-6575 yards, par 71.
M-6338 yards, par 71.
W-5721 yards, par 73.

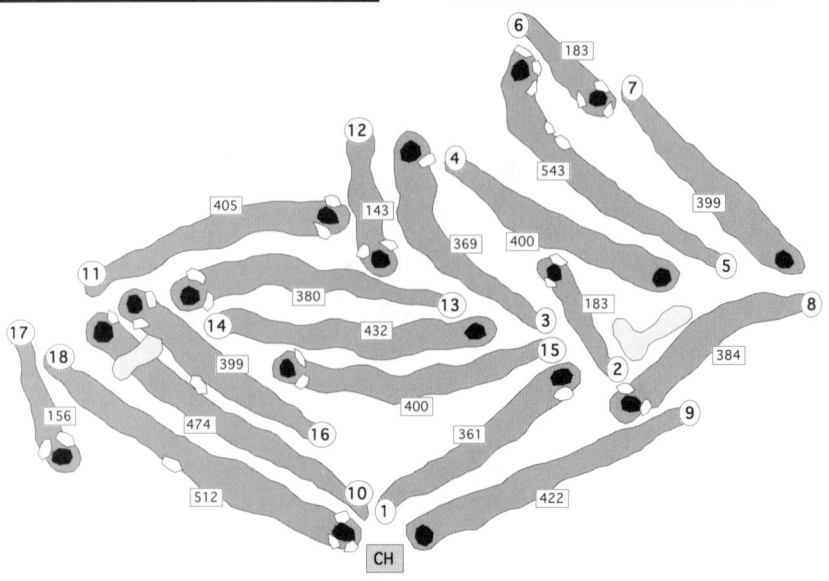

Mountain Crossroads Golf Club (public, 9 hole exec. course)

100 Hwy 206; Creston, Montana 59901
Phone: (406) 755-0111. **Fax:** (406) 752-2869. **Internet:** none.
Pro: Peter LeDonne, PGA. **Superintendent:** unavailable.
Rating/Slope: C 67.9/110; M 66.7/107; W 69.3/112. **Course record:** 24.
Green fees: W/D $17/$10; W/E $17/$10; no special rates; M/C, VISA, DIS.
Power cart: $16/$8. **Pull cart:** $4/$2. **Trail fee:** $2 for personal carts.
Reservation policy: tee times are on a first come first served basis.
Winter condition: the golf course is closed from December 1st thru March 1st.
Terrain: flat, some hills. **Tees:** all grass. **Spikes:** soft spikes only.
Services: pro shop, lessons, snack bar, beer, wine, liquor, putting green.
Comments: the Mountain Crossroads Restaurant is currently open for business. The course features small to medium sized greens that are fairly flat. Fairways are wide open. The course is on the short side but is enjoyable for all ages.

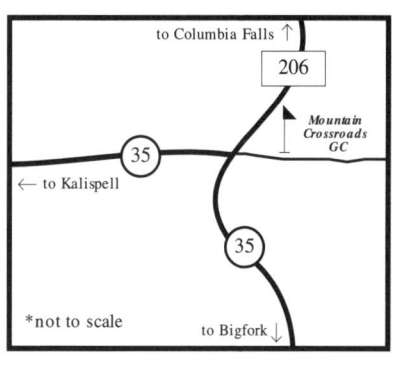

Directions: from Kalispell, take Hwy 35 east for 7.3 miles to the intersection of Hwy 206 and Hwy 35. Turn left on Hwy 206. Course is on the right hand side.

Course Yardage & Par:
C-1393 yards, par 30.
M-1254 yards, par 30.
W-1124 yards, par 30.
F-870 yards, par 30.

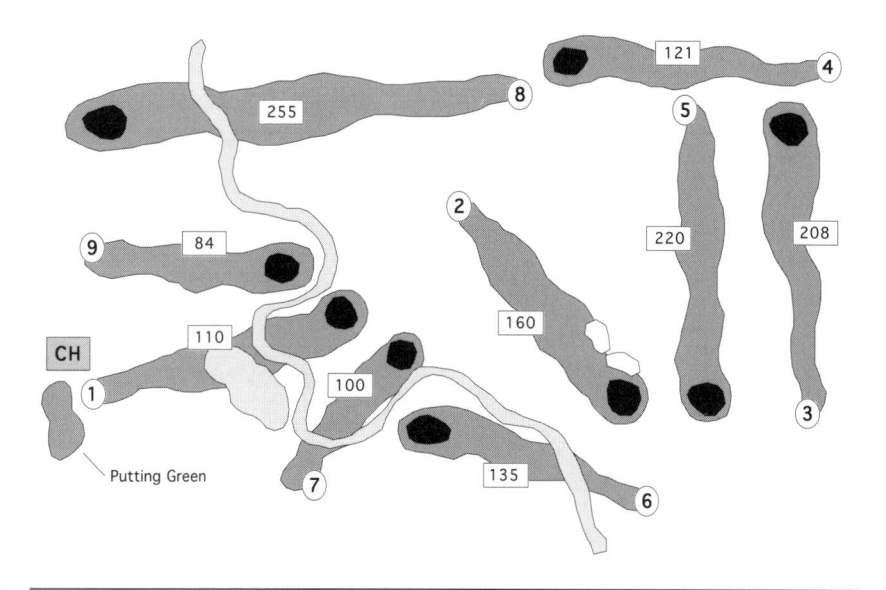

Northern Pines Golf Course (public, 18 hole course)

3230 Hwy 93 North; P.O. Box 1257; Kalispell, Montana 59901
Phone: 800-255-5641 or (406) 751-1950. Fax: none. Internet: www.golfmt.com
Pro: Tom Clary, PGA. Superintendent: unavailable.
Rating/Slope: T 72.5/121; C 70.7/119; M 68.6/115; W 69.9/118. **Record:** 67.
Green fees: W/D $44; W/E $44; off season rates; M/C, VISA, AMEX.
Power cart: $14 per person. **Pull cart:** $3. **Trail fee:** not allowed.
Reservation policy: please call in advance for your tee-times.
Winter condition: the golf course is closed November thru March.
Terrain: flat, some hills. **Tees:** all grass. **Spikes:** soft spikes required.
Services: club rentals, lessons, pro shop, driving range, restuarant, liquor, beer, wine, beverage cart in season, putting & chipping greens, club memberships.
Comments: the golf course is registered with the Audubon Cooperative Sanctuary Program which promotes wildlife and birds. Designed by 2 time U.S. Open Champion Andy North, this course is one of the best courses in the state.

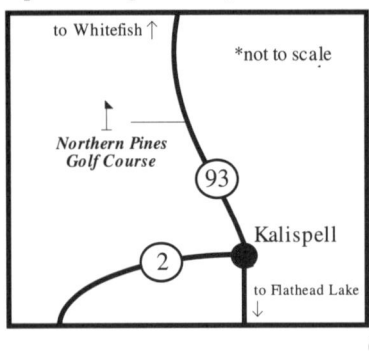

Directions: the golf course is located 2 miles north of Kalispell off of Hwy 93. Look for signs posted at your turn.

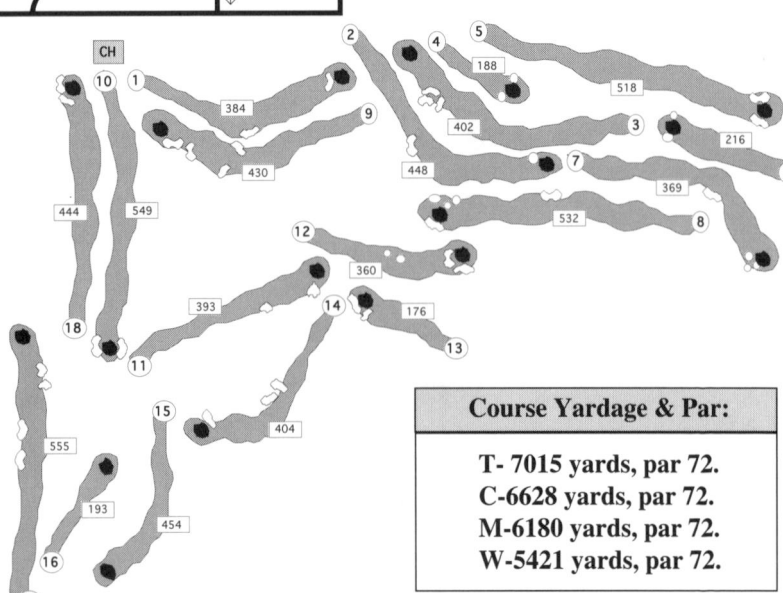

Course Yardage & Par:

T- 7015 yards, par 72.
C-6628 yards, par 72.
M-6180 yards, par 72.
W-5421 yards, par 72.

Old Baldy Golf Course (public, 9 hole course)
Delger Road; Townsend, Montana 59644
Phone: none. **Fax:** none. **Internet:** none.
Pro: none. **Superintendent:** none.
Rating/Slope: M 68.2/109; W 71.1/113. **Course record:** 32 (9 holes).
Green fees: W/D $10; W/E $10; all day $15; no special rates; no credit cards.
Power cart: $15/$10. **Pull cart:** available. **Trail fee:** $5.
Reservation policy: all tee-times are on first come first served basis.
Winter condition: the golf course is open all year long, weather permitting.
Terrain: flat (easy walking). **Tees:** all grass. **Spikes:** no spike policy.
Services: pop machine, driving range, very limited services for the golfer.
Comments: a rustic golf course which is often on the honor system. Place your green fee in an envelope and turn it in. The course is flat and easy to walk. It has small firm greens that can be tough to hold. Fair public track off the beaten path.

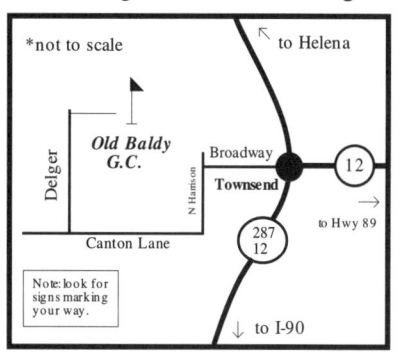

Directions: from Highway 287 turn east on Highway 12 (Broadway) in Townsend. Proceed thru town .5 miles to N. Harrison. Turn left. Proceed on N. Harrison, it will become Canton Lane. Travel 1.4 miles to Delger Road. Turn right. The golf course entrance is .5 miles ahead on your right.

Course Yardage & Par:
M-3150 yards, par 36.
W-2810 yards, par 36.
Dual tees for 18 holes:
M-6300 yards, par 72.
W-5620 yards, par 72.

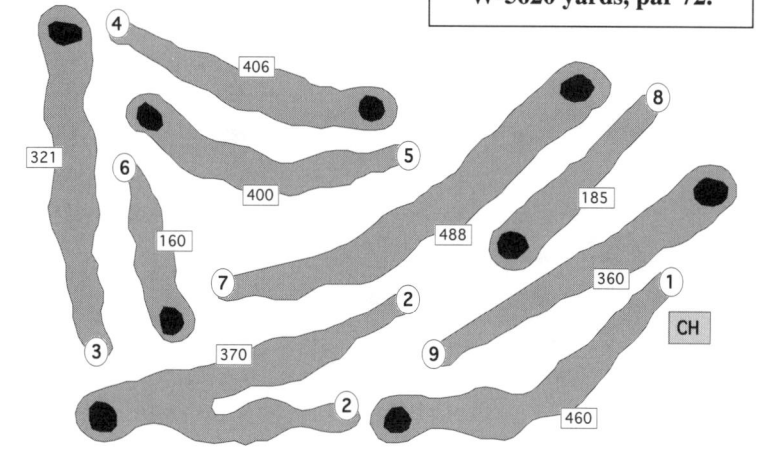

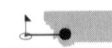

Old Works Golf Club (public, 18 hole course)

1205 Pizzini Way; P.O. Box 100; Anaconda, Montana 59711
Phone: (406) 563-5989. **Fax:** (406) 563-3033. **Internet:** www.oldworks.org
Pro: Steve Wickliffe, PGA. **Superintendent:** unavailable.
Rating/Slope: T 75.7/131; C 73.2/125; M 70.7/121; W 69.4/112. **Record:** 68.
Green fees: $38/$28 (peak season); $29/$19 (off season); M/C, VISA, AMEX.
Power cart: $24/$14. **Pull cart:** $5/$3. **Trail fee:** personal carts not allowed.
Reservation policy: 3 days in advance. 30 days with credit card reservation.
Winter condition: the course is closed from November thru April.
Terrain: flat, some hills. **Tees:** all grass. **Spikes:** soft spikes only.
Services: club rentals, lessons, lounge, snack bar, beer, wine, liquor, pro shop,
driving range, putting & chipping greens, 3 hole golf course around the range.
Comments: the golf course was designed by Jack Nicklaus and is truly one of a
kind. Built on the site of Anaconda's historic copper smelter, the Old Works
Golf Course is destined to be one of the best courses in the state of Montana.
Old Works features unique black sand bunkers and the area's most spectacular
practice facility incuding three practice holes. The December '98 issue *Golf
Digest* rated Old Works as "one of the best new affordable public courses."

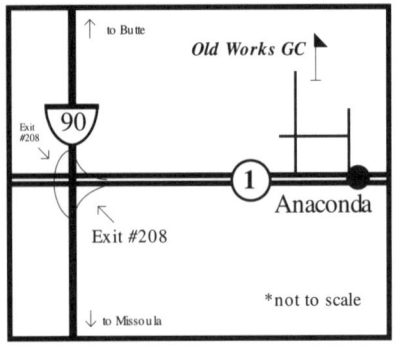

Directions: the golf course is located in
Anaconda at the Old Works site. From
I-90 E&W take exit #208 (Hwy 1) go
south to Anaconda. Turn north of Hwy
1 at Cedar Street and then a right on
Pizzini Way to the course entrance.

Course Yardage & Par:
T-7705 yards, par 72.
C-7211 yards, par 72.
M-6766 yards, par 72.
M-6144 yards, par 72.
W-5348 yards, par 72.

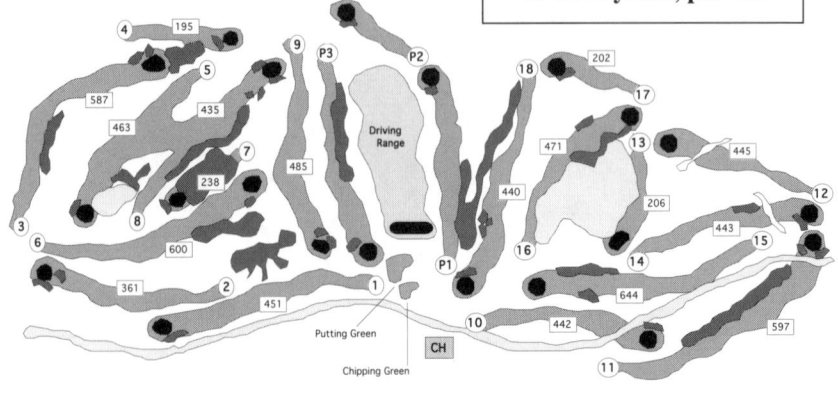

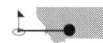

Overland Golf Course (public, 9 hole course)

1 Mile E Highway 10; P.O. Box 1091; Big Timber, Montana 59011
Phone: (406) 932-4297. Fax: none. Internet: none.
Pro: Ken Nelson. Superintendent: unavailable.
Rating/Slope: C 69.7/110; M 69.0/108; W 69.9/111. **Course record:** 68.
Green fees: $18/$11 all week long; $25 all day; M/C, VISA.
Power cart: $14/$8. **Pull cart:** $2.50/$1.50. **Trail fee:** $7/$4.
Reservation policy: you may call up to 5 days in advance for tee times.
Winter condition: the golf course is closed November 1st to March 15th.
Terrain: flat, some hills. **Tees:** all grass. **Spikes:** soft spikes preferred.
Services: club rentals, lessons, lounge, snack bar, beer, wine, pro shop, driving range, putting green, club memberships. **Comments:** the course is located in the plains area of the state with a backdrop of the Crazy Mountains and the Absaroka Range in the distance. You will find the greens and course in excellent condition

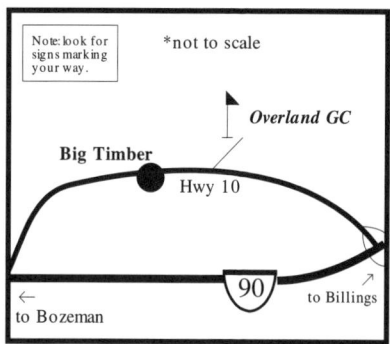

Directions: the course is located .25 miles west of East Interchange on I-90. Take the Big Timber exit off of I-90. Travel to town on Hwy 10 for 1.1 miles to the turn golf course.

Course Yardage & Par:
C-3393 yards, par 36.
M-3087 yards, par 36.
W-2828 yards, par 36.
Dual tees for 18 holes:
C-6786 yards, par 72.
M-6171 yards, par 72.
W-5656 yards, par 72.

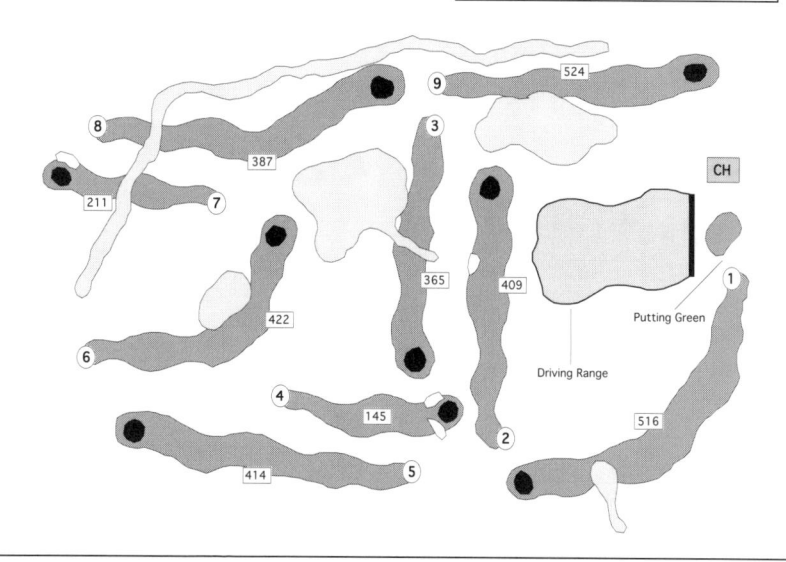

Par 3 on 93 Golf Course & Driving Range (public, 9 hole par 3 course)
Highway 93 South; Whitefish, Montana 59937
Phone: (406) 862-7273. Fax: none. Internet: none.
Pro: none. Superintendent: unavailable.
Rating/Slope: the golf course is not rated. **Course record:** 21.
Green fees: W/D $10; W/E $10; M/C, VISA.
Power cart: $7. **Pull cart:** $2. **Trail fee:** personal carts not allowed.
Reservation policy: call ahead but most times on a first come first served basis.
Winter condition: course is closed November 1st to March 1st. Pro shop open.
Terrain: flat (easy walking). **Tees:** all grass. **Spikes:** soft spikes preferred.
Services: club rentals, lessons, pop, pro shop, driving range, putting green, lounge, casino, restaurant on adjoining property, Par T virtual golf, mini golf.
Comments: par three courses are excellent for practicing your iron play on or take the whole family for a fun day of golf. Nice facility for practicing your iron play. It also offers a full service pro shop for all your golfing needs.

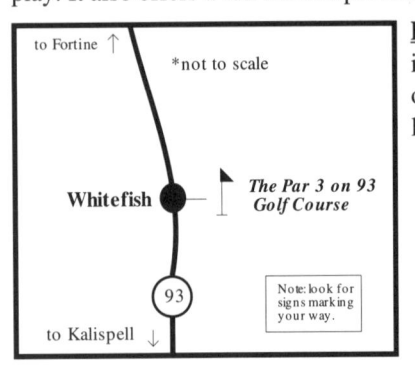

Directions: the course and driving range is located on Hwy 93S, between the cities of Kalispell and Whitefish, the course is located right on Hwy 93 in Whitefish.

Course Yardage & Par:
M-1065 yards, par 27.
W-1065 yards, par 27.

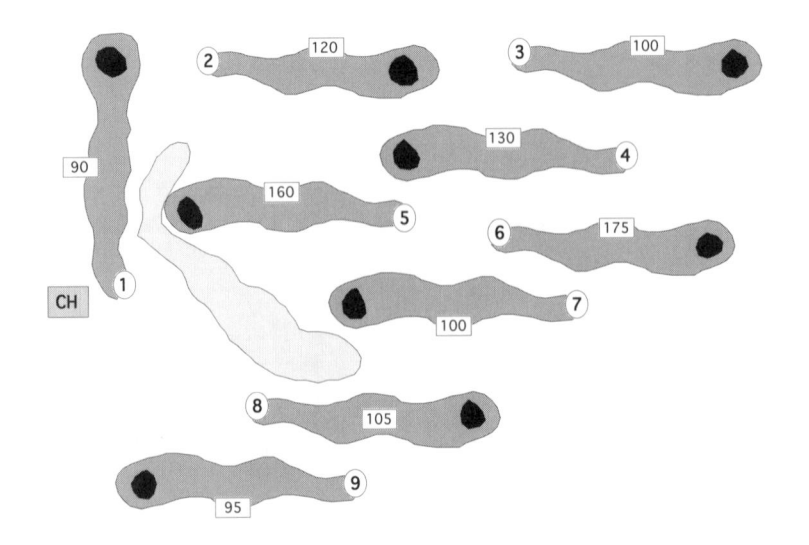

Pete's Pitch & Putt (public, 18 hole par 3 course)

Mailing address: P.O. Box 3207; Missoula, Montana 59806
Physical address: 901 Lakeside Drive, Montana 59847
Phone: (406) 273-3333. **Fax:** (406) 728-9479. **Internet:** none.
Manager: Duane Petterson. **Superintendent:** Duane Petterson.
Rating/Slope: the golf course is not rated. **Course record:** 21.
Green fees: Adults $6; Youth $4; M/C, VISA.
Power cart: $4. **Pull cart:** $1. **Trail fee:** personal carts not allowed.
Reservation policy: call ahead but most times on a first come first served basis.
Winter condition: closed November 15th to March 1st.
Terrain: flat (easy walking). **Tees:** mats. **Spikes:** no spike policy.
Services: club rentals, lessons, pop, pro shop, driving range, putting green.
Comments: this par three course is on the short side. Excellent on course driving range to practice on. The facility is very popular in the summer months.

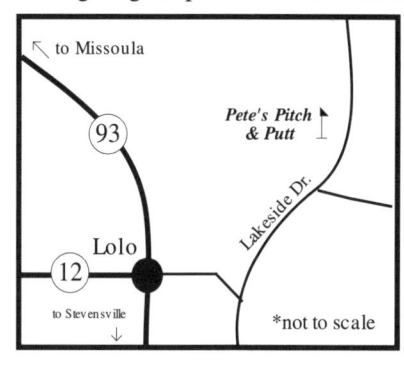

Directions: the course and driving range are located on Hwy 93S in the town of Lolo. Proceed on Glacier Drive or Taylor Way. Proceed to Lakeside Drive and turn left. Proceed to the course on the left.

Course Yardage & Par:
M-899 yards, par 54.
W-899 yards, par 54.

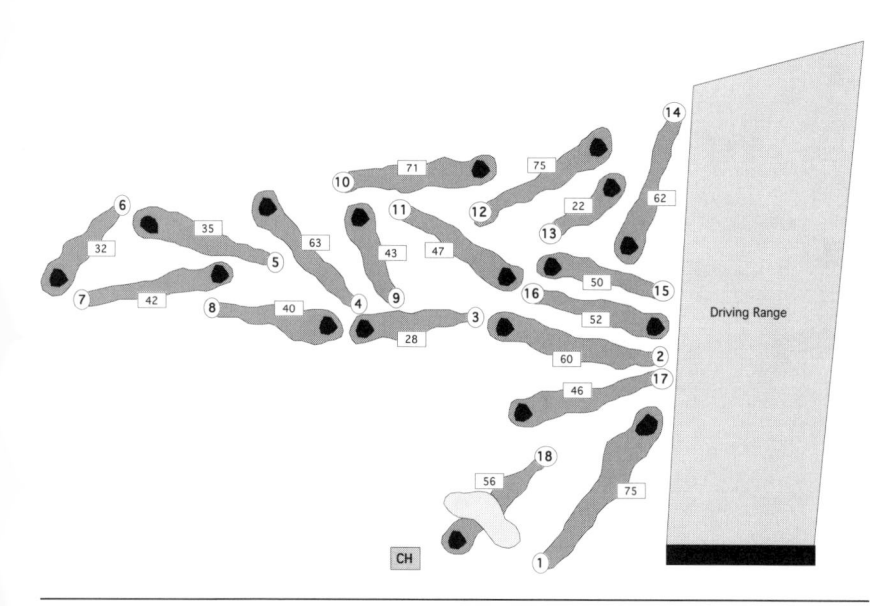

Peter Yegen Jr. Golf Course (public, 18 hole course)

3400 Grand Avenue; Billings, Montana 59102
Phone: (406) 656-8099. Fax: none. Internet: none.
Pro: Randy Northrop. Superintendent: unavailable.
Rating/Slope: C 69.7/112; M 68.2/110; W 67/109. **Course record:** 58.
Green fees: W/D $16/$11; W/E $18/$12; M/C, VISA.
Power cart: $20/$10. **Pull cart:** $3/$2. **Trail fee:** personal carts not allowed.
Reservation policy: call up to 3 days in advance to make your tee times.
Winter condition: the golf course is closed from November 1st to March 1st.
Terrain: flat, some hills. **Tees:** all grass. **Spikes:** soft spikes required.
Services: club rentals, snack bar, beer, wine, pro shop, driving range.
Comments: the course offers wide open, mounded fairways with few trees. The primary hazard on this course is a host of ponds to catch those errant shots. A popular public golf course in the summer months which is well groomed.

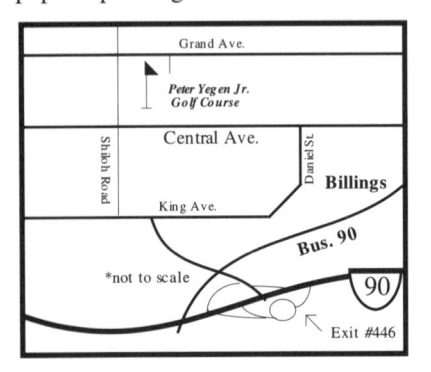

Directions: the golf course is located on Grand Avenue and 34th in Billings, Montana. From Billings, head west on Grand Avenue, look for the golf course 3.2 miles beyond Billings Montana.

Course Yardage & Par:
C-6617 yards, par 71.
M-6220 yards, par 71.
W-4994 yards, par 71.

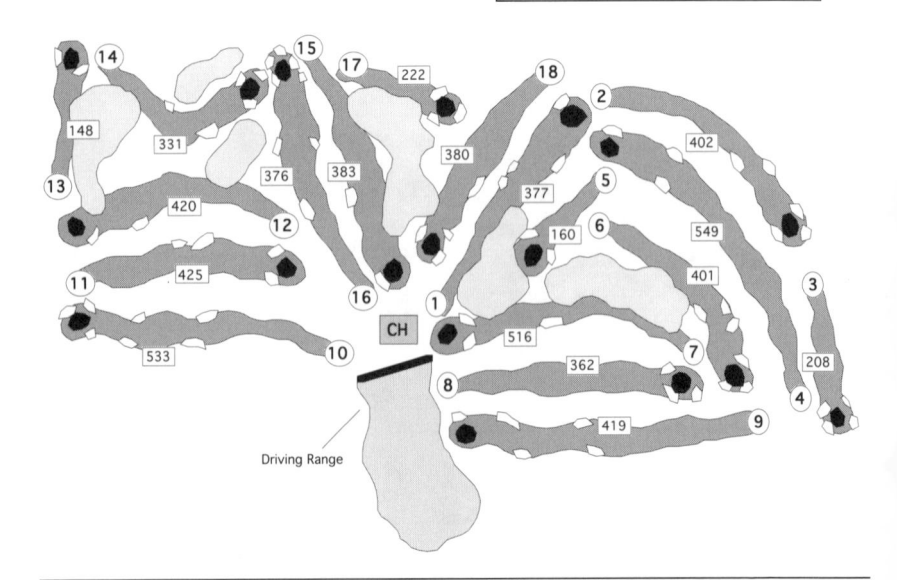

Pine Meadows Golf Club (semi-private, 9 hole course)

Country Club Drive; P.O. Box 719; Lewistown, Montana 59457
Phone: (406) 538-7075. Fax: none. Internet: none.
Pro: Ken Sipes, PGA. Superintendent: Morey Ray.
Rating/Slope: M 69.4/109; W 71.1/111. **Course record:** 30.
Green fees: W/D $14; W/E $16; Jr., Sr. and twilight rates; M/C, VISA.
Power cart: $18/$11. **Pull cart:** $2. **Trail fee:** personal carts not allowed.
Reservation policy: call 14 days in advance for all your tee times.
Winter condition: the golf course is closed November 1st to March 1st.
Terrain: some hills. **Tees:** all grass. **Spikes:** soft spikes preferred.
Services: club rentals, lessons, small pro shop, putting & chipping greens.
Comments: set in a valley and surrounded by mountains this is a very scenic
course. Their fairways have many rolling hills so sidehill lies can present a real
challenge. Dual sets of tees are available for a full eighteen hole round of golf.

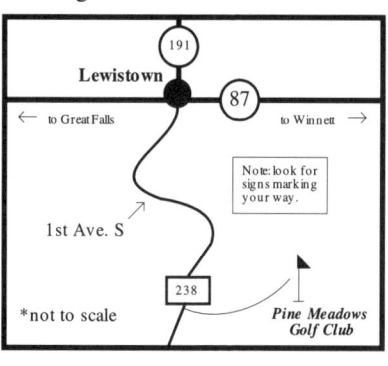

Directions: from Highway 238 proceed
southbound for 1 mile to the golf course
which will be located right off the
highway in Lewistown. Look for a sign
indicating your turn to the golf course.

Course Yardage & Par:
M-3332 yards, par 36.
W-2896 yards, par 37.
Dual tees for 18 holes:
M-6602 yards, par 72.
W-5853 yards, par 74.

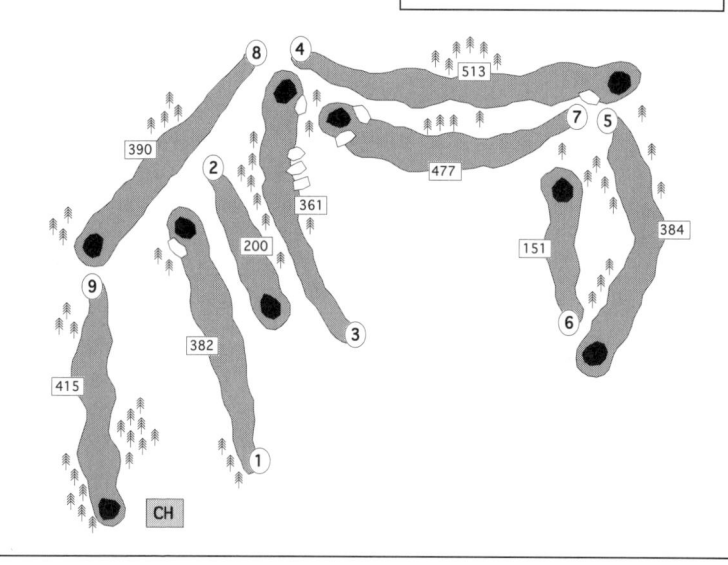

Pine Ridge Country Club (public, 9 hole course)

71 Golf Course Road; P.O. Box 604; Roundup, Montana 59072
Phone: (406) 323-2880. Fax: none. Internet: none.
Manager: T. West. Superintendent: T. West.
Rating/Slope: M 36.0/97; W 36/96. Course record: 33 (9 holes).
Green fees: $10 for 9 holes all week long; M/C, VISA.
Power cart: $15/$10. **Pull cart:** $2. **Trail fee:** daily rate available.
Reservation policy: you may call up to 2 days in advance for tee times.
Winter condition: the golf course is closed from November 1st to March 15th.
Terrain: relatively hilly. **Tees:** all grass. **Spikes:** soft spikes preferred.
Services: club rentals, lessons, snack bar, beer, small pro shop, driving range.
Comments: well kept public course that was a nice surprise to find. The greens
are medium in size with few hazards fronting them. Water comes into play on
three holes and will be a factor off the tee or on your approach shots. The
course offers dual tees for those wanting a different look on your 2nd 9 holes.

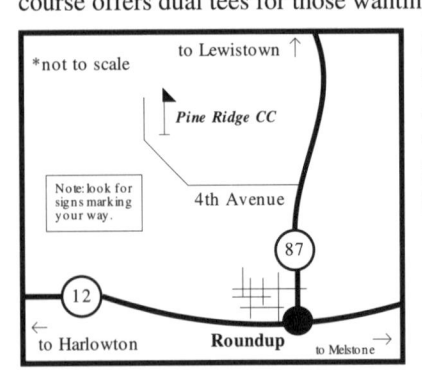

Directions: from Hwy 87 in Roundup
turn east on 4th Avenue. Proceed on 4th
Avenue to Golf Course Road where you
will turn right. The golf course entrance
is .7 miles up the gravel road. The course
is located a little north of Roundup.

Course Yardage & Par:
M-2849 yards, par 36.
W-2516 yards, par 36.
Dual tees for 18 holes:
M-6007 yards, par 72.
W-5032 yards, par 72.

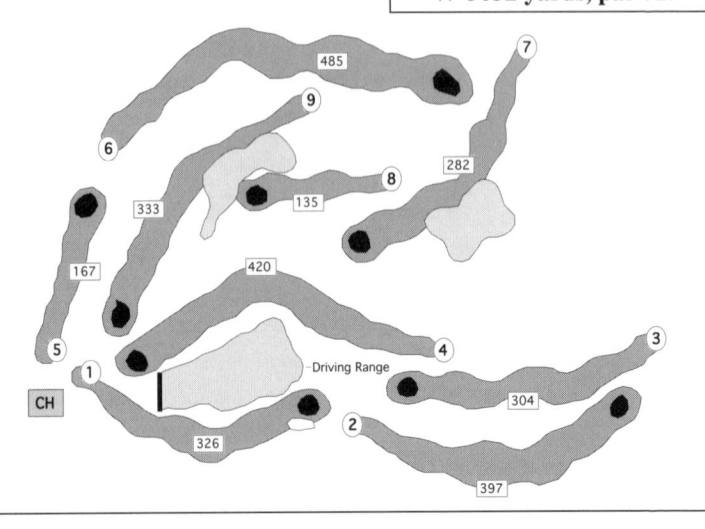

Plains Golf Club (public, 9 hole course)

Highway 200; P.O. Box 995; Plains, Montana 59859
Phone: (406) 826-3106. Fax: none. Internet: none.
Pro: Walter Martin. Superintendent: unavailable.
Rating/Slope: M 65.7/102; W 65.5/101. **Course record:** 31 (9 holes).
Green fees: W/D $9; W/E $10; M/C, VISA, AMEX
Power cart: $14/$8. **Pull cart:** $2. **Trail fee:** no trail fee.
Reservation policy: tee times are on a first come first served basis.
Winter condition: the golf course is open all year, weather permitting.
Terrain: relatively hilly. **Tees:** all grass. **Spikes:** soft spikes preferred.
Services: club rentals, lessons, snack bar, beer, small pro shop, driving range.
Comments: fair public course that varies in terrain. Greens are medium in size, leaving the golfer with a lot of chipping and putting if you miss the green. The course sports narrow tree-lined fairways.

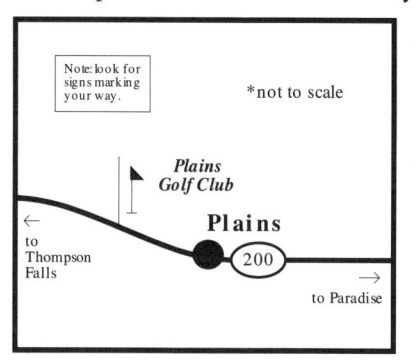

Directions: the golf course is located north of Plains Montana on Highway 200 on the east side of the road (near Milepost 73). Look for a sign to the golf course.

Course Yardage & Par:
M-2900 yards, par 36.
W-2474 yards, par 36.

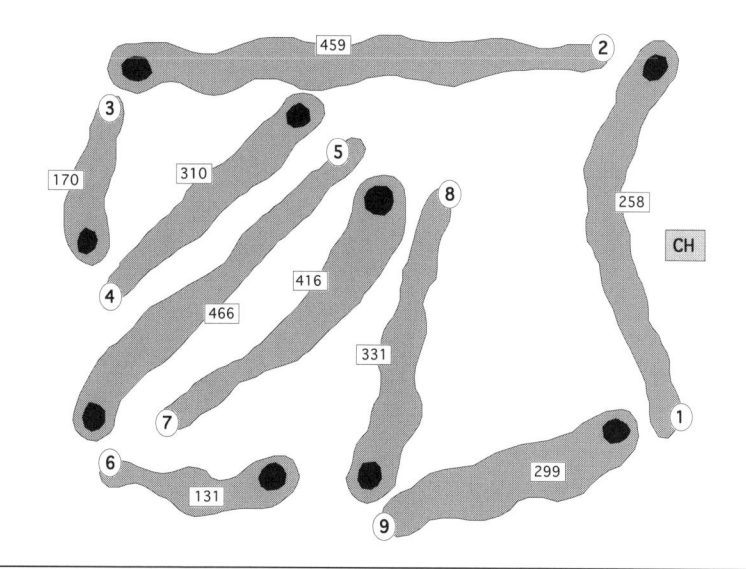

Plentywood Golf Club (semi-private, 9 hole course)

709 North Sheridan Street; Plentywood, Montana 59254
Phone: (406) 765-2532. Fax: none. Internet: none.
Pro: Keith M. Berezay. Superintendent: Keith M. Berezay.
Rating/Slope: C 68.1/106; M 67.7/103; W 67.5/102. **Course record:** 60.
Green fees: W/D $15/$10; W/E $18/$12; no credit cards.
Power cart: $16/$10. **Pull cart:** $2. **Trail fee:** daily rate available.
Reservation policy: you may call up to 7 days in advance for tee times.
Winter condition: the course is closed from November 15th to March 15th.
Terrain: relatively hilly. **Tees:** all grass. **Spikes:** soft spikes preferred.
Services: club rentals, lessons, snack bar, beer, small pro shop, driving range.
Comments: some of the tee-times are restricted to club members so be sure to
call ahead for a tee-time. The course has varied terrain and wide open fairways.
Greens are small in size but very receptive to your approach shots. The golf
course has a driving range for those wanting to brush up on their golfing skills.

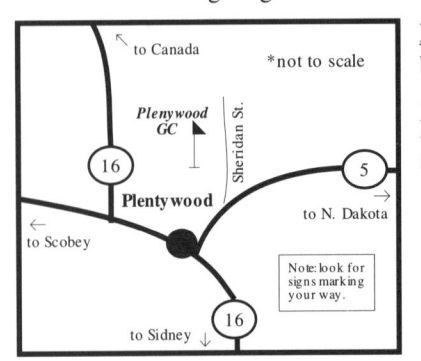

Directions: from Highway 5 turn northbound on Sheridan Street and proceed for
.8 miles to the golf course on your left
hand side. Look for signs that are posted
at your turn.

Course Yardage & Par:
C-2972 yards, par 36.
M-2818 yards, par 36.
W-2630 yards, par 36.

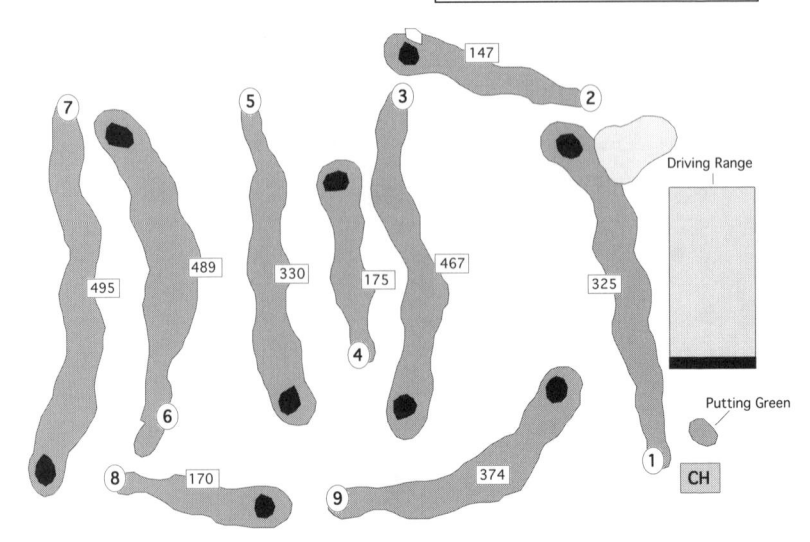

Polson Country Club (public, 27 hole course)

111 Bayview Drive; Polson Montana 59860
Phone: (406) 883-2440. Fax: none. Internet: (e-mail) polsoncc@digisys.net
Pro: Roger D. Wallace, PGA. Superintendent: Larry Newlin.
Rating/Slope: C 70.9/119; M 67.9/115; W 68.4/114. **Course record:** 64.
Green fees: $25/$15 all week long; M/C, VISA, AMEX.
Power cart: $22/$12. **Pull cart:** $3/$2. **Trail fee:** $10/$6.
Reservation policy: 2 days in advance. Call anytime w/ credit card.
Winter condition: the course is closed from December 1st to March 1st.
Terrain: flat, some hills. **Tees:** all grass. **Spikes:** soft spikes required.
Services: club rentals, lessons, lounge, beer, wine, restaurant, pro shop, driving range, putting & chipping green, gambling. **Comments:** this beautifully maintained golf course is located on the south shore of Flathead Lake. You will find great views of the lake and Rocky Mountains from almost every hole. The golf course plays very tough from the back tees. Great track that is worth a trip.

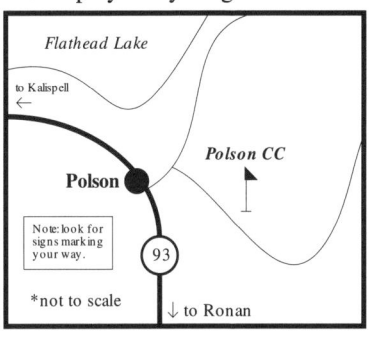

Directions: the golf course is located adjacent to Highway 93 at the south end of Polson Montana. Look for signs.

18 hole Course

Course Yardage & Par:
T-6964 yards, par 72.
C-6271 yards, par 72.
M-5785 yards, par 72.
W-5413 yards, par 72.

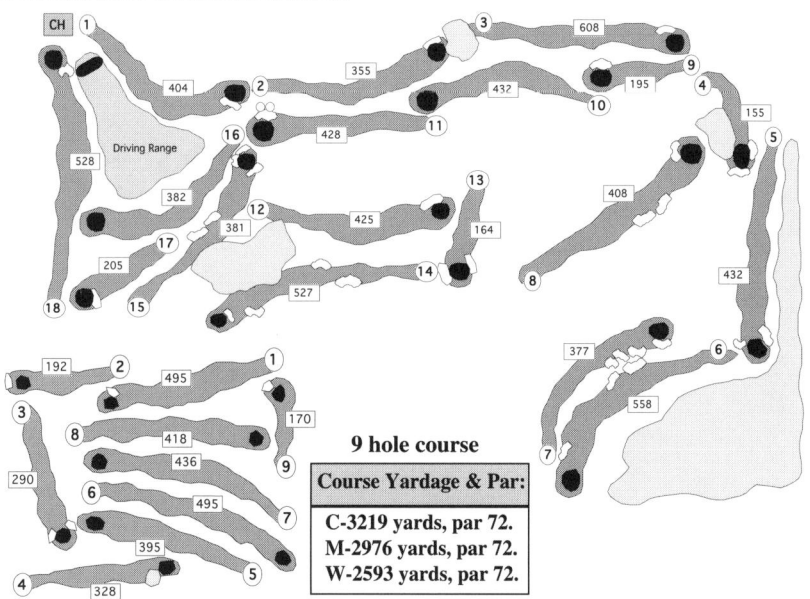

9 hole course

Course Yardage & Par:
C-3219 yards, par 72.
M-2976 yards, par 72.
W-2593 yards, par 72.

Pondera Golf Club (public, 9 hole course)

4th Avenue South; P.O. Box 1354; Conrad, Montana 59425
Phone: (406) 278-3402. Fax: none. Internet: none.
Manager: Randy Manzy. Superintendent: Randy Manzy.
Rating/Slope: C 68.0/106; M 66.8/103; W 69.3/105. **Course record:** 30.
Green fees: W/D $10; W/E $11; no special rates; M/C, VISA.
Power cart: $15/$10. **Pull cart:** $2. **Trail fee:** daily rates available.
Reservation policy: please call 7 days in advance for your tee-times.
Winter condition: the golf course is closed from November 1st to April 1st.
Terrain: flat (easy walking). **Tees:** all grass. **Spikes:** soft spikes preferred.
Services: club rentals, lessons, lounge, beer, wine, restaurant, pro shop, driving range, putting & chipping green. **Comments:** the golf course is fair conditioned. The terrain is flat leaving the course very walkable. Few hazards are in play off the tee except one creek. Greens are on the large size with very few undulations.

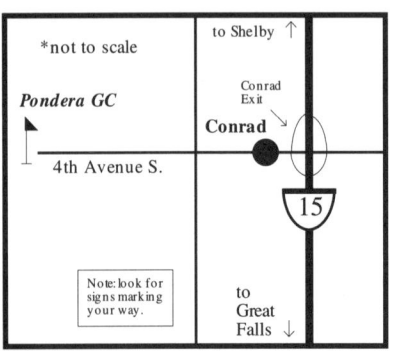

Directions: from Highway 15 in Conrad Montana turn west on 4th Avenue South. Proceed 1 mile to the golf course. The golf course is located 1 mile west of Conrad. Look for signs along the route.

Course Yardage & Par:
C-3079 yards, par 36.
M-2947 yards, par 36.
W-2729 yards, par 36.

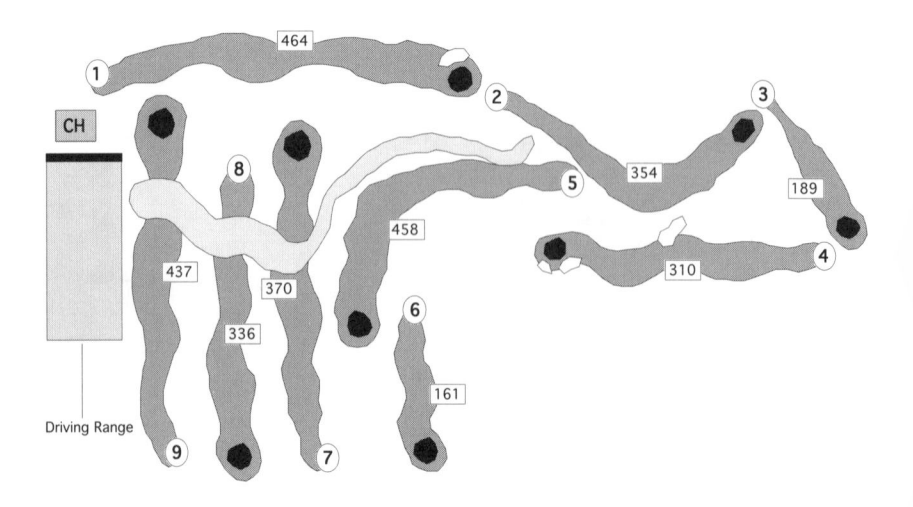

Ponderosa Butte Public Golf Course (public, 9 hole course)

1 Long Drive; P.O. Box 127; Colstrip, Montana 59323
Phone: (406) 748-2700. **Fax:** none. **Internet:** none.
Pro: Don O'Neil, PGA. **Superintendent:** Fred Ackley.
Rating/Slope: C 69.8/116; M 68.0/112; W 68.3/110. **Course record:** 67.
Green fees: W/D $14/$8; W/E $12/$8; M/C, VISA.
Power cart: $15/$8. **Pull cart:** $3/$2. **Trail fee:** call for prices.
Reservation policy: you may call up to 7 days in advance for tee times.
Winter condition: the golf course is closed November 1st to March 15th.
Terrain: flat, some hills. **Tees:** all grass. **Spikes:** soft spikes required.
Services: club rentals, lessons, lounge, snack bar, beer, wine, pro shop, driving range, putting & chipping greens. **Comments:** great course that is tucked away in the small town of Colstrip Montana. This course will challenge you at every turn. Greens are undulating and well bunkered. Fairway bunkers and water come into play on almost every tee shot. Great pro shop and restaurant to serve you.

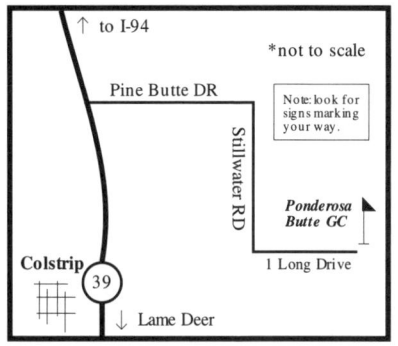

Directions: from Highway 39 exit on Pine Butte Drive and follow to the course entrance .4 miles ahead. The course is located north of Colstrip Montana next to the high school. Look for signs.

Course Yardage & Par:
C-3164 yards, par 36.
M-2880 yards, par 36.
W-2488 yards, par 36.
<u>Dual tees for 18 holes:</u>
C-6469 yards, par 72.
M-6050 yards, par 72.
W-4976 yards, par 72.

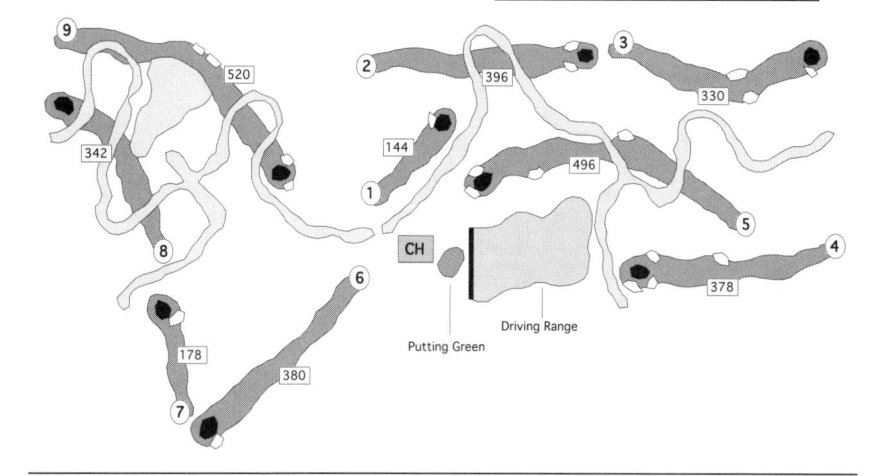

Pryor Creek Golf Club (private, 27 hole course)

Pryor Creek Road; P.O. Box 365; Huntley Montana 59037
Phone: (406) 348-3900. Fax: none. Internet: none.
Manager/Pro: Joe Link, PGA. Superintendent: unavailable.
Rating/Slope: West/North: C 71.1/121; M 69.2/118; W 71.7/118. **Record:** 64.
Rating/Slope: North/South: C 71.6/116; M 69.1/116; W 70.9/117.
Greens fee: private club members & guests only; reciprocates.
Power cart: private club. **Pull cart:** private club. **Trail fee:** not allowed.
Reservation policy: private club members & guests only.
Winter condition: the golf course is closed from November 15th to March 15th.
Terrain: relatively hilly. **Tees:** all grass. **Spikes:** soft spikes only.
Services: club rentals, lessons, beer, liquor, snack bar, full service private club, pro shop, lockers, driving range, putting green. **Comments:** private course that plays very tough. Greens are well bunkered and large. The course is built over varied terrain giving the golfer a wide variety of lies from the fairway.

Directions: the golf course is located right off I-94. Take exit #6 in Huntley. Proceed to the golf course that is just south of I-94 on top of the hill.

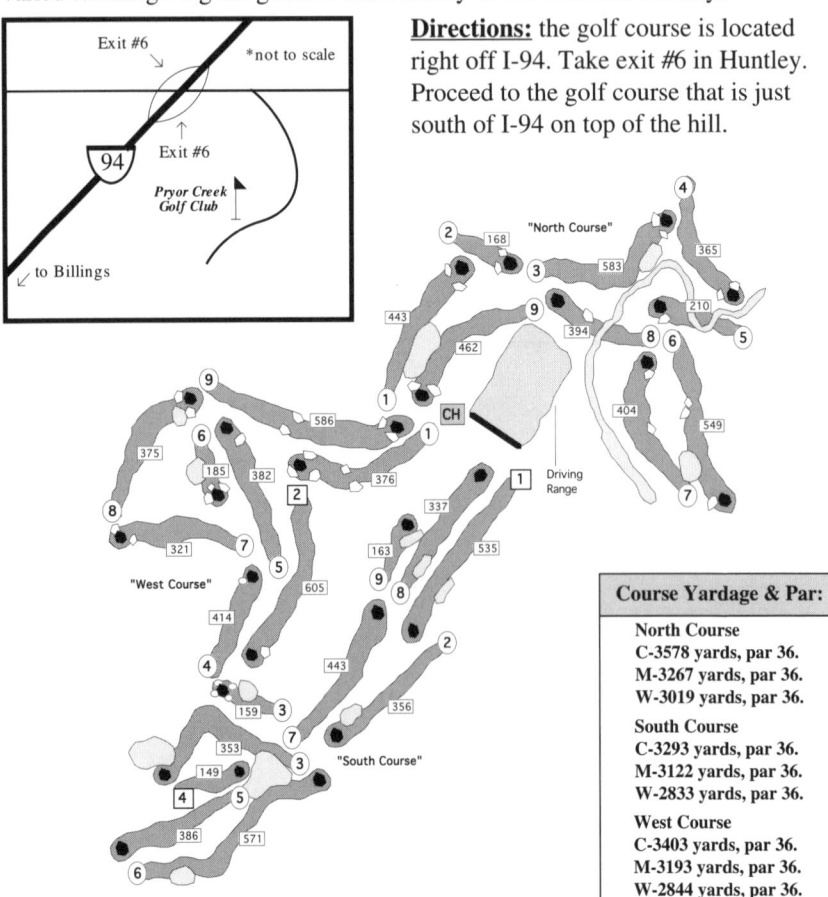

Course Yardage & Par:

North Course
C-3578 yards, par 36.
M-3267 yards, par 36.
W-3019 yards, par 36.

South Course
C-3293 yards, par 36.
M-3122 yards, par 36.
W-2833 yards, par 36.

West Course
C-3403 yards, par 36.
M-3193 yards, par 36.
W-2844 yards, par 36.

Red Lodge Mountain Golf Course (public, 18 hole course)

828 Upper Continental Drive; P.O. Box 750; Red Lodge, Montana 59068
Phone: (800) 514-3088 or (406) 446-3344. Fax: none. Internet: none.
Pro: unavailable. Superintendent: unavailable.
Rating/Slope: C 69.8/118; M 69.3/115; W 70.4/115. **Course record:** 67.
Green fees: W/D $24/$15; W/E $24/$15; MC, VISA.
Power cart: $18/$10. **Pull cart:** $2. **Trail fee:** no personal carts allowed.
Reservation policy: call 14 days in advance for information for all tee times.
Winter condition: the golf course is closed from November 1st to March 1st.
Terrain: rolling terrain. **Tees:** all grass. **Spikes:** soft spikes only.
Services: club rentals, lessons, retaurant, lounge, beer, wine, pro shop, driving range, putting green. **Comments:** with its red rock trails, rustic bridges, and the surrounding Beartooth Mountains this course is surely one of the most scenic in all of Montana. The course will challenge even the best golfer. Shot placement is a must as you drive into tight, tree lined fairways. Water hazards abound.

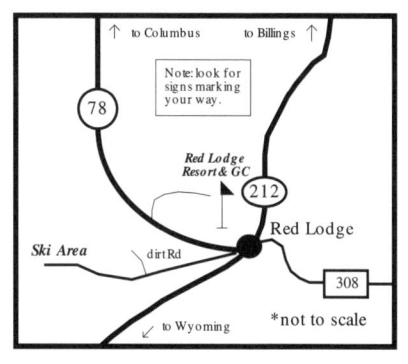

Directions: from US 212 turn west onto Highway 78 (just north of Red Lodge). Proceed up the hill to the golf course located on Upper Continental Drive. The course is well marked.

Course Yardage & Par:
C-6863 yards, par 72.
M-6483 yards, par 72.
W-5678 yards, par 72.

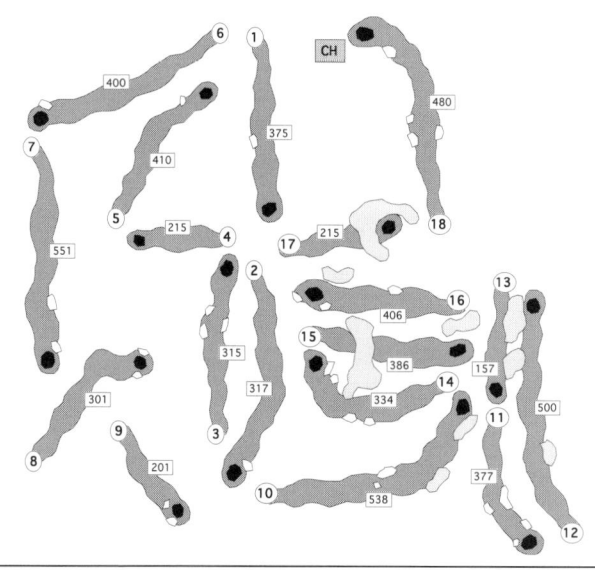

River's Bend at Thompson Falls (public, 9 hole course)

46 Golf Course Road; P.O. Box 372; Thompson Falls, Montana 59873
Phone: (406) 827-3438. Fax: none. Internet: none.
Manager: unavailable. Superintendent: unavailable.
Rating/Slope: M 67.2/109; W 68.9/112. Course record: 33 (9 holes).
Green fees: W/D $14/$10; W/E $16/$12; no special rates; M/C, VISA.
Power cart: $16/$10. Pull cart: $2. Trail fee: $10 all day.
Reservation policy: call up in advance to confirm tee times. No time limit.
Winter condition: the golf course is closed November 1st to March 1st.
Terrain: flat, some hills. Tees: all grass. Spikes: soft spikes only.
Services: club rentals, snack bar, beer, driving range, putting green, RV park.
Comments: course winds through a stand of Ponderosa Pines along the lower
Clark River in a very secluded part of the state. The course is naturally beautiful
and very tough with small, quick greens and many out-of-bounds. I definitely
recommend this course, bring your RV and stay the night. Good 9 hole track.

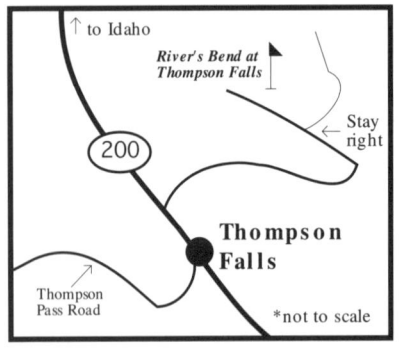

Directions: from Hwy 200 take the exit
for the golf course located 1 mile north
of town. The course is on the east side of
Hwy 200 and the way is well marked.

Course Yardage & Par:
M-3022 yards, par 36.
W-2670 yards, par 36.
__Dual tees for 18 holes:__
M-5995 yards, par 72.
W-5386 yards, par 72.

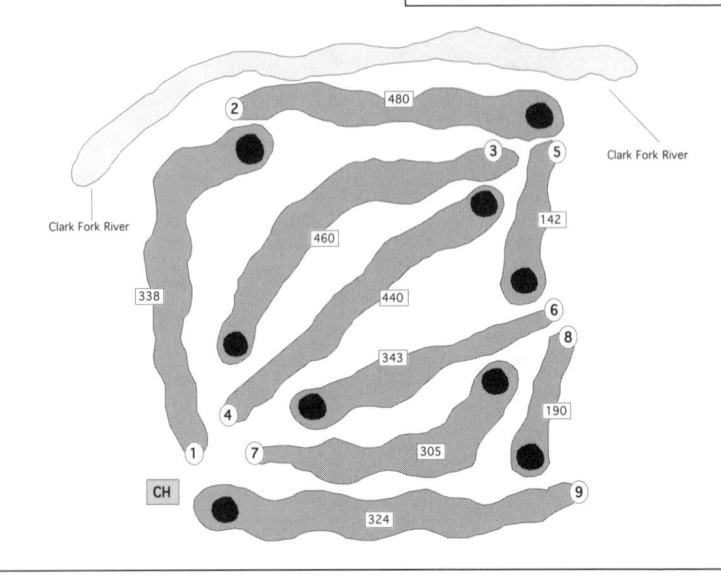

Riverside Country Club (private, 18 hole course)
2500 Springhill Road; Bozeman, Montana 59715
Phone: (406) 586-2251. Fax: (406) 587-5107. Internet: none.
Pro: David Baucom. Superintendent: unavailable.
Rating/Slope: C 70.3/119; M 68.8/115; W 71.5/119. **Course record:** 63.
Greens fee: private club members & guests only; reciprocates.
Power cart: private club. **Pull cart:** private club. **Trail fee:** not allowed.
Reservation policy: private club members & guests of members only.
Winter condition: the golf course is closed from November 1st to April 1st.
Terrain: flat (easy walking). **Tees:** grass. **Spikes:** soft spikes only.
Services: club rentals, lessons, beer, wine, liquor, snack bar, full service private club, pro shop, showers, lockers, driving range, putting & chipping greens.
Comments: the track offers spectacular views of the Bridger Mountain Range in the distance. The course can be found in great condition during the season.

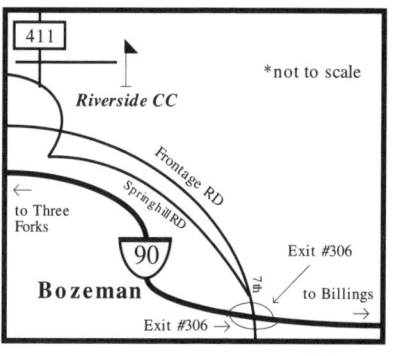

Directions: proceed north on North 7th Avenue out of Bozeman, over I-90. Springhill Road will be on the right. Turn on Springhill Road to the golf course entrance which will be on your right hand side. Look for a sign to the parking lot.

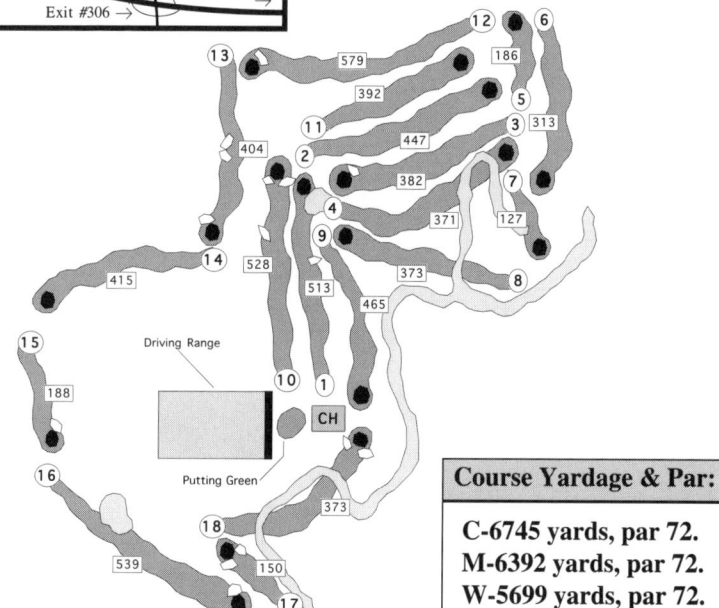

Course Yardage & Par:
C-6745 yards, par 72.
M-6392 yards, par 72.
W-5699 yards, par 72.

Robert O'Speck Golf Course (public, 18 hole course)

29th & River Drive North; P.O. Box 5021; Great Falls, Montana 59401
Phone: (406) 761-1078. Fax: none. Internet: none.
Pro: Connie Cramer-Caouette, LPGA. Superintendent: unavailable.
Rating/Slope: C 69.3/118; M 68.7/111; W 69.7/115. **Course record:** 64.
Green fees: W/D $18/12; W/E $18/12; M/C, VISA, AMEX.
Power cart: $16/$8. **Pull cart:** $2. **Trail fee:** personal carts not allowed.
Reservation policy: call 14 days in advance for all your tee times.
Winter condition: the golf course is closed from November 1st to March 1st.
Terrain: flat, some hills. **Tees:** all grass. **Spikes:** soft spikes preferred.
Services: club rentals, lessons, snack bar, beer, wine, pro shop, driving range, putting & chipping greens. **Comments:** the golf course is one of the most popular in the area. Many fairways are tree lined although this is really the extent of the hazards, you will not find water or sand bunkers on this course.

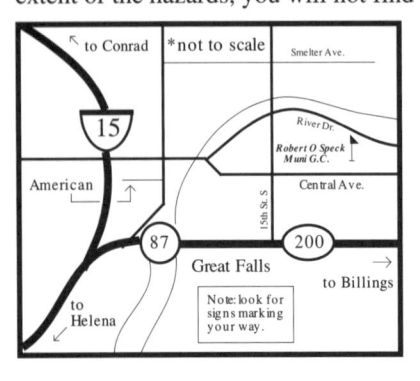

Directions: from Highway 87 turn on River Drive. Proceed .8 miles to 25th Street N. Turn into the golf course and baseball park complex. **Note:** Your turn is on River Drive not River Road.

Course Yardage & Par:
C-6830 yards, par 72.
M-6525 yards, par 72.
W-5817 yards, par 72.

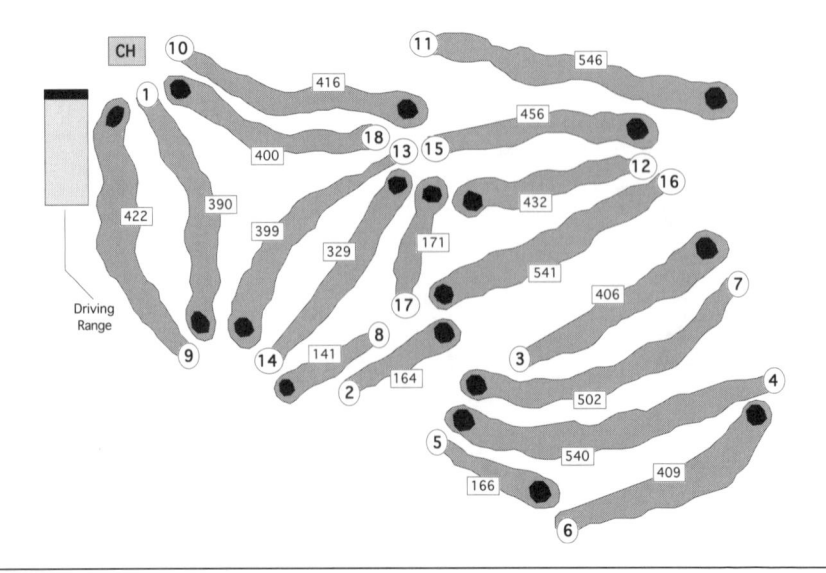

Rolling Hills Golf Course (public, 9 hole course)

Hwy 212 West; Broadus, Montana 59317
Phone: (406) 436-9984. **Fax:** none. **Internet:** none.
Manager: Curt McCamish. **Superintendent:** Curt McCamish.
Rating/Slope: M 68.1/104; W 67.2/103. **Course record:** 32.
Green fees: W/D $14/$9; W/E $17/$12; All day $20; VISA, M/C, AMEX.
Power cart: $16/$8. **Pull cart:** $2/$1. **Trail fee:** no trail fee.
Reservation policy: you may call in advance. You can usually walk on anytime.
Winter condition: the golf course is closed November 15th to April 1st.
Terrain: relatively hilly. **Tees:** all grass. **Spikes:** soft spikes preferred.
Services: club rentals, lounge, snack bar, beer, wine, lockers, pro shop, driving range, putting & chipping greens. **Comments:** this is a very friendly golf course which welcomes visitors anytime, even during their leagues. Water comes into play on holes no. 1 and 9, otherwise there are few hazards. There is a campground right next door to the golf course for those who want to spend the night.

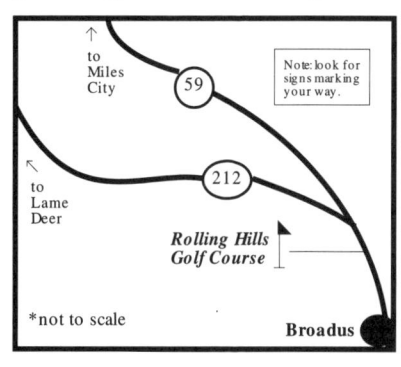

Directions: the course is located 3 miles west of Broadus. It is south of Jct Montana Highway #59 and US 212.

Course Yardage & Par:
M-3064 yards, par 36.
W-2501 yards, par 36.
Dual tees for 18 holes:
M-6128 yards, par 72.
W-5202 yards, par 72.

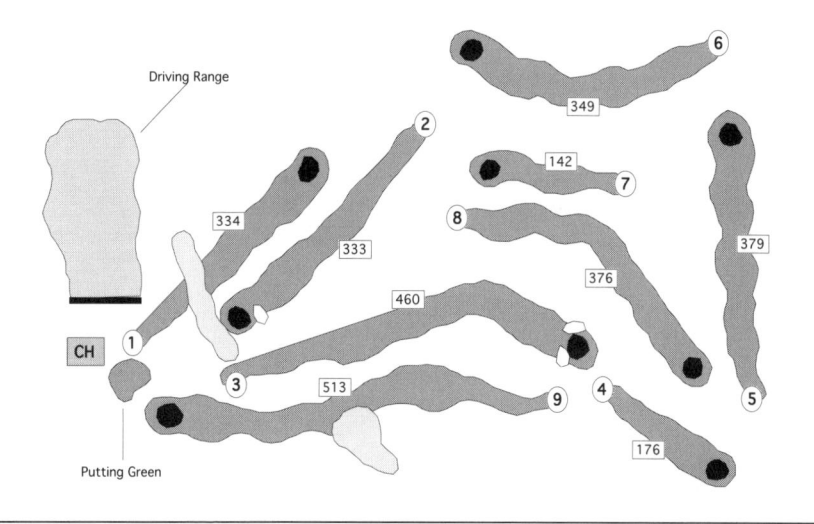

Scobey Golf Club (semi-private, 9 hole course)

Floor County Road; P.O. Box 754; Scobey, Montana 59263
Phone: (406) 487-5322. Fax: none. Internet: none.
Manager: Glorianne Fouhy. Superintendent: none.
Rating/Slope: M 66.8/104; W 70.7/112. **Course record:** 33 (9holes).
Green fees: W/D $14/$9; W/E $18/$13; M/C, VISA.
Power cart: $15/$10. **Pull cart:** $2. **Trail fee:** call for prices.
Reservation policy: call 14 days in advance for information for all tee times.
Winter condition: the golf course is closed October 15th to March 15th.
Terrain: flat, some hills. **Tees:** all grass. **Spikes:** soft spikes preferred.
Services: club rentals, snack bar, beer, wine, putting/chipping green.
Comments: the rolling terrain on this golf course will give the golfer a variety
of lies which will challenge your skill. The course was renovated in the mid
1980's to created elevated greens and tees while retaining some of the original
1927 features. Combine a day of golf with a trip to pioneer town right next door,
a truly unique experience!

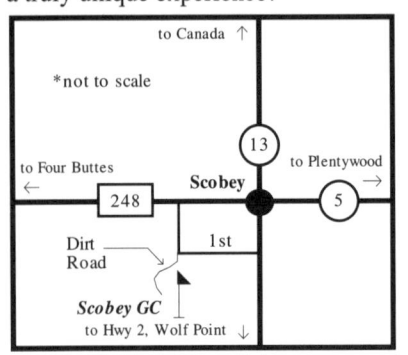

Directions: from Highway 13 turn west
on First Street. Proceed to the end of the
road and turn left on the gravel road.
Proceed past the ghost town to the golf
course entrance which is straight ahead.
From Hwy 248 turn south on the gravel
road just west of Scobey. Look for a
sign marking your turn.

Course Yardage & Par:
M-3059 yards, par 36.
W-2842 yards, par 36.

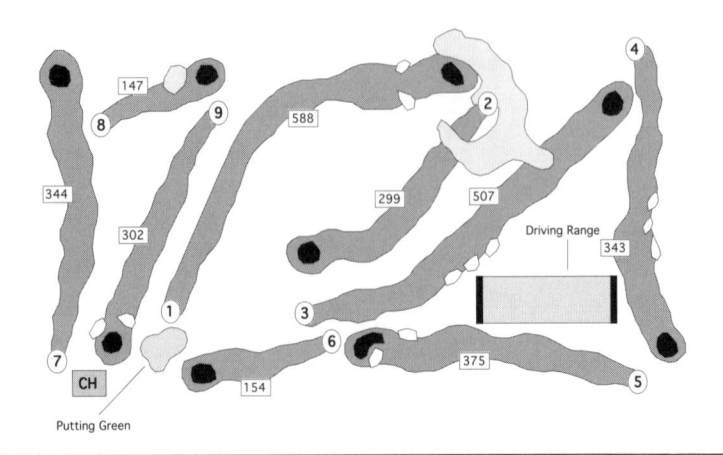

Sidney Country Club (semi-private, 9 hole course)

Highway 16 North; P.O. Box 548; Sidney, Montana 59270
Phone: (406) 482-1894. Fax: (406) 482-1894. Internet: none.
Pro: Jeff Nelson, PGA. Superintendent. Damon McLaughlin.
Rating/Slope: C 69.2/112; M 69.7/114; W 70.6/115. **Record:** 64 (18 holes).
Green fees: $20/$18 all week long; M/C, VISA, AMEX.
Power cart: $18/$10. **Pull cart:** $2. **Trail fee:** $8 for personal carts.
Reservation policy: reservations are required, call 14 days in advance.
Winter condition: the golf course is closed October 1st to March 31st.
Terrain: flat (easy walking). **Tees:** all grass. **Spikes:** soft spikes only.
Services: club rentals, snack bar, pro shop, driving range, putting green.
Comments: the course sports rolling fairways lined with cottonwood and elm trees. Greens are medium to large in size, sand bunkers guard them on some of the shorter holes. For a quiet, relaxing day of golf give Sidney Country Club a try while traveling through Montana. New 9 holes opening in 2000 or 2001.

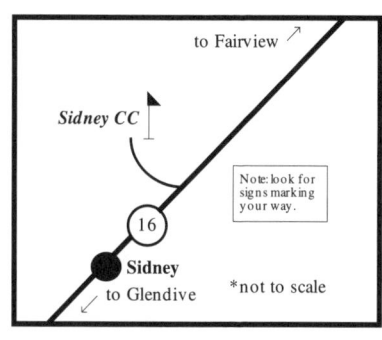

Directions: the country club is located on Hwy 16, just east of the town of Sidney. Look for a sign marking your entrance (on right if traveling southbound, left if traveling northbound).

Course Yardage & Par:
M-3148 yards, par 36.
W-2750 yards, par 36.

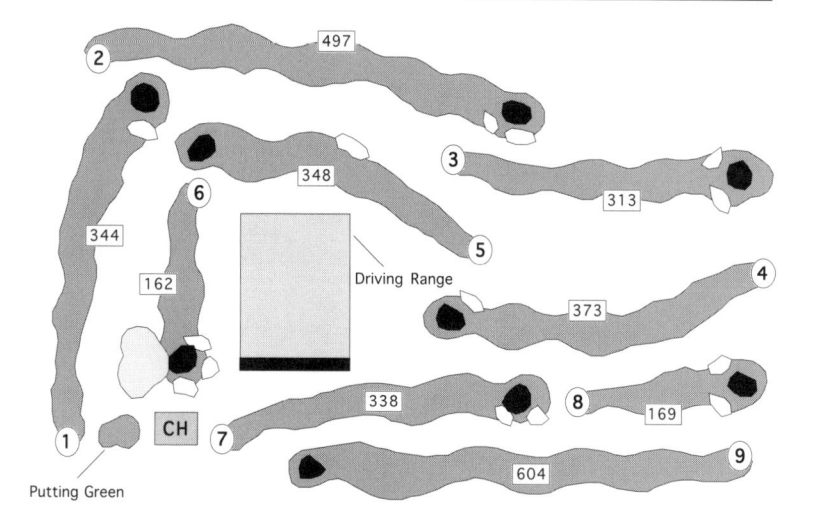

Signal Point Golf Course (public, 9 hole course)

Airport Road; P.O. Box 1134; Fort Benton, Montana 59442
Phone: (406) 622-3666. Fax: none. Internet: none.
Pro: Scott Nance. Superintendent: unavailable.
Rating/Slope: C 72.0/117; M 70.8/115; W 73.2/119. **Course record:** 65.
Green fees: W/D $18/$10; W/E $20/$11; Sr. rates; M/C, VISA.
Power cart: $18/$10. **Pull cart:** $3/$2. **Trail fee:** $5 for personal carts.
Reservation policy: call 14 days in advance for information for all tee times.
Winter condition: the golf course is closed from October 15th to April 15th.
Terrain: flat, some hills. **Tees:** all grass. **Spikes:** soft spikes required.
Services: club rentals, snack bar, beer, small pro shop, driving range.
Comments: Signal Point gets it's name from the rich history of the area, the location was used to watch for approaching steamships coming up the Missouri River from St. Louis. The golf course overlooks the town, the river, and the surrounding plains. Terrain varies with many trees and bunkers coming into play.

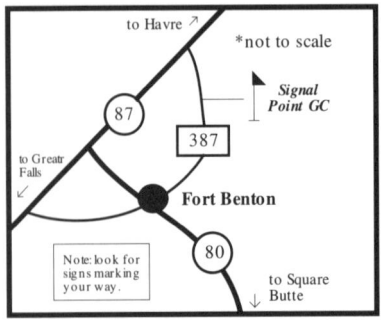

Directions: from Hwy 87 turn off onto Hwy 387 and proceed to the golf course. Note: the course is located next to the airport. Look for signs to the golf course.

Course Yardage & Par:
C-3327 yards, par 36.
M-3457 yards, par 36.
W-3123 yards, par 37.

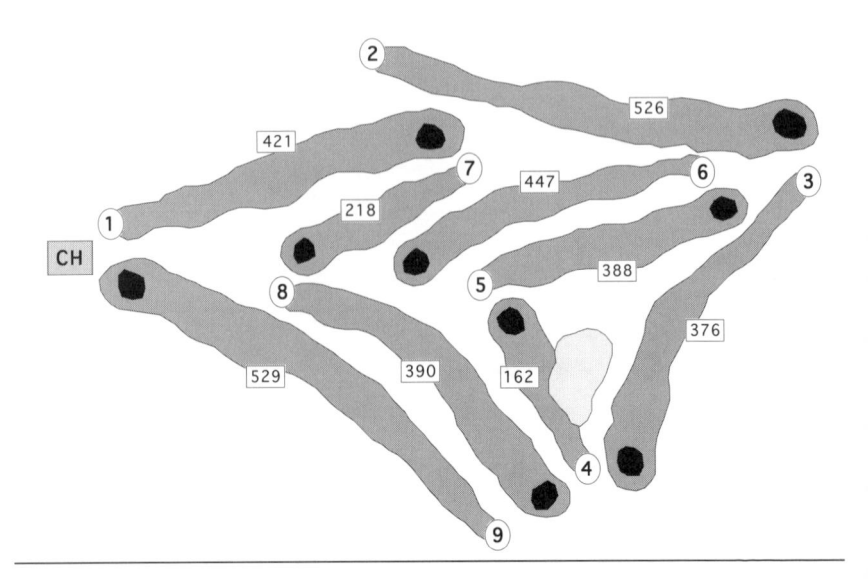

Sleeping Buffalo Golf Course (public, 9 hole course)

Rural Route 1; P.O. Box 13; Saco, Montana 59261
Phone: (406) 527-3370. **Fax:** none. **Internet:** none.
Pro: none. **Superintendent:** none.
Rating/Slope: the golf course is not rated. **Course record:** 66.
Green fees: W/D $18/$10; W/E $18/$10; M/C, VISA.
Power cart: $14/$8. **Pull cart:** $2. **Trail fee:** call for prices.
Reservation policy: call 14 days in advance for information for all tee times.
Winter condition: the golf course is closed from October 15th to April 15th.
Terrain: flat, some hills. **Tees:** all grass. **Spikes:** soft spikes preferred.
Services: club rentals, snack bar, beer, wine, liquor. **Comments:** the course is
located within the Sleeping Buffalo Hot Springs Resort. The golf course is wide
open. Other amenities at the resort are a motel, camping facilities, pool,
waterslide and natural mineral hot springs all near the Nelson Reservoir.

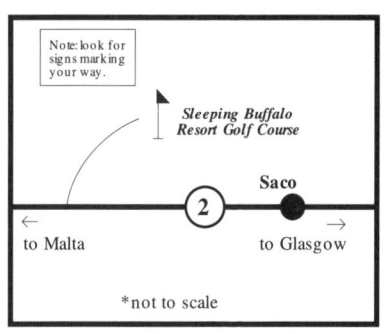

Directions: the course is .5 miles off of
Hwy 2 at the Sleeping Buffalo Resort 10
miles west of Saco, 17 miles east of Malta.
Turn north to the resort from Hwy 2.

Course Yardage & Par:
M-3282 yards, par 36.
W-2988 yards, par 38.

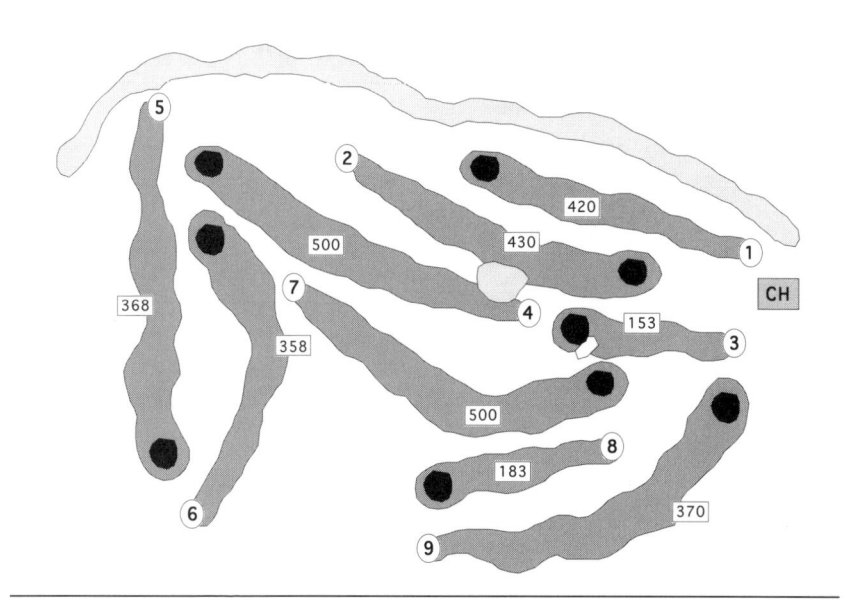

Stillwater Golf & Recreation Association (public, 9 hole course)

Airport Road; P.O. Box 727; Columbus, Montana 59019
Phone: (406) 322-4298. Fax: none. Internet: none.
Manager: Cindy Buechler. Superintendent: unavailable.
Rating/Slope: M 67.9/108; W 67.1/105. **Course record:** 29 (9 holes).
Green fees: W/D $18/$10; W/E $18/$10; no special rates; M/C, VISA.
Power cart: $9. **Pull cart:** $2. **Trail fee:** personal carts not allowed.
Reservation policy: call 7 days in advance for information on all tee times.
Winter condition: the golf course is closed November 1st to March 31st.
Terrain: flat (easy walking). **Tees:** all grass. **Spikes:** soft spikes only.
Services: snack bar, beverages, small pro shop, driving range, putting green.
Comments: this is a great course to take the whole family for a day outing or for seniors. The course is easy to walk and not overly long. Water comes into play on a few holes and greens are fronted by bunkers. The Beartooth Mountains are the backdrop for the golf course. This course will be worth the trip.

Directions: from Hwy 78 turn east on Airport Road (just beyond the bowling alley) to the course entrance ahead on your right hand side (right across from the airport). Look for signs to the course.

Course Yardage & Par:
M-3105 yards, par 36.
W-2640 yards, par 36.
Dual tees for 18 holes:
M-6295 yards, par 72.
W-5295 yards, par 72.

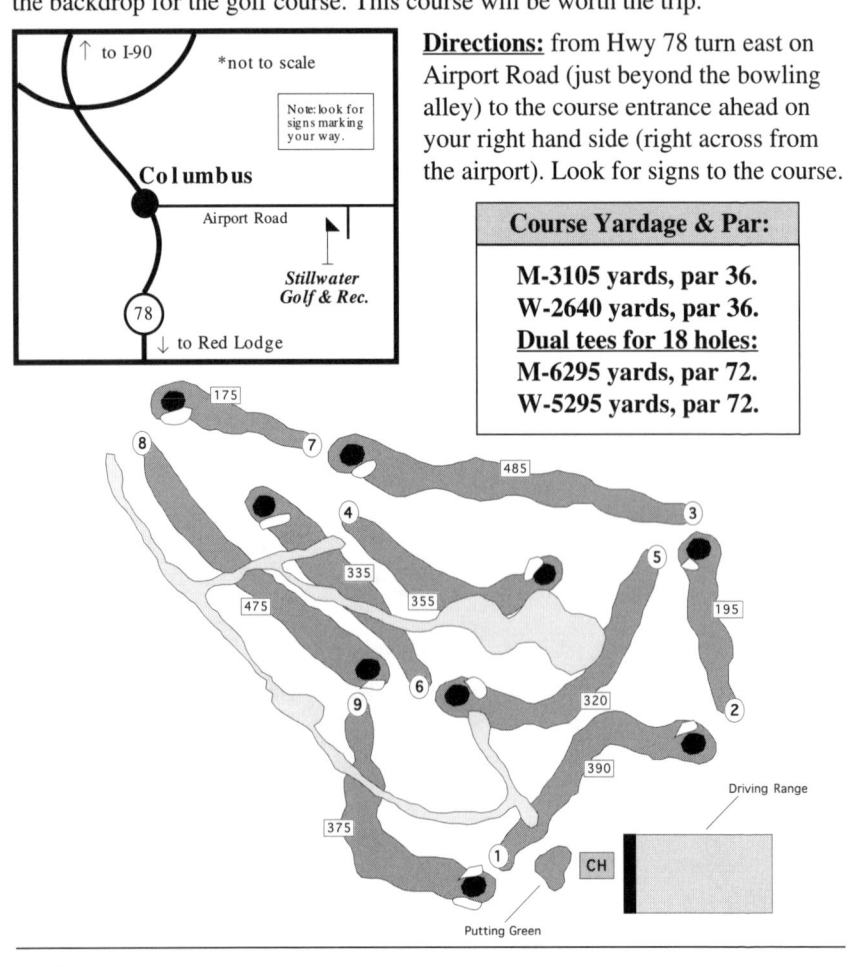

Sunnyside Golf & Country Club (semi-private, 9 hole course)

Skylark Road; P.O. Box 704; Glasgow, Montana 59230
Phone: (406) 228-9519. Fax: none. Internet: none.
Pro: unavailable. Superintendent: unavailable.
Rating/Slope: C 69.4/113; M 69.4/113; W 68.1/112. **Course record:** 32.
Green fees: $18/$12 all week long; no special rates; M/C, VISA.
Power cart: $15/$9. **Pull cart:** $2. **Trail fee:** personal carts not allowed.
Reservation policy: call up to 1 day in advance to confirm tee time availability.
Winter condition: the golf course is closed November 1st to March 1st.
Terrain: flat (easy walking). **Tees:** all grass. **Spikes:** soft spikes preferred.
Services: club rentals, snack bar, beer, pro shop, driving range, putting green.
Comments: the course offers some tree lined fairways and many lateral water
hazards which can make it tough to score on. Flat terrain make this a good
walking course. If traveling through Montana take the time to stop at Sunnyside.

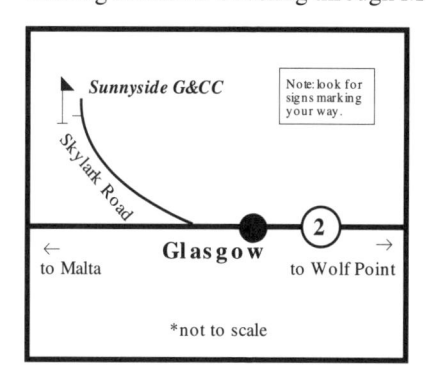

Directions: from Hwy 2 turn northwest
on Skylark Road, proceed approximately
1 mile to the course entrance on your left
hand side. The course is just west of the
outskirts of the town of Glasgow. Look
for signs to your turn to the course.

Course Yardage & Par:
C-3233 yards, par 36.
M-3152 yards, par 36.
W-2548 yards, par 36.

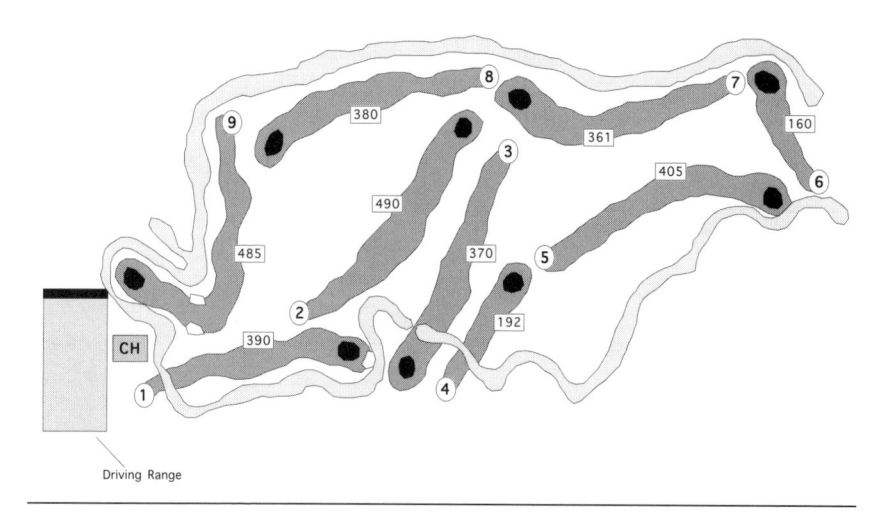

Trestle Creek Golf Club (public, 9 hole course)

1 Trestle Creek; Saint Regis, Montana 59866
Phone: (406) 649-2680. **Fax:** none. **Internet:** none.
Pro: Marv Clover, PGA. **Superintendent:** Rick Meier.
Rating/Slope: M 69.9/119; W 68.5/116. **Course record:** 66.
Green fees: W/D $16; W/E $10; M/C, VISA.
Power cart: $16/$8. **Pull cart:** $2/$1. **Trail fee:** $4.
Reservation policy: call 14 days in advance for information for all tee times.
Winter condition: the golf course is closed from November 1st to March 1st.
Terrain: rolling terrain. **Tees:** all grass. **Spikes:** soft spikes preferred.
Services: club rentals, lessons, small pro shop, beverages, putting green.
Comments: the course sits atop a plateau overlooking the Clark Fork River and is cut out of a mature stand of towering Ponderosa Pines. The course is tight in many spots and offers small greens, the combination of which, make it very difficult to score on. A very scenic location with homesites available.

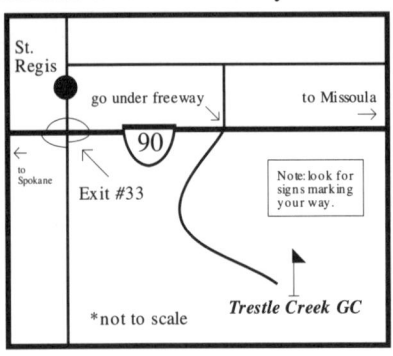

Directions: from I-90 take exit 33. Turn north to the first stop sign and turn right. Proceed for .8 miles to a dirt road, turn right. Proceed .2 miles to the clubhouse (you must travel under the freeway).

Course Yardage & Par:
C-3227 yards, par 36.
M-3052 yards, par 36.
W-2839 yards, par 36.

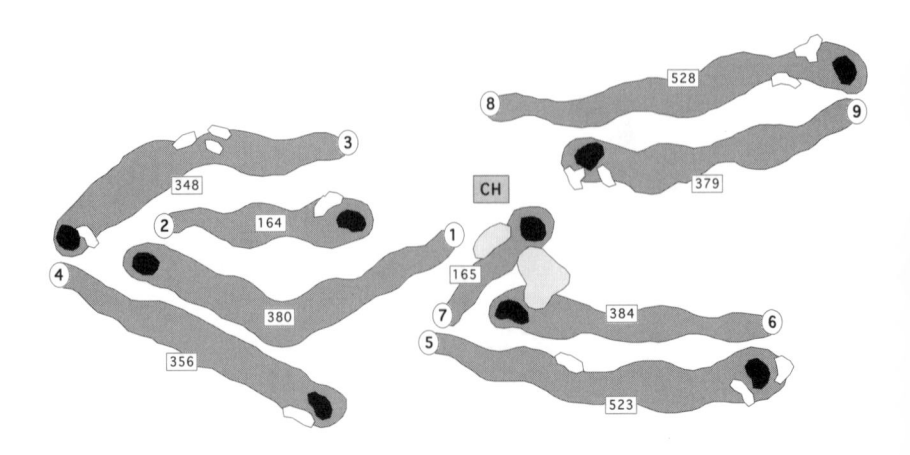

University Golf Course (public, 9 hole course)

515 South Avenue East; Missoula, Montana 59812
Phone: (406) 728-8629. Fax: none. Internet: none.
Pro: Bob Crandall, PGA. Superintendent: unavailable.
Rating/Slope: M 68.6/110; W 72.4/116. **Course record:** 31.
Green fees: W/D $16/$10; W/E $18/$12; Student, Sr. rates; MC, VISA.
Power cart: $20/$10. **Pull cart:** $2/$1. **Trail fee:** $6 for personal carts.
Reservation policy: call 14 days in advance for information for all tee times.
Winter condition: the golf course is closed from November 1st to March 1st.
Terrain: flat, some hills. **Tees:** all grass. **Spikes:** soft spikes preferred.
Services: club rentals, lessons, small pro shop, driving range, putting green.
Comments: the course sits at the foot of Mt. Sentinel, a favorite hiking location to the big "M" behind the University. Greens here are small and guarded by sand bunkers on many holes. The course plays longer than the yardage indicates.

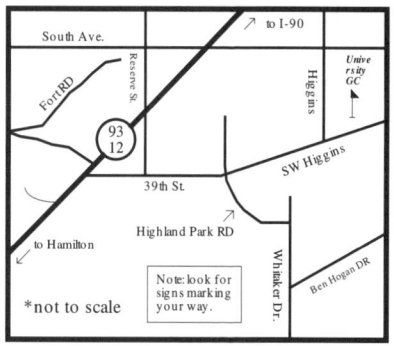

Directions: from I-90 E&W take the Van Buren exit. Turn left off the exit. Proceed to Broadway and turn right. Proceed to Authur and turn left. the course is 1.7 miles ahead. Look for signs.

Course Yardage & Par:
M-3086 yards, par 35.
W-2986 yards, par 36.
Dual tees for 18 holes:
M-6450 yards, par 71.
W-6072 yards, par 72.

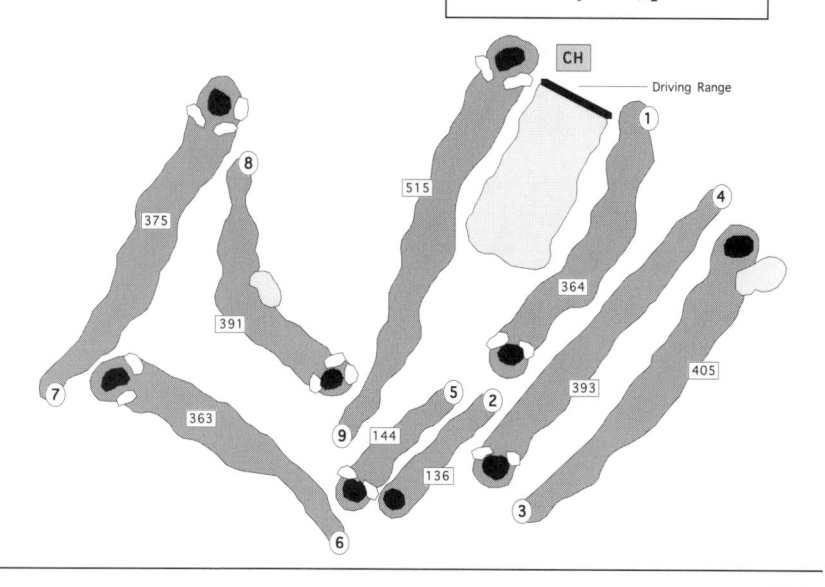

Valley View Golf Club (semi-private, 18 hole course)

P.O. Box 207; 302 East Kagy; Bozeman, Montana 59715
Phone: (406) 586-2145. Fax: none. Internet: none.
Pro: Scott Kremmel, PGA. Superintendent: R. Scott Woodhead.
Rating/Slope: C 68.7/118; M 67.1/116; W 69.2/113. **Course record:** 66.
Green fees: $37/$22 (non-member guest); MC, VISA.
Power cart: $18/$11. **Pull cart:** $2. **Trail fee:** personal carts not allowed.
Reservation policy: call 14 days in advance for information on all tee times.
Winter condition: the golf course is closed November 1st to March 31st.
Terrain: flat (easy walking). **Tees:** all grass. **Spikes:** soft spikes required.
Services: club rentals, lessons, restaurant, beer, wine, pro shop, driving range.
Comments: the course is meticulously maintained with a nice variety of trees, shrubbery, and flowers. Greens are small and difficult to read, water hazards abound. These factors equal a very challenging round of golf for any skill level.

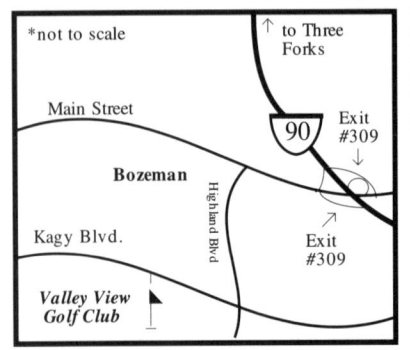

Directions: from Hwy 191 turn south on 19th Avenue South. Proceed to Kagy Blvd. and turn right. The course is located on Kagy Blvd. ahead on your right side.

Course Yardage & Par:
C-6262 yards, par 70.
M-5841 yards, par 70.
W-5308 yards, par 70.

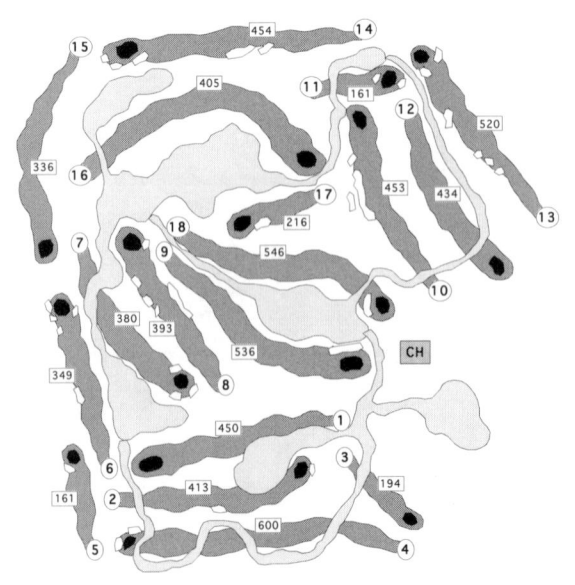

Village Greens (public, 18 hole course)

500 Palmer Drive; Kalispell, Montana 59901
Phone: (406) 752-4666. Fax: (406) 752-4658. Internet: www.montanagolf.com
Pro: Ryan Malby, PGA. Superintendent: Mark Salisbury.
Rating/Slope: C 69.8/114; M 67.6/109; W 68.3/114. Course record: 63.
Green fees: $27 all week long; $20 after 2pm Sunday-Thursday; M/C, VISA.
Power cart: $18/$9. Pull cart: $4. Trail fee: call for prices.
Reservation policy: call 3 days in advance for information on all tee times.
Winter condition: the golf course is closed November 1st to March 31st.
Terrain: flat (easy walking). Tees: all grass. Spikes: soft spikes required.
Services: club rentals, lessons, deli, pro shop, driving range, putting green.
Comments: the course features lush fairways, meticulously maintained bent
grass greens, white sand bunkers and magnificent lake and mountain views.
Village Greens also offers properties for sale in this active community.

Directions: from Hwy 93 exit east on Hwy 2. Turn left on 7th Avenue E. Travel 1.3 miles to W. Evergreen Dr. where you turn right. Proceed .3 miles to the course entrance on your left.

Course Yardage & Par:
C-6401 yards, par 70.
M-5907 yards, par 70.
W-5208 yards, par 70.

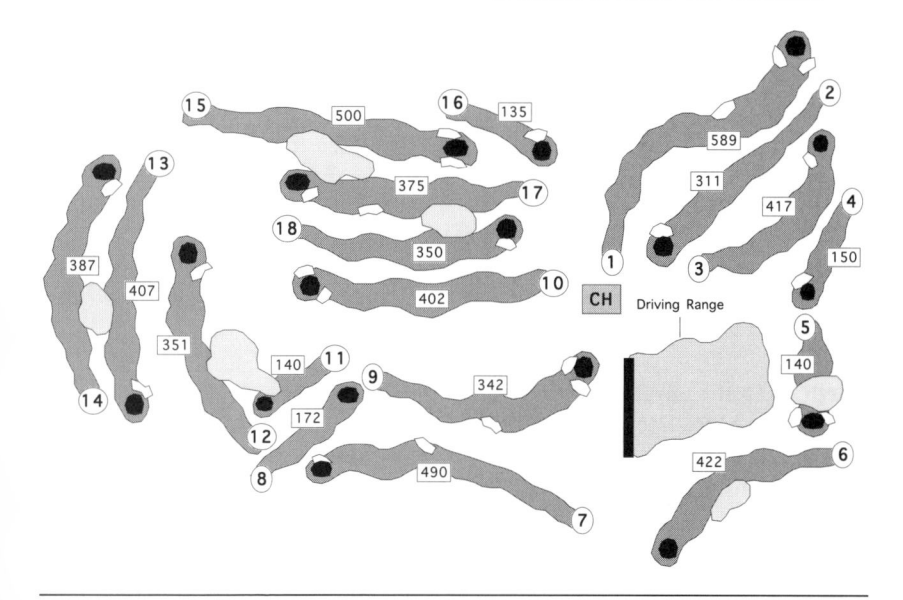

Whitefish Lake Golf Club (public, 36 hole course)

Mailing address: P.O. Box 666; Whitefish, Montana 59937
Physical address: Highway 93 North; Whitefish, Montana 59937
Phone numbers: call (406) 862-5960 for information; (406) 862-4000 starter.
Fax: unavailable. **Internet:** unavailable.
Pro: Tim Olson, PGA. **Superintendent:** Dick Collins.
Rating/Slope: *please see below for your course ratings. **Course record:** 64.
Green fees: $39 or $35 with 2 day advance (regular season); $34 or $32 with
2 day advance (value season); M/C, VISA, AMEX, DISCOVER.
Power cart: $12.25 per person. **Pull cart:** $2. **Trail fee:** not allowed.
Reservation policy: please call 2 days in advance for all your tee times.
Winter condition: the golf course is closed November 1st to March 31st.
Terrain: flat, some hills. **Tees:** all grass. **Spikes:** soft spikes required.
Services: club rentals, lessons, lounge, restaurant, snack bar, beer, wine, liquor,
beverages, pro shop, driving range, putting/chipping greens, club memberships.
Comments: the courses offers spectacular scenery, lakes, sand, and each hole is
surrounded by towering pines. You must be very straight off the tee as the
somewhat narrow fairways give little room for error. You will use every club in
your bag over this 36 hole layout. This is one of the finest public golf courses in
the state of Montana. A track that is definitely worth a special trip. If you are
looking for a meal after your round of golf be sure to stop in the Log Clubhouse
Restaurant and Lounge that was built in 1936. Dinner reservations are suggested
so be sure to call ahead at (406) 862-5285.

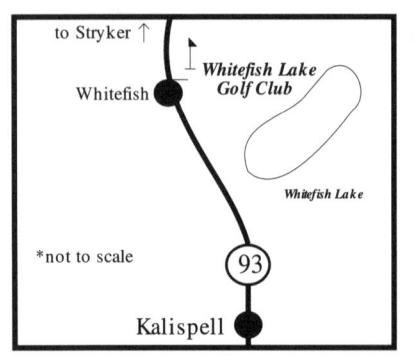

Directions: the golf course is located at
the northend of Whitefish Montana on
the east and west sides of Highway 93.
Look for signs that are posted for your
turn into the golf course parking lot.

***course yardage on
the following page.**

Golf course ratings and slope:

North 18 Golf Course:
C 69.8/118; M 68.7/116; W 70.1/115.

South 18 Golf Course:
C 70.5/122; M 69.0/120; W 70.3/120.

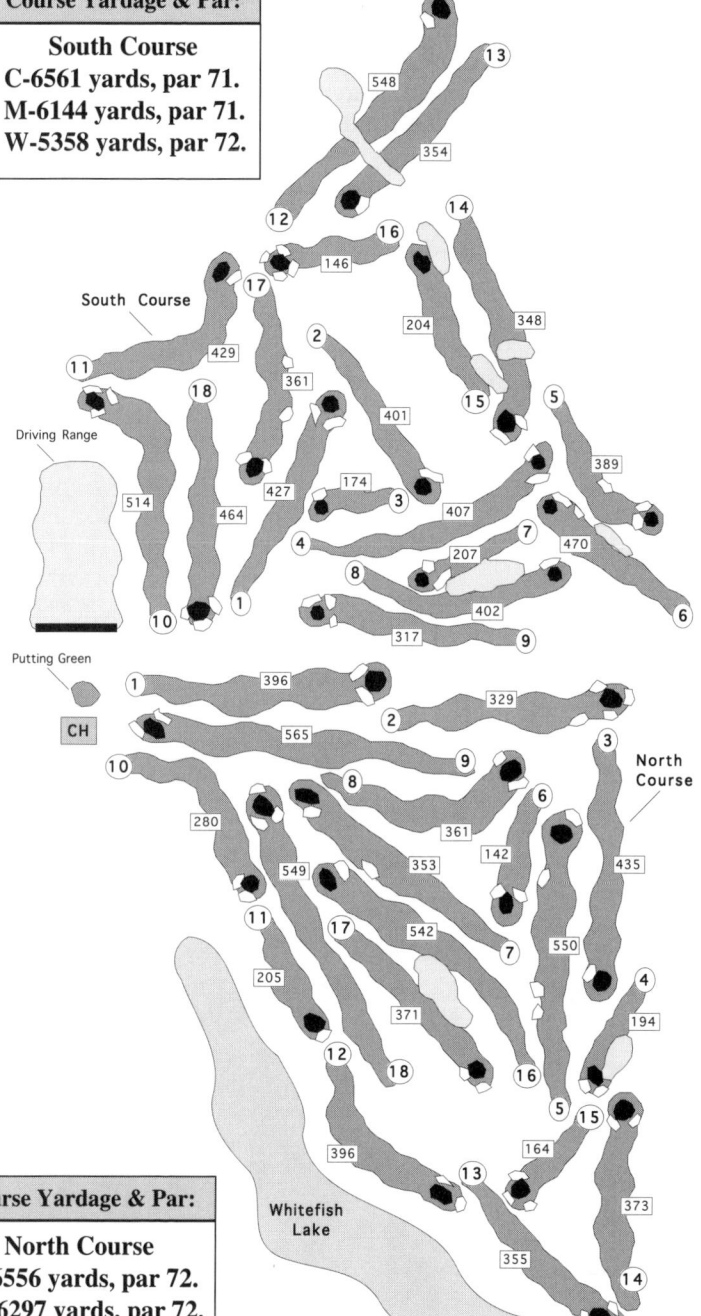

Course Yardage & Par:

South Course
C-6561 yards, par 71.
M-6144 yards, par 71.
W-5358 yards, par 72.

South Course

Driving Range

Putting Green

CH

North Course

Whitefish Lake

Course Yardage & Par:

North Course
C-6556 yards, par 72.
M-6297 yards, par 72.
W-5556 yards, par 72.

225

Whitetail Golf Club (public, 9 hole course)

4295 Wildfowl Lane; Stevensville, Montana 59870
Phone: (406) 777-3636. **Fax:** none. **Internet:** none.
Pro: David Aller. **Superintendent:** unavailable.
Rating/Slope: M 65.8/104; W 67.9/107. **Course record:** 36.
Green fees: W/D $10; W/E $11; M/C, VISA, AMEX.
Power cart: $16/$10. **Pull cart:** $2. **Trail fee:** call for prices.
Reservation policy: call 14 days in advance for information on all tee times.
Winter condition: the golf course is closed November 1st to March 31st.
Terrain: flat (easy walking). **Tees:** all grass. **Spikes:** soft spikes preferred.
Services: club rentals, snack bar, limited pro shop, driving range, (irons only).
Comments: a very scenic course located in the Lee Metcalf National Wildlife
Refuge at the base of the Bitterroot Mountains. The course offers bentgrass greens,
tree lined fairways and one pond. Come enjoy the serenity and beauty of area.

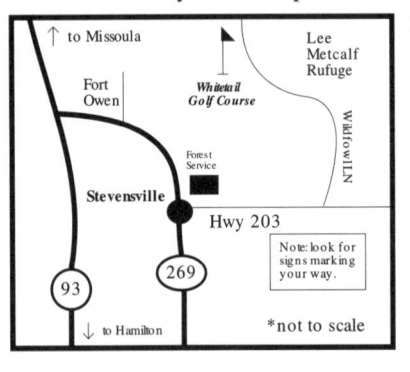

Directions: from Hwy 93 turn southeast onto Hwy 269. Proceed 1.3 miles to Hwy 203. Turn left onto Hwy 203. Proceed .3 miles to Wildfowl Lane. Turn left and travel 2.5 miles to the gate to the golf course which is on your left. The parking lot is .5 miles ahead. **Note:** The course is located in the Lee Metcalf Wildlife Refuge, 3 miles from Highway 203.

Course Yardage & Par:
M-2844 yards, par 35.
W-2596 yards, par 35.

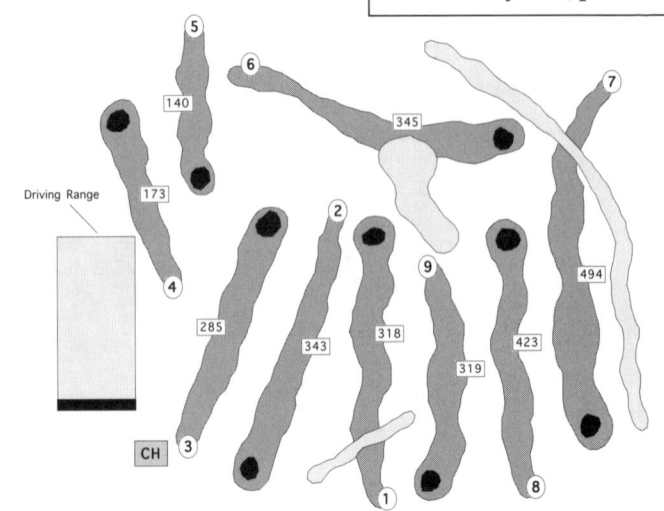

Yellowstone Country Club (private, 18 hole course)

5707 Bobby Jones Boulevard; Billings, Montana 59106
Phone: (406) 656-1701. Fax: none. Internet: none.
Pro: Paul Allen, PGA. Superintendent: Joe Stribley.
Rating/Slope: C 71.4/122; M 69.6/118; W 73.4/118. **Course record:** 62.
Green fees: private club members & guests only; reciprocates.
Power cart: private club. **Pull cart:** private club. **Trail fee:** private club.
Reservation policy: private club members & guests only.
Winter condition: the the golf course is closed during the winter months.
Terrain: flat, some hills. **Tees:** all grass. **Spikes:** soft spikes only.
Services: club rentals, lessons, beer, liquor, snack bar, pro shop, driving range, putting green. **Comments:** the course offers spectacular views of the Rimrocks, the cliffs on the north end of the Yellowstone Valley. Fairways are tree lined and greens are well bunkered. These factors, together with the length (7121 yards from the tips) make this a tough course. Call for the reciprocation agreement.

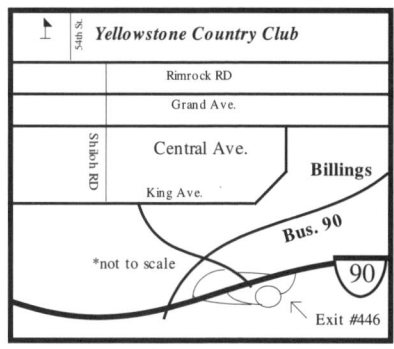

Directions: proceed west of Billings on Rimrock Road approximately 4 miles to the sign. Turn right. Proceed two blocks and turn left to the club entrance.

Course Yardage & Par:
C-7121 yards, par 72.
M-6690 yards, par 72.
W-6027 yards, par 76.

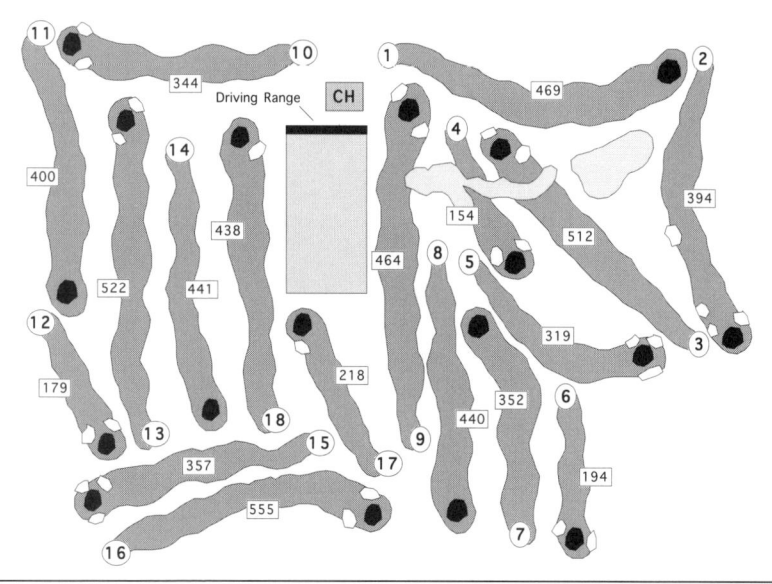

National Golf Driving Range
3159 Highway 93 North; Kalispell, MT 59901
(406) 752-4653. Pro: Ken Olson.
Hours: hours vary depending upon season.
Lights: yes. **Covered:** yes.
Putting & Chipping: yes.
Services: lessons, club fitting,
large retail golf shop, putting green.
Directions: the driving range is located right
off of Highway 93, north of Kalispell.
<u>**R1; Map 1; Grid B2**</u>

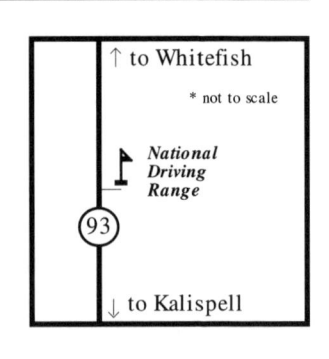

Skyline Driving Range
2324 26th Street South; Great Falls, MT 59405
(406) 453-2265. Pro: none.
Hours: hours vary depending upon season.
Lights: yes. **Covered:** yes.
Putting & Chipping: none.
Services: lessons, club fitting,
large retail golf shop.
Directions: the range is located in Great Falls.
<u>**R2; Map 2; Grid B3**</u>

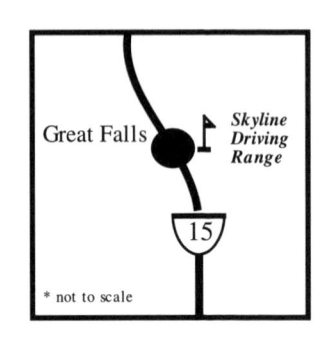

Bob's Golf Carts
3507 S Arizona Street: Butte, Montana; (406) 494-3668
Services: golf cart sales and service.

Carliq Custom Golf & Repair
1402 Broadwater Avenue; Billings, Montana; (406) 245-2533
Services: custom clubs, club repair.

Diamondback Golf
1629 W Main Street; Bozeman, Montana; (406) 586-7545
Services: retail golf store.

Diamondback Golf
906 S 1st Street; Helena, Montana; (406) 442-2648
Services: retail golf store.

Golf Center
1305 9th Avenue S.; Great Falls, Montana; (406) 452-3061
Services: retail golf store.

Golf Time
412 Central Avenue; Great Falls, Montana; (406) 727-8613
Services: retail golf store.

Golf USA
1812 Grand Avenue; Billings; Montana; (406) 655-1000
Services: lessons, indoor range, club repair, computer club fitting, retail store.

Golf USA
2304 N 7th Avenue #B; Bozeman, Montana; (406) 587-1412
Services: indoor range, club repair, computer club fitting, retail merchandise.

Golf USA
3703 Harrison Avenue; Butte, Montana; (406) 494-2424
Services: club repair, custom clubs, club refinishing, retail merchandise.

Golf USA
38 1st Avenue E #A; Kalispell, Montana; (406) 756-7123
Services: club repair, custom clubs, club refinishing, retail merchandise.

Golfmasters
1801 S 3rd Street W; Missoula, Montana; (406) 543-8816
Services: club repair, custom clubs, club refinishing.

Knoyle's Kustom Klubs
1801 South 3rd West; Missoula, Montana; (406) 543-8816
Services: club fitting, lessons, video your swing, indoor driving net, refinishing.

Mitchell Golf Company
1117 Central Avenue; Billings, Montana; (406) 245-8691
Services: club repair, custom clubs, club refinishing, retail merchandise.

Montana Academy of Golf
210 Parkhill Drive; Whitefish, Montana; (406) 862-1222
Services: golf instruction school.

National Golf
529 24th Street West; Billings, Montana; (406) 656-4653
Services: club repair, custom clubs, club refinishing, retail merchandise.

National Golf
3159 US Hwy 93 N; Kalispell, Montana; (406) 752-4653
Services: club repair, custom clubs, club refinishing, retail merchandise.

Outlaw Golf
1310 6th Street E; Polson, Montana; (406) 883-6822
Services: club repair, custom clubs, club refinishing, retail merchandise.

Pin High Custom Club Fitting
166 Ridgeview Drive; Kalispell, Montana; (406) 257-4293
Services: club repair, custom clubs, club refinishing.

Scheels Sport Shops
1233 24th Street West; Billings, Montana; (406) 656-9220
Services: retail golf merchandise.

Scheels Sport Shops
3 Holiday Village; Great Falls, Montana; (406) 453-7666
Services: retail golf merchandise.

Anaconda: Anaconda Country Club, Fairmont Hot Springs Resort, Old Works Golf Club
Baker: Lakeview Country Club
Big Sky: Big Sky Golf Club
Big Timber: Overland Golf Course
Bigfork: Eagle Bend
Billings: The Briarwood, Circle Inn Golf Links, Exchange City Par 3, Hilands Golf Club, Lake Hills Golf Course, Peter Yegen Jr. Golf Course, Pryor Creek Golf Club, Yellowstone Country Club
Bozeman: Bridger Creek, Cottonwood Hills Golf Course, Riverside Country Club, Valley View Golf Club
Broadus: Rolling Hills Golf Course
Butte: Butte Country Club, Highland View Golf Club
Chinook: Chinook Golf & Country Club
Choteau: Choteau Country Club
Colstrip: Ponderosa Butte Golf Course
Columbia Falls: Meadow Lake Resort
Columbus: Stillwater Golf & Recreation
Conrad: Pondera Golf Club
Creston: Mountain Crossroads Golf Course
Cut Bank: Cutbank Golf &Country Club
Deer Lodge: Deer Lodge Golf Club
Dillon: Beaverhead Golf Course
East Glacier: Glacier Park Golf Course
Ennis: Madison Meadows Golf Course
Fairfield: Harvest Hills Golf Course
Forsyth: Forsyth Country Club
Fort Benton: Signal Point Golf Course
Fortine: Meadow Creek Golf Course
Frenchtown: King Ranch Golf Course
Glasgow: Sunnyside & Country Club
Glendive: Cottonwood Country Club
Great Falls: Anaconda Hills Golf Course, Emerald Greens, Meadow Lark Country Club, Robert O Speck Golf Course, Skyline Driving Range
Hamilton: Hamilton Golf Club
Hardin: Fort Custer Golf Club
Harlowton: Jawbone Creek Country Club
Havre: Beaver Creek Golf Course
Helena: Bill Roberts Municipal Golf Course, Fox Ridge Golf Course, Green Meadow Country Club
Huntley: Pryor Creek Golf Club
Kalispell: Buffalo Hill Golf Club, National Driving Range, Northern Pines Golf Course, Village Greens
Laurel: Laurel Golf Club

Lewistown: Judith Shadows Golf Course, Pine Meadows Golf Club
Libby: Cabinet View Country Club
Livingston: Livingston Golf & Country Club
Lolo: Pete's Pitch & Putt
Malta: Marian Hills Golf Course
Miles City: Miles City Town & Country Club
Missoula: Highlands Golf Club, Larchmont Golf Course, Linda Vista Public
Golf Course, Missoula Country Club, University Golf Course
Plains: Plains Golf Club
Plentywood: Plentywood Golf Club
Polson: Polson Country Club
Red Lodge: Beartooth Golf & Country Club, Red Lodge Mountain Golf Course
Ronan: Mission Mountain Country Club
Roundup: Pine Ridge Country Club
Saco: Sleeping Buffalo Resort
Saint Regis: Trestle Creek Golf Club
Scobey: Scobey Golf Club
Seely Lake: Double Arrow Golf Resort
Shelby: Marias Valley Golf & Country Club
Sidney: Sidney Country Club
Stevensville: Whitetail Golf Club
Superior: Cedar Creek Golf Course
Thompson Falls: River's Bend at Thompson Falls
Three Forks: Headwaters Public Golf Course
Townsend: Old Baldy Golf Course
West Glacier: Glacier View Golf Club
Whitefish: Par 3 on 93, Whitefish Lake Golf Club
Wolf Point: Airport Golf Club

Montana State Regional Map

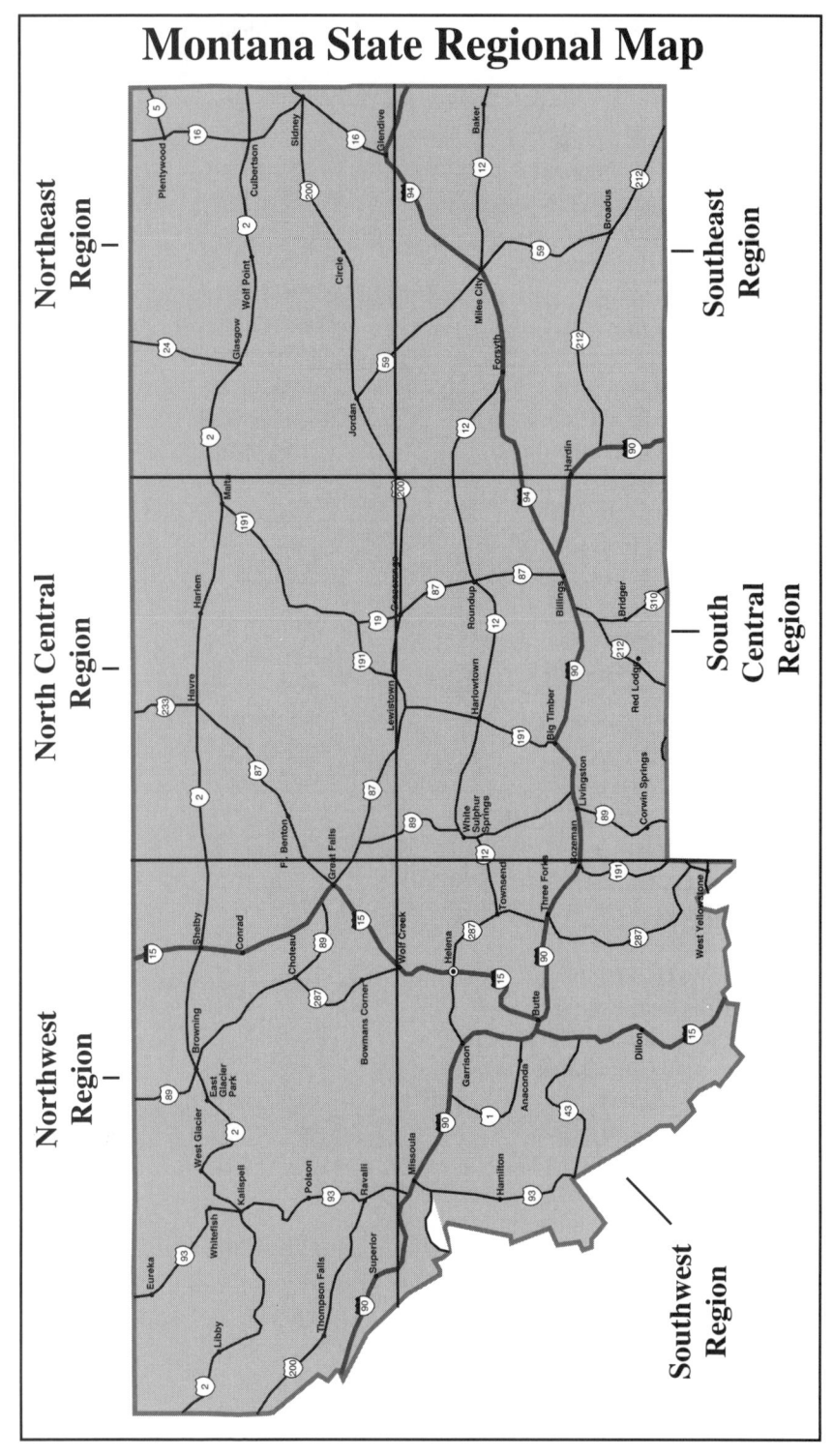

North Central Region

Beaver Creek Golf Course
Chinook Golf & Country Club
Marian Hills Country Club
Pine Meadows Golf Club
Signal Point Golf Course

Northeast Region

Airport Golf Club
Cottonwood Country Club
Plentwood Golf Club
Scobey Golf Club
Sidney Country Club
Sleeping Buffalo Golf Course
Sunnyside Golf & Country Club

Northwest Region

Anaconda Hills Golf Course
Buffalo Hill Golf Club
Cabinet View Country Club
Cedar Creek Golf Course
Choteau Country Club
Cut Bank Golf & Country Club
Double Arrow Golf Resort
Eagle Bend Golf Club
Emerald Greens
Glacier Park Golf Course
Glacier View Golf Club
Harvest Hills Golf Course
Marias Valley Golf & Country Club
Meadow Creek Golf Course
Meadow Lake Resort
Meadow Lark Country Club
Mission Mountain Country Club
Mountain Crossroads Golf Course
National Golf Driving Range
Northern Pines Golf Course
Par 3 on 93 Golf Course & Driving Range
Plains Golf Club
Polson Country Club
Pondera Golf Club
River's Bend at Thompson Falls

Robert O' Speck Golf Course
Skyline Driving Range
Trestle Creek Golf Club
Village Greens
Whitefish Lake Golf Club

South Central Region
Beartooth Golf & Country Club
Briarwood, The
Bridger Creek
Circle Inn Golf Links
Cottonwood Hills Golf Course
Exchange City Par-3 Golf Course
Fort Custer Golf Club
Hilands Golf Club
Jawbone Creek Country Club
Judith Shadows Golf Course
Lake Hills Golf Course
Laurel Golf Club
Livingston Golf & Country Club
Overland Golf Course
Peter Yegen Jr. Golf Course
Pine Ridge Country Club
Pryor Creek Golf Club
Red Lodge Mountain Golf Course
Riverside Country Club
Stillwater Golf & Recreation Association
Valley View Golf Club
Yellowstone Country Club

Southeast Region
Forsyth Country Club
Lakeview Country Club
Miles City Town & Country Club
Ponderosa Butte Public Golf Course
Rolling Hills Golf Course

Southwest Region
Anaconda Country Club
Beaverhead Golf Course
Big Sky Golf Club
Bill Roberts Municipal Golf Course
Butte Country Club
Deer Lodge Golf Club

Fairmont Hot Springs Resort
Fox Ridge Golf Course
Green Meadow Country Club
Hamilton Golf Club
Headwaters Public Golf Course
Highland View Golf Course
Highlands Golf Club, The
King Ranch Golf Course
Larchmont Golf Course
Linda Vista Public Golf Course
Madison Meadows Golf Course
Missoula Country Club
Old Baldy Golf Course
Old Works Golf Club
Pete's Pitch & Putt
University Golf Course
Whitetail Golf Club

I have been writing golf books since 1986 and watched how the golf industry has changed over these years. Titanium. Who had heard of it in 1986? Well...you know the story.

The internet is growing at an incredible rate. It is quickly becoming the medium of choice for purchasing everything from cars, toys, airline tickets, even groceries. In only the first four years it reached over 50 million users, something that took radio 38 years to achieve and 13 years for television. With this tremendous growth, access to information and many other services is growing daily. The technology is revolutionizing the way we live, and play. I am pleased to say that this new medium is bringing golf reservations into the 21st century. **MAC Productions** is dedicated to providing the most accurate, up to date information available for each and every book. When we go to press we go to great lengths to make sure that the information is the best available at the time. I take pride in my product and in the service I provide to my customers. In all my years of business **LinksTime.com** is the first service that has been presented to me that complimented my books. Like myself, **LinksTime.com** is also, truly dedicated to customer service to golfers and the golf industry alike. I am pleased to be a part of this emerging network.

Internet based golf reservations are here. At the time that this edition of *Golfing in Oregon* went to press, **LinksTime.com** was in the process of launching a national network of golf courses to join this service, with the Pacific Northwest as the initial market. Willows Run in Redmond Washington is the very first course to use the service in this area. There are currently almost 30 participating golf courses and the network is growing daily. I suggest that you visit the web site frequently to see who has been added as it is sure to continue to grow at a rapid pace. Participating courses that have the LinksTime.com logo on the bottom of their page.

The advantages to this technology are many. You can go to the golf course's web page to get instant information on the course, pro shop specials at the time, tournaments, rates, driving directions, just to name a few features.

The most compelling feature, however, is the ability to make reservations without calling the course. This service is available 7 days a week, 24 hours a day. Making a tee time couldn't be easier. In fact, you can even inquire about tee time availability at multiple courses at the same time. You can book mark your favorite courses, request a time and day that you want to play, and the service will tell you which of your courses of choice have that tee time available for the number of players you want.

Imagine....you are sitting in your office, it is Monday...lunchtime. Stale sandwich in hand, followed by a lukewarm soda, you are dreaming of Saturday afternoon at your favorite course. You know that getting a tee time can be tough if you don't call right away the first available day that the reservations are taken for the weekend times. You can't take 20 minutes to call course after course to find one that has the slot you want, nor can you make long distance calls from work.

Solution! LinksTime.com

The golf course now stores it's tee times on a computerized tee sheet. This tee sheet is connected to the internet. When you put in your request you are actually communicating with the Tee Sheet, real time! A response will come back telling you if the time is available as well as the nearest time before and after. If you want to play, select the time, fill out your profile and reserve it. **LinksTime.com** will charge you a small convenience fee at the time of booking. No more busy signals, no more endless phone calls, no more wasted long distance charges...it couldn't be easier or more convenient. Now all you have to worry about is improving that golf swing...